POP
ULAR
MUSIC

MENU

SAGE has been part of the global academic community since 1965, supporting high quality research and learning that transforms society and our understanding of individuals, groups, and cultures. SAGE is the independent, innovative, natural home for authors, editors and societies who share our commitment and passion for the social sciences.

Find out more at: **www.sagepublications.com**

TARA BRABAZON

POP
U LAR
MUSIC

TOPICS, TRENDS & TRAJECTORIES

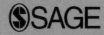

Los Angeles | London | New Delhi
Singapore | Washington DC

SAGE Publications Ltd
1 Oliver's Yard
55 City Road
London EC1Y 1SP

SAGE Publications Inc.
2455 Teller Road
Thousand Oaks, California 91320

SAGE Publications India Pvt Ltd
B 1/I 1 Mohan Cooperative Industrial Area
Mathura Road, Post Bag 7
New Delhi 110 044

SAGE Publications Asia-Pacific Pte Ltd
33 Pekin Street #02-01
Far East Square
Singapore 048763

Library of Congress Control Number: 2010942408

British Library Cataloguing in Publication data

A catalogue record for this book is available from the British Library

ISBN 978-1-84787-435-1
ISBN 978-1-84787-436-8 (pbk)

Typeset by C&M Digitals (P) Ltd, Chennai, India
Printed in India at Replika Press Pvt Ltd.
Printed on paper from sustainable resources

Contents

About the Author   vii
Acknowledgements   viii

Introduction: Walking On the Dance Floor   1

I   APPROACHES   11
Listening to Music   13
Visualizing Music   18
Dancing to Music   23
Thinking About Music   30
Writing About Music   36

II   MUSIC SPACES   45
Sonic Architecture/Soundscape   47
City Music and Urban Spaces   53
Recording Spaces   59
Clubs and Pubs   66
Soundtracks and Filmic Spaces   71
Music Video and Televisual Spaces   77
Radio, Podcasting and Listening Spaces   82
MP3 and Downloading Spaces   86

III   INSTRUMENTS OF/FOR STUDY   91
Guitar Cultures   93
Keyboard Cultures   100
Drumming and Percussion   105
Voice   110
Turntablism   114
iPod   118

IV   GENRE AND COMMUNITY   125
Country   127
Folk   132
The Blues   136
Rock and Roll   141

Soul	147
Reggae and Ska	152
Salsa	157
Metal	161
Punk and Indie	166
Hip Hop	171
Disco	176
House and Post-House Musics	180
World Music	185
V DEBATES	**191**
Intellectual Property	193
Censorship and Regulation	200
Race, Appropriation and Commodification	206
Girl Groups and Feminism	212
Boy Bands and Men's Studies	218
Gay, Lesbian, Bisexual and Transgenderist Musics	222
Digitization, User Generated Content and Social Networking	228
Music: Politics, Resistance and Protest	233
Conclusion: Walking Off the Dance Floor	**241**
References	**246**
Sonic Sources	**269**
Visual Sources	**274**
Index	**279**

About the Author

Tara Brabazon is Professor of Communication at the University of Ontario Institute of Technology (UOIT). She has previously held academic posts in the United Kingdom, Australia and Aotearoa/New Zealand. Tara has won six teaching awards throughout her career, including the National Teaching Award for the Humanities.

Tara values both higher education and lifelong learning. She holds three bachelor degrees, three masters degrees, a graduate diploma in internet studies and a doctorate in cultural history. She has a long-standing interest in sound, orality, aurality and popular music. Tara remains interested in how to use the complexities of sonic media in scholarship.

Tara has published ten books and over one hundred refereed articles. Her best known monographs include *Digital Hemlock, The University of Google, From Revolution to Revelation* and *The Revolution Will Not Be Downloaded*. She has also written journalism for arts publications and *Times Higher Education* in the United Kingdom.

For further information, or to contact Tara, please visit www.brabazon.net

Acknowledgements

Most authors thank sponsors, funding agencies and benefactors for grants, facilities and study leave. This book is different. It was written early in the morning before long teaching days. It was drafted through weekends filled with hope that Manchester City would win, or at least not lose.

This book was built on the support, care and time of four people. It would not have been possible without the range of music that filled (and fills) the house of my parents, Doris and Kevin Brabazon. Between Doris's lap steel guitar and Kevin's trumpet, this book was started – albeit unintentionally – many decades ago. My brother Stephen Brabazon packed my childhood with piano scales and his old beat-up Volvo with Rick Wakeman's *Six Wives of Henry the Eighth*. Without him, keyboard cultures would have remained a mystery.

Finally, I wish to thank Steve Redhead. He is not only the best husband a short Australian woman could hope to find, he has also saturated my life with laughter, love, joy, dancing and music. From our iPod quizzes ('You have four bars to guess this song') through to our shared devotion at the Rickenbacker tabernacle, this book would not have been as punchy or percussive without his comments.

Everything within it – except the references to Bob Dylan, Rick Wakeman, Louis Armstrong and Johnny Cash – remains my responsibility.

Introduction

Walking On the Dance Floor

Look around you. Allow your eyes to dart around the landscape. Perhaps you are in a library or on the train. Maybe you are flicking through my book in a bookshop. Possibly, you are watching television while sampling a chapter on a Kindle or visiting the iPad's iBookstore. For a moment, be conscious of how you are gathering information about the world and the position of your body in the surrounding environment. Be aware of what you see and how you understand the behaviour of people around you.

Now I am going to ask you to do something else. Instead of seeing, we are going to experiment with your hearing and the role your ears have in locating your body in space. In a moment, I want you to close your eyes and let the waves of sound enfold you. Note what you hear. Consider the different types of information you receive when listening to the world.

Close your eyes now.

Upon reopening your eyes, think about the information blind listening gave you. Perhaps you heard sounds, noises and voices that were not obvious when your eyes were open and flitting around the landscape. When sight is not dominant in understanding the world, loops of sound enter our consciousness. Some are recognizable. Some are unusual or disturbing. Perhaps you hear strains of a melody or beat bleeding from a car stereo or iPod. A trace of another person's life will enter our attention through the leakage of sound.

There is a reason for our experiment. In the hierarchy of senses, vision blocks and marginalizes sound, touch, taste and scent. Our understanding of the world comes via our eyes. Seeing is believing. That cliché suggests we have less developed literacies and strategies to deploy other senses in a conscious and reflexive way. Since September 11, we replay in our minds horrific images of airplanes crashing through the Twin Towers. Terrorism is visual. So is racism. Mostly, these judgements are unaccompanied by sound. Web 2.0 initiatives and social media are enabled through screen-based environments. Twitter, YouTube, Flickr and Facebook emphasize text, images and visuality. Sound and sonic media are underplayed, under-discussed and secondary in their influence. The sounds of our culture are muffled through the accelerated visuality of Twitter's 140 characters and the glossy sheen of the iPad.

While recognizing the burgeoning screens of our lives, it is also a booming time for sonic mobility through the iPod, mobile phones and audio books. Sound is increasingly mediated, filtered and channeled through visual media. Handheld communication platforms invented to receive a voice call now service a range of computing functions, including web searching, applications, social networking and games. 'Talking' and 'listening' are visualized through text. The only sound is the clicking of keypads or the beeping arrival of a message. While we seem to live in the age of sound, actually we live in a time of screens. The iPad is a confirmation of this statement. Henrik Hansson and Sylvia van de Bunt-Kokhuis realized that,

> A century ago, virtually no images were used; today, pictures are large and important, increasingly expanding at the expense of the text … International places like hotels and airports mainly use icons to indicate toilets, luggage, keys and other services. This use of symbols is spreading to other areas. Browsers and computer interfaces use icons universally, a kind of 'visual Esperanto'. Visual language is considered one of the hottest areas in the humanities. In one way, written language is moving back to its origins, since the earliest examples of writing were pictorial (2004).

The movement away from orality and aurality silences sound and speech. Uncomfortable or inconvenient sounds, noises and music are filtered or ignored by overlaying other sounds. In such a context, iPodification reveals profound consequences for how we think and write about listening, particularly to popular music.

Popular Music: the dancing definition

Popular music changes in its definitions as it moves through time and space. It continues the etymological trajectory of the word 'popular,' connoting inferiority and the material of 'the masses'. As Stuart Hall stated, this label creates an 'assumption … that you might know before you looked at cultural traditions in general what, at any time, was a part of the elite culture or of popular culture' (1978: 6–7). In other words, any judgement or valuing of culture is not intrinsic to the song, film or photograph. Hall – even when he wrote these words in 1978 – noted that this division between high and low culture as 'untenable'. Such assumptions and biases lock the phrase 'popular music' into a semiotic system that defines the term by what it is not. Supposedly, popular music is *not* classical music or folk music. Actually, the boundaries between different forms and modes of music are permeable. Instead, it is more appropriate and useful for scholars to ignore the loaded labels of genres and explore popular music through its audiences. Inspired by the disciplines of sociology and psychology, popular music becomes part of the shared experiences of a group or community, offering pleasure, resistance and narratives of love, romance, sex, masculinity, femininity and desire. A further definition that is increasingly relevant explores the relationship between popular music and its modes of dissemination through diverse – but digitally convergent – technological platforms. Popular music refers to the sonic content that is migrated between the analogue and digital, vinyl and MP3.

Definitions of popular music are volatile but useful. The phrase captures an important part of our mediated lives and experience. The term refers to diverse genres, many histories and the myriad platforms on which music is produced, played and consumed. As suggested by the adjective 'popular,' it refers to the songs that have a currency beyond the local audience of a pub or club. These songs move through space and time to gain new audiences, meanings and contexts. While disconnected from folk music and classical music, these distinctions are not as clear as they may seem, with the songs of Bob Dylan, Joan Baez, the Three Tenors and Il Divo moving between categories. Indeed, David Toop, in his *Ocean of Sound* (1995), affirms that there is no need to write about categories of music. It is much more productive to probe and explore the remaking of sounds in their environment or context. We, as students of popular music, require less pigeonholing and labelling of music and more attention being paid to how sounds shape our identity.

Why does *Popular Music: Topics, Trends and Trajectories* exist?

In *Popular Music: Topics, Trends and Trajectories*, I take Toop at his word and apply his argument that we should move beyond unproductive categorizations and explore how sounds create identity as they move through history and geography. It is important – with the overstuffed lists of books about popular culture, popular music, media and cultural studies – that there are concrete reasons and justifications to add another text to your reading list. There are four reasons this book exists. The first motivation for offering these pages to you is that **writing about popular music is incredibly difficult**. It can feel like we are draining the life from the beat, image, fabric or feeling. Music is difficult to understand because so much of it is non-linguistic, incorporating fashion, hairstyles, bodies, dancing, rhythm, spaces, cities, screens, computer files, gaming, clubs and pubs. Therefore, this book offers assistance in how to write about popular music.

There are millions of words written about music on blogs, in magazines, newspapers, biographies, interview books and band histories. Nevertheless, discussing popular music in an academic environment must be distinct from fan-based enthusiasm. Academic writing on popular music can use journalism, but must not be journalism. It offers opinion and subjective assessment but is tempered by interpretation, research and critical argument. Examples and evidence are required. Academic writing about popular music extends beyond an album review or a fan response to a great dance track or important guitarist. This passion, fandom and opinion can and should feed into academic work. Our pleasure and personal commitments are the *start* of our scholarly writing, not the end of it. One of the finest popular music academic writers, Andrew Goodwin, realized that, 'there are too many academic books on pop that fail because the author lacks three basic qualities: knowledge of facts, understanding of music, ability to write' (1998: 122). My goal is to help students fulfil Goodwin's criteria, becoming great writers about popular music. This book is a foundation and scaffold to start your journey to remake pop and pop prose for a new era. Do not agree with my words: question, probe, challenge, think and change them.

It is the right moment for this change. I have participated in exam boards for a decade. It is always the popular music module, course or unit that will pick up the critiques and concerns from external examiners. The comments are always similar: students do not extend themselves. The academic papers and essays are not at a high enough standard. Students think that opinion substitutes for research. Such statements are rarely offered in response to film, television or media policy courses. Popular music is the focus of examiners' concern. Put another way, how students research and write about popular music in an academic setting is a long-term, complex and deep academic challenge. One of my aims when I started this book was to focus on the 'how to write' aspect of popular music. Each chapter in *Popular Music: Topics, Trends and Trajectories* aims to help students activate an idea, theory or method about which they are most passionate. Arching beyond opinion, I want students to move out of their sonic comfort zone and encounter new sounds, think about new ideas, and connect research and music in innovative ways. To repeat: fandom is not enough. It is only the starting point for scholarship. Loving music is an excellent and important beginning in the journey through popular music studies. It is not the end. It is necessary to note that the study of popular music borrows, reconfigures and applies ideas and concepts from a range of academic disciplines. A range of theories and methods should punctuate our work. Our writing includes media policy, textual analysis, theories of technological change, musicology, ethnography, sociology, men's and women's studies, geography and history.

It is important that all of us share and discuss the difficulty and the potential of studying popular music in universities. Research in and with music faces two great problems. Firstly, it is part of popular culture and confronts judgements and questions about cultural value. It is rarely recognized or acknowledged by those who define themselves as the elite. The second difficulty is that music is *music*, rather than words or script. Many – perhaps too many – cultural critics still take the easy option of analyzing lyrics like the lines of a poem, rather than asking more complex questions about instrumentation, rhythm, harmony or trans-genre hybridities.

Besides the difficulties involved in writing about music, the second pivotal change that has propelled the writing of this book is **digitization**. This is the first post-iPod popular music textbook. It is also the first to embed the potential, capacity and consequences of digital compression and convergence on the music industry. Not one sentence of this book was written during the period when compact discs and cassettes were in their ascendancy. Instead, my work takes MP3s, iPods, home recording, remixing and file sharing as a starting point. This is the environment described by Lawrence Lessig as a "'hybrid economy," transforming both "art" and "commerce."' (2008)

One agent for this transformation is the iPod. The product emerged in 2001 and within six years, music charts were no longer lists of the sales of physical platforms such as compact discs. *Popular Music: Topics, Trends and Trajectories* acknowledges that while the record industry is facing great difficulty in managing these changes, the music industry has never been more important. It is necessary to observe what has happened to record companies and log the changes to popular music history that are emerging around us as a result of downloading. Louis Barfe – in his evocatively titled *Where have all the good times gone? The rise and fall of the record industry* – recognized the scale of this transformation.

> The old certainties have disappeared from markets all around the world. Record companies can no longer relieve music fans of their cash with the ease that they once did. If you want a particular song and you have an internet connection, chances are that you can download it from someone, somewhere on the world wide web. The record company doesn't get paid and neither does the artist. However, for established artists, there is a silver lining to this particular cloud. They can now abandon their corporate paymasters and start selling direct to their punters, primarily over the internet. Sales are inevitably lower, but the proportion of cash going straight to the talent is much, much higher (2004: xiv).

Barfe makes the point that through to the 1980s, the record business was based on a way of thinking about 'products' that had been created 100 years earlier (2004: 293). Basically, the record companies' inability to see the consequences of digitization was not 'caused' by the iPod, rather by conservative approaches to the relationship between sound and technology. Their commercial model was nostalgic long before Napster. The key for researchers is to understand the connection between record companies and the music industry, e-commerce and pop. To explore such a link, it is necessary to investigate audiences and fans. Occasionally piracy – in the form of mix tapes and illegal taping – is part of this story. However, illegal downloading communities deploying the mobility of MP3 files have challenged and transformed the business model of popular music. Part of the function of *Popular Music: Topics, Trends and Trajectories* is to understand this transformation.

To explore this change requires the investigation of new and provocative relationships between production and consumption. Digitization – and its consequences on music – is a foundational reality in each chapter in this book. It has changed not only particular topics, like the marketing and distribution of popular music, it has also altered how this book is structured. I know that the reader of this book, at the point I mention a song, can enter iTunes or the hundreds of other file sharing sites and either purchase a copy of an important track, illegally download the song, or hear streamed seconds for free or after an advertisement on Spotify. This is liberating for the writer of a popular music textbook. If it is important for you to hear a sample of Leadbelly, I know that as a student you can do so without buying an album or missing out on this sonic experience because of a lack of access. At the end of each chapter, further reading and listening opportunities are listed. Many singles are mentioned that capture a sound or historical moment. This book has a soundtrack and if you wish to listen to this music while you are reading, then digitization opens a database of songs and sounds. The book deploys rather than ignores this potential. It is singles-led, not an album-based book. Alongside further listening and reading is an array of important websites to explore. Key questions are asked at the end of each chapter to confirm knowledge and provide a pathway to further research topics and essays.

The iPod matters. The highest selling digital audio player in history, it has multiple platforms, including the Classic, Nano, Touch, iPhone and iPad. Like a jukebox in our pockets it can hold an entire music library, transferred from the user's computer. The first iPod was launched on October 23, 2001 – just six weeks after the trauma of September 11. Therefore, iPodification works against conventional studies of popular music, with attention given to nations, genres, bands and eras. The 'iPod moment' not only changed how music is written, recorded, distributed, bought and sold, but also has transformed the way in which to study sound and fans, spaces and history. Early reviewers of the iPod underestimated the scale of the change. In 2001, Brent Schlender stated that,

> like the Walkman before it, the iPod, if it really catches on, could change the format in which music lovers 'consume' much of their music. Most will still buy their music, which will keep the record companies and recording artists happy. But after ripping their CDs into MP3s and loading them onto the iPod, they'll leave the disks on the shelf in their cases for months at a time.

Schlender nearly predicted the alienation of behavioural habits. Ripping compact discs is now rare. There are few mediating media between a computer and iPod. Music downloads from a portal to a platform, often in wireless environments. A particular version of Zygmunt Bauman's *Liquid Modernity* (2000) – perhaps called Liquid Music – has emerged. The (iPod) player is the platform for both the storage and the playing of music. There is no need to refer back to a hard copy of vinyl, cassettes or compact discs. Such a behaviour and practice changes how we think about, understand and write about popular music. The fluidity and mobility of music – alongside the intimacy and inwardness of carrying a personal database of music with us through our daily life – requires the development of new strategies and theories.

The third rationale for this book is a desire **to construct a more complex and contemporary musical history that is post-rock and post-genre.** Too often in past studies, there has been an (over)emphasis on a particular period of music – the 1950s, 1960s or 1970s – and particular guitar-based genres of music. My task in *Popular Music: Topics, Trends and Trajectories* is to show the complexity of popular music and its capacity to hook into a range of other media. There is not only attention to music or lyrics, but also to study the art of iTunes' banners and advertising, screen cultures through music videos and gaming soundtracks, user-generated content and the influence of dancing. Popular music is so important because it moves between media, beyond sound and into the screens, visions and bodies. I want to capture some of that textual complexity.

When defining this simple phrase 'popular music,' we reveal movement, arguments and controversies about quality and cultural value. Popular music patrols its boundaries. It connects in intimate ways with an audience of listeners, providing information about identity, while also working with mature and new media to create communities of listeners and innovative modes and models for listening. Too often, popular music collapses into the category of rock music. While rock music is worthy of consideration, it is an historical term that requires contextualization, not naturalization. Popular music is much larger than rock music.

The fourth motivation in writing this book is the imperative **to position popular music into creative industries initiatives, strategies and policies**. Popular music is a business. Tracks are produced to make money. It is a corporate, capitalist, creative industry. While performers – particularly from 'indie' genres – will confirm their love of music rather than business, the emergence of creative industries initiatives, including Richard Florida's (2005) work with the creative class and creative cities and Charles Leadbeater's and Kate Oakley's (1999) research into 'The Independents', has increased the connectivity between 'creativity' and 'commerce'. Grassroots capitalism is enabled through illegal downloading communities and Web 2.0 social networking sites that share music through YouTube and – to a lesser extent – Facebook and Twitter. Throughout the 2000s, both popular music and capitalism changed. New business models emerged through creative industries' strategies.

Musical platforms always change. The movement from vinyl to cassettes to compact discs to MP3s is not a linear story of progression, but offers insight into how listening communities transform. Instead of isolating genres from their communities, my goal is to explore the fluid new relationships between sound and auditory cultures. It is no longer – was it ever? – easy to determine the relationship between 'the underground' and 'the overground'. The accelerated movement between popular and unpopular music ensures not only dynamism in genres, but also the inherent difficulty in writing about a formation as it is changing. Not only does this speed of change create challenges for music journalists and academics, but also for fans.

The structure of *Popular Music: Topics, Trends and Trajectories*

Five sections organize *Popular Music: Topics, Trends and Trajectories*. The first – **Approaches** – embraces the interdisciplinary study of music. Instead of isolating songs and sounds along with the disciplines like musicology, sociology and history that have studied them, the goal is to orient students through a much more active and engaged process of study. These chapters show students how to study not only music, but also dancing, music videos and music journalism. The goal is to move them away from the act of listening to music towards the process of writing about it.

The second section – **Music Spaces** – is located in and explores how sounds create an environment. The role of music in filling out the spaces of cities, clubs, pubs and recording studios is enlarged and enhanced by the digital spaces created through MP3s. Because it is so difficult to write about popular music and convey in words what it feels like to listen to a great song or dance to a pulsating rhythm, I introduce a series of writing strategies and tools to anchor music into a physical space. One strategy to simplify, clarify and solidify the meaning that comes from sound is to construct an imaginary connection between music and place. For example, acid house was linked with Ibiza and the Hacienda nightclub in Manchester. Techno grasped the industrial decay of Detroit, which was influenced by the cold modernity of Kraftwerk's Düsseldorf. Narratives of urbanity and rurality, modernity and traditionalism play out in the space between a song and location. So often, these clichés compress and simplify the relationship between place and sound. Ponder phrases like Hawaiian Guitar, Delta Blues or East Coast Rock. This fusing of place and sound is an attempt to transform music into (hi)story, activating representations of a city or landscape that may not be accurate or real, but still offer a hook into popular music, and particularly the writing about it. Music is more than digital files. It tells stories about place and identity.

The third section – **Instruments of/for Study** – explores the sound boxes of popular music. Moving from guitars, keyboards and drumming cultures through to the voice, turntable, iPod and mixing software, I explore how objects of music creation are the basis of subjective experiences of a life through sound. The goal is to show how particular instruments configure not only a sound but also a community.

The fourth section – **Genre and Community** – returns to conventional topics and concepts in popular music studies. Most books on popular music will use genre as the basis of their study. Indeed, Dan Laughey stated, 'music is delivered and sold to youth audiences, and young people on the whole are fans of one music genre or another' (2006: 1). Such a reality has changed. By digitizing the sonic back catalogue, many genres are resurrected from historical interest and re-introduced into the contemporary mix. The dialogue between past and present manifestations of country, soul, punk and dance music is more direct, immediate and intimate than was possible in the analogue age. As Dawe and Bennett realized, 'there can be no doubt that musical styles serve as important marketing devices for the global music industry, allowing for the categorization and packaging of music to appeal to certain audiences' (2001: 4). Genres offer a feedback loop to musicians. A categorization of 'Emo' or 'Handbag House' allows musicians and DJs to position their work in both history and context. *Popular Music: Topics, Trends and Trajectories* does not present a review of the genres from an historical, industry or musician's perspective. Instead, this section explores the consequences of such labeling for an audience of popular music. There are assumptions about the audience for rap, when compared to country music or metal. Particularly after Bing Crosby's retirement from popular music in 1954 and the emergence of rock and roll, popular music was assumed to be the music of youth, with a 'generation gap' constructed and studied in the 1960s. This research was based on assumptions about the audience and genre. There is a reason for this simplification of song and listener, just as there is a reason why genre is problematized in this book. The goal is to understand the complexities of research into popular music, fandom and audiences. Listening to popular music is as it is likely to be conservative as it is radical, reinforcing our attitudes about love, sex, politics and rhythm as much as challenging us to think differently. Genre is an intellectual shorthand that prevents more complex and new ways of thinking and writing about music.

The final section of the book – **Debates** – takes on eight topics of controversy and challenge. Moving from the weeping wound of intellectual property, censorship and regulation of Web 2.0 through to the long-standing concerns with race, appropriation and the commodification of difference, I also explore questions about men, women and sex. The key debates of the book, with regard to digitization and user generated content, are matched by a renewed questioning of the role of resistance, politics and protest in contemporary music.

These sections have a single aim: to probe how digitization has agitated conventional methods and modes of studying popular music. One of the greatest problems that emerges in courses about popular music is that students write using subjective judgements alone, rather than grasping how sound engages with diverse audiences in different ways. The importance of interpretation and research in popular music studies – rather than opinion and conjecture – is a constant theme of this book. As we travel through this historical moment of change – with our iPhone earbuds firmly pressed into our ear canals or our Skullcandy headphones creating a secondary supportive cranium – we can hear and feel the pervasive impact of music on our lives. The goal now is to disturb our iPod isolation in order to build a community in and through digitized music. With more music available to download than was ever possible to buy or tape in an analogue environment, both the benefits and problems of consumerist choice emerge.

Popular music matters for its complexity, inter-textuality and accessibility. What makes it an important source and basis for our daily lives and university study is its capacity to be 'pop,' to capture a moment and channel an experience. While popular music is a sign system shaped by history, geography, conventions and genres, it will always be about something more. Discovering, mapping and understanding that 'something' is the task set for the pages that follow.

Key Questions

1. Which disciplines and approaches can assist the study of music?
2. What are the challenges involved in studying popular music?
3. Why is it difficult for students to write about popular music?
4. What is the difference between fan and academic knowledge of popular music?

Further Reading

Elborough, T. (2008) *The Long-player Goodbye*. London: Hodder & Stoughton.

Knopper, S. (2009) *Appetite for Self-destruction: The Spectacular Crash of the Record Industry in the Digital Age*. New York: Simon & Schuster.

Lewis, J. and Miller T. (eds) (2003) *Critical Cultural Policy Studies: A Reader.* Malden: Blackwell.

Wall, T. (2003) *Studying Popular Music Culture.* London: Hodder Arnold.

Sonic sources

Henry Jenkins, Johanna Blakley, David Carr, Stephen Duncombe (2009) 'Politics and popular culture', MIT, iTunes U.

Joy Division (1979) 'Digital', released on *Still* (1981). Factory.

Linkin Park (2003) 'Nobody's Listening', *Meteora.* Warner Bros.

Undertones (1978) 'Teenage Kicks'. Good Vibrations.

Visual sources

Dylan, B. (2006) 'Someday Baby' iTunes Commercial, *YouTube,* http://www.youtube.com/watch?v=X450KgAlgIQ

Florida, R. (2003) 'Richard Florida: The Rise of the Creative Class', *YouTube,* http://www.youtube.com/watch?v=iLstkIZ5t8g

Jobs, S. (2001) 'Apple Music Event 2001', *YouTube,* http://www.youtube.com/watch?v=kN0SVBCJqLs

The Beatles (2009) 'The Beatles Rock Band Twist and Shout Trailer', *YouTube,* http://www.youtube.com/watch?v=h3YlnQze028

Web sources

Against Pop, http://nomuzak.co.uk

Creative Class, http://creativeclass.com/

Harris, J. (2009) 'Don't look back', *The Guardian,* (June 29) http://www.guardian.co.uk/music/2009/jun/27/music-writing-bangs-marcus

International Association for the Study of Popular Music, http://www.iaspm.net/

Section I

Approaches

Section 1

Approaches

Listening to Music

The first issue to consider in *Popular Music: Topics, Trends and Trajectories* is the difference between hearing and listening. If we do not want to see a person or image that troubles us, then we can close our eyelids or look away. We do not have to see what we do not want to see. Hearing is different. Our ears do not have lids. As we move through daily life, we hear sharp and unexpected noises, arguments on the street, crying children and cars in need of a service as they grind around corners. Unless we remove our bodies from a location, we hear unintended and unwanted sounds. Often these unexpected sounds are termed noise. To close our ears to these 'foreign' sounds, a range of strategies can be deployed, including the use of iPod buds or headphones to block other people's noise with a listener's preferred soundtrack. Schafer described this as 'an attempt to modulate information intake' (2004: 28). A refusal to listen is also a refusal to fit into an environment. Mobile devices enable us to control what we hear and therefore create a sonic world of our own choosing.

Listening is different from hearing. It is intentional, conscious and active. Listening is literacy for the ear. It is a social act and involves making choices in filtering and select-ing our sonic environment. While we may *hear* noise, we *listen* to music. Listening is a reading strategy for sounds that involves choices to make music relevant to a context and environment. Listening is underestimated in our daily lives and undertheorized in academic literature. Jean-Luc Nancy confirmed that hearing is 'to understand the sense' and listening 'is to be straining towards a possible meaning' (2007: 6). He argued that listening requires work, decoding the unknown and inaccessible into the realm of interpretation and understanding. The overwhelming majority of information we receive to understand the world emerges through our eyes. We believe what we see. Most of what constitutes knowledge and methods of study – like ethnography and participant observation – attaches meanings to behaviour, derived primarily from the information we gather through vision. Since September 11, terrorism has been captured on live news. Differences between people are judged visually. Racism emerges from the differences that we observe, rather than the diverse accents that we hear.

With this saturation of visuality, Michael Bull and Les Back probe 'the opportunities provided by thinking with our ears' (2004: 3). When moving beyond the visual, there is an opportunity to explore and test other senses. For example, music also activates tactil-ity through playing musical instruments or feeling the groove of records as they spin on a turntable or touching the screen of an iPhone. When listening to sound with our consciousness, we experience our world differently, beyond the visual.

The bedroom. The lounge. The car. The train. The street. These are some of the spaces for listening in our lives. The desire to control our listening spaces and reduce the influence of the noises emanating from those around us is best revealed through the proliferation of personal stereos. The intimacy and isolation created by users with Sony Walkmans in the 1980s and iPods in the 2000s unearthed critics who lambasted the alienation and disconnection of young people. A great advocate of the classics, Allan Bloom, nominated personal stereos as a sign that a generation was deaf and blind to high culture and literature.

> As long as [my students] have the Walkman on they cannot hear what the great tradition has to say. And, after its prolonged use, when they take it off, they find they are deaf (1987: 81).

Bloom is making a comment not only about the loudness of music, but also about the literacy of popular music listeners. Similarly, in 1985, Steven Chaffee stated – flatly and without comment – that 'listening to music is the most universal mass communication behaviour, requiring neither literacy nor advanced electronic media' (1985: 416). Such dated statements from both Chaffee and Bloom confirm that listening to popular music has been misunderstood in our recent history. University academics have too often judged, rather than understood. As the 1980s progressed, such judgements about cultural value were questioned through postmodern theory, deconstruction, popular music studies, media literacy theory and ethnographic research into auditory cultures. To misunderstand listening is to ignore the literacy, choices and intelligence of groups and individuals who are unlike us. Listening to music provides the form and context for a different history of desire, hope, love and social change to emerge.

We read sound through our ears as much as we read print on paper or text on a screen. Through our sonic literacies we hear a voice, a combination of notes or a rhythm and assess its quality, effectiveness and appropriateness. Every act of listening is based on recalling a prior hearing experience. When we hear, we learn. Because we lack ear lids, we accidentally build literacies, learning about ourselves through what we hear and how we judge it. When reading the novel *High Fidelity* or watching the film, it is easy to see how views about listening become statements about identity and judgements of others. A fan of Bob Dylan has credibility. A follower of Chris de Burgh is assessed less favourably. The tether between listening choices and constructing a sense of self establishes boundaries of belonging, community, inclusion and exclusion.

Most literacies are learnt, improved and disseminated through media. Radio has been the crucial medium of transmission for popular music. Until the mid twentieth century, it was described as 'the wireless', but this word has been recently appropriated to describe short-range networking through a Wireless Local Area Network, WiFi and Bluetooth. Radio refers to the transceiver device. Wireless describes the method used for the delivery of communication. The influential moment that entwined the history of radio and the history of popular music began in 1960, when Sony introduced the first transistorized radio. Demonstrating many of the innovative features of the iPod, including its small size and weight and durability, it allowed music to be much more portable. It also disconnected teenagers' listening locations and genres away from the central family radio cabinet. Digitization has built on these earlier innovations, influencing radio, with Digital Audio Broadcasting (DAB) increasing the selection of channels. Significantly, many of the features of talk radio have influenced podcasting, which involves a series of digitized media files being distributed over the internet using syndicated feeds (RSS). These podcasts are played on either a computer or portable media device. Podcasts – like radio – can refer to the content of programmes or the means by which it is distributed. The attraction of podcasting is that individuals can create what seem to be their own radio shows in the home with domestic software and hardware, including their preferred content. Listeners can then move the material to a convenient time and place. Most popular music genres, performers, DJs and fan communities have a series of regular podcasts produced by enthusiasts. For podcasters, listening has been transformed into the production of sound.

Listening has a history and this changes. The popularity of iPods for example has changed listening. Firstly, digitized formats like the ACC and MP3 have compressed sonic files, removing data from music. Secondly, through much of the history of iPods, consumers have heard music through ear-bud headphones with heavy leakage or small computer speakers (Milner, 2009: 354). Mobility, ease of downloading and low cost (or free if illegally obtained) music became more important than sound quality. Peter Gotcher realized that 'the reality is that the generation coming up may never own a stereo' (Gotcher in Milner, 2009: 354). One consequence of such an argument is that the literacy to recognize and appreciate high quality sounds and music may be declining. There is however an alternative narrative to this history of compressed files, tinny speakers and leakage from the iPod buds. Skullcandy have inverted the market, creating a new group of consumers who choose to wear large and bulky headphones with little or no leakage (Skullcandy, 2009). The parallel to the 1980s is obvious. Even in a period of Walkman miniaturization, boom boxes and ghetto blasters had started to appear on the street. These high quality, visible headphones also change how we listen. Compression freshens old sounds. When sonic information is removed, other sounds buried in the mix emerge. For example, Carly Simon's blistering revenge song 'You're So Vain' gains new layers of meaning as Mick Jagger's backing vocal is peeled away from the instrumental track after compression is applied. Conversely, the other famous backing track recorded by Jagger for 'Out of Time', the song co-written with Keith Richards for Chris Farlowe, dissolves in the mix, melted by the extraordinary paint-stripping voice of Farlowe. In other words, the combination of removing sonic material from sonic files and increasing the auditory capacity of the headphones such as the Skullcandy range is creating new modes of listening, a new way of hearing popular music.

Digitization is also reducing the range of musical platforms. The decline of the CD has had a major economic impact on recording industries. Downloaded sonic files are the new product. Such a change is also creating new opportunities, with innovative ways to combine the content of music with the form of media that can present it. Ralf Hutter from Kraftwerk asked,

> What is an album? In that format, it was 40 minutes, by a decision made by vinyl: side A, and side B. And then the CD was longer – and now, it could be endless. We could do an endless album … because for me, music is like 24 hours. We created the 168-hour week for Kraftwerk (Hutter in Harris, 2009: 3).

The change of platform has shaped listening in new ways. The iPod has altered how listeners think about and categorize music. The white ear buds signify a type of sonic experience, even if a range of iPods now features screens and touch. The iPod can encourage safe listening, only hearing what we have uploaded and downloaded, but radically transforms how we store, access, distribute and move music.

Listening is intensely personal. As Peter Szendy asks, 'what summons us to listen?' (2008: 142). It involves making choices about our environment and identity. Each new musical technology creates artificial ear lids to develop a new intimacy between the self and sound. The transistor radio in the 1960s disconnected teenagers from their family. The iPod has allowed diverse groups to claim space through sound, whether it is commuters, students or drivers. When sharing listening practices, communities of interest are built. On social networking sites like Facebook and MySpace, a list of shared listening choices confirms a much deeper level of connection between 'friends' than only sharing music. Listening builds commonality and difference. Hearing and listening is an underutilized skill and literacy in all forms of research, which prioritizes eye over ear. Mark Smith et al. have realized that 'historians have only just begun to overcome their deafness to the aural worlds of the past' (Smith, Snay and Smith, 2004: 365). Our role as students and scholars of popular music is to render significant and resonant the sounds and sensibilities from the past and present.

Key Questions

1. Why has listening to popular music been denigrated by conservative writers and researchers?
2. Is listening to popular music passive?
3. What are the consequences to the study of popular music of not having ear lids?
4. What is the relationship between hearing and power? The panopticon was the visual mechanism for surveillance. Is there an equivalent aural mechanism for surveillance, empowerment and disempowerment?

Further Reading

Bull, M. and Back, L. (2004) *The Auditory Culture Reader*. Oxford: Berg.

Erlmann, V. (ed.) (2005) *Hearing Cultures*. Oxford: Berg.

Morley, P. (2003) *Words and Music*. London: Serpent's Tail.

Wittkower, D. E. (2008) *iPod and Philosophy: iCon of an ePoch*. Chicago, IL: Open Court.

Sonic sources

British Library Sound Archive (2009) http://www.bl.uk/nsa

Hear in this place (2009) Public Radio International, iTunes.

Kraftwerk (1974) *Autobahn*.

Joy Division (1979) *Transmission*.

Visual sources

High Fidelity (2000) Bueno Vista Home Entertainment.

Noise.io – The iPhone Synthesizer (2008) *YouTube*, http://www.youtube.com/watch?v=u8yhQHJUll8

Radio Days (1986) MGM.

White Noise for iPhone and iPod Touch (2008) *YouTube*, http://www.youtube.com/watch?v=s9h-sWQRC0k

Web sources

Noise Abatement Society (2009) http://www.noiseabatementsociety.com

Noise Act (1996) http://www.opsi.gov.uk/acts/acts1996/ukpga_19960037_en_1

Noise Pollution (2009) Environmental Protection Agency, http://epa.gov/air/noise.html

Ross, A. (2009) *The Rest is Noise*, http://www.therestisnoise.com/audio/

Visualizing Music

Songs summon visuality. Story songs in particular use words and instruments to paint a visual picture and evoke imagination. Al Stewart's 'The Year of the Cat' (1976) paints a Casablanca-inflected exoticism, using saxophone, piano and the lyrical mention of Peter Lorre. Maximo Park's 'Books from Boxes' (2007) is anchored to a rain-swept day in the north of England and Sunderland's football ground, the Stadium of Light. Many songs evoke images, colours and sensations. Visuality and the visual media are woven through music, whether these involve seeing a busker perform on a street, watching a DJ in a club, the wash of music videos providing wallpaper for gyms or creating new relationships between sound and vision on an iPad.

Such saturated visuality offers a stark contrast to the nineteenth century. The aspirational abstraction of 'classical' music aimed to give it social status and an equivalence to painting. The artistic form was cold, aloof and disconnected from the realities and struggles of daily life. The best art and culture was socially aspirational, summoning our best selves and embodying the excellence and highest achievements of individuals. To enact this project, 'art' was disconnected from live music and the historical conditions that created its production and performance. Before the infiltration of such a high cultural agenda, music was unthinkable without performers. Viewers could see as much as hear the music being played. With the arrival of both the radio and the gramophone, the purity of music involved its separation from its means of production. To this day, the visuality of music remains a site of controversy and threat, whether describing the scarcity of clothes worn by women in hip hop videos, the decadence of Roxy Music album covers, the fashion of Lady Gaga, or the quirky clichés of films like *Moulin Rouge* or *High School Musical*.

When visuality was tethered to popular music through the twentieth century, the 'threat' to youth via music increased. The conservative critic Allan Bloom, who featured in the last *Popular Music: Topics, Trends and Trajectories* chapter for 'Listening to Music', not only disliked the Walkman, he also exposed the threat and horror of music videos.

> Picture a thirteen-year-old boy sitting in the living room of his family home doing a math assignment while wearing his Walkman headphones or watching MTV … A pubescent child whose body throbs with orgasmic rhythms; whose feelings are made articulate in hymns to the joys of onanism or the killing of parents; whose ambition is to win fame and wealth in imitating the drag-queen who makes the music. In short, life is made into a nonstop, commercially prepackaged masturbational fantasy (1987: 74–75).

Bloom rendered popular music a threat because it encouraged rampant sexuality, violence and short cuts to success. It was seeing – rather than the listening to – music that made it onanistic. On similar grounds, Julian Johnson abused popular music, particularly its ubiquity, repetition and the 'manipulation' of sound through technology. The visual elements provided the greatest threat.

> The surface is everything. We live in a visual culture that attaches primary significance to the exchange of signs – of power, attraction, status, wealth, desire – that are overwhelmingly visual. Even in music visuals are everything: hence the ubiquity not only of the music video but the marketing of the star. And when it comes to the music the surface sheen is everything; the music is literally one-dimensional (2002: 58).

Even through the critique, Johnson confirms that music is attended by visual elements. The link between sound and vision was not invented by MTV. In venues for live performances, the singer, DJ or band members are seen, admired and watched as much as heard. Magazines present the smiling face of performers. The album cover – in its largest and most expansive form as the packaging for long-playing records – was a design opportunity to visualize music. An album sleeve protected the vinyl but was also an advertisement that distinguished one record from another product. Its project was a complex one, giving visuality to sound and a soundtrack to design. The most famous covers are from the height of the album's success as a format, including The Beatles' *Sgt. Pepper's Lonely Hearts Club Band* (1967), Pink Floyd's *Dark Side of the Moon* (1973), Roxy Music's *Country Life* (1974) and two conceptual covers: The Velvet Underground's *The Velvet Underground* (1968) and The Rolling Stones' *Sticky Fingers* (1971).

The era of the LP was a critical moment in the visual history of popular music. Peter Gammond stated at the height of the long-playing record's popularity,

> Records are no longer brittle objects in brown paper wrappers. They are permanent documents, and it is expected that they will come in tastefully designed covers with full and accurate information on their contents (1980: 27).

While the visual elements of popular music were enhanced through record covers, this mode of visuality has declined with a change in platform. Through the downloading of MP3s, these 'permanent documents' have not survived. The iPod Video, the iPhone and iPad have instead created different relationships between visuality and music. Music videos are self-standing cultural artifacts and products to be purchased and downloaded. These digitized sonic and visual files are not permanent, but convenient and mobile. The iTunes Store added the sale of videos to its music range in October 2005 and full-length movies followed in September 2006. A platform that started playing music and audio files is now using the iPod's screen to play texts of visual culture, including music videos, film and television, games and a suite of applications.

While applications and album covers show how music can be visualized, the most obvious example remains the music video. Activating visual and sonic literacies, music videos are texts of excess, incorporating thousands of editing cuts within a three-minute period. Music videos are advertisements, promotional materials that accompany – most frequently – a single song. The 1980s are particularly associated with music videos. While there are many full-length musical films that create a powerful relationship between a song and image, including Paul Robeson's 'Ol' Man River' from *Show Boat*, the longer form and narrative construction of these musicals meant that the song's function was subsumed in the story. Conversely, music videos are forms of short film that trial new visual techniques. Abstractions and non-narrative techniques are common. The earliest music videos – particularly those from The Monkees and The Beatles – were used to promote singles without performers touring.

In the 1970s and 1990s, music videos offered a distinct visual history of popular music. Aural and visual codes were collapsed, with musical genres like the New Wave and New Romantic movement gaining from this tight dialogue. Music videos have circulated via clubs, television programmes, videos, DVDs and now portable music devices. Music videos also hooked into a range of other histories, including

- the history of film
- the history of television
- the history of popular music
- the history of dance
- the history of postmodernity.

Music videos found their natural home in the segmented flow of television. Occasionally they accessed a bigger culture, as shown by Ultravox's *Vienna* or Michael Jackson's *Thriller*. The use of film noir or horror codes enabled the deployment of sophisticated editing and a reshaping of the boundaries between high and popular culture. Music video enabled new cinematic options. Peter Gabriel's *Sledgehammer* and A-ha's *Take On Me* blended new modes of animation with live footage. Because music video moves between commerce and art, popular and avant-garde, realism and modernism, the visual and sonic possibilities of a four-minute music video are radically distinct from a ninety-minute film. The impact of music videos on cinema, from *Risky Business* to *Moulin Rouge*, is obvious and important to recognize.

The proliferation of screen cultures has ensured the development and expansion of new ways to see music. Video games use sound effects to convey interactivity and the relationship between a player's behaviour and the screen action. A range of composers has gained great success for their work in writing game soundtracks. Koji Kondo is known for his work with Nintendo. As the sound cards improved, soundtracks for games became increasingly complex. *Grand Theft Auto* is an example of how found sounds can capture an environment and move the player through both the streets and the game. The Xbox also increased the level of interactivity, by allowing players to create customized soundtracks for some games by inserting a compact disc into the platform. This gaming market matters to popular music. One in every four dollars spent in the USA on entertainment is linked to gaming (2008 Gaming Industry Data, 2009), and it delivers music to consumers in new ways. For example, the unsigned band Avenged Sevenfold had their music launched on the Madden NFL 2004 Xbox game, while Electronic Arts (EA) games have included a range of performers on their releases, including Kings of Leon, Blink-182, Green Day and Fatboy Slim.

While popular music is positioned best within a wider history of sound, its visual history is also provocative, complex and dynamic. With the growth in both gaming and screen-enabled mobile music platforms, the visual elements of popular music are areas of development and growth. Computers have created new visual opportunities for music. For example, whenever a Windows environment was activated, 3.25 seconds of music played. Brian Eno created this 'song' in 1995. It is probably the most played sample of music in the world, yet it is forgotten because primacy is given to the screen. Computer-mediated environments are transforming the relationships between sound and vision. The screen has become a new space for a visual communication about music. Particularly through YouTube, not only music but also screen-based communication can be the basis of a marketing campaign. Social networking sites allow a free release of music from both new and established performers, along with the accompanying videos. Domestic platforms such as the range of Flip cameras, with resident editing software, allow bands to produce visual accompaniments to their songs at low cost and with limited expertise in film making and editing. Direct uploading to YouTube is also possible. Frederick Levy rewrote Andy Warhol's famous slogan for this Web 2.0 environment, titling his guide to the portal as *15 Minutes of Fame: Becoming a Star in the YouTube Revolution* (2008). Such social networking sites confirm that music is not only visible, but also that screens are preserving and disseminating new histories of sound.

Key Questions

1. How does seeing a performer change how you think about music?
2. What was the role of the album cover in advertising the songs included in a package?
3. Now that songs are downloaded without visual covers, has the visuality of popular music declined?
4. What potentials and problems do social networking sites and YouTube offer to new bands, performers, DJs and producers?

Further Reading

Austerlitz, S. (2007) *Money for Nothing: A History of the Music Video from The Beatles to The White Stripes*. London: Continuum.

Frith, S. (ed.) (1993) *Sound and Vision: Music Video Reader.* Abingdon: Routledge.

Hanson, M. (2006) *Reinventing Music Video: Next-generation Directors, Their Inspiration and Work.* Cheadle: Rotavision.

Vernallis, C. (2004) *Experiencing Music Video: Aesthetics and Cultural Contexts.* New York: Columbia University Press.

Sonic sources

Buggles (1979) *Video Killed the Radio Star.* Island.

Electronic Arts (2006-), podcast, iTunes.

The Music of Grand Theft Auto IV (2008) Rock Star Games.

The Sims 2 (2005-), podcast, iTunes.

Visual sources

Human Traffic (1999) Fruit Salad Films.

I'm Not There (2007) Paramount.

Moulin Rouge (2002) Bazmark.

Shine a Light (2008) Paramount Vantage.

Web sources

MySpace, www.myspace.com

Revogaming, www.revogaming.net

Soundtrack Collector, www.soundtrackcollector.com

YouTube, www.youtube.com

Dancing to Music

Dancing is a cultural practice. Diverse intellectual strategies and theories are required to research and write about it, including history, sociology and leisure studies. The rarity of documentation and evidence about dancing practices raises questions about the techniques and analytical models used to gather source material and develop a coherent approach. Dance studies is an important field that has much to offer popular music studies. Methods deployed include ethnography, participant observation and archive-based historical research. Dance studies is part of a wider study of the body in society and has been part of cultural studies since the late 1980s. Stories of identity are told through dance. It was the great theorist of postmodernity and popular culture, Dick Hebdige, who offered the greatest statement about the purpose of dancing: 'knowledge that comes up through the feet' (1987: 68). The question is how to move this knowledge from the feet and write about it.

Through its history, dance studies has been Eurocentric and focused on concert-based dance, particularly ballet. Now, through the impact of sociology, cultural studies and media studies, new histories of bodies and identity are emerging. There are difficulties and challenges in writing about dance. The problem is that there are few sources available for scholars to understand and document dancing practices. Dancing is of the moment. It is a series of transient kicks, flicks, stretches, shapes, behaviours and actions. How this experience is transcribed into words raises scholarly challenges and difficulties. Too often 'Western' dance studies becomes lost in theories of 'art', which means that popular cultural dance practices are either devalued or ignored. Even amid new and interdisciplinary subject areas, dance is neglected. Angela McRobbie realized that, 'it is surprising how negligent sociology and cultural studies have been of dance' (2006: 207). It is also surprising how negligent dance studies has been of sociology and cultural studies. When populations move, so do their rhythmic patterns and dances. Andrew Ross argued, 'the dance floor has always offered a safe haven for the socially marginalised' (1994: 10). While thinking about the role of the body in music, it is important to consider the interplay between subversion and seduction, social acceptance and sonic and spatial invasion. Through the impact of acid house – developing into techno, trane, jungle and drum 'n' bass – new relationships were formed between dancing spaces and architecture, technology and drugs. Important interdisciplinary approaches are being developed to investigate dance as a social activity and a way to participate with and enjoy music. Such an influence has moved the study of dance from a formalist or aesthetic perspective to a contextual foundation, from sociology or cultural studies (Thomas: 2003). The goal is to understand dancing in context, rather than as isolated choreography.

There are three ways to understand the link between dancing and living, movement and meaning.

> Dancing is an affective experience that operates in a transitory and ephemeral way. For moments in a dancing experience, the dancer can transcend discourse.

OR

> Dancing directly performs the social positioning of the dancer.

OR

> There is a separation between the dancing space and the living space. The feelings and experiences while dancing gain meaning later, when the dance floor has been vacated.

In other words, dancing is either disconnected from daily life, embedded in daily life or a transitory pause in daily life. Whichever perspective is deployed, rules and restrictions limit the movements on the dance floor. Primarily, the body is disciplined through rhythm.

While choreography maps and tracks steps, it is difficult to reconstruct a dance as it was first executed. In the case of dancing to popular music, the lack of formal, pre-planned and executed steps ensures that it is almost impossible to reclaim and reproduce the ephemeral form. There were and are particular bodily shapes and movements that have been associated with dancing to popular music, such as the Twist, the Hucklebuck, the Time Warp and the Hustle. More frequently, a much more gentle and subtle relationship between bodies and space, bodies and beat is formed. While ballroom dancing is part of popular culture and increasing in its popularity through the mainstream television success of *Dancing with the Stars* and *Strictly Come Dancing*, social dance culture transformed after disco, acid house and techno. Dance is part of the history of femininity and masculinity, sexuality and intimacy. It is also a part of wider struggles about economic and social injustice. Emma Goldman is attributed with the evocative statement that, 'If I can't dance, it's not my revolution' (in Steinem, 1995: 4). If we think about dancing as a site of knowledge, rather than as a corporeal response to rhythm, then it creates new ways of learning about bodies, histories, politics and memory. Dancing is difficult to understand and so is dance music, because it is non-linguistic and involves the social transcriptions of space.

There is a justification of this resistance through movement. Dancing is a celebration of an event, emotion or experience, ending Shakespearian comedies, confirming freedom for heroines from Eliza Doolittle in *My Fair Lady* to Baby Houseman in *Dirty Dancing*, and virility for heroes from Fred Astaire's character Jerry Travers in *Top Hat* to Kevin Bacon's Ren McCormack in *Footloose*. Dancing captures freedom, self-confidence and community. Emotion and time are invested in dancing. It is an act of participation, to cut through and share a complex rhythm and pattern of movement. When describing the meaning in dance music and dancing, Kodwo Eshun argued, 'The body is a large brain' (1998: 2). This bodily brain transforms dancing into an opportunity to think about music through movement. Most popular culture encourages people to sit down: reading newspapers, surfing the web, playing video games or watching television. Music encourages a physicality of response to sound, from singing to tapping feet in time through to dancing. Therefore, the study of dance is not only part of the history of aesthetics, but also part of affectivity, style, music and sexuality. The body is framed and restricted by ideological normalities of femininity, masculinity, sexuality, religion and class. Even the dancing body cannot escape history.

One of the disciplining limitations on the dancing body is rhythm. Dancing is a way of reading a beat through the feet, legs and body. It is a rhythmic movement of the body to music and an expressive, non-verbal mode of communication. While it can hold ceremonial, competitive, or erotic functions, it can also be part of a corporeal vocabulary to signify belonging to a social system. A large part of the response to popular music has been physical, moving the body in a particular way. The role and place of consciousness and reflection in the dancing experience has been a topic of debate, with rave culture creating Temporary Autonomous Zones. From the Jive to the Jitterbug, from jacking to moshing, body shapes are formed that capture and perform the changes in music.

There is also a discourse of dancing. Movement to music is positioned into diverse frameworks of meaning by corporate and cultural institutions, including journalism, recording companies, television, fashion-houses and film industries. Occasionally when we dance we will feel something, a rush or explosion of emotion that summons the euphoric sensation that we can do anything, be anything and that this feeling will last forever. How we think, feel and behave on the dance floor – even if that dance floor is our lounge, kitchen or bedroom – is different from how we move, dress and think away from the dance floor. Humans used their bodies to interpret, understand and remember sounds throughout history. Sign language is based on translating spoken words, sentences and ideas into a corporeal representation. Dancing to music interprets rhythm rather than words through our feet and translates sound into meaning. Dance music in particular has been based on a desire to move to recorded – rather than live – music (Butler, 2006: 35).

Dancing has been underdiscussed in popular music studies. The arrival of dance culture in the late 1980s and the early 1990s through house and techno meant that these movements could no longer be ignored as either a form of community or as a way to 'read' music. While dance leaves few traces in historical records, it offers a way for disempowered groups such as young people, women, citizens of colour, gay, lesbian and working class communities to grasp the gaze of dominant groups and then twist the surveillance into the pleasure of being watched. Dancing is a product of popular music and a process through which meaning can be formulated. It is therefore remarkable how often dancing is absent from academic and journalistic understandings of popular music. Jeremy Gilbert and Ewan Pearson recognized that 'scholarly writing on music – "classical" or "popular" – has been astonishingly neglectful of the importance of the relationship between music and dancing' (1999: 47). Perhaps part of the reason for this absence is that rock music encourages serious listening with respect, rather than dancing to create pleasure, euphoria or community belonging. The interventions of punk, emo and metal fans created new opportunities for men to move and shapes for them to assume.

Most post-1950s music is in 4/4 (or common) time. This has become the default time signature for dance music, particularly disco and house derivatives. The evenness of this beat, sometimes used to critique the simplicity of popular music, creates a predictability of rhythm to enable dancing. In other words, the rhythmic patterns of popular music are difficult to understand without grasping how beat enables movement. The history of intimacy and social relationships between men and women is conveyed through watching the shift in dancing styles. In the years before and just after World War One, the Foxtrot and Tango presented smooth, stylish and sexual movements where male and female dancers embraced as one and moved with great precision. The Tango opened a world of new Latin rhythms, which remains part of the mix within contemporary dance music. By the 1940s, one of the most exciting of dances, the Jitterbug, had arrived. It was essentially a gymnastic dance. The air step involved one dancer in the couple leaving the floor. Couples were freer to 'do their own thing'. The movement in the Jitterbug known as the breakaway allowed a show-off solo for the male dancer, predating disco's fascination with the man in the flared white suit. The next great transformation emerged through the 1960s when the choreography was individualized. The Twist, Mashed Potato, Frog, Swim, Pony, Jerk and Boogaloo all emerged, each with their own song. The Twist was the first dance that separated couples and provided the basis of contemporary club culture. Disco built on the separation of men's and women's bodies, changing the rules for dancing. The disco era created a highly integrated relationship between dancing and music. While the 1977 film *Saturday Night Fever* is controversially positioned in the history of disco because of its heteronormativity rather than acknowledging the gay foundation of the genre, the filmic narrative linked dancing with social mobility. This was empowering music for a recession era. Dancing became a shortcut to success. Similarly, films such as *Fame*, *Flashdance* and *High School Musical* linked dancing with social and economic achievement.

The 1980s and 1990s had their own movements and emotional restrictions, from voguing and slamming, the Lambada to the Macarena. Acid house, with its aerial hand motions, increased the space occupied by each dancer, just as Goth-induced dancing, clad in black and termed 'shoe gazing', compressed bodily space. The mosh pit was and is a site of stage diving and aggressive clashes of (generally male) bodies. Slamming, where two or more people run into each other in beat to the music, defamiliarizes the idea of acceptable kinesthetic coupling on a dance floor. The body is pummeled and bruised.

After the fall of acid house at the end of 1988, the dance floor splintered into acid jazz, deep house, garage, the Belgium-based new beat and rave. This fracturing continued through jungle and drum'n'bass. Raves were incredibly significant to this history of dance. Located originally outside of club culture, raves became the archetypal niche, entrepreneurial industry in the post-industrial age. Derelict industrial spaces and open fields were the venues for huge parties. The (official) raves returned to the clubs when these parties became the target of legislation in the UK and Australia. The Entertainment (Increased Penalties) Act of 1990 in the UK was an evocative finale to the end of the decade party. Touted as the Acid House Bill, this legislation served to police night life. The British courts had the power to impose a twenty thousand pound fine for holding 'unlicensed public entertainment'. There were protests in response to this bill, and the freedom to dance became one of many nodes of political action against Margaret Thatcher's government. Yet dancing was not curtailed by this legislation. It was not forced to go underground. Instead, dance music became part of popular music. Kylie Minogue and the Pet Shop Boys enabled the movement of high house and dark dub to enter the charts and combine popular music and dance culture in new ways. Local sounds infiltrated international mixes. As Susan Luckman realized, 'local manifestations of dance music exist within a global network of linked cultural practices but have evolved in their own unique fashion' (2003: 315). Much of the popularity of British dance music in 1987 and 1988 translated and transformed dance music around the world. Its influence can still be seen in the performances of The Pussycat Dolls, Lady Gaga and Justin Timberlake.

The study of dancing offers much to intellectual life. To ignore this dancing space is to reduce the methodologies and theories deployed in and through popular music. Electronic dance music involves the movement from analogue to digital and the explosion of hybrid genres through remixing. It moves through national borders. It is inflected by colonialism and postcolonialism. It is sexual, dangerous and experimental. The dance floor is an unusual space. It is dark, hot and packed. Similarly, dance music is odd because it is made for the dark. It has a repetitive structure, resists clear analysis through a lack of lyrics and lacks the easy claims for originality and authenticity derived from analogue instruments. Its 'politics' is difficult to determine. Irvine Welsh, best known for his novel *Trainspotting*, captured some of this power in the party in his follow-up fiction, *Ecstasy*.

> It was the party: he felt that you had to party, you had to party harder than ever. It was the only way. It was your duty to show that you were still alive. Political sloganeering and posturing meant nothing; you had to celebrate the joy of life in the face of all those grey forces and dead spirits who controlled everything (1996: 26–7).

Dancing teaches movement, change and politics. In returning dancing to popular music studies, experience connects with knowledge. Much of dancing history is situated in the space between self expression and collective recognition. For women particularly, dancing is a way to bring bodies back to popular music history. Leslie Gotfrit suggested that,

> Dancing precipitates an incredible longing. To recover the pleasure – in the imagining and re-membering, the connecting again with my limbs, my breath, my body – is to ignite desire. These are rare moments of realizing my body and mind as not distinct, and of feeling the power of creativity when embodied. This is my history, and investment in dance, always in the shadow of the writing (1991: 176).

Dancing feet leads a writing hand. The task for dancers who attempt to write about it is to build connections between bodies and politics, beat and meaning, self and sensibility. Dance conflates many histories of bliss, economic dislocation, sexual experimentation, race-based prejudice, affirmative feminism and generational memory. While a record spins or a remix builds in software applications, dancers and dance writers circulate, sample and scratch notions of revolt, change and transformation.

There is a new way of dancing and new ways of moving. iPod Raves and Silent Discos do not feature loud music. Instead, a specialist mode of flash mob asks that participants bring along a media player, listen to their own music through headphones and dance to it. While this music is not heard by observers, the participants form a community of dance, unified in space but differentiated by soundtrack. Dancing is an active history that is translated by different feet. Dance is a creativity emerging in the dark, but is written about in the morning.

Key Questions

1. What is the relationship between dancing and popular music?
2. What difficulties exist in writing about dancing?
3. Why has the study of dance been neglected in popular music studies?
4. What did Dick Hebdige mean when he stated that dancing is 'knowledge that comes up through the feet'?

Further Reading

Buckland, T. (2006) *Dancing from Past to Present: Nation, Culture, Identities*. Madison: University of Wisconsin Press.

Daly, A. (2002) *Critical Gestures: Writings on Dance and Culture*. Middletown, CT: Wesleyan University Press.

Desmond, J. (2006) *Meaning in Motion: New Cultural Studies of Dance*. Durham: Duke University Press.

Thomas, Helen (2003) *The Body, Dance and Cultural Theory*. Houndmills: Palgrave.

Sonic sources

Chubby Checker (1961) *Let's Twist Again*. Parkway Records.

Donna Summer (1977) *I Feel Love*. Casablanca.

Martha Reeves and the Vandellas (1964) *Dancing in the Street*. Motown.

Snap (1998) *Rhythm is a Dancer*. Anzilotti & Munzing.

Visual sources

Dirty Dancing (1987) Vestron.

Grease (1978) Paramount.

High School Musical (2006) Disney.

Saturday Night Fever (1977) Paramount.

Web sources

Beyonce, 'Single Ladies,' *YouTube*, http://www.youtube.com/watch?v=x1nixzYHDus

Camp Jitterbug, http://www.campjiterbug.com/

Evolution of Dance, *YouTube*, http://www.youtube.com/watch?v=dMH0bHeiRNg

Fantasia, http://www.fantazia.org.uk/

Thinking About Music

Thinking about popular music in schools and universities requires the application of diverse scholarly disciplines and methods. Sociology, media studies and cultural studies have been used along with the attendant methods of ethnography, semiotics and unobtrusive archival research. The goal of these approaches and methods is to create a considered, rigorous, repeatable and valid series of interpretations from the ephemeral, subjective and volatile sounds of and audiences for popular music. To think about popular music is to control, limit and manage its interpretation and organize it so that it can be translated into scholarly prose.

The first decision to make when thinking about music is how to demarcate sound and noise. We all tend to claim particular sounds as pleasant and other as damaging or objectionable. This difference is sometimes generational, but other social variables may also be involved. Hearing and listening to music requires literacy. To be literate in what we hear, patterns are identified and particular aural signifiers (or forms) can be described through signifieds (or content). In other words, a particular combination of keyboard and bass patterns is a signifier. A signified for what we are hearing may be 'reggae'. Music is different from noise. There is a greater number of signifieds to describe musical signifiers. Those signs that cannot be recognized will often have one signified: noise.

As a mode of communication, music sequences emotion, ideas and attitudes to melody, harmony and rhythm. Morris stated, 'A song is a shot to the heart. A song is an excuse to share an emotion with someone else. A song is a way of saying something in the most direct way possible. A song is something that sneaks up behind you and tells you what you always suspected' (2003: 13). The reason why popular music is popular is because particular musicians are able to build a relationship with audiences through sound and vision. The relationship between performers and fans is based on cycles of personal allegiance and alliance. Popular music is a form of symbolic interaction. The encoding and decoding of sounds, rhythms and lyrics is mediated through the marketing of music as a commodity for consumption. It is also moderated between the forces of tradition and forces of resistance, providing a pattern of behaviour and the soundtrack for identity.

When studying popular music, it is important to remember that scholars are investigating a part of popular culture. It is not only a question of notes, rhythm, melody and sounds, but also a network of landscapes, relationships, links and matrixes. To move beyond listening and towards thinking requires strategies and techniques to transform the ephemeral and transitory into structures of thinking, evaluating and comparing. To theorize music is complicated, delicate and difficult. Indeed, because of its complex relationship between the aural and visual, aural and corporeal, sonic and spatial, rhythm and identity, many disciplinary strategies and techniques are required to understand music.

Thinking about music is a way to ponder and process controversial topics encircling youth, violence, drugs, work, consumerism, race and alienation. Throughout the 1960s, music was seemingly so important that subsequent generations could supposedly never feel or care as much about it. From the perspective of the early 1990s, music academics were concerned that 'young people' underestimated the impact of music in their lives. Simon Frith stated in 1991 that,

> The average teenager listens to pop music for 4 hours a day, 3 times more, it's claimed, than teens spent listening to pop in the 1970s. The poll also reveals that pop is 'very low' on the list of 'the most important things in life' ... The young listen to more and more and it means less and less (1991: 18).

The pervasiveness of pop has markedly increased since Frith wrote these words. Nevertheless, he was not alone in arguing that Baby Boomers had a special relationship with popular music. There was an implicit and special relationship between youth and music in the 1960s. Further, what Simon Frith described as a 'valorization of youth' (1992: 181) has infused the sociology of popular music with nostalgia, which continues with every reissue, remaster and repackaging of The Beatles' albums. Rock critics and academics bring forward their 'youth' as they age, overwriting the study of contemporary music (and youth). Digitization has shredded such seamless and simple connections between age and sound. Indeed, when popular music was reducible to youth culture (between the late 1950s to the late 1970s in particular) it was easier to think about, label and understand. Popular music, through its link to youth culture, could be framed as a resistive cultural force. Yet it was – and is – produced from businesses and corporations. This ambivalent capitalism – buying music to resist the commodification of culture – continues through the new platforms and software innovations, such as MP3, sampling and web-based sales. Lawrence Grossberg affirmed that,

> The various post-baby boomer generations seem barely able to use the music to mark any generational difference, and totally unable to mark intragenerational differences. While the music matters, it matters in not quite the same way ... Rather than dancing to the music you like, you like the music you can dance to (1994: 56).

Another interpretation is that there is simply more popular music history to explore and more of this music is accessible on new mobile media platforms.

There is a hierarchy of knowledge in thinking about popular music. Academics are supposedly at the top of the credibility pile, followed by journalists and then fans. Yet personal musical narratives – often documented through social networking sites – rupture such structures. The movements in the ranking of musical knowledge and expertise become particularly complex in user-generated environments such as

Wikipedia. The best entries, evaluated internally by Wikipedia's star ranking system, are invariably in the area of popular culture, and particularly focused on genres and performers of popular music. Collective fan knowledge tends to construct a thorough, empirical review of particular bands, albums and sounds. Often, though, the empirical information spills into empiricism, where 'facts' blot out alternative interpretations and readings of music. The blurring of fan and academic knowledge through wiki-enabled and social networking sites adds confusion and complexity to thinking about popular culture in a scholarly context.

Many academic disciplines offer fresh paradigms and approaches to popular music. Simon Frith and Andrew Goodwin, from the cusp of the 1980s and the 1990s, stated that 'the academic study of popular music is rooted in sociology, not musicology (for which, even now, popular music is at best of marginal interest), and the sociology of pop and rock is, in turn, rooted in two non-musical concerns; the meaning of 'mass culture' and the empirical study of youth' (1990: 1). In other words, musicology rarely explores the specificities of popular music. Sociology though has tended to focus on theories of youth and deviance. Each subject area and discipline offers advantages and disadvantages to the scholar of popular music. The best strategy is to create new knowledge and methods through the alignment of history, musicology, geography, leisure studies, media and cultural studies, men's studies and women's studies.

Popular music studies emerged in the 1980s and focused around the *Journal of Popular Music Studies*, which began in 1981. The International Association for the Study of Popular Music (IASPM) was formed and this created an academic community around the study of popular music. The growth of popular music studies was assisted by the parallel development of cultural studies, which validated the place of popular culture in universities. Theories of cultural value started to shift, along with the relationship between high and popular culture (Frow, 1995).

Musicology remains important, even though it has been associated with a classical musical history of 'the West', enjoyed by elite, affluent and educated groups. Nothing within the discipline is rooted to these musical forms. All music cultures can be evaluated and assessed through musicological methods. From the late 1980s onwards, the 'new musicology' focused more attention on the cultural investigation of popular music, concentrating postcolonial, feminist and Marxist perspectives. Richard Middleton offered a considered and powerful critique of the social, political and intellectual limitations of the older modes of musicology, revealing the profound consequences of popular music being ignored. He described musicologists as 'both contemptuous and condescending … and they generally find popular music lacking' (1990: 103). A revision of the field created grafts with history, ethnology and sociology. While the disciplines of history, philosophy, anthropology and acoustics have applications and relevance to the field, there are also two practice-based research areas within musicology that include performance practice and composition that can be deployed in forms that are more popular. With the rise of higher education institutions such as LIPA, the Liverpool Institute of Performing Arts, founded by Paul McCartney, popular music is being studied and taught in new ways.

When thinking about popular music, it is important to log this history and build connections between disciplines, sounds and communities. Just as musicology can be critiqued for ignoring pop, so popular music can be questioned for avoiding a wider consideration of sound. It is important to avoid separating sounds from our studies. In addition, there is a tendency for academics to study pop in the same way as prose and poetry. Simon Frith realized the problems that a disconnection between music and scholarship could create.

> I ... wanted to respond to a feeling of unease I've got about the apparent distance between the people in here discussing popular music and the people involved – whether as producers or consumers – in popular music itself. The conference assumption seems to be that 'popular music' is an object outside, out there, to be held still, observed, revealed. I'm not sure that popular music is that kind of object and I am sure that it take such a detached view of pop is to pass over its politics (1981: 142).

In collapsing the distance between intellectual and fan, music and everyday sounds, Frith has acknowledged that there are other ways of thinking about popular music that cannot always been observed 'from the outside'. To think and write about music requires a detachment from popular music. The strength of creating a critical environment around music is that assumptions, ideologies and the listener's values are probed and questioned.

Scholars of popular music should use a range of perspectives. Scholars and students could activate a textual analysis of a song or music video. They could also deploy a musicological analysis, paying attention to instrumentation, time signature, key, melody, harmony or chord progression. Another option would be to create an institutional analysis of record companies or governmental agencies charged with developing creative industry initiatives, or monitoring how legal representatives deployed copyright law. For those wanting more detailed evidence of a particular moment in music, ethnography enables scholars to understand a group of fans, musicians or managers – to suggest a few examples – and probe the detailed workings of a community. Another option would be to present an historical analysis, moving beyond a chronological narrative, to show the relationship between a social environment and the development of music.

Music and musical technology are changing at speed. However, the modes and models of thinking about popular music have slowed. Steve Redhead tracked this problem from the early 1990s.

> As post-war sociologists have got older, and research grants to hire postgraduate students have become fewer, the inevitable has happened and social scientists have tended to lose touch – as both fans and professions – with what 'your actual young person' does and thinks today (1993: 193).

This gap in experience and expertise has had a consequence on the research conducted about youth and music. The imaginative personal and social use of music encompasses physical participation, including singing, dancing, air guitar and gaming programmes like

Guitar Hero. There is also an emotional use of music, where a special song is used to summon personal experiences or to offer opportunities for relaxation and escape. It can provide a soundtrack for life, including driving, exercising, studying and shopping. Therefore, insider information and experiences are required as much as detached observation.

One of the most common critiques of students' interpretation and writings about music is the blurring between fan and academic knowledge. The key strategy is to find a way to arch beyond personal interests and passions and discover a method to place music in many contexts and not only within personal meanings. It is important to be conscious and reflective about the position from which we think about popular music. Rosalind Brunt commented that,

> What worries me more are academics who go on about being fans. I'm deeply suspicious of that, and I think it's more honest to say that yes I'm a fan but also I'm differently located, and that has certain implications and responsibilities (1992: 80).

While musicians, fans and academics often configure popular music as a textual site of choice, taste and judgement, the freedom, choices and resistance can be overemphasized here. Musical scales, pre-programmed rhythms, genres, samples and musical histories all frame, shape and limit the choices available to the listener. They also limit our thinking about the border or boundary between sound and noise. Some options are not available to select, stylistically, commercially or musically. Musical notes, chords and time signatures limit the options available. While thinking about popular music involves making choices, it is worthwhile to remember that music is structured by genres, repeated on playlists and recycled through advertising. Music moves and the way scholars think about it must follow its trajectory.

Key Questions

1. Which disciplines are involved when thinking about popular music?
2. What is the difference between fan and academic knowledge when researching popular music?
3. Is music more or less important now, when compared to the 1960s?
4. Which strategies can you deploy to move the study of popular music beyond the study of youth culture?

Further Reading

Clayton, M., Herbert, T. and Middleton, R. (2003) *The Cultural Study of Music*. New York: Routledge.

Cox, C. and Warner, D. (2004) *Audio Culture: Readings in Modern Music*. New York: Continuum.

Moore, A. (1997) *The Beatles: Sgt. Pepper's Lonely Hearts Club Band*. Cambridge: Cambridge University Press.

Negus, K. (1999) *Music Genres and Corporate Cultures*. London: Routledge.

Sonic sources

Bocelli, A. (1995) *Time to Say Goodbye*. Polygram.

Enya (1988) *Orinoco Flow*. Geffen/Warner Bros.

The Who (1965) *My Generation*. Decca.

The Who (1971) *Won't Get Fooled Again*. Polydor.

Visual sources

Il Divo (2006) Encore, Sony.

Josh Groban in Concert (2002) WMV.

Richard Thompson's 1000 Years of Popular Music (2006) Cooking Vinyl.

Rick Wakeman: The Classical Connection (2004) Beckman Visual Publishing.

Web sources

'Adorno about popular music,' *YouTube*, http://www.youtube.com/watch?v=Wn_ lF3o8QXQ&feature=PlayList&p=96735ED98C0DA542&index=14&playnext =2&playnext_from=PL

International Association for the Study of Popular Music (IASPM), http://www. iaspm.net

Jasonmit, 'Music Today Sucks,' *YouTube*, http://www.youtube.com/watch?v=n GvkSFWr1qs

Punk Rock Academy, http://www.punkrockacademy.com/

Writing About Music

In 1976, Frank Zappa made the often-repeated statement: 'rock journalism is people who can't write, preparing stories based on interviews with people who can't talk, in order to amuse people who can't read' (in Jones, 1994: 39). About the same time, Elvis Costello (supposedly) described 'writing about music [is] ... like dancing about architecture' ('Dancing about architecture': 2002). If music is to survive beyond ephemeral chart success, the joy of an individual playlists or a crowd jumping together in a club, then it is *writing* that grants meaning, importance, relevance and the survival of sounds. There is as much bad writing about music as there is bad music. The key to improving pop writing is to think carefully about the structures and links between the sound and its reception, the music and its audience. Popular music does not 'reflect' its time or the people who listen to it. It constructs, teaches, frames, negotiates, disconnects and challenges listeners. Therefore, it is necessary to understand the space between sound and ear, guitar and brain, beat and feet.

Writing about popular music is controversial because music is contested and ambiguous, both socially trivial and personally crucial. In moving from sound to words, the sonic to scriptory, there are questions about whether writing about music is beneficial or useful. Both academics and journalists fight over 'cred,' which may refer to either credibility or credentials. Both groups proclaim their right to speak about – and 'represent' – the investment of fans. These judgements are made in an attempt to render ephemeral and transitory popular culture into a series of objects holding credibility. The best of popular music writing challenges us to move beyond our own ears, beyond our assumed categories, listening practices and iPod playlists. The best of music writing is not only about the music. It also uses rhythm, melody and lyrics as a starting point to probe critical commentary and create discussion of social concerns. At its best, wordplay and soundplay converge to create both meaning and a melody.

The gap between experiencing and understanding popular music is vast. Bridging such a chasm is not assisted by most popular music writing, which is not significant, revelatory or important (Herbert, 2001). It is composed of pop biographies, rapidly composed blogs and tweets, CD notes and concert programmes. While such sources can be the foundation for academic research, this mode of writing is too conversational, immediate and unreferenced for musical scholarship. There is money in music writing and the publishing industry has realized the value of the music market. Chart books, biographies, autobiographies, instrument histories, software and hardware guides and tour reviews create a glut of words about sounds. Simon Reynolds' recognition is correct: 'what excites people in pop, and what they manage to articulate of those feelings are generally two very different things' (1990: 9). He argues that – particularly in rock criticism – there is a desire to create order and genre-based stability from the confusion and contradiction. This 'rock discourse' (Reynolds, 1990: 9) labels volatile judgements of quality and cultural value. Fortunately, there are continual moments of innovation that freshen the schematics assembled by rock writers. The key challenge for those of us who write about music is to move out of the predictable structures and clichés of rock writing, including fetishizing the origins of music from a particular city, town or club and over-validating the public relations' narratives offered by performers to journalists.

By 1998, Reynolds had developed a 'pet theory' about the relationship between writing and music.

> I have a pet theory that the vitality of a pop genre is in inverse ratio to the number of books written about it. Compared with the thousands of biographies, essay collections and critical overviews that clog up rock's arteries, only a handful of tomes (academic efforts included) have addressed the dance-and-drug culture – despite the fact that in Europe it's been the dominant form of pop music for nearly a decade (1998: 432).

There are some ironies in Reynolds' position. He is complicit in his own argument by regularly writing about rock, albeit in its indie formation. Nevertheless, he has a point. Those of us who study popular music must ask and justify why we are writing about popular music in an academic context. The goal is not only to capture 'the real' or 'the authentic' experience, but also to widen the thinking spaces of research into the imaginary, the possible and the potential of sound and identity. To write about music transforms the affectivity, emotion and ephemera of sound into the realm of mediated abstraction. There is no definitive or correct position from which to write about music. Certainly, there are many puffed up statements about one view having value over others. For example, Peter Gammond and Raymond Horricks justified their investigation of the record industry by dismissing alternative views and perspectives.

> After the appearance of a number of books by star-struck outsiders, it's about time that the professionals began to have their say (1980: viii).

In other words, for Gammond and Horricks, experience is more important than expertise. While it is extremely difficult to write about dance music and electronica in a way that captures its energy and ephemerality, the function of rock writing is distinct. Ulf Lindberg, Gestur Gudmundsson, Morten Michelsen and Hans Weisethaunet confirmed that the role of rock criticism is to transform the musical genre into '"serious" music' (2005). The desire to pass judgement and slice up cultural fields blurs the relationship between fan and expert. Magazines such as *Q* and *Rolling Stone* render rock music significant, worthy and countercultural.

The consequences of some genres being written about and other areas neglected mean that much of what makes music popular is ignored, undervalued or decentred from 'serious' writing. Indeed, most pop music is not deemed worthy of study, simply being left to the musings of music fans as they narrate their daily experience. There is a search for the masculine, the credible and supposedly important. While journalists abuse scholars in the field studying music, academics similarly discredit the writing of others.

> The increasing number of scholarly articles on rap music by academics is one symptom of this celebration of the marginality of rap in which a taste for the vicarious thrills of African-American hip hop becomes synonymous with academic hipness (Mitchell, 1996: 31).

This statement by Tony Mitchell raises a question about how much space is available for academic writing about race, slavery and blackness, alongside the role of contemporary sounds and ideas in scholarly work. With journalists attacking academics and academics attacking academics, it is difficult to construct a stable position from which to write about music in universities.

It is a political action to translate into words what is heard through the ears and stomped through the feet. Writing about all forms of popular culture is difficult. It always feels like we are draining life from the beat, image and fabric of feeling. Because so much of popular music is non-linguistic, there is a need to access, understand and translate the meanings of fashion, rhythm, beat and harmony. Writers about popular music are often intellectual trolls, watching shadowy bodies through smoke and mirrors, chasing the coat-tails of fashion and hearing phantoms of meaning. By attempting to match the beat of music with the syncopation of syntax, changes in sonic history can be traced, captured and remembered. Conversely, the more the body moves, the lower the quality of writing is about it. The remarkable Kodwo Eshun described most dance writing as 'nothing more than lists and menus, bits and bytes: meagre, miserly, mediocre' (1998: 006). The best music writing is strange and also able to capture and explain a moment in the best popular music. Writing occupies a specific and important place in particular genres. For colonized or 'world' music, dance genres and tracks without lyrics, writing occupies a site alongside the music, translating, negotiating, claiming and affirming. The crucial recognition is that writing about popular music must enact critical distance and detachment. Once this realisation is acknowledged, its contested, conflictual and textured nature can be grasped. While much is made of what is lost from music through its transcription into words, writing provides a way to chart its pedagogic, social and political potential.

Music journalism commenced in the eighteenth century, reporting on classical music. While perhaps more correctly termed music criticism, Charles Avison published his 'Essay on Musical Expression' in 1752. An English composer, he used the essay to critique the music of George Frideric Handel, one of his contemporaries/competitors. Increasingly through the nineteenth century, music became a more common topic within mainstream journalism and newspapers. During this century, music writers were less frequently musicians. This separation between 'writing' and 'doing' survives to the present day. In this new millennium, music journalism is part of a wider entertainment reportage, including profiles on singers and bands, concert reviews, album and single reviews and discussions of music technology. There are magazines that focus on music, such as *Rolling Stone* and the *New Musical Express*. Celebrity magazines also include musicians in their pages.

A difficult terrain for writers about popular music to negotiate is the relationship between journalists and academics. There are strong sentiments from journalists denying the potential contribution of academic commentary. Simon Reynolds has occupied the metaphoric role of bouncer at the club of popular music writing.

> Just as punk and rap became grist for the cult studs mill, rave music may be next on the academy's menu. Once upon a time, rave was just a case of London proles escaping workaday drudgery by losing it on the dance floor every weekend. But where once there was mere madness soon a thousand dissertations will bloom (1996: 35).

Other writers who work the space between journalism and academia are far more comfortable with their poaching, questioning, moving and thinking. Greil Marcus's books, including *Dead Elvis* (1999), stretch and test the limits of writing about popular music. In *The Fascist Bathroom* he probed the power of punk.

> I'd never heard anybody talk like that before. I am a cliché, I don't even exist, there's nothing you can do to hurt me, I am a zero, I can start from nothing, you made me up out of your fantasies and now reality is up to me (1993: 404).

Marcus captures the complexity of writing about popular music. He leads the way in commentary on rock genres and finding ways to move beyond them. Most journalists who write about popular music follow in some way Greil Marcus's *Stranded: Rock and Roll for a Desert Island* (1998). Written in 1978, it was based on a response to the imaginary problem of which rock album one would take to a desert island. Ironically, Marcus has become his own cliché, capturing the challenges and excesses of writing about popular music.

The critical tradition of rock and roll writing involves white men shaping a narrative of struggle between the forces of art and big business. There is an assumption that most musicians struggle against capitalism and much discourse has emerged from the journalists and academics who want to find social significance in such sonic resistance. As long as there has been rock music, there has been writing about rock. This act of writing transformed ephemeral songs and feelings into an archive of importance, history and tradition. The notion that dance music was not important – being repetitive and cyclical in structure – offered particular challenges in writing about it. Kodwo Eshun realized that 'allegedly at odds with the rock press, dance press writing also turns its total inability to describe any kind of rhythm into a virtue, invoking a white Brit routine of pubs and clubs, of business as usual, the bovine sense of good blokes together' (1998: 7). Eshun is evocatively accurate here. There is an inability to describe, analyze and write about music without falling back to the default setting of lyrical analysis, political resistance and masculine authenticity.

Writing about popular music gives credibility and longevity to the ephemeral. Yet journalists and academics do not write about *all* music, they instead select and value the topics and songs. Dave Hickey stated that,

> During the nineteen seventies, when I was writing rock criticism and popular songs, and playing music, I used to wonder why there were so many love songs. More specifically, I wondered why ninety percent of the pop songs ever written were love songs, while ninety percent of rock criticism was written about the other ten percent (1997: 15).

The impact of this desire is that the specificity and specialness of popular culture – what makes pop popular – is lost in a debate over cultural value and quality. This is why much of the writing about popular music dismisses dance culture in favour of rock and under-plays women's role in production and consumption by celebrating a few men who play guitar and focus on 'political' lyrics rather than love songs.

The best writers about popular music are able to work with the complexity and pro-found difficulty of translating sounds into written language. One of the greatest academ-ics of rock music who embodies this quality is Simon Frith. He moved between diverse roles and functions in popular music studies.

> In order to pursue my interests I had to live a double life: on the one hand going through the paces of an academic sociological career – respectable research on the history of education, on youth as a social phenomenon – and on the other hand ringing the changes as a semi-professional rock writer (1978: 9).

To write about popular music is to engage in this uncomfortable exercise of critical compromise. To fix (however temporarily) the meaning of a beat, a photograph and a feeling is to dissociate the hearing/seeing/dancing/reading/writing experience. Popular music has a fluid and dynamic structure, resulting in a complex relationship between an/the audience and a/the text. This ephemerality adds honesty to the writing process. As Dave Godin described,

> Social history is notoriously difficult to record because, by its very nature, it is fleet-ing, ephemeral and experienced in many different ways, and on various levels, by different people … Memory plays strange tricks: events overlap, time sequences get out of kilter, and above all, the wisdom of hindsight often colours and exagger-ates how it really was (2001: viii).

Godin wrote these words as a foreword to Keith Rylatt and Phil Scott's book *CENtral 1179: The Story of Manchester's Twisted Wheel Club*, which was a hub for black American music in England. There remain methodological problems, to (over) emphasizing a particular club, performer or style of music as 'central', 'important' or even 'relevant'. Where does personal experience end and a wider history commence? How is opinion managed against evidence?

To make the situation even more complex, the greatest of popular music writers can often be the most opinionated. Nik Cohn – in one of his best known books *Awopbopaloobop Alopbamboom* – expressed the newness and innovation of rock and roll in the 1950s. While logging the combination of black rhythm and blues and white romantic crooning and country, he realized that,

> What was new about it was its aggression, its sexuality, its sheer noise and most of this came from its beat. This was bigger and louder than any beat before it, simply because it was amplified. Mostly pop boiled down to electric guitars (1969: 11).

The dialogue between rock journalism and academic writing about popular music has proven controversial to map and track. Punk for example has been well served by the journalists Jon Savage, Julie Burchill, Tony Parsons and Greil Marcus and scholars such as Dick Hebdige. Rock and punk gave writers the permission to be arrogant, confident, self assured and cocky. Paul Morley captured this attitude.

> You wanted to be a writer because you believed that writing changed the whole world, and you wanted to be a music writer because you knew that writing changed your own world, and your whole being was fused with this notion of change, and music, and writing, and change, and making people know that things could be better, stranger, darker, faster, newer (2003: 15).

With the arrival of new sites and platforms for writing such as blogs, fans with fervour have gained new energy and spaces for expression. A fan's relationship with popular music operates in the domain of emotion, summoning a popular knowledge that is expressed in a diversity of language styles and modes. The intensity of fandom when expressed in this time of instant publishing is able to reveal the transitory obsessions of popular music. For those moments when a song is important in a person's life, it defines the nature of the rest of that life. It is the filter for the social/political moments that are active at the time. That is why the phrase 'they're playing our song' is so crucial. It is a clichéd reminder of how popular music provides a trigger for memory. Through user-generated content platforms, this transitory – but deep – passion can be expressed through writing.

The online environment has offered a series of new sites and spaces to write about music. However these digitized spaces – of Facebook wall posts, tweets and instant text messaging – are marked by generational, classed and gendered divisions. Particularly in writings about popular music – on analogue or digital platforms – women's position to claim expertise is unstable. Most of the pop writers cited in this chapter are men. There is of course a reason for this. As Norma Coates realized,

> For women to be heard, they must temporarily assume the expert position normally held by men in the [rock] formation. That is, they must talk like a man, or more accurately, as if they were men (1998: 83).

An important corrective necessitates remembering that there are few women academic and journalistic writers about popular music. Web 2.0 environments provide the space and opportunity for new voices and views to emerge.

What is effective writing about popular music? The best of writing conveys and holds onto a moment of the best music. Writing occupies a different place in particular genres. For dance music, it translates, negotiates, claims and affirms. The most successful popular music – like the most successful writing – occupies and claims the present, without being dragged forward by the techno futurists or backward by the desires of heritage consumption. Music and writing that can live in the present and claim their topicality do readers, dancers and listeners a service. That service is the interpretation and translation of the time and sounds of our lives.

Listening, dancing, visualizing and thinking about popular music are not enough. Listening to and writing about popular music is part of a war of position. Academic writing in popular music is now healthy, coinciding with the final realization that rock and punk are not the epitome of excellence and that many modes of music require diverse modalities of writing. Researchers of popular music have come a long way since Philip Tagg noted in 1982, 'one of the initial problems for any new field of study is the attitude of incredulity it meets. The serious study of popular music is no exception to this rule' (p. 37). The future of music – on and offline – will be built via writing.

Key Questions

1. What is the difference between academic writing and journalism about popular music?
2. Why do few journalists write about love songs?
3. Why is it difficult to write about dance music?
4. Does writing about popular music change when it is online?

Further Reading

Eshun, K. (1998) *More Brilliant Than the Sun*. London: Quartet.

Heylin, C. (1992) *The Penguin Book of Rock & Roll Writing*. London: Penguin.

Lindberg, U., Gudmundsson, G., Michelsen, M. and Weisethaunet, H. (2005) *Rock Criticism from the Beginning: Amusers, Bruisers And Cool-Headed Cruisers*. New York: Peter Lang.

Terkel, S. (2006) *And They All Sang*. London: Granta.

Sonic sources

Morley, Paul (2007) 'Control: the podcast', iTunes.

Simply Syndicated (2007–) 'Albums you should hear', iTunes.

The Q Podcast (2006–) iTunes.

Travis (1999) 'Writing to reach you', Independiente.

Visual sources

'An interview with Lawrence Grossberg,' (2007) *YouTube*, http://www.youtube.com/watch?v=NZoDG6tfxHg

Authors@Google: Greil Marcus, (2007) *YouTube*, http://www.youtube.com/watch?v=J0O9ISIAbCE

'Greil Marcus on the shape of things to come', (2007) *YouTube*, http://www.youtube.com/watch?v=n4CnseuDLtw&feature=PlayList&p=346E2C690F02E6D4&playnext=1&playnext_from=PL&index=4

'Simon Reynolds discusses rip it up and start again,' (2008) *YouTube*, http://www.youtube.com/watch?v=W1Ov09YdchQ

Web sources

Nguyen, M. (2009) 'Writing about popular music,' Suite 101, April 11, http://magazinepublishing.suite101.com/article.cfm/writing_about_music

Rock's Backpages, http://www.rocksbackpages.com/

Rockcritics.com, http://rockcritics.com/

This business of dance and music, http://www.thisbusinessofdanceandmusic.com/

Section II

Music Spaces

Sonic Architecture/
Soundscape

A soundscape emerges when fusing sound and landscape. In the context of *Popular Music: Topics, Trends and Trajectories*, this word offers a strategy to link a place with popular music. A soundscape is much more expansive than popular music alone. Andrew Blake stated that,

> Music surrounds us so thoroughly that we hardly ever ask what it means. Part of the answer is that it helps to give a sense of place. It is time to explore this geography of sound, the relationship between sound and space. Listen to your environment. You'll hear some or all of: birdsong, wind, traffic, office or domestic equipment such as fans or kettles, and music. Music from cars, out of doors and windows, from your own radio. Television, walkman or hi-fi (1996: 175).

Sonic media are expansive, deeply rooted in our surrounds and hook into our identity. Sound is a mode of communication that slows the interpretation of words and ideas, heightens awareness of an environment and encourages quiet interiority and reflection. It punctuates buildings, workplaces, streets and family life. The visual bias in theories of truth and authenticity means sounds are silenced or ignored in empowered knowledge systems. CCTV cameras rarely capture sound. Seeing individuals and their behaviour is enough to diagnose crimogenetic behaviour. Our interpretations of sound – particularly through writing – can rarely match this visual sophistication. Formal educational structures like schools and universities are geared towards developing literacies in managing print, text and artefacts that we can see. In opening our ears to other rhythms, melodies, intonations and textures in the sonic palette, we realize that sound creates a shape and architecture in our environment that is fragile, changeable and under researched. Through sound, we discover systems and structures of belonging, inclusion and exclusion.

Soundscapes reveal layers of sound that operate like the textures of skin. They are uneven and delicate and create spaces of separation and difference. While visual media are implicated in debates about representation, race, gender and generation, there are more subtle and perhaps more damaging modes of displacement and marginalization that emerge from the waves of distinction created and perpetuated through sound. While this cultural role is clear, there is also a science to sounds. The study of acoustics – like researching perspective in classical art – summons an analysis of angles, dimensions and architecture. The investigation of how sound 'fills out' our sonic reality requires a combination of both artistic and scientific approaches. Part of the design – not only of buildings but also of cities – necessitates an understanding of how sound travels through space and architecture. The difficulty (and the strength) of sound is that it bleeds through walls. It can be inconvenient. It extends and travels beyond social rules and manners. As R. Murray Schafer has argued, 'the amplifier was also invented by an imperialist: for it responds to the instinct to dominate others with one's own sound' (2004: 35). While much of the history of popular music focuses on the famous instruments – the Fender Stratocaster, the Moog and the Roland TR-808 – there is a key area of research in understanding the impact of volume in creating audiences for popular music. Amplification and amplifiers are overlooked in music history. A few books, such as Tom Wheeler's *Celebrating 60 years of Fender Amps* (2007), take the amplifier rather than the instrument as a focus. Even Keith Richards realized that the amplifier has been a neglected part of popular music history.

> I had a lot of experimentation, eventually having these beautiful guitars and never having the right amp to go with them, or very rarely. I knew they could sound better. Then one day I picked up my Fender guitar and went through a beautiful Fender Twin and … Oh yeah! There it is! Meet the wife! (Wheeler, 2007: 12).

In understanding how popular music – and particularly rock – gathers ideologies from youth culture and resistance, it is necessary to monitor the role of volume in this history. The amplifier allowed the guitar to cut through the brass section of big bands. The amplifier enabled sound to move beyond one location and to stretch into sonic space. It also alters the tone from electric instruments. While there is much focus on instruments and the distortion or chorus pedals that can shape their sound, the amplifier creates the tone and volume. It moves the music through territory.

Visual communication is limited by the parameters of our gaze. Our eyesight restricts what it is possible to see. Sound is rarely limited to the immediate vicinity of our ears. Hearing gives us information from around corners and through buildings and even spills from a moving car. We hear at different angles and in different ways when compared to what we can see. Don Ihde has described how the visual field 'remains before me in its finite roundness. The space of the visual field is limited to being in front of me' (2007: 206). Instead, sound surrounds our bodies and creates an immersive environment. These spaces of sound can be productive and destructive, challenging and damaging. Because we have no ear lids, private sounds often become public. The pervasiveness of MP3 portable music players is a way to control a personal soundscape, to ensure that private music moves through public experiences and shields us from sounds we do not choose. The capacity to reproduce and carry a personal soundtrack mediates our experience with the environment. We can travel, walk with, exercise and shop to music. Michael Bull termed this process 'aesthetic colonization' (2002: 89), which in his research described the experience gained when wearing the Sony Walkman.

Soundscape, Sound Art and Sonic Architecture were phrases used with increasing frequency through the 1980s. While Sound Art as a phrase is often accredited to Canadian composer/audio artist Dan Lander from the mid 1980s, soundscape and sonic architecture have been deployed more widely, linked with geography, urbanity and city living. Attention is focused on how sound creates spaces and structures for daily life. Sonic architecture is intentional. Urban planners, performers and artists actively construct the environment for sonic encounters with residents, tourists, audiences, communities and citizens. Soundscape often describes a more random and accidental alignment of sound and landscape. As an example, Brian Eno mused in response to walking through Cologne Airport in 1977, 'I started to wonder what kind of music would sound good in a building like that' (2004: 96). While 'elevator music' has become a label for accidental, incidental and often random sound, most of the spaces in our lives – from supermarkets to museums – will feature an often underappreciated soundtrack. As the iPhone and iPad have proliferated – along with the Apple iTunes Store – a significant range of applications is available that can create soundscapes with, for, and through the mobile platform. Indeed, Brian Eno has continued his innovations in this area, creating with Peter Chilvers the 'Bloom' (2009) and 'Trope' (2009) applications for the iPhone.

While mobile telephony appears to have created new ways of negotiating between sonic media and movement, light moves faster than sound. Our sense of sight is more widely used than hearing in our daily life. We depend on what we see to understand our environment. Visual literacy is more highly developed than auditory literacy. The consequences of these maxims are that we gather most of our information about reality, truth and life through our eyes as they flick over the visual landscape. Yet Alan Licht has realized that sound also provides a different kind of information about life.

> Both visual and aural information are not only essential to survival in any environment, to hear something that may be unseen and pose a threat, but sound can also indicate aliveness (2007: 15).

Because vision tends to marginalize other sensory experiences, what Douglas Kahn described as 'blind hearing' (2001: 4) is a rare experience. Invariably sight swamps the more subtle senses. It is only when noise is heard and labeled that we confront our biases, boundaries and assumptions about sound and place. Paul Hegarty realized that 'what is judged noise at one point is music or meaning in another' (2008: ix). While noise is a negative category, it is a label applied retrospectively. Sound is organized and categorized. Noise is defined as that which is not sound. However, there is movement between these categories. Put bluntly, when listeners lack literacies in a sound, it is defined as noise. Neighbours and passing drivers share the boom boom boom of their personal sound track with residents. Buskers infiltrate shopping malls. It is a rare day when sounds not chosen or produced by us and our personal interests do not enter our hearing. The parameters and limitations of sound and noise are constantly changing and impact on the determination of popular music. In unsettling the relationship between sound and noise, the aural palette is extended. New sonic literacies are formed when new styles of music and noise combine. The technical possibilities of electronic music have particularly enlarged sonic possibilities.

Noise is a problem, a disordered sound that is unpleasant to the ears. Noise and music are not objective terms, but are relative to perception. The relationship between noise and music changed as new genres developed, from jazz through to rock and roll, with an increasing role for the guitar via electrification. The loudness of guitars – through punk and metal genres – crossed the boundaries of sound and noise. When Jimi Hendrix played 'The Star Spangled Banner' at Woodstock, the response was both applause and offence. Innovative music often straddles these categories while listeners develop and negotiate new auditory literacies. Nothing is intrinsic to the notes, chords or rhythm that differentiate between the categories of music or noise. Radio expanded the limits and parameters of sound, broadcasting information, chat, talkback, music and drama. Social and institutional decisions about recording, distribution and marketing, moderate and manage the sonic experiences that enter our daily context. Paul Hegarty confirmed, 'there is no sound, no noise, no silence … without listening' (2008: 197). All sound reaches our ears through the same physics of transmission. However, how we process and interpret the information entering our body through our ears is socially determined by our history, literacies and surrounding architecture.

This determination of noise 'pollution' was a serious problem in cities through the twentieth century because a particular culture of planning dominated debates about space and sound. Will Alsop argued that,

> For much of the twentieth century, especially the second half, sensible planning was regarded as the savior of the city. Much of this activity concentrated on denial and impermissible activity, unless you happened to be driving a car. There was an assumption that suburban dwelling was a common goal for most people, accompanied by car ownership, a sizable garden and modern schools for your children with large windows and playing fields (2005: 1).

The problem with this planning culture is that sounds permeate with through physical structures and do not behave in a predictable way. They disturb, rupture and question, bleeding from freeways and motorways into suburban gardens. Planned cities always create unplanned sound. By the end of the 1990s, Richard Rogers' study, which he titled *Towards an Urban Renaissance,* argued for the importance of increased density, reduced travel distances from home to work, and a reduced reliance on the car in favour of public transport. Also important to this strategy was a focus on public spaces to increase the intensity of urbanity. Bars, coffee shops and restaurants would be the basis not only of commerce, but also of creativity. He argued that good architecture should create relationships between people and the spaces they inhabit. Obviously, sounds flow between these structures of community and belonging. Yet they also reverberate between the global, regional and local. The sonic flow allows many unexpected relationships to develop between time and space, technological causes and social effects.

For Karl Marx, cities provided opportunities for revolution and political change. Architecture from earlier – particularly industrial – ages left scars of inequality from older models of urban planning. Importantly, though, sounds move faster than vision in terms of regeneration. Architecture takes time to build, demolish and renew. Sounds are more flexible and can transform old buildings and spaces for new uses. While the Walkman, iPod and car radios create a specific soundtrack to shape and augment our visual engagements with the world, there are also intentional interventions that defamiliarize our accustomed relationship between sound, landscape and identity. For Douglas Kahn, sounds are much more than a soundtrack for history: 'they are also a means through which to investigate issues of cultural history and theory' (2001: 4). In popular music studies, there has been too much focus on an individual song or performer and too little on determining how these diverse sounds travel to different contexts and summon new meanings.

Sonic media, sonic art, sonic architecture and soundscape all describe how what we hear constructs and positions our identities and bodies in space. In addition, a branch of sonic arts focuses on the local sound environments of particular groups such as migrant communities, youth and the elderly. A soundscape can speak of alternatives and choices, offering new forms of belonging. For example, Maria Pini created a study of women and dance music, showing how femininity could be transformed in the movement from a home environment to house music. While women are often absent in the history of dance and club cultures, her research showed how rave created 'the emergence of new ways of being women-in-culture' (2001: 95). A new soundtrack and soundscape enabled this identity.

Students and teachers who gain the greatest success have mastered print and visual literacies. The focus rests on reading and writing, rather than hearing and listening. Yet by activating the diversity of our senses, we can not only return the body to our academic lives, we can also increase our awareness of auditory space. Technology is important to such a project. The remarkable writer David Toop has increased our consciousness of how sounds – intentionally or unintentionally – can create architecture for experiences and meaning. He realized that 'digital communications have pitched the idea of space into confusion, so the relationship of sound to space has become an immensely creative field of research' (2004: 3). All of us who read, write and research in popular music studies operate in this new 'creative field' of sound, rather than remaining anchored to the nostalgic and frequently limiting labels for genres, performers and songs.

Key Questions

1. What is a soundscape?
2. How are sounds consumed? Does this process involve distinct practices to the consumption of images?
3. How do we control the sounds that we hear?
4. What is the role of silence in our aural life?

Further Reading

Connell, J. and Gibson, C. (2003) *Soundtracks: Popular Music, Identity and Place.* London: Routledge.

Hegarty, P. (2008) *Noise/Music: A History.* New York: Continuum.

Licht, A. (2007) *Sound Art: Beyond Music, Beyond Categories.* New York: Rizzoli.

Ross, A. (2008) *The Rest is Noise: Listening to the Twentieth Century.* London: Fourth Estate.

Sonic sources

Eno, B. (1983) *Apollo: Atmospheres and Soundtracks.* Virgin Records.

Future Sound of London (1996) *Dead Cities.* Virgin Records.

PLAY, *Sound Salon*, iTunes podcast.

Tangerine Dream (1974) *Phaedra.* Virgin Records.

Visual sources

AC/DC, Rock and Roll ain't noise pollution, *YouTube*, http://www.youtube.com/watch?v=3HyxdRO2i9o

Blue (1993) Basilisk Communications Ltd.

Icke, D. (2004) *The Freedom Road.* UFO TV.

Theremin: An Electronic Odyssey (1993) Orion.

Web sources

Positive Soundscapes, http://www.positivesoundscapes.org/

Sonic Architecture, www.sonicarchitecture.com

Soundscapes, http://soundscapes.info/

Space Weather, www.spaceweather.com

City Music and Urban Spaces

Each city is distinct, shaped by different histories, industries, economic choices, topologies and immigration policies. Occasionally, these factors align to create a branded music industry. This emerged in San Francisco during Haight-Ashbury's 'summer of love' in 1967 (Hoskyns, 1997). Music is a way to mark a city as distinct. The relationship between geography and sound is taken for granted, but music is linked with particular places. Seattle and Liverpool are each recognized as a hub and home for their music and musicians. Creative industries' strategies and policies build on or attempt to initiate such a sonic branding. Writers such as Richard Florida (2005), Charles Leadbeater (1999) and Kate Oakley (2004) research the role and function of 'creative people,' including musicians, as drivers of an economy. Basically, 'the creative class' enjoys living in a city with a vibrant music 'scene'. In such an environment, cities become a focus for the creative industries of fashion, film, publishing, gaming, sport, architecture and design. Music is more than a self-standing industry, it becomes a facilitator for other activities like film making, fashion design and website production. Popular music industries are a siren's song for creativity, enabling other industries to function, grow and develop. This emphasis on creativity supposedly facilitates a transition from a managerial to entrepreneurial form of government, enabling cities to adapt to a new economic, social and political context. Phil Hubbard confirms, 'Place-marketing is inevitably accompanied by the fabrication of a new urban landscape, which can therefore be seen as both an expression and a consequence of attempts to re-image the city' (1996: 444). Paying attention to the marketing of a place enables a city to be sold to students, business people and entrepreneurs, leading to local economic development. Popular music is the soundtrack for this transformation of a city's image.

After the decline of manufacturing in the formerly once great industrial cities, new reasons needed to be found for their existence. Once car production declined in Detroit, the steel industry was lost to Sheffield and the cotton industry waned in Manchester, new industries were needed to prevent (or at least slow down) depopulation and languishing investment. Without intervention, vacant inner cities would result. Throughout the 1990s and early 2000s, cities were 'managed' by incorporating new economic, social and political principles. With increasing importance being placed on tourism, sport and music, cities were branded and marketed to assist with economic development. This commercialization relied on music to develop a night-time economy of clubs, pubs and restaurants as a strategy to bring consumers back into cities. Richard Florida's series of books, commencing with *The Rise of the Creative Class*, confirmed that 'cities like Seattle, Austin, Toronto and Dublin recognize the multidimensional nature of this transformation and are striving to become broadly creative communities, not just centers of technological innovation and high-tech industry' (2002). He realized that the 'creative' centres were also musical centres. A music industry improves the 'lifestyle' and leisure of the 'creative class' so that they will 'cluster' and sustain their innovativeness. This type of language – of hubs, clusters, precincts and districts – is derived from management and business studies rather than media studies. Yet the relationship and relevance of the music industry to urban planning and cultural policies is also clear.

Richard Florida's interest in both cities and music fused in the concept of the Bohemian Index. This maps, logs and ranks the acceptance of alternative subcultures and a range of urban professionals enjoying the experiences of artists and musicians. Florida has based his career on the supposition that human creativity has replaced raw materials, physical labour and finance capital as the builder of economic value. While the causes or origins of creativity are debatable, his work has served as a reminder that the music industry is much larger and more important that the sale of compact discs, downloads and concert tickets. It creates the positive creative environment that facilitates the development of other industries (Florida, 2005). The music industry provides a 'lifestyle' for creative workers. This realization – which seems self-evident – was excluded from arts and urban planning decisions through much of the twentieth century, with full attention being placed on dividing 'high' and 'low' culture in cultural policy. A foundational if implicit definition of 'good culture' was that it did not make any money. Popular music was drawn into this binary opposition of good and bad culture. This meant that popular music and popular musicians were neglected both critically and financially. As the creative industries' new economic vocabulary sliced through the divisions between art and pop, music could no longer be ignored, ridiculed or trivialized as a leisure pursuit of youth, but would trigger and frame new strategies for economic development. Enhanced by the movement of digitally convergent compressed music files, the economic potential of music in a globalized economy was more obvious and held greater potential than this happening through the movement of analogue and physical objects such as compact discs.

In such stories of regeneration and development, the phrases 'new economy' and 'creative cities' are used too often and frequently without definition. The characteristics of the new economy, of which the popular music industry is a part, are:

- globalization
- digitization
- recognition of the economic value of education
- increasing awareness of copyright and intellectual property rights
- increased diversity of working practices and models
- convergence of work and leisure practices
- increased role of consumption rather than production in the formulation of identity.

The reason that both popular music and the fashion industries have been visible and promoted within the creative industries literature is that they deploy elements that enable this 'new economy' to make money, including patents, copyrights and intellectual property rights. This is one reason why digital rights management has been a key 'problem' or 'solution' in the e-commerce marketing plan for popular music.

Much of the creative industries' literature advocates the potential of cities and policy-based interventions in the urban environment. A city is more than a collection of streets, shops and houses. It also offers a series of sonic spaces and opportunities for unofficial, illegal and dangerous alternative communities. Paul Du Noyer confirmed this role for the city that commenced the beat explosion: 'Liverpool is more than a place where music happens. Liverpool is a reason why music happens' (2002: 1). Similarly, for a decade, most of the important indie bands in Britain came from Manchester, such as The Smiths, Joy Division, New Order, The Buzzcocks and The Fall. Two of the early innovators of house – a Guy called Gerald and 808 State – and the three significant guitar bands, The Stone Roses, Inspiral Carpets and Happy Mondays, all came from the city. In addition, clubs, like The Hacienda in Manchester and Cream in Liverpool, have been the basis of the rejuvenation of these deprived areas. Dave Haslam confirmed that,

> There's an identity crisis at the heart of the story of the modern city. Manchester, like England, is now re-creating itself, looking for a new role, a life without manufacturing industry. Like a middle-aged man made redundant after a lifetime in a factory, Manchester is either facing years drawing charity, welfare and government handouts, or it's going to retrain, reorganize, and find something to keep it occupied (1999: xi).

Similarly, post-punk Sheffield produced a range of bands based on electronic music and experimentation as the steel industries declined and closed. The Human League, Cabaret Voltaire, Chakk, ABC and Hula reconfigured the history of the steel industry to generate experimentations with industrial music. In a regenerated Sheffield, the producers/event managers Gatecrasher used the leisure and service industries to create pleasure and profit, instead of foundries and coalmines. Indeed, when monitoring the history of industrial music, hip hop, techno, jungle and drum 'n' bass, there is a disruption – a defamiliarization – in the mapping of urbanity.

There are many characteristics of a music city. They are connected via transportation networks. They are compact and often walkable (Rogers, 1997). They also encase a large number of university students, ensuring an audience for a music industry and disposable income without the burdens of family and a mortgage. However, there must also be an environment that will bring together music with local businesses. As Barry Shank has explained,

> When people – musicians, journalists, sound technicians, booking agents, fans – now speak of the scene, they mean the activity surrounding those successful musicians who have attracted such attention, or who are believed to be on the verge of doing so, and are in the process of shifting the marketing mainstream of youth-oriented music (1994: 240).

This extract comes from Barry Shank's *Dissonant Identities: The Rock 'n' Roll Scene in Austin, Texas*. What makes this book a leader in the field of city music is that he mapped the musical venues in the city, including record and music shops, nightclubs, rehearsal rooms, streets, trains and buses. In describing a music 'scene,' he showed both the fragmentation and subcultures that kept it buoyant and dynamic. To cite Bennett and Peterson's (2004) book title *Music Scenes: Local, Translocal and Virtual*, in a digital age files move through geographical spaces with ease, but there are key anchors of music to streets, clubs, transportation networks and shops.

Popular music is not a national industry. It comes from cities, but negotiates with myths and narratives of the urban and pastoral past. Through popular music, new groups and communities negotiate the meaning of a city to find an identity. Dominant groups in the culture organize not only space, but also how it is represented. Architects, urban planners, lawyers, engineers, politicians and city councils all designate and define who uses the land and why. Popular music is what Iain Chambers described as the 'urban alphabet' (1986: 3). From such a metaphor, it seems logical to argue for the specialness of a city's sound or musical dialect. Each place constructs its sonic sentences differently. In a parochial haze, we can 'hear' Detroit in the mechanical precision of the pulses of early 1990s techno; the swirls and screeches of acid house spiral out of post-industrial Manchester; Seattle's dark, brooding weather marinates the aggression of grunge. While such connections provide the basis for outstanding journalistic hyperbole, the truth of the music and its interpretation is invariably more complex to study. Without doubt, music allowed a revival and reinterpretation of Manchester's industrial past. Stefan Pierlejewski confirmed that,

> During 1989 and 1990 Manchester's popularity rocketed. It was virtually all the press was writing about. Manchester had all the top bands: Stone Roses, Happy Mondays, New Order, 808 State, Inspiral Carpets and N-Joi. The Hacienda and the Eastern Bloc had reached near legendary status and people were flocking to Manchester as if the Holy Grail were here. Even Manchester University was receiving thousands more student applications than it had ever had before as potential students rushed to become part of the thriving scene (1997: 130).

Manchester is the model for a music-led recovery of an urban environment. However there are many cities that are not known for their music industry and do not have articles and books written around them. One city without the fame and marketing of a music city but has still been studied is Milton Keynes. Ruth Finnegan's *The Hidden Musicians: Music-making in an English Town* (2007) researched the amateur musicians of Milton Keynes and generated ethnographies of music practice. Finnegan realized that 'it is easy to underestimate these grass-roots musical activities given the accepted emphasis in academic and political circles on great musical masterpieces, professional music, or famed national achievements' (2007: xvii). Her work is a profound intervention in the assumptions about city music. She explores the continuum between amateur and professional music and musicians, locating where and how performers learn about music. She also recognizes how difficult it is to map and understand the behaviours that form the practice of popular music. For those of us who study music and musicians, her methods and models of research are both innovative and inspirational.

While the sounds of the city seem to permeate pop, there have been losses and closures in the spaces of music, most specifically the record shop. In 2008, Graham Jones decided to conduct 'one last tour' of what he believes will be the last fifty record shops in the United Kingdom. Yet the shutting of these shops has not – he believed – been caused by downloading. He stated, 'downloading will continue to grow, but it is important for the record companies to recognize that the vast majority of the general public prefer to obtain their music on a physical format' (2009: 288). Such a statement is debatable. However his study shows that successful record shops have diversified the genres stocked and increased the imports and music-related products such as books, musical instruments, posters and t-shirts (Jones, 2009: 303).

The city's function within popular music studies is as a resistive localism against the homogenization and standardization of global sounds. The local, national and global are interdependent, not adversarial. The local – the specific city music – remains interesting, not because it is more authentic and real than trans-Atlantic musics, but because it demonstrates what happens to global formations and popular culture in specific contexts, probing how differences are negotiated. Writing a history of music through a history of cities confirms the value of place in creating both sounds and an audience for them. Examination of creative industries-enabled policy has shown that music has a role in international strategies for urban regeneration. The key issue to avoid when studying popular music through cities and urban spaces is that we do not simplify the complexity of music by making it fit into the requirements of creative industries' policy or urban regeneration. The relationship between cities and music is not linear or causal. Liverpool does not 'explain' The Beatles. Manchester does not 'explain' house music. In bringing the city back to popular music studies, it not only enables scholars to place songs in context but also to understand how a music industry can form the basis for economic development, city imaging and regional branding.

Key Questions

1. Why is a popular music industry important to creative industries researchers?
2. Why is music production encouraged in post-industrial cities?
3. What are the characteristics of successful music cities?
4. Why has Manchester shown a pattern of musical success?

Further Reading

Crawford, R. (2001) *America's Musical Life in New York*. London: Norton.

Finnegan, R. (2007) *The Hidden Musicians: Music-making in an English Town*. Middleton, CT: Wesleyan University Press.

Shank, B. (1994) *Dissonant Identities: The Rock 'n' Roll Scene in Austin, Texas*. Hanover, NH: Wesleyan University Press.

Swiss, T., Sloop, J. and Herman, A. (1998) *Mapping the Beat: Popular Music and Contemporary Theory*. Malden: Blackwell.

Sonic sources

Fat Boy Slim (1998) 'You're not from Brighton'. Skint.

Reed, L. (1989) *New York*. Sire Records.

The Beautiful South (2006) 'Manchester'. Sony.

The Clash (1979) 'London Calling'. CBS.

Visual sources

Morrissey – Who Put the 'M' in Manchester (2008) Sanctuary Visual Entertainment.

Nirvana: Spirit of Seattle (1995) S. Gold and Sons.

Shadowplayers: Factory Records 1978–81 (2006) LTM.

Something in the Water (2008) WBMC.

Web sources

'Music and The Beatles,' Visit Liverpool.com, http://www.visitliverpool.com/site/experiences/music-and-the-beatles

Pride of Manchester, http://www.prideofmanchester.com/music/

South by southwest, http://sxsw.com/

Urban sounds, http://www.urbansounds.com

Recording Spaces

Recording sound is the way to ensure its survival through time and enable its movement through space. It does not capture 'real' sound but provides the potential for music to transcend the place of its original performance and for new sonic literacies to develop in listeners. Greg Milner, in *Perfecting Sound Forever: The Story of Recorded Music*, realized that 'a record is absolutely meaningless unless it is played. As an object, it signifies nothing. If you don't play a CD, it's nothing but a coaster. A record is a text that cannot be "read". It must be decoded' (2009: 22). This process of decoding – or understanding – sound is naturalized. This means that all of us tend to assume that the recorded representation of sound is the reality of sound. It is important to remember that recordings are illusions of sounds that never existed. They are mixed, remastered, edited, cut, reordered and reorganized to render them suitable for the dominant sonic platform of the day.

Recording sound electronically requires a resonating surface, termed a microphone. (Milner, 2009: 53). Recording a song seems to be a simple enough process of connecting a microphone to a computer and clicking a large red button on a screen with a mouse or via a touch screen. While the technical skills for recording have been reduced through digitization and the availability of cheaper laptop computers and mobile telephony, other skills remain more costly and difficult to attain. To record, mix and master music requires an expertise in melody and rhythm, as much as in software and hardware. Much of *Popular Music: Topics, Trends and Trajectories* is inflected and informed by digital convergence, compression files and mobile music players. Under discussed in this narrative of change is the function of domesticated musical software and hardware on how music is created, produced and distributed. The range of cheap and effective software and hardware for sound recording has had an extraordinary impact on the places and spaces of music production. Through much of the twentieth century music was not recorded at home, but in specialist studios or through live performance. The key contemporary change is that this live recording can be changed, augmented and edited at a low cost and at home. Suddenly, the quality of the 'demo' recording is higher and much more than a guide track for studio production. V.V. Brown for example, combined and recorded her interest in soul, electronica and doo-wop. When recording *Travelling Like the Light*, she remembered that,

> I did it all myself … I wrote every song on it, and I produced the album as well. I'd program the beat at home on Logic and bounce it on to Pro Tools in the studio. The engineer would clean it up, then press record, and I'd go off and play the keys and the synth parts and the bass parts (2009: 11).

Suddenly the separation of performers, producers and engineer evaporated. Auto-Tune ensured that vocal tracks could be pitch perfect, even when double tracked. While engineers could correct pitch before Auto-Tune through sampling and using the pitch wheel, Auto-Tune meant that this complex task of correcting pitch was deskilled. In such a time, the tendency is to downplay the role of recording studios in musical history. The proliferation of domestic recording technology and software means that the importance of a commercial environment for recording is minimized. Through the trans-national movement of sonic files, where a song is recorded is insignificant. What matters is how it is recorded.

This 'how' of recording is changing. In December 2008, Olympic Studios in London were closed by EMI. The online response to this decision varied from nostalgia in remembering the music that had been produced in the studios, through to a recognition that the business models in the music industry had changed. Nick Coleman at the point of Olympic's closing, offered a more wide ranging commentary about the transformation of the industry.

> There is something unquestionably sad about the news. There is more to a great studio than machinery. There is what 'the studio' means to musicians; what it means to the very sound of music; and what a studio brings to the story of music, as a component in a narrative shaped as much by myth as it is by reality (2009).

Recording a hit song has remained a mysterious process for much of rock history. Indeed Howard Massey stated, 'for many people, record production seems to be a kind of black art, imbued with an almost mystical secrecy' (2000: v). Particular exponents – like Brian Wilson, George Martin, Brian Eno and Phil Spector – have used the studio as an instrument to build a song. These famous producers extended the innovations coming from the early inventions of Edison and Berliner, the pioneers of recording machine development at the end of the nineteenth century. For them, recording was mechanical and acoustic. Through electrical recording in the 1920s, electromagnetic transduction was possible. While recordings were in mono, there was some flexibility in microphone positioning. By the Second World War, the first AC-biased tape recorders had emerged, which both increased the quality of the recording and enabled editing. The paper-coated tape was replaced by plastic to increase its durability, leading to BASF's chromium dioxide innovations in the early 1970s.

All these recording platforms and processes were analogue. Analogue recording captures sound by converting differences in sound pressure into a variable electrical voltage. The channel for that conversion was and is a microphone. Digital recording converts the electric wave from the microphone and into a binary code. These binary numbers capture the amplitude of the sound. Home recording via analogue and digital platforms has been possible since the arrival of cassettes. Bands recorded tracks on audio cassettes and DATs (Digital Audio Tapes) from 1987, years before iTunes and the iPod were even design concepts. Jyoti Mishra, better known as White Town, and A Guy Called

Gerald famously recorded their best known tracks in their bedrooms. The DIY ideology of both punk and indie not only enabled a different type of live performance but also a new way of validating home recording, simplified through domesticated digitization. Throughout the 1990s, more performers arrived at studios with almost completed tracks. Alanis Morissette's *Jagged Little Pill* was recorded on DATs in a home studio.

Hip hop and rap foreshadowed this trend. As David Toop showed, New York's hip hop genre was based on using already existing music with mixing and producing emerging 'in real time' (2000: 92–93). The use of found sounds enabled a new range of genres and musical styles. The hip hop DJ showed that re-using music through samples could build new sounds and sonic structures. Hundreds of software applications and samples followed this example. Through broadband, compression files and cheap software with accessible interfaces and freely available loops, new potentials for making music emerged.

Technology does not create music, it provides new metaphors, tropes and possibilities to think about and combine sounds in different ways. Rodney Brooks stated that,

> We've always thought of our brains in terms of our latest technology. At one point, our brains were steam engines. When I was a kid, they were telephone-switching networks. Then they became digital computers. Then, massively parallel digital computers. Probably, out there now, there are kids' books which say our brain is the World Wide Web. We probably haven't got it right yet (2008: 3).

Such metaphors try to make the new platform or idea understandable through positioning it in relation to older knowledge. While recording and mixing using digital and domestic platforms has allowed new groups access to older sounds, this software is based on the principles and practices of analogue recording, mixing and sampling. The conversion of sound into bits and bytes means these can be manipulated and moved in different ways. Obviously, recording music requires much more than managing hardware and software. It also necessitates active listening and a capacity to make choices about microphones, levels and control. Through the invention of the Musical Instrument Digital Interface (MIDI) in 1981, one computer could control a range of sounds, synthesizers and sequencers. In addition, the MIDI interface created what Michael Berk described as a 'visual dimension to audio editing' (2000: 196). As we have discussed through *Popular Music: Topics, Trends and Trajectories*, the visual dominates the sonic. Through software packages such as Adobe Audition, the open source Audacity, Magix Music Maker and Acoustica Mixcraft, sounds are visualized on a screen and edited via the sound waves that we see, perhaps more than the sounds emerging from often small computer speakers. Users can see sound waves as well as hear them. New literacies for production and editing emerge. To trim loops and samples by ear required very precise auditory literacies and calculated guesswork. When editing was enabled through visual and graphical interfaces, the speed of decision making and mixing increased exponentially. It is practical to micro-edit and manage sounds in a way that was not possible before the visual interface. The composer/performer is now able to work with their sounds in a way that circumvents the role of engineers and producers. For example, Moby, also known as Richard Hall, recorded his 1999 album *Play* at home using Cubase software. With Apple's GarageBand, Sony's Acid xPress and a range of copyright-free loops now available, there are challenges to analogue notions of authenticity, originality and creativity (Blake, 2007: xi).

Such an argument may suggest that the history of recording studios has ended. There is a reason – even with the availability of home recording options – that there remains a focus on the recording studio in popular music studies. Frankly, it is much easier to write a history of popular music using recording studios. These anchor music to a particular space and time. For example, the histories of dub reggae are easier to describe and explain through King Tubby's studio in Waterhouse and Lee Perry's Black Ark studio in Washington Gardens in Kingston than by investigating more complex theories of race, colonialism and resistance. When music production disperses into individual houses and computers and can be remixed to a professional standard by amateurs, then the authentic narrative of rock music, composed and produced by talented technicians who have specialist expertise in a tailor-made recording location, can be is questioned. Lawrence Lessig separates these environments into two economies: commercial and sharing (2008: 117). He describes it as the Read-Only (RO) economy and the Read-Write (RW) economy (2008: 116). Read-Only is protected and copyrighted. Read-Write is the culture of sharing and remixing or, put another way, copyright violation.

The improvement in both hardware and software has rendered redundant most of the functions of a recording studio. A Digital Audio Workstation (DAW) enables the recording of sound, the activation of effects on that sound, mixing down to – most commonly – an MP3 or WAV file and subsequent burning of a CD or distribution online. However a range of other web-aligned audio files is available, including Audio Interchange File Format (AIFF), which is the standard Mac format for audio, Windows Media Audio (WMA), RealAudio, which is used for streaming, and OGG, which is open source software. To create an effective DAW, it is necessary to have a computer with available RAM, an intuitive audio interface and multi-track recording and editing software. Home recording has meant that for electronica in particular, the technical reasons for entering a studio are now redundant. Yet studios were always more than a source and site for technology. They were also a hub for expertise, a vibrant social community and an economic powerhouse. They in turn became a brand and the symbol of a genre. Sun Records became an origin for rock and roll, recording Elvis Presley, Johnny Cash, Jerry Lee Lewis and Roy Orbison. Even in this analogue history, there were famous recording studios that were not purpose-built. The Band famously recorded their first two albums in houses, Big Pink and the converted pool room of Sammy Davis's residence. Recording studios, throughout much of the history of popular music, allowed amplified voices and instruments to be recorded, mixed, mastered and distributed to an audience. Now that recording and mixing can be accomplished at home and music may be distributed on the web, the recording studio is losing its purpose.

A range of high quality microphones, samples and loops is available at low cost, along with an assortment of free and open source options. Similarly, the great instruments – the Rickenbackers, Fenders and Gibsons – that few musicians would see in their towns and cities are now available from a local music store or to purchase online. The skill of mastering remains the element of recording that is locked within the jurisdiction of the professional. Mastering has two functions: enhancing sound and repairing problems. These functions are still necessary and not redundant in a domestic digital age. Chris Gibson stated 'high-level mastering and post-production facilities will survive, but are likely to remain rare, and centralized in urban areas, and they will probably not acquire the notoriety or fame of their predecessors' (2008: 205). This demarcation of digitized home software and hardware to record and mix music, which may later enter post-production in a professional studio, ensures that the number and function of studios will reduce.

This mastering expertise is reducing in importance. Bob Katz stated that, 'within the home, the listening experience is deteriorating' (2007: 19). Because of compression files, listeners are now attuned to sonic files that, by necessity, have had data removed from them. The quality of sound is thus not as high. The argument – and it is debatable – is that listeners are becoming accustomed to inferior sound because of increased home recording and declining demands for excellence through mastering. Recognizing this social change, writers and musicians have found great strength in the new process. Karl Coryat terms it guerrilla home recording (2008). He argues that digital recording creates an array of options that are affordable and flexible. Coryat summons the key metaphor that, 'the best-stocked kitchen with the most professional pots and pans won't magically turn you into a brilliant chef' (2008: 2). As with the flattening of professional writing through citizen journalism, there has been a flattening of sound production through domestic hardware and software. But simply because the software and hardware is available does not mean it is used well. Conversely, simply because a musician was recorded, mixed and mastered in a studio did not guarantee a hit record.

Particular mastering functions may be preserved by residual studios. Now there is an increasing interest in what Erik Hawkins called a *Studio-in-a-box* (2002). The key development in home recording was the need for a personal computer with large amounts of RAM that could run the virtual studio software. Now there are many recording and mixing software options available, it is important to log the historical importance of Cubase at the key moment of change. Used by dance producers, it introduced virtual instruments into a virtual recording environment. Loops could be integrated into an already existing track, matching the beats per minute. Similarly, Cakewalk's Sonar was the first generation virtual studio written for a Windows environment.

While logging the social and technological importance of these software programmes, there remain important 'symbolic meanings' (Gibson and Connell, 2005: 193), for the best studios. They exist in urban spaces and create a hub for the music industry. Sun Records' relationship with Memphis and Factory Records links with Manchester are two examples of this relationship. While critical attention is placed on the studios, often

the resident session musicians made the most important contribution. Columbia's
Wrecking Crew, the Funk Brothers at Motown and Booker T and the MGs at Stax are
the best examples of this Gibson and Connell realized that,

> Why recording studios are mythologized more than other stages and spaces of
> production (even if still neglected in academic work) is partly a product of the
> meanings we invest in them, beyond their importance in the production process
> (2005: 195).

Again, because music consumption and fandom are difficult to understand and write
about, it is easier to over-emphasize the production process. Actually, consumers, audiences and fans are the ones who make meaning from music. It is much harder to research
and control the behaviours of illegal downloaders than retell the history of Abbey Road,
Strawberry Studios, Big Pink or Motown.

Recording – in a studio or in the bedroom – matters. The capacity to hear music after
its live performance is a characteristic of modernity. A century ago, a song was heard
and was silenced when the musicians stopped playing. Now, through recording, the best
and worst performances can be captured and repeated. It is important to remember
where we started this chapter for *Popular Music: Topics, Trends and Trajectories*: recording
does not capture the real sound. Through a supposedly artificial environment of loops,
samples and matched rhythm, melodies and effects can be created that could not have
been imagined. Sound can also be distorted, looped and micro managed. The point of
recording is to preserve music and allow it to move through space and time. Without this
function, a popular music industry could not emerge. The industry begins in the spaces
of recording, wherever these may be.

Key Questions

1. In an analogue age, what was the purpose of a recording studio?
2. Which functions in the recording process can now be completed at home
   and at low cost rather than in a studio?
3. What is mastering? Is it still important to a finished recording?
4. How does the new domestic software and hardware alter how researchers
   write about popular music?

Further Reading

Miller, P. (ed.) (2008) *Sound Unbound: Sampling Digital Music and Culture*. Cambridge,
MA: MIT Press.

Milner, G. (2009) *Perfecting Sound Forever: The Story of Recorded Music.* London: Granta.

Shapiro, P. (ed.) (2000) *Modulations: A History of Electronic Music.* New York: Caipirinha.

Theberge, P. (1997) *Any Sound You Can Imagine: Music Making/Consuming Technology.* Hanover, NH: Wesleyan University Press.

Sonic sources

Corner House Studio, podcast, iTunes.

Long, M., *Home Studio and Audio Review*, podcast, iTunes.

Miller, D. and Chick, D., *Inside Home Recording*, podcast, iTunes.

No Place Like Home Studios, podcast, iTunes.

Visual sources

Everything You Need to Know About Setting Up a Bedroom Studio (2006) Wise.

Good Rockin' Tonight: The Legacy of Sun Records (2001) Image Entertainment.

Home Recording Basics (2006) Hal Leonard.

Tom Dowd & the Language of Music (2003) Palm Pictures.

Web sources

Acoustica Mixcraft, http://www.acoustica.com/mixcraft/

Audacity, http://audacity.sourceforge.net/

Audition, http://www.adobe.com/products/audition/

Home Recording, http://homerecording.com/

Clubs and Pubs

Music is produced and heard in spaces. These locations may be as diverse as the family home, a shopping centre, an elevator or a sporting stadium. However, the incubators, nurseries and archives of popular music are nightclubs and pubs. Richard Rogers reminded us that, 'buildings are not merely commodities. They form the backdrop of our lives in the city. Architecture is the art form to which we are continually exposed. It enhances or hinders our lives because it creates the environment in which all our everyday experiences take place, be they commonplace or seminal' (1997: 68). Buildings are a frame for public life, a structure for the creation and consumption of popular music, and allow for the connection of music with its audience.

Nightclubs and pubs facilitate the performance of music. They provide the foundation for future music success and a reminder of past sounds and experiences. They are also the lifeblood of the night-time economy. While a series of moral panics have emerged about knife crime, binge drinking, guns and violence, economic activity at night is also a default feeder of urban regeneration (Talbot, 2007: 2–10). And while the loss of manufacturing jobs in Detroit, Manchester or Sheffield leads to economic decline, the building of a music, restaurant, club and pub environment is seen as a way for urban developers and policy makers to return money, people and employment. There are paradoxes in such a development. While validating breweries and pubs and encouraging the consumption of alcohol, there is a parallel moral panic that discredits the behaviour of young people as 'binge drinking'. Economic development through music and entertainment is located in the same places where social problems and 'deviant behaviour' emerge. The '24 hour city' is a result of the abolition of statutory closing times for pubs and clubs, which inevitably has led to a fear of the night, triggered by alcohol-fuelled crime, drug use and youthful drinking. It also perpetuates and naturalizes the need to regulate and control music and/or noise throughout the night.

While such policies arbitrarily divide day- and night-time consumption and spending practices, it is also part of a naturalization of leisure activities, using popular music as a way to increase economic development and regeneration. Creative industries' policies have created 'cultural quarters' that incorporate not only pubs and clubs, but also restaurants, galleries, museums, cinemas and inner city loft apartments. Only the activities with an audience of young people are deemed harmful to law and order. A couple of married professionals living in Manhattan and visiting the Museum of Modern Art are not social pariahs. Young people drinking and dancing in a club are the threat.

Nightclubs are not the equivalent of galleries or museums. They are essentially spaces of transformation, to create and imagine many possible identities. Through glimpses of exposed flesh through smoke and oblique mirrors, they operate late at night, when families, children and married couples have vacated the streets. Nightclubs offer the promise of eroticism rather than the certainty of gratification. Nightclubs are not only places to question and test the limits of sexuality and gender, they are also a source to understand the function of both work and leisure in the configuration of identity. Robert Fitzgerald described his life as a New York club bouncer and found a strict demarcation of club and non-club behaviour.

> I don't know where the world keeps nightclub customers when they're not drinking and dancing, because I don't see people like them anywhere else but inside (2007: 3).

He suggests that nightclub behaviour is different and disconnected from the rest of life. Pubs are different spaces where drinking is granted a priority over both music and dancing. Certain genres, like rock music, gain important opportunities for exposure through pubs. 'Pub rock' is not only a description *of* a genre, it is also a genre *in* a place. It describes a music that has been tested, changed and workshopped in diverse audiences with expectations of it varying from being a soundtrack for drinking through to a way to begin a (long) Friday night of entertainment. Cover bands dominate the venues of most cities, but receive very little attention in the rock press or academic literature. The focus is on 'original' music, generally played by men and using conventional instrumentation, chord structures and time signatures. Actually, much of the supposedly pub-based original music is derivative, either creatively or historically.

There is a reason for this. Cover music and cover bands form the bulk of pub-based performers. The attraction is clear: the desire to hear a song that is known. It is not only easy listening, it is also easier sonic literacies to hear what we already know. The economic contribution of cover bands is under recognized and researched. In the search for the 'next Beatles,' what is often forgotten is how much of The Beatles' first album was composed of covers. Similarly, their residencies in Hamburg clubs and the Cavern are often credited with tightening their sound. In these venues, they performed other people's material to gain their start in the industry.

The music in pubs and clubs has been managed very differently by cultural critics, journalists and researchers. While pub rock is framed as masculine, innovative and edgy, dance music and the club culture is rarely granted musical credibility. Sarah Thornton claimed that,

> Dance cultures have long been seen to epitomize mass culture at its worst. Dance music has been considered standardized, mindless and banal, while dancers have been regarded as narcotized, conformist and easily manipulated (1995: 1).

The irony is that even though club-based music appears to be playing already existing tracks rather than creating a live sound, through mixing and techniques from turntablism, new sets emerge each night. The same box of vinyl can create different soundtracks in the same venue at various times. While pubs have the credibility of men drinking together, clubs are associated with women dancing (stereotypically around their handbags) or the community-building dancing practices of the gay and lesbian community. The power held by the audience determines the value of the music they hear.

Recognizing the limitations of this history, only a few books have been written on influential pubs and clubs. There are five clubs in particular that have transformed popular music since the 1960s, with their notoriety felt to this day. The Cavern Club, on Mathew Street in Liverpool, was opened as a jazz venue in 1957. By 1961, it had become a beat club and was the stage for most of the Merseybeat groups. Brian Epstein met The Beatles there in November 1961, with Gerry & the Pacemakers and the Swinging Blue Jeans (originally The Blue Genes) also performing. The response from the early Liverpool audience foreshadowed what was to follow throughout the world. The original Cavern Club was demolished, later rebuilt, and still features live music. It is now a hub for Beatles' tourism around Mathew Street in the city.

CBGB, owned by Hilly Kristal, provided the stage for Talking Heads, New York Dolls, Television, Johnny Thunder & the Heartbreakers, the Voidoids, Blondie, the Ramones and Patti Smith. The club's full acronym – CBGB&omfug – stood for Country, Blue Grass, Blues and Other Music for Uplifting Gormandizers. The club was opened in New York in December 1973, but gained its profile when – in March 1974 – the band Television was featured. A few weeks later, they played again with The Ramones as their support band. In 1975, Patti Smith famously logged a seven-week residency at the club, playing two gigs a night. This collective of bands was originally termed street rock, but by 1976 the label of 'punk' had started to be used.

Overlapping chronologically with CBGB was Studio 54, which captured disco in its sexual and drug-fuelled excesses. Gaining fame after Bianca Jagger held her thirtieth birthday party at the venue, it featured a tough door policy from Steve Rubell, the club owner. Based in New York, it was the first great celebrity club. Famous for its dancing, drugs and sexual promiscuity, it was known as much for its 'beautiful people' as its music. Disco gained a hub and a context through Studio 54, giving the music glamour, danger and humour.

The Warehouse became the home of house music, the club that gave it its name. In the late 1970s and early 1980s, the DJ Frankie Knuckles specialized in mixed disco, soul and European electronica. The club was positioned in a decaying industrial part of Chicago in a three-storey factory building. His audience was young, gay and black. The combination of Knuckles' innovation and a risk taking, experimental group of dancers meant that this club was responsible for founding a genre. The 125–145 beats per minute, the warbling divas and the relentless high hat rhythm became key characteristics of house. Building on the best of disco, house music from the Warehouse was able to stretch and cut rhythm, building to a crescendo that created ecstatic dancing experiences. Later recordings would follow the pattern created in the club.

The Hacienda, owned by Factory Records and New Order, linked the Happy Mondays, New Order and wider electronica, also providing the venue for Madonna's first gig in the United Kingdom in 1983. Like the Warehouse, it was located in a post-industrial wasteland. It was the UK's first superclub and was the crucible for house in the UK. Opened in May 1982, it lost money until Mike Pickering made Friday nights a house event – called Nude – in 1986. The Hacienda name was derived from the heart of Situationism. Ivan Chtcheglov's new urbanism mentioned its potential.

> And you, forgotten, your memories ravaged by all the consternations of two hemispheres, stranded in the Red Cellars of Pali-Kao, without music and without geography, no longer setting out for the hacienda … Now that's finished. You'll never see the hacienda. It doesn't exist. The hacienda must be built (1981: 1).

Tony Wilson, a founder of Factory Records, took this slogan literally and decided to build and name the Manchester-based club The Haçienda. It was planned to become a venue of live performance. It became the crucible of house music. The seeds for techno and rave were planted in The Haçienda. While the arrival of 'Madchester' was replaced by Gunchester and drug scares inside and outside the venue, every nightclub since has poached something from the design, aspiration or the staging of The Haçienda.

Like much of the city music literature, the popular music books and articles focusing on clubs and pubs attempt to 'explain' or 'justify' distinct sounds through the emergence of a particular location for music. However, the parallel characteristic of most of the great pubs and clubs is that they eventually close. They are temporary. New York's Paradise Garage closed in 1983. The Warehouse in Chicago ceased in 1987. This was not the end of an era. Dance culture survived, grew and exploded when it was released around the world and into a diversity of clubs. Shoom, Spectrum and The Trip, the famous clubs from 1987–8, also ended. They were not only located in a precise geographical location but also in a distinct moment in history.

Pubs and clubs capture the joy and excitement of a remarkable night or a great summer. To write about these important venues is also a way to assemble a golden age. Contemporary pubs will never be as important as the Roxy. Every club dances in the shadow of the Hacienda. Yet there is – through Web 2.0 – a great capacity to remember a special night of live music. The website songkick.com emerged in 2007 as an alert service for fans of future live events. However, by June 2009 the site had also added a database of over one million gigs from the previous fifty years. Users can log their participation at gigs, find friends and share experiences. The great pub, the great club and the great night-out are now preserved online, even when the venue has closed and the group has disbanded.

Key Questions

1. Which types or genres of music thrive in pubs?
2. Why do great clubs close?
3. Why are the venues of and for popular music neglected in the popular music literature?
4. Why do you think Sidekick.com extended its service from promoting future gigs to remembering past sessions and concerts?

Further Reading

Fitzgerald, R. (2007) *Clublife*. New York: HarperCollins.

McCarthy, C. (2008) *Fly by Night: The New Art of the Club Flyer*. London: Thames and Hudson.

Pickering, M. and Green, T. (1987) *Everyday Culture: Popular Song and the Vernacular Milieu*. Milton Keynes: Open University Press.

Savage, J. (1992) *The Hacienda Must Be Built*. London: International Music Publications.

Sonic sources

A Guy called Gerald (1988) *Voodoo Ray*. Rham.

Chic (1978) *Le Freak*. Atlantic.

Mr Fingers (1986) *Can You Feel It*? Trax Records.

New York Dolls (1973) *Personality Crisis*. Mercury.

Visual sources

24 Hour Party People (2002) Pathe.

CBGB Final Night, YouTube, http://www.youtube.com/watch?v=7bZkFkJRBQs&feature=related

Studio 54 (1999) Walt Disney.

Studio 54, YouTube, http://www.youtube.com/watch?v=_dl726_FKhc&feature=related

Web sources

CBGB's Online, http://www.cbgb.com/

Club Equinox, http://clubequinox.com/index.html

Fake Bands, http://www.fakebands.co.uk/

Songkick, www.songkick.com

Soundtracks and Filmic Spaces

Sound and vision – hearing and seeing – activate distinct modes of communication. The movement between visual and sonic media has a major effect on both viewers and listeners. Similarly, the film and popular music industries are distinct, requiring varying professional production techniques, diverse marketing strategies and academic skills to decode and interpret. There are increasing and productive relationships between these industries and media. New audiences and new literacies emerge when linking media. There is a precedent for such a confluence. Film music has been important since Al Jolson crooned 'Mammy' in *The Jazz Singer*. Musicals from the height of the golden age of Hollywood, featuring such performers as Judy Garland, Mickey Rooney and Fred Astaire, propelled the narrative of love and loss with song and dance. Over half a century later, films such as *Human Traffic* and *Trainspotting* offered micro memories of club experiences through visual re-presentations of music. There have been many films about music. From Vince Everett (Elvis Presley) in *Jailhouse Rock* in 1957, to *Velvet Goldmine's* rendering of 1970s glam rock, from *24 Hour Party People's* interpretation of Manchester's music and *8 Mile* with B-Rabbit (Eminem) guiding the audience through hip hop and Detroit's 8 Mile Road, there have been key moments that have transformed both popular music and cinematic industry.

    The Blackboard Jungle is credited with being the first rock and roll film. Released in 1955, it was the moment where youth culture not only saturated the Hollywood screen, but also when 'youth' was recognized as a distinct audience for film. The key moment in both the narrative and fame of the film emerged when Bill Haley & The Comets performed 'Rock around the Clock'. The following year, this song title was to provide the title for Fred F. Sears' film. Bill Haley & The Comets once again appeared. In this early moment of confluence between rock and cinema, Bill Haley signified 'youth' and 'rock and roll'. Considering his age and origins in country music, he was an odd choice for an icon. A more appropriate embodiment was Elvis Presley who appeared in *Jailhouse Rock* 1957. Such examples show how particular films became a vehicle for a pop star or group and as a way to draw a youthful audience to an old medium. Elvis Presley's films embody this tendency, but David Bowie's occasional sojourns into cinema, from *The Man Who Fell to Earth* to *Labyrinth*, are examples that are more modern. It is significant to note the particular performers who have been selected to 'represent' popular music in a visual form. Most frequently, these have been white, male, young and (relatively) safe under a parental gaze.

Cliff Richard and The Beatles are clear examples for this argument. Film made popular music – particularly rock and roll – understandable and controllable. It placed it in a wider context of entertainment. The reason why The Beatles became loveable mop tops is due in no small part to their work in and with cinema. The Richard Lester-directed Beatles' film, *A Hard Day's Night*, foreshadowed MTV with the 'Can't Buy Me Love' sequence. The rapid montage sequence integrated film, television and popular music (Carr, 1996). Similarly, the animated *Yellow Submarine* introduced generations of children to Beatles music.

The three minute pop song has proved an ideal structuring device for filmic montages to signify the passing of time or an emotional transformation. *Pretty in Pink* and *Peter's Friends* used a single track to develop a plot, extend a character and create an emotional shorthand with the audience. Lyrics can propel a narrative and prioritize content. Instrumental tracks will create atmosphere or mood. There are also discursive conflicts between classically constructed film and the structures of popular music. Claudia Gorbman made the observation that,

> The stanza form of popular song, the presence of lyrics to 'compete' with the viewers reception of film narrative and dialogue, and the cultural weight and significance of the stars performing the songs all work against classical Hollywood's conception of film music as an 'inaudible' accompaniment, relying on the anonymous yet familiar idioms of symphonic Romanticism, its elastic form dictated by the film's narrative form (2000: 43).

This means that a pop song will be frequently used to signify the passing of time – whether a day, night, season or years – or to capture a developing relationship. A fine example of this usage is from the film *Notting Hill*. When the two protagonists separated, Al Green's 'Ain't No Sunshine' captured the passing of the seasons and the cost of their physical and emotional disconnection.

Popular music draws particular filmic audiences to the cinema and DVD purchase, and holds a specific function in the plot. The role of particular songs in a film is a way to bring forward sound in what is primarily a visual media. Mostly music is background and backgrounded. A recognizable song can enable 'background' music to jut through and reconfigure the relationship with visuality. It also increases a song's ability to be marketed to an audience after a film has concluded (Smith, 1998: 5). New songs can be written for a film, but – with more frequency since the 1960s – pre-existing songs will be deployed. Powerful examples of found songs will be included Steppenwolf's 'Born to be Wild' in *Easy Rider*, the use of Joy Division's 'Love Will Tear Us Apart' in *Donnie Darko* and entire soundtracks for Quentin Tarantino's films, including *Pulp Fiction*. These tracks add to a film's narrative and emotional range. They are integral to its funding, marketing and promotion. Alexander Doty suggested that,

> Perhaps Hollywood's growing awareness of a large and moneyed 'youth market' finally led industry publicists to fully recognize the potential for music-and-movie exploitation implicit in the conglomerate entertainment networks (1988: 72).

Popular music serves a purpose in the filmic text. It also has a commercial role. The familiarity of popular music feeds into the marketability of film, transforming subcultural sounds into a popular cultural currency.

Easy Rider is important to this history. Directed by Dennis Hopper and written by Peter Fonda and Dennis Hopper, it was described by the latter as 'the first film to use found music. Everything previously had been soundtracks before that' (2004: 46). *Easy Rider* collated already existing music and used it to both create and confirm particular themes in the film. The myth of the soundtrack construction is seemingly correct. The rough cut of the film used Peter Fonda's record collection, assuming that Crosby, Stills and Nash would write the soundtrack. However, from this rough cut, Fonda and Hopper realized that the existing form could not be improved (Hill, 1996). In the sequence when Jack Nicholson rides pillion on Peter Fonda's chopper, the only required voiceover was Steppenwolf's 'Born to be Wild'.

There are multiple moments of interrelationship and hybridity between rock and film. A key moment of alignment between new cinematic forms and popular music was D.A. Pennebaker's *Dont Look Back*. Using *cinéma verité* techniques to create a visual style, it provided the template of half a century of rock documentaries. Dylan's seeming unawareness of the camera while talking, singing, walking and playing his guitar constructed a 'real' persona that he was to manage, reinforce and transform throughout the rest of his career. Martin Scorsese's *No Direction Home*, released in 2005, looped back into Pennebaker's films of Dylan (including footage from the unreleased *Eat the Document*), thereby creating another revisioning of his part in popular music history.

Lester Bangs recognized that this style of rock and roll image making was particularly important, ensuring that film still had an audience after Hollywood's golden age.

> Rock 'n' roll is an attitude: it's not a musical form of a strict sort. It's a way of doing things, of approaching things. Writing can be rock 'n' roll, or a movie can be rock 'n' roll. It's a way of living your life (2000: xv).

Bangs was using rock and roll as an ideology and an aesthetic. Other genres of music have also influenced cinema. Indeed, it is hard to separate Underworld's 'Born Slippy' from its sequence in *Trainspotting*. The rock era for cinema remains particularly important because it moved cinema away from family entertainment and into a diversity of markets.

Television and the music video have replaced many of the functions of the musical as a 'star vehicle'. There remains a small and influential portfolio of films continuing this early history, with popular music shaping the soundtrack. *West Side Story* in 1961 was an attempt to modernize the Hollywood musical. This project has been continued by Baz Luhrmann throughout all his films, particularly *Moulin Rouge*. He argued that,

> You have to find a code for any particular place and time. In the 30s the contract with the audience was clear: you had Fred Astaire singing to Ginger that he loves her as they dance across a gloss floor. You get to the 60s and you've Julie Andrews

running up a real hill outdoors singing 'the hills are alive with the sound of music'. In 1970 the music is Greek-chorused and Joel Grey is singing 'money makes the world go round' while the Nazi's are beating someone up. You get to the late 70s and you cut away to a needle dropping on a record while John Travolta moves to the groove (2001: 16).

Luhrmann understands the complex role of popular music in film, not only incorporating big band, rock and house into the soundtrack of *Moulin Rouge* but – by deploying Norman Cook as the music supervisor of the film – also activating a wide dance culture. He moderated and managed the relationship between family entertainment and youth culture, popular culture and the counterculture. Soundtracks have moved on since Rogers and Hammerstein. *Hair*, *Saturday Night Fever*, *Grease* and *The Rocky Horror Picture Show* captured a particular version of youth culture that was safe and aspirational but with a touch of danger. While the musical is no longer a key genre in contemporary filmmaking, the popularity of reality television talent shows has meant that particular aspirational forms of the musical have remained popular. The cultural profile of *High School Musical* and *Glee*, cleaning up the darker aspects of *Fame* and *Flashdance*, has meant that the 'Star is Born' narrative to singing success is still part of both film and music.

The sounds popularized by film are cut away from the vision to remain a significant area of sales for the record industry. Soundtracks – the recorded music that is synchronized to video games, films and television programmes – are frequently released commercially and generate new audiences and commercial opportunities for popular music. However the origin of the term from the film industry is derived from a 'sound track' (two words), which referred to the recording of sound either during film production or it being added during post-production. There are multiple sound tracks featuring dialogue, sound effects and music. When aligned, a composite track is formed. A dubbing track can also be added when moving a film into different languages. The soundtrack – as one word – entered popular culture when 'soundtrack albums' were released. Most frequently it was music from the films, with dialogue and effects absent from the recording. *Grease* and *Saturday Night Fever* are two high-selling examples of this form. In the case of films such as *Bend it Like Beckham* and *Pulp Fiction*, some of the dialogue remains on the soundtrack album as a memory of the cinematic context. The contemporary soundtrack also includes music recorded or found ('found music') for the soundtrack, such as in the case of *Fame* and *High School Musical*, or portions of the score, in such films as *The Piano* and *Donnie Darko*. By convention, a soundtrack can include music 'inspired by' or 'influencing' the film, but a score will only contain the original composer's music. The soundtrack is particularly important for the filmic genre of the biopic which re-creates the life of a performer, such as Johnny Cash or Ray Charles. Often these films and soundtracks will reactivate a back catalogue.

The influence of film can also work the other way, by changing music. Madonna's *Material Girl* played freely with Howard Hawks' *Gentlemen Prefer Blondes*. Other examples include Julien Temple's 30-minute short film for David Bowie's 'Blue Jean' and

Derek Jarman's extended video for The Smiths' 'The Queen is Dead'. Jarman also filmed a range of Pet Shop Boys' videos and the projections for their first world tour. While popular music films may be rare, the techniques used have been continued and improved through the music video. Music videos have also funded more serious avante garde projects for directors, with Temple and Jarman being clear examples here. While popular music has been more comfortably woven into the fragmented medium of television, it has both transformed and marketed film. Popular music has transformed cinema, particularly in the way it is edited and advertised. It has also amalgamated sound and vision to create new alignments and possibilities for performers and their audiences.

Key Questions

1. What is a soundtrack (one word)? How is it different from a sound track (two words)?
2. Why are soundtracks released?
3. Why do films feature music? For example, what is the function of the *Donnie Darko* soundtrack in comparison with that of *Walk the Line*?
4. What role do films hold in the marketing of music?

Further Reading

Crenshaw, M. (1994) *Hollywood Rock: A Guide to Rock 'n' Roll in the Movies*. London: Plexus.

Denisoff, R.S. and Romanowski, W. (1994) *Risky Business: Rock in Film*. New Brunswick: Transaction Publishers.

Romney, J. and Wootton, A. (1995) *Celluloid Jukebox: Popular Music and the Movies Since the 50s*. London: British Film Institute.

Smith, J. (1998) *The Sounds of Commerce: Marketing Popular Film Music*. New York: Columbia University Press.

Sonic sources

Berry, C. (1964) *You Never Can Tell*. Chess.

Haley, B. and the Comets (1954) *Rock Around the Clock*. Decca.

Joy Division (1980) *Love Will Tear Us Apart*. Factory.

Steppenwolf (1968) *Born to be Wild*. Dunhill.

Visual sources

Moulin Rouge (2001) 20th Century Fox.

Pulp Fiction Dancing, *YouTube*, http://www.youtube.com/watch?v=zoUEMZnibS8

Steppenwolf, *Born to be Wild*, *YouTube*, http://www.youtube.com/watch?v=rMbA Taj7Il8

The Blackboard Jungle (1955) Metro Goldwyn Mayer.

Web sources

Movie Music.com, http://www.moviemusic.com/

Soundtrack.net, www.soundtrack.net

STLyrics, http://www.stlyrics.com/

The Quentin Tarantino Files, http://www.tarantino.info/

Music Video and Televisual Spaces

At their most basic, music videos are advertising. They are a way to sell music. In an e-commerce environment they have also become a self-standing product and alternative revenue stream. Before iTunes and downloading communities though, the music video had a key role in the medium of television. The 1980s are known as the decade of the music video, framed by the arrival of MTV, on August 1, 1981. The broadcast started with The Buggles' 'Video Killed the Radio Star'. While much of the scholarly discussion focused on sex and violence, a new mode of marketing and presentation was formed through these televised music videos. For example, Christine Hall Hansen and Ranald Hansen were concerned that 'a generation is coming of age while watching sex and violence on television' (1990: 212). Performers like Madonna developed an image through music videos as much as via music. The most significant music video of this early period was Michael Jackson's *Thriller*, with Peter Gabriel's *Sledgehammer* using a mixture of live footage and animation techniques.

The function of music videos is clear. They are short promotional films that borrow many of the techniques of cinema, gaming and live performance. Working between commerce and art, new visual languages were generated through this innovative televisual text. The narrative and visual possibilities of a four minute video were and remain different to those of a full-length film. Not only are there questions about scale and length, but the techniques required to make a music video also require thousands of editing cuts and effects in a few minutes. Music video transformed television programming and filmic construction. Sharp narratives and heightened visual literacies emerged from the music video. A generation of young people learnt to 'read' and manage micronarratives and create new relationships between sound and vision.

A key year in the prehistory of the music video was 1966 and this was pioneered by The Beatles. When they finished touring in 1966, their promotional films for 'Rain' and 'Paperback Writer' became more elaborate and significant, culminating in the videos for 'Strawberry Fields Forever' and 'Penny Lane' the following year. Music videos were a replacement for touring so that fans could see a band or performer without attending a live performance. Bob Dylan, in the midst of D.A. Pennebaker's *Dont Look Back*, presented an iconic version of 'Subterranean Homesick Blues'. Dylan neither sang nor mouthed the lyrics, but held up cards featuring some of the song's lyrics. The Kinks and The Who both probed and extended the genre in mini films with plots through *Dead End Street* and *Happy Jack* respectively.

Throughout the 1970s, the music video changed along with musical formats. Popular music was included as part of variety entertainment, with such programmes as *The Sonny & Cher Comedy Hour* and *Morecombe and Wise*. For groups such as Abba, the music video performed a similar role to that which it had done for The Beatles, as a replacement for touring. Music programmes like *Top of the Pops* and *Solid Gold* showed videos. The break-through video that rejuvenated the genre once more was Queen's *Bohemian Rhapsody* which – although it deployed simple visual effects – demonstrated that new relationships between sound and vision were being formed. For many nations outside of Europe and the Americas, music videos were incredibly important in building a fan base for particular performers. Particularly in Australia, the success of Abba and Meatloaf could be linked almost directly with the expansive videos produced for their songs. These promotional music videos were featured on the national show *Countdown* and interspersed with live and local performers like Skyhooks and Sherbet. For remote nations, the only way to see Abba, Madonna or Duran Duran was through the release of the music video.

Recognizing this earlier history, the 1980s music industry is most associated with the music video. There are technological reasons for this. Cheaper video recording and edit-ing equipment was developed which meant a greater variety of bands could produce promotional videos, rather than having to deploy film stock. Because of the pervasive-ness of domestic film equipment, by the middle of the decade it was expected that every single would feature an accompanying video. Videos accompanying complete albums would also emerge, most notably from Duran Duran, Blondie and Split Enz.

This history of music videos tracks a decline in live concerts throughout the 1980s. Music videos not only circulated in the family home throughout the television in the lounge, they also did the same in pubs and clubs. They are currently well represented in MySpace and YouTube. The history of music video inter-relates and interplays with numerous other histories:

- the history of film
- the history of television
- the history of popular music
- the history of dance
- the history of postmodernism
- the history of Web 2.0 and the read–write web
- the history of home recording

Music videos are a complex textual form because they resonate with these other histories. There is no single academic method or approach to grasp music video. While there is fre-quently an obvious connection between the narrative of a song and video, occasionally a music video such as Ultravox's *Vienna* accessed a bigger culture – incorporating film noir codes, with the femme fatale, decadent imagery and very sophisticated editing, and the high culture of ballet, architecture and sculpture. Codes from melodrama frame the ending. Similarly, New Order's *True Faith* combined Bauhaus-style costumes, seventeenth-century

Rococo iconography, sign language and Punch and Judy-like violence. Such videos are both exceptional and the exception. The overwhelming majority of videos will present an – albeit heavily edited – 'live performance'. But even this conventional 'live' presentation can be shaken and reordered as witnessed in the Ting Tings' video for 'That's Not My Name'.

Videos problematize the crisp divisions between aural and visual, pop art and high art. The video format has been used to try out new techniques such as Aha's 'Take On Me', which featured a blending of animation and live footage. No matter which techniques are deployed, music videos remain part of pop culture. They operate through Web 2.0 participatory sites and environments and engage with dance culture and the fashion industries. They also colonize time during non-peak television periods such as Saturday and Sunday mornings and late at night. Specialist and niche music video channels are part of pay television packages.

A clear example of this re-purposing of music for a new digital life(style) has emerged for the music videos as much as the music, being purchased from iTunes and other commercial portals. This is an innovative service, recognizing the independent role of the music video in popular music history. The improvements in mobile screen media through the iTouch, iPhone and iPad have ensured that videos can be viewed with clarity. Indeed, the navigation system for the newer music players is increasingly icon- rather than text-based. The internet has created a new platform for videos, particularly since broadband access became more widely available. Besides MTV streaming music videos and Apple's iTunes Store, YouTube, and MySpace have also become channels for music videos. The difference is that – through user generated content – the diversity of material available to download and view has increased exponentially. The selected video can be viewed at any time of the day. The 1980s commercial applications for music video have been updated, digitized, uploaded, downloaded, shared, mashed up and discussed.

All media have been effected by digital convergence. A diversity of music television channels form a large part of pay television services and some specialist music programming remains on free to air. Internet-housed radio is also being accompanied by pictures, vodcasts, video clips and show notes. As a result, although music videos seemed to be the archetype of the compressed, segmented flow of television, they have ended up moving beyond television.

Music videos and/in televisual spaces have provided the impetus for new relationships between screen and sound. Music-based console games have created new and interactive relationships between screens and audience, with guitar- and drum-shaped controllers offering innovative interfaces. Other modes of interaction are included in games such as Dance Dance Revolution that allow players to become part of the songs and music videos from the 1980s. Of particular note here is gaming music. For example, Grand Theft Auto has created imagined radio stations such as 'Head', with songs and advertisements for Scatwerk (a gaming version of Kraftwerk). Music has become integral to all interactive screen play. Online communities are now forming around video game music.

One such example is OverClocked ReMix, which involves musicians transforming the arrangements and structure of original gaming music. As a way of aligning a desire to see and hear music along with a capacity to play an instrument through a gaming console, music fans can now be part of the action. They can not only watch, they can also become part of the music video.

Key Questions

1. What is the purpose of a music video?
2. What are the characteristics of a music video?
3. Besides television, what are the other ways to see a music video?
4. As television has declined in its influence, have music videos become more or less important?

Further Reading

Banks, J. (1996) *Monopoly Television: MTV's Quest to Control the Music*. Boulder, CO: Westview.

Hanson, M. (2006) *Reinventing Music Video: Next-generation Directors, Their Inspiration and Work*. Cheadle: Rotovision.

Missingham, A. (2007) *Why Games are Bigger than Rock 'n' Roll*. London: Youth Music.

Schwartz, L. (2007) *Making Music Videos: Everything You Need to Know from the Best in the Business*. New York: Billboard.

Sonic sources

David Bowie (1977) *Sound and Vision*, RCA.

Etchart, M. (2006) *Sound and Vision Radio*, podcast, iTunes.

Robbie Williams (2009) *Reality Killed the Video Star*, Chrysalis.

The Sports (1978) *Who Listens to the Radio*, Mushroom.

Visual sources

Beyonce, *Single Ladies (Put A Ring On It)*, music video, iTunes.

Duran Duran, *Rio*, music video, iTunes.

Green Day, *Wake Me Up When September Ends*, music video, iTunes.

Ultravox, *Vienna*, music video, iTunes.

Web sources

Anime Music Videos, http://www.animemusicvideos.org/home/home.php

Music Video Games, http://www.musicvideogames.net/

OverClocked ReMix: Game Arrangement Management Community, http://www.ocremix.org/

Video Cure.com, http://www.videocure.com/

Radio, Podcasting and Listening Spaces

Towards the end of the nineteenth century, pre-recorded music for the home was provided by either the gramophone or the pianola. There were few options to either record or replay music. By the 1920s music had become invisible, a sonic experience that separated the performer from the listener. Radio was an important medium that has often been underplayed in its significance. It was both – as Brian Regal realized – 'machine and ... media' (2005: xii). It invoked histories of design and radio communications, yet was also integral to the disconnection of a human voice from a body, creating a desire for mobile media. The interwar years (1919–1939) were the period that moved radio from a mode of private communication and into the basis of public discourse. Like all media, it combined a series of earlier developments, including electricity, the telegraph and the telephone. Through radio, music and sounds could be moved from their original location of performance. Music and spoken word programming could be distanced from a live experience. Voices and sounds could pass through a microphone and be transmitted to other locations. Through the internet, radio signals could be digitized and become part of a network. Local stations gained international audiences. Podcasting extended the potential of radio, enabling both space and time shifting. Now listeners can hear, at their convenience, the form and type of any presentation rather than fitting in with the schedule of a radio producer. The radio and music industries did not predict that podcasting could be so successful. This widened the opportunities not only for music, but also for DJ sets and a range of spoken word programming.

This flexibility and customization of podcasts was based on the post-television configuration of radio in the spectrum of broadcasting. As Jody Berland described, radio is a 'secondary medium' (2003: 230), an accompaniment to the other activities that make up our social life. Radio, after its initial height in popular culture, has been continually displaced by the new medium or platform of the time. Such a process continued as radio was replaced by iPod-compatible units in motor vehicles. Certainly, radio was the dominant broadcast medium up until the mid-twentieth century. It was through the advent of sonic and screen cultures, and the integration of sonic and visual platforms, that the role of radio declined in the portfolio of popular culture. This has meant that it has had to transform its role in daily life, in response to the new mix of media, listening and viewing behaviours. Andrew Crisell extolled 'how extraordinarily resilient radio is' (2006: vii). No longer needing to cater to a general population, alternative and specialist communities form around particular types of music and subjects.

Radio is a secondary medium that is continually displaced by new platforms. Currently, new and productive relationships are being created between radio and podcasting. A vast network of listening spaces has evolved. Varying from commercial to community media, a series of hybrid formations has been generated through the time and space-shifting potentials of web-enabled podcasts with RSS (Really Simple Syndication). From June 28, 2005, the iTunes Store has also enabled the downloading of podcasts, the overwhelming majority of which have been free of charge. While radio separated listeners and broadcasters, podcasting has enabled listeners to become both programmer and producer.

Radio has been crucial to making music popular, shaping and framing the charts. With Web 2.0 platforms music can be selected, customized and inserted into a personally appropriate time and place. Before the pervasiveness of the web in music marketing through MySpace and YouTube, radio airplay was integral to chart success. Richard Cook complained that 'If I want to hear modern bebop, severe heavy metal, one reggae, old rockabilly, fresh ambient or any other kind of strain that programmers have filtered out of their schedules, I have to go somewhere other than radio' (1999: 46). Commercial radio forced its audience to listen to advertizing before hearing the next track. The iPod and MP3 players created personal playlists without interruptions. David Kusek and Gerd Leonhard realized that 'digital music has become the new radio for the Internet generation' (2005: 6). This is however not quite accurate. Portable media players allow listeners to hear commercial-free music of their choice at their own convenience. It is more – and less – than radio.

Kusek and Leonhard declared that, 'radio is no longer the primary way that people discover new music' (2005: 26). Certainly traditional radio stations now use the web as a portal for their product, but podcasting derived from communities and individuals without advertising content is transforming not only music radio but also talk radio. Significantly, a strong survivor in this new environment is community radio. Focused on the building of community and the development of democracy a specialist broadcasting product is offered, addressing religion, radio for citizens with print disabilities or indigenous and migrant media in an array of languages. This desire is what Kerrie Foxwell et al. have described as 'the cornerstone of the sector's philosophy, providing a conduit to embrace, legitimize and validate difference and diversity' (2008: 16). The creation of a 'communicative democracy' (Foxwell, 2008: 16) slices through globalized, homogenized, digitized media. Community radio has been readily incorporated into the new imperatives of the age, with a focus on local and specific concerns. As Rodriguez has suggested,

> Citizens' media do not have to compete for global markets; they do not have to reach all audiences; they do have to 'talk to everyone' and therefore, local dialects, local issues, and local codifications of social reality find their way into citizens' media programming … citizens' media are in a privileged position to delve into, to explore, and to articulate differences between subordinate groups – unlike mainstream media which tends to generalize and smooth away such differences (2001: 154).

Community radio performs a role in a digitized, fragmented and diffused media environment. In terms of popular music, it can service diverse sonic and subcultural communities without a direct link to the music charts. When this specialist programming is repackaged and rebranded for an international podcasting audience, special interest musical communities can transcend a particular place and time. This means that reggae, emo or metal fans who may be minority interest groups in their city and unserviced by commercial radio can seek out fans with similar interests online.

The question is how does the integration of digital platforms – such as MP3 players and mobile phones – enable or discourage new audiences in the discovery of a diversity of music? Now that the physical retailing of music has declined, consumers are able to locate a range of music from diverse sources. Online music has created new sonic communities. This is a post-radio culture. There is a large group within the population that no longer accesses radio in any form, with the function of talk radio being replaced by podcasts. Music radio is today being bypassed by personalized song lists or iPod-generated genius playlists. Radio is not the place to hear challenging or different music. This new material can be sourced through tie-ins with gaming, film and television, social networking sites and digital music services such as MSN, iTunes and Amazon. Without the intervention of record or radio companies, the capitalist relationships between music and consumers are changing.

Key Questions

1. What is a podcast? What is the role of a podcast for music of a genre such as reggae or ska?
2. Berland described radio as a 'secondary medium'. What did she mean?
3. What is community radio?
4. What is the future for commercial radio?

Further Reading

Hutchinson, T. (2008) *Web Marketing for the Music Business*. Boston, MA: Focal.

Jensen, E. and LaBelle, B. (2007) *Radio Territories*. Los Angeles, CA: Errant Bodies.

Osborne, J. (2009) *Radio Head: Up and Down the Dial of British Radio*. New York: Simon and Schuster.

Regal, B. (2005) *Radio: The Life Story of a Technology*. Westport, CT: Greenwood.

Sonic sources

Josh Highland, notPopular.com, podcast, iTunes, 2008–

Ministry of Sound Podcast, podcast, iTunes, 2007–

The Pete Tong Tongcast, 2005–

Trance Tuesday Podcast, podcast, iTunes, 2009–

Visual sources

Good Morning Vietnam (1988) Walt Disney.

'Podcasting in plain English,' *YouTube*, http://www.youtube.com/watch?v=y-MSL42NV3c

Radio Days (2009) MGM.

The Boat That Rocked (2009) Universal.

Web sources

Free Internet Radio, http://www.shoutcast.com/

Live 365, http://www.live365.com/index.live

Podcast.com, http://podcast.com/

Podcast Alley, http://www.podcastalley.com/

MP3 and Downloading Spaces

Recording technologies have shaped and structured the music industry. Expensive recording equipment, matched by complex production and distribution mechanisms for music, ensured that large corporations and a few entrepreneurial independents dominated the music industry. Only when high quality reproductions could be created and mixed in domestic and small commercial environments did the power and reach of record companies decline. This was accelerated by readily available and intuitive hardware and software and the capacity to distribute (and sell) tracks online through social networking sites. Record companies had previously maintained control not only of recording spaces but also the pathways of distribution. Now that songs can be recorded and mixed in the home and distributed as compression files via the web, sales are not limited by the production of a physical release such as a compact disc, cassette or vinyl album. The business model for record companies has dissipated, creating new spaces not only for commerce but also for creativity.

When sound is digitized, it is separated from its original time and space. Digitization samples a sonic wave. The quality of the wave is dependent on the number of samples of the data. All digital representations are incomplete. Digital compression increases the amount of data that is removed from the file. The advantage of moving a file through the online environment mitigates and justifies this loss of sonic quality. Mobile phones, laptops, netbooks, iPads and MP3 players are new portals for broadcasting, recording and remixing. The quality of the songs played and recorded is lower, but the convenience and mobility overcome this disadvantage.

The irony of the changes instigated by MP3s on the music industry is that the file format was developed for the motion picture industry as a standard for the digitization of video and audio. Even in this media context, the goal was to compress data so these could be exchanged and stored on computers. The German-based Fraunhofer Institute for Integrated Circuits in Germany created the MPEG-1 in 1992, removing some data to facilitate compression. There were three levels of data compression. The first two layers or levels enabled high quality recording. However the third layer was of a lower specification, more suitable to domestic and personal use. This third level was dismissed as an unimportant discovery and was stored on a German university computer until a Dutch programmer, known only as SoloH, found the file, improved it and then sent it to the open source community for further development. Because of this collaboration, better MP3 encoders eventuated (SoloH, N.D.). Yet the popular cultural currency in the early 1990s was limited, meaning that very little was known about this MP3 (Fasoldt, 1998).

It was only through the P2P (peer-to-peer) networks and a company named Napster that the threat of file compression to the recording industry suddenly started to be recognized. Napster is often credited with having initiated Web 2.0. A small and free software programme, it was written by eighteen year old Shawn Fanning. In 1998, Napster's network made it easy for music fans to go online, find a copy of a song, and download it for no cost. It operated on a central server controlled by Fanning and his uncle. Napster users searched the directory and downloaded from other users' computers. Such a practice violated copyright and so record companies rapidly sought the closure of such enterprises through the application of existing analogue law. Peer-to-peer sharing of music became the target of legal action. Instead of realizing that the recording industry had been slow in acknowledging the impact of digitization on music and providing alternative e-commerce models, lawyers sued individual downloaders who had been identified as sharing music online, with each downloaded song attracting a penalty of US$230,000:

Corporate panic triggered by the shift in platforms created excessive reactions. Music had been 'shared' for decades via analogue tapes. Digital downloading only increased the speed of the practice. John Alderman (2001) offered a powerful and consistent understanding of downloading spaces, not only considering distribution frameworks but also by reviewing the new relationships that had been formed through production and consumption,

> A shift towards synthesizers, sampling, and digital production studios means that in many cases songs nowadays are created that exist from beginning to end as purely digital code. The switch to online digital distribution fits in perfectly with these developments, just as occupations as diverse as journalist, stock trader, and office manager have found themselves less concerned with physical objects and more concerned with playing roles within a larger datascape of networked computers. Almost all recently commercially released music has been digitally recorded, or at the very least, mastered. To go to the trouble of actually pressing a song's data onto a CD, when there are faster, more efficient ways of distributing the ones and zeroes, is increasingly anachronistic (2001: 34).

Alderman was prescient, writing these words a decade ago. He suggested that when music was produced digitally, digital distribution would follow. Instead, downloading cultures were 'the new punk' and 'the new house' (Mewton, 2001: 12–13). The integration of music production and consumption was naturalized. Fans not only became producers, but distributors as well. Intriguingly, record companies who committed to the CD single as a way to distribute individual songs were too slow to notice the social transformations of listening, consuming and purchasing music through downloading. Users, rather than the legal owners, of music started to share and distribute music using methods that were beyond the control of performers or producers. Literacies changed, creating new relationships between screen and sound.

Napster closed after legal action in the summer of 2001, but it had provided a model for a new way of thinking about community and consumption online. Flickr, MySpace, Facebook, World of Warcraft, YouTube and blogs were built on this realization. Kazaa was also founded following Napster's innovation, becoming the most downloaded software in

history. Apple's Steve Jobs saw in Kazaa's example that a centralized downloading process and portal, rather than a file sharing system, would be possible. In response, iTunes
launched on April 28, 2003. The downloading software, BitTorrent, began its rise in
2004, with the file sharing protocols developed in 2001 and operating independent of
a server. Using many intermediate servers, it maintained the anonymity of the peer-to-
peer users. The deployment of peer networks to transmit data reduced the bandwidth
required and meant that files could be sent in smaller components and at greater speed.
It was indeed a torrent of bits. For a user to download a file, BitTorrent client software
needed to be installed on their computer and be able to locate a torrent file and a
tracker file, which manage the distribution of files. Significantly, Kazaa's innovator Niklas
Zennstrom moved on from music and established Skype, the world's first effective and
free internet telephone service.

The difficulty in managing the il/legality of music downloading is that nothing – no
physical product – is actually moved, bought, sold or exchanged. A copied digital file is
unlike analogue tape recording. There is no loss of quality in each subsequent generation. This
transformation was devastating for the business models that had sustained record companies for
the previous half-century. The success of the early record companies was determined by their
capacity to produce systems of and for recording. As the costs of recording reduced, encouraged through sampling and mixing, music moved away from a conflict between commerce
(industry) and creativity (the artists) (Negus, 1999). It was necessary to offer both recording
and playing equipment for the consumer, which doubled sales. Up until the 1920s, there
had been two competing systems for recording technology: Edison's cylinder and Berliner's
disc. Both were superseded by the vinyl record, and by the end of the Second World War
the United States had become the leading record-producing country in the world.

A change in music platforms will shift the marketing, selling, storage and audiences of
recorded music. Vinyl records had occupied an important place in musical culture throughout much of the twentieth century, developing from the earliest trials in the recording of
sound through to the movement of popular music into the home. Yet the mobility of
this music was limited by the weight of record players and the fragility of vinyl. Other
platforms such as the analogue cassette would move music into the car and create opportunities for personal stereos like the Sony Walkman and mix tape culture (Moore, 2004:
12). The cassette – developed in the 1960s – was small and portable. The 1970s were the
decade for cassettes as part of home stereos, portable boom boxes and walkmans. They permitted the home copying of vinyl. Through the 1980s, the mix tape became what Dean
Wareham described as a 'form of "speech" particular to the late twentieth century, soon
replaced by the "playlist"' (Wareham, 2004: 24). They took time to construct and conveyed
a message to the recipient: love, regret or pride in the quality of the mixer's musical taste.

The cassette inevitably declined with the arrival of the compact disc. Every redundancy
in music platforms will offer productive opportunities for new gadgets and appliances and
increased revenue for both hardware developers and record companies. The supercedence
of vinyl in mainstream music cultures was a result of the arrival of the compact disc
in the 1980s. Introduced by Sony in 1982, it became the main medium for recording

and distributing music in the 1980s. It created a boom in the music industry and a large profit for record companies because the vinyl back-catalogue was reissued. Surprisingly, the smaller and more durable compact discs increased the value of vinyl records for dance, electronica and hip hop communities. The turntable and vinyl – while displaced from chart-based music cultures – became DJ instruments for scratching, cutting and mixing.

While home taping was a battle between producers and consumers, the MP3 triggered a sonic and legal war. MP3s held enormous advantages: it became possible to find music and freely download it. At an early stage in its history there was little alternative to illegal downloading, as record companies tried to deny the exchange and purchase of music online. Only when legal online musical stores and portals were created, particularly through the iTunes Store, were there alternatives to the illegal file sharing sites. Finally, there was an avenue for those who did not want to continue to pay high prices for compact discs, but also wanted to support artists and avoid criminal prosecution.

Intriguing, the iTunes Store does not utilize MP3s. Apple used the AAC audio format, which deploys a different code and compression mechanisms for audio files. AAC had an improved sound quality of an equivalent file size. Until March 2009, the tracks were available with Digital Rights Management that meant they could only be played on a finite number of platforms. It was a way to block the illegal copying of legally purchased sonic files. Yet even this restriction was modified because of consumer complaints.

Music capitalism requires waste and obsolescence to create a profit. A focus on innovative technology ensures that the purchasing of songs, albums and equipment is ongoing, rather than consumers living in their own back catalogue with an ageing stereo. While histories are currently being written around and about the iPod and MP3 player, the easy accessibility of the musical back catalogue – with thousands of songs available at the touch of a screen, click of a mouse and turn of a wheel – means that a love for new music is tempered by the sheer range, diversity and simplicity of clicking through sonic history. With a century of recorded music available via tactile scrolling through a screen listeners can live in a constantly changing shuffle of songs, without the need to be challenged by the new or the different.

When reviewing the last fifty years of popular music history, this reveals the survival of the single, through iTunes, MP3 files and BitTorrent, and the decline of the album, masked by a twenty-year detour through the compact disc era. While the compact disc 'replaced' vinyl, it also replicated vinyl structures, genres and presentational modes for music. The length of albums and the role, function and selection of singles remained the same, applying analogue and vinyl standards while underestimating the possibilities of digital convergence. Because the CD was perpetuating the limitations of an older platform, when the next technological change emerged, the transformation was swift. Instead of applying the analogue standards of vinyl singles and albums, with particular lengths and structures, the 'new' downloaded single could be 45 seconds long or a two-hour DJ session. While the compact disc continued vinyl history without the vinyl, the iPod and MP3 players did not perpetuate an analogue nostalgia. They were different and changed the spaces for how music would be purchased, sold and consumed.

Key Questions

1. How has the purchasing of music transformed through digital downloads?
2. Why did the iPod become part of popular culture so quickly?
3. How has listening to music been transformed through the downloading of music files?
4. Could record companies have predicted the speed of decline in both the compact disc and the physical retailing of music? What future transformations in the relationship between music, mobility and identity do you predict?

Further Reading

Bell, D. and Hollows, J. (eds) (2005) *Ordinary Lifestyles: Popular Media, Consumption and Taste.* Milton Keynes: OUP.

Bull, Michael (2007) *Sound Moves: iPod Culture and Urban Experience.* London: Routledge.

Jones, D. (2005) *iPod, Therefore I Am.* London: Weidenfeld and Nicolson.

Merriden, T. (2001) *Irresistible Forces: The Business Legacy of Napster.* Oxford: Capstone.

Sonic sources

Edison Media Research (2008) *Music Royalties,* iTunes.

Kusek, D. (2005) *The Future of Music,* iTunes.

Moonah, J (2007–8) *Online Music Marketing,* iTunes.

Quail, M. (2006) *The Music Law podcast,* iTunes.

Web sources

Apple Corporation, http://www.apple.com

DJDownload, www.djdownload.com

Madden, M. and Rainie, L. (2005) *Music and video downloading moves beyond P2P,* PEW Internet and American Life Project, http://www.pewinternet.org.PPF/r/153/report_display.asp

Sony, http://www.sony.com

Section III

Instruments of/for Study

Guitar Cultures

The guitar is a stringed object that when strummed or picked creates sound. Often made of wood, other materials of construction include a range of metals, most famously deployed in the case of the Dobro guitar, also labeled the national steel. Electric guitars, while featuring a timber base, incorporate plastic and metal pickups. Nylon and steel strings are also common. Because of this diversity in construction, the role of the guitar in music is complex and extensive. As a mobile instrument, it has been used in urban and rural environments and by a range of performers in an array of genres. In the late nineteenth century, cheap guitars became available throughout the United States of America, providing the origin and impetus for many of the narratives and genres described in this book. Andy Bennett and Kevin Dawe described the guitar as 'in every respect a global phenomenon' (2001: 2). Its proliferation captures both the complexity and simplicity of popular music. The guitar is easy to play, but difficult to play well. It requires manual dexterity, with a capacity to create chords or shapes with the left hand while independently building melodies and rhythm through strumming and picking. This technique is inverted for left-handed players. Within a few hours, the most inexperienced of players can structure a chord and create some form of sound. Often the degree of simplicity or complexity of chord structures and picking styles will determine a style of music. For example, Luther Perkins was as important to creating Johnny Cash's popular success as his legendary bass-baritone voice. The boom-chicka-boom-chicka picking style was simple but startling, creating a melodic space for the subtlety, volume and timbre of Cash's voice.

Playing the guitar differs from the piano, which requires a similar technique with both the right and left hand. The guitar necessitates separate actions from each hand. This principle is common to the playing of instruments in the violin family; however in the case of a guitar, finger picking and/or a combination of a plectrum or finger picks replace the bow. While there are left- and right-handed guitars, generally the dominant hand is most frequently designated the more complex task of strumming and finger picking. The less dominant hand is used on the fretboard, with fingers depressing strings either individually or in chord combinations. The fret markers are located in precise positions along the fret board, determining the length of the string's vibration. This vibration determines the pitch. Chording is often a task of strength rather than dexterity, particularly with regard to barre chords. While much attention is focused on the famous guitars and guitarists, it is also important to remember the special connection between the human body and the instrument. The relationship between physical gestures and musical object permits a dynamic range of options for each guitarist. While the function of guitarists in rock genres is differentiated between 'lead' and 'rhythm', in practice, performers will move between these categories. For every Eric Clapton lead break in The Beatles' 'While My Guitar Gently Weeps', there is Buddy Holly playing on 'Peggy Sue' or Keith Richards on '(I Can't Get No) Satisfaction' that transgresses between the designation of lead and rhythm guitar.

A guitar has many advantages over other instruments. It has both acoustic and electric versions and can be carried and played in a range of places. A range of sounds can emerge from the same six strings by augmenting the finger positions and rhythmic technique with the right and left hand. There is also a capacity to use electronic effects and pedals to alter the sound. These differences are created by altering the combination of chords, hammers on and off, picking and strumming patterns and amplification. Electrification increased the place and function of guitars so they can be heard above the drums, percussion and brass. As an example of this moment of transition in terms of genre when guitars were amplified, listen to Bill Haley and The Comets 'Rock Around the Clock'. The brass and guitars duel for ascendancy, each claiming a lead break in this short but influential moment in popular music history.

As the electric guitar became lighter and more portable, and the techniques to bend and vary the tone of strings increased through the developments in pedals, it moved from being a backing instrument in big bands to a lead instrument in rock music. Throughout the 1960s, the distortion of sounds from an electrical signal increased by interfacing effects, stomp boxes and pedals through the signal path. These are employed by the foot while playing and can create diverse tones within a single song. The most common effects are the chorus and compression/sustain, delay and reverb, fuzz, wah-wah and flanging. Examples of pedal use include compression on Roger McGuinn's Rickenbacker for 'Mr Tambourine Man' and the chorus pedal on Johnny Marr's Rickenbacker on 'How Soon is Now' for The Smiths. The electric guitar is integral to popular music, with over 700,000 sold each year (Millard, 2004: 3). The history of the guitar in popular music therefore is not only a question of construction or technique. Steve Waksman described electric guitars as 'instruments of desire' (1999). It is an inspiration and aspirational object expressing creativity and belonging.

Guitars combine both the art and craft of music. Famous brands such as Martin, Gibson, Fender and Rickenbacker have moved through the trends in music to shape and transform the sound emerging from a fret board, wooden body, strings and a sound hole. Guitars have a history that originated long before the twentieth century and rock music. Connections can be seen and heard with ancient instruments such as the sitara and the smaller sitar in India and Central Asia. They featured a curved body and a fretted neck. By also noting the etymology of the word 'guitar,' a trace of its history can be seen. The English word is derived from the Spanish *guitarra*, which comes from the Latin *cithara* and was based on the Greek word *kithara*, which also shows links with the Persian *sihtar*. This movement through language and history confirms its long-term influence in musical history.

The guitar as used today has a relationship with the *cithara* that the Romans brought to Hispania in 40AD. Moving through experimentations with lute tunings, different numbers of strings and transformations of the body shape, the acoustic guitar started to stabilize in its construction throughout the nineteenth century, particularly through the design innovations of Antonio de Torres Jurado in Seville and Louis Panormo in London. The body of the guitar creates the sound quality. The soundboard – the top of the guitar – is an incredibly thin piece of wood that is reinforced by internal bracing. The quality of the tone emerges through the vibration of strings through the guitar top. For the electric guitar – particularly the solid body – a shortage of suitable hardwood since the 1970s has meant that guitars are rarely built from one solid piece. The body is carved so that electronic components can be recessed into the wood. The electronics on guitars allow aspects of the sound to be controlled by the player, particularly the volume and – even without pedals – the tone. However, the mechanism through which the vibration of the strings hits the soundboard is the bridge. Without the bridge, the strings would not hold their place on the body of the guitar. Some guitar models allow the raising or lowering of the bridge, often referred to as 'the action'. A low action is necessary for finger picking styles. A high action increases the harmonics often associated with reggae and jazz. The importance of the species of the wood chosen for construction of the bodies and the materials used for the strings influences both the tone and the role of the guitar in the melody and rhythm.

There are two types of guitar played in popular music: acoustic and electric. Acoustic guitars include the classical guitar, which is intended for solo performances, and flamenco guitars, that offer greater rhythmic and percussive possibilities created through the gauge of the strings and a high action. Mariachi bands, for example, include a range of guitar sizes, from the smallest *requinto* to the *guitarron*, which is larger than a cello. Acoustic models include the Portuguese guitar, featuring twelve strings, and the flat-top guitar with a larger body and reinforced neck to manage the strain of six steel strings. This guitar is louder and has been used in diverse genres, particularly country, bluegrass, mountain music, jazz, blues and country. Dobro or Resonator guitars have (as the name suggests) a metal resonator in the top of the body to amplify the sound. Even after amplification, these guitars are still popular because of their distinctive sound. Archtop guitars exist in both acoustic and electric forms, featuring an f-hole design, similar to a violin. The deep hollow body creates diverse modes of resonance and remains popular in jazz music. Both Gibson and Rickenbacker constructed versions of the Archtop for their models of electric guitar. Similarly, the 12-string guitar exists in both acoustic and electric forms.

Diverse string arrangements are possible on the guitar, including the four, seven, eight and nine, but the six and twelve string configurations are the most common. The twelve string version features six paired strings, with four (E, A, D and G) tuned one octave above the conventional pitch. The rationale for the twelve strings is to increase volume, but this format also creates a distinctive tone. They are difficult instruments to play both in terms of chording and finger picking, and are often used as a rhythm guitar because of this complexity. Leadbelly, George Harrison, Roger McGuinn and Richie Sambora all played the twelve string. While Harrison only played the twelve string on a few tracks during his Beatles' career, McGuinn – after seeing Harrison play it in the film *A Hard Day's*

Night – bought the guitar. The Byrds' sound was based on the innovations he instigated in both left and right hand techniques. He deployed a picking style from the banjo and innovative shapes of chords to manage twelve strings, while freeing fingers for hammer ons and pull offs.

While much of the guitar's design history is about wood and strings, there is also a history of technology to overlay, along with discussions of practice and performance. The electric guitar is a hybrid instrument. Even an electric guitar features acoustic elements. It has shadowed a range of sonic transformations, including analogue electrical experimentation, the MIDI and digitization. Electric guitars contain an array of circuits and an opportunity for incorporating new technological developments, with signal processing, amplification and an 'on board' interface that allows a transformation of the resultant sound. Electric guitars feature diverse body constructions, varying from solid to semi-hollow (often-termed semi-acoustic) to hollow bodies. They make little sound without amplification and require transducers (pickups) that transpose the vibration of the strings into an electrical signal. This signal passes through a cable to the amplifier. Through this passage, electronic devices such as effects pedals change the modulation and tone. Amplification has meant that a series of techniques rarely used on acoustic instruments, such as legato (through a sustain pedal) and harmonics, have emerged.

While it is a simple task to convey this history of the physical construction of a guitar, it is the sociology of the guitar – who plays it, how is it played and its social function – that requires most attention. Electric guitars are the foundation of many musical genres, including jazz, rock music, country and blues. Rickenbacker Electro Instruments was founded in 1931 by Adolph Rickenbacker and George Beauchamp. They developed the first modern electric guitars by attaching a magnetic pickup to the body of the instrument. The problem was feedback, triggered by the hollow body of the guitar. Les Paul and Leo Fender independently invented solid-body guitars that resolved this problem. Fender went on to found the Fender Electric Instrument Manufacturing Company and Paul worked with Gibson guitar manufacturers. Once the manufacture of solid body guitars began, a diversity of shapes was possible.

The Fender Stratocaster remains the world's best-selling guitar. It features a light-weight design with an added pickup to the standard design of the Fender Telecaster. With the addition of a vibrator arm, versatility in sound was possible. Significantly, the early Telecaster featured a bolt-on neck. Leo Fender wanted the design to be modular to manufacture, so that it could be Fordist in construction, cost-effective and easy to repair. By 1953, the Stratocaster was being produced and was seen as an improvement on the Telecaster as it included a synchronized tremolo and three single-coil pickups. The Fender Precision Bass also emerged from this period of development, being released in 1951. While there have been famous players of the Stratocaster, its early use by Hank Marvin from the Shadows propelled the guitar into fame. Marvin's control of the tremolo arm made it an instrument of aspiration. Listening to his lead melody in songs like 'Apache' demonstrates an expertise and physical dexterity which tested the limits of right-hand technique. Similarly, Jimi Hendrix, a left-hander playing a right-handed model, demonstrated the scale, speed and rhythm in matching technique with the capacities of amplification. 'Hey Joe' is the archetype of this innovative combination.

The Gibson Les Paul solid body guitar originated in 1952, predating the development of the Fender Stratocaster. Both these guitars crossed musical genres, from blues to country. The 'sustain' quality of this early Les Paul model was legendary, creating innovative opportunities for harmonics. Hearing the early rock tracks from the 1950s, from Elvis Presley, Bill Haley and Buddy Holly (Laing, 1971: 104), the clean single string lead breaks and the frantic strumming patterns of 'Peggy Sue' and 'See You Later Alligator' emerge through these early electric guitar cultures. Throughout the 1960s, the sound emerging from guitars could be modified through effects pedals, such as the wah wah – used most famously by Jimi Hendrix.

While many instruments have been transformed through digitization, the guitar has changed more slowly in this narrative. A range of new and alternative materials is now being used, particularly as the availability of timbers and materials for inlays in the fret board is reducing. Instead of solid wood, high-pressure laminate (HPL) is used to layer and bond material together with higher quality woods featured on the outer layer. Digitization is transforming the guitar. A range of digital guitars has been proposed and produced since 2003, with both Gibson and Variax being innovators here. The goal of the 'digital guitar' project was to convert sound from analogue to digital on the guitar/device and then deliver a digital signal over an Ethernet cable. Signal processing for each individual string was possible. When the amplifier manufacturer Line 6 released the Variax guitar, the electromagnetic pickups were replaced by piezoelectric sensors. An internally-fitted computer modified the guitar's sound. While these innovations have not gained widespread popularity, Gibson has continued the development, moving from the HD.6X-PRO Digital Guitar, the appropriately named Robot Guitar that amalgamated an analogue instrument with self-tuning guitar, to – in December 2009 – the Gibson Dark Fire. This instrument increased the range of onboard tonal choices, autotuning and myriad sonic possibilities through supplied software (Gibson.com, 2009).

While these innovations have not gained widespread currency, the use of a Les Paul Guitar shape as a games controller in Guitar Hero World Tour ensured the continued centrality of the instrument in the digital age. Similarly, the Rickenbacker controllers in The Beatles' Rock Band game have continued and enhanced the profile and branding of the instrument. The link between the guitar, popular culture and gaming is an important one. As Mott asserted,

> Things change. The way people access their music has changed. The way people buy their music has changed. Above all else, Guitar Hero changed the way people saw music games permanently (2007).

Guitar Hero has altered how researchers, students and players think about a guitar. The guitar is an important – perhaps the most important – object in popular music history. Guitar Hero continued this historical role through gaming. Many inventors, guitar makers, effects innovators and musicians have created new sounds and techniques for the instrument. It has also played a key role in articulating the specificity of local music and – for genres such as indie – the selection of guitar and amplifier is a crucial element in gaining credibility for music and performers.

As the original audience for rock music has aged, there has also been an increasing market for vintage guitars that the now fifty-something men can afford. These guitar collectors are well educated and earn a high income (Ryan and Peterson, 2001). They also provide the market for a series of magazines including *Vintage Guitar, Guitar Player, Guitarist, Guitar World, Total Guitar, Guitar Techniques, Guitar International* and *Acoustic Guitar*. Recognizing these nostalgia-charged magazines, it is understandable that the guitar has not been greatly affected by 'the revolution' in digitization, with productive exceptions such as the Guitar Hero World Tour Les Paul-shaped controller. There is a reason. Even in its analogue form, the guitar is difficult to improve. There are promising design possibilities in integrating the expressive qualities of the analogue instrument with digital audio interfaces. Flexible, mobile and changeable with diverse histories and genres, the guitar remains the core and foundation of popular music.

Key Questions

1. Why was the electric guitar developed?
2. Besides increasing the volume of the guitar, which innovations in sound were possible through amplification?
3. Why is the guitar easy to play but hard to master?
4. Why did Guitar Hero World Tour use the shape of a Les Paul guitar as a game controller?

Further Reading

Bennett, A. and Dawe, K. (eds) (2001) *Guitar Cultures*. Oxford: Berg.

Fiestad, S. (2007) *Blue Book of Electric Guitars*. Minneapolis: Blue Book.

Ingram, A. (2001) *A Concise History of the Electric Guitar*. Pacific: MelBay.

Millard, A.J. (2004) *The Electric Guitar*. Baltimore, MD: Johns Hopkins University Press.

Sonic sources

Jimi Hendrix (1968) *All Along the Watchtower*.

Led Zeppelin (1971) *Stairway to Heaven*.

Oasis (1994) *Live Forever*.

The Byrds (1965) *Mr Tambourine Man*.

Visual sources

Air Guitar Nation (2008) Contender Entertainment Group.

Extreme Guitar Metal Edge (2008) Quantum Leap.

Legends of Bottleneck Guitar (2003) Music Sales.

The Strat Pack: Live in Concert – 50 Years of the Fender Stratocaster (2005) Eagle Rock.

Web sources

Fender, http://www.fender.com/

Gibson Les Paul, http://www.lespaulguide.com/

Guitar Hero, http://hub.guitarhero.com/

Rickenbacker, http://www.rickenbacker.com/

Keyboard Cultures

Keyboards are percussion instruments formed by adjacent keys that convey melody. When a key is pressed on a piano, a small hammer strikes a string. Electronic keyboards involve pressing a key that connects to a circuit. The Western musical scale of 12 notes, differentiated by colour, is the most common structure of a keyboard. These adjacent keys play the notes of the chromatic scale, running left to right. Sharps and flats are black (C Sharp/D Flat, D Sharp/E Flat, F Sharp/G Flat, G Sharp/A Flat, A Sharp/B Flat). The C major scale (C, D, E, F, G, A, B) is white keys. These octave patterns repeat throughout the keyboard, whatever its length. Most pianos have 88 keys, extending to the Bosendorfer 290 Imperial model with 97 keys. Synthesizer keyboards most frequently have 61, 76, or 88 keys. MIDI controllers often feature as few as 25 keys, but can comprise 49, 61, or the full 88. Other instruments such as the glockenspiel, marimba and xylophone deploy the conventional keyboard layout but are made of different materials, with the notes being struck by varied means. The relationship between striking the keys with the fingertips and creating a range of notes, chords and scales ensures that a diversity of sounds, genres and rhythms emerges via a keyboard. Listening to Jerry Lee Lewis or Little Richard playing the piano is like hearing drums with a melody. When Little Richard covered Johnny Cash's 'Get Rhythm', transposing the famous guitar track into a piano-propelled cover version, the primary rhythmic instrument was the piano. The diversity of sounds possible through keyboard instruments is created because many notes can be played simultaneously, including melodies, harmonies and chords. Comparing the scope of melodies and sweeping sonic landscapes created through Rick Wakeman's layers of keyboards with Chris Lowe's minimal set-up with the Pet Shop Boys, the spectrum of keyboard cultures is confirmed.

A range of techniques is required to play a keyboard. While guitars necessitate different uses for the left and right hands, keyboard technique permits the hands to be used in either different or similar ways. Most frequently, the right hand plays the melody and the left hand accompanies with chords or rhythm. This is a custom rather than a mechanical requirement of the instrument. However very subtle techniques are required. For pianos, the harder or lighter the key is pressed, the louder or softer the volume. On electronic keyboards, such manual shaping of sound is less noticeable.

This keyboard culture, involving pianos and their electronic replicants, is only one part of the story. Musical culture has moved from the piano keyboard to the computer keyboard that is now used to record, mix, burn, upload, download and copy. A keyboard is part of both computers and mobile devices, but is situated in a separate history from the piano, derived from the typewriter. Instead of keys organized through a chromatic scale, the QWERTY keyboard, developed in the 1870s, still survives in telephony and gaming. The bridge between these two keyboards was the MIDI, which created a matrix of relationships between analogue and digital systems of music. Computers are integral to the creation, editing, mixing and performing of electronic music. The availability of the microprocessor in 1971 enabled the movement from large mainframe computer music into personal computing. The interface for this new mode of music making was the keyboard. Striking the keys of a computer keyboard continues and develops the range and influence of keyboard cultures. There were many moments of interfacing from (musical) keyboard to (computer) keyboard, but in 1979 the development and popularity of the Fairlight Computer Musical Instrument was a key moment in this history. It continued the history of the Theremin, the Hammond organ, the Moog and Buchla synthesizers. While the Hammond organ (1935) and the Moog synthesizer (1965) used piano-modelled keyboards, Leon Theremin's Theremin (1917) and Don Buchla's Buchla Box (1965) deployed non-standard interfaces. Because musicians recognized the conventional black and white notes of a keyboard, these interfaces gained popular success and were used as controllers in popular music. The Theremin and Buchla Box were commercial failures. Part of the reason for this was the loss of the conventional piano keyboard interface.

There are many points in musical history where the keyboards from the music world and computers combine. A key moment emerged in the most unusual of places. The Fairlight was invented in Australia and enabled fast and effective sampling and sequencing (Twyman, 2004). It was the world's first digital synthesizer-sampler. It embedded and embodied the consequences of the development of microprocessors in the 1970s. One of the reasons for its success was that it applied the design lesson of the Hammond organ and Moog by deploying a conventional piano keyboard and a computer keyboard (Fairlight Instruments, 1982). This dual interface predicted the future of both computing and music, combining their two histories into a package and a meshed future. Two different communities – computing and musical – were able to mobilize their literacies and learn new skills and relationships. The development of the light pen also enabled musician/users to change a sound by drawing and augmenting the waveform represented on the Computer Musical Instrument (CMI). Series I of this first digital synthesizer-sampler was released in 1979 and used to effect by Peter Gabriel, Kate Bush and Stevie Wonder. Early applications of this model included Gabriel's use of a string sample on 'Start', released in May 1980, and perhaps even more famously, Kate Bush's use of the sampled sound of breaking glass on 'Babooshka'.

While the Fairlight was a musical instrument, it also had the great advantage of being a computer. Because it was digital, it did not have the heating and tuning problems of the Moog analogue synthesizers. Similarly, because the Fairlight was based on software, it could be continually upgraded and improved. In 1979, the use of Page C and Music Composition Language (MCL) meant that not only was the Fairlight a synthesizer and sampler, it also incorporated musical composition abilities. By 1982, a real-time programmable sequencer was added. In 1983, the Musical Instrument Digital Interface (MIDI) and Society for Motion Picture and TV Engineers time code (SMPTE) were supported through a plug-in card (Pressing, 1992). The Fairlight in its three series not only changed music, it also amalgamated the history of keyboards. The company would lose its market dominance as Casio started to take a component of Fairlight's sampling abilities and sell it at a fraction of the price. However the influence of the Fairlight throughout the music industry was so pervasive that Phil Collins mentioned it on the liner notes of his Grammy award-winning 1985 album *No Jacket Required*: it was a 'Fairlight-free album': (Collins, 2004). Even as late as 2004 on the album *Body Language*, Kylie Minogue mentioned the Fairlight in the lyric for 'Sweet Music', (Minogue, 2004). The greatest impact of the Fairlight was to integrate musical and computer keyboards to create new keyboard cultures. They merged these histories by developing an intuitive interface (Shneiderman, 1998). This narrative of the Fairlight not only captures a part of the history of Human-Computer Interaction (HCI), it also becomes a specialist study to understand the interaction between musicians and keyboard. Because ethnomusiciology tends to focus on cultural identity and musical performance, technology remains an under-studied variable within the discipline. This means that the social relationships and performance opportunities created around and through musical platforms require further research. There is an array of primary data to use. A burgeoning range of musical software and hardware magazines will be of use for future research in this area.

To understand contemporary popular music we are required to track the movement from keyboard to keyboard, from the pattern on the original piano through to the musical instrument modeled on a typewriter. However, our work on keyboard cultures would be incomplete without one further instrument and agent of change. A synthesizer is an electronic instrument that blends and harmonizes electrical signals that are then converted into a sound through a speaker. It not only produces sound, it also shapes and changes it. They are instruments in their own right, but are also present in every home computer. There are three types of synthesizer: analogue, digital, and via software. An assortment of interfaces has also been used, including foot pedals, keyboards, wheels and sliders. More recently embedded software has allowed a computer keyboard user to transform sound.

The synthesizer has been used on a range of popular music tracks, perhaps most famously when Giorgio Moroder used the Moog on Donna Summer's 'I Feel Love'. The first electric synthesizer has a much earlier history, invented by Elisha Gray in 1876. Originally entitled the 'Musical Telegraph', it was part of the technological development of the telephone. Gray realized that when sound vibrated from an electromagnetic circuit, it could be controlled. This discovery created the first single note oscillator. Gray later built a basic loudspeaker – a vibrating diaphragm in a magnetic field – to render these oscillations audible. From this early experiment, other inventors such as Ivor Darreg and Evgeny Murzin developed methods to synthesize both voice and music. Throughout the 1960s, synthesizers could be played in real time but could not be utilized in live performances because of their size. Robert Moog's innovations created a synthesizer that was practical for musicians. While it was difficult to set the machine for a new sound, it was small and intuitive. While thought of as an early gimmick, the Moog started to enter popular culture. Micky Dolenz of The Monkees bought one of the first Moog synthesizers and it was featured on the Monkees' fourth album, released in 1967, *Pisces, Aquarius, Capricorn & Jones Ltd*. Moog established the standards for controlling the interfaces, at one volt per octave pitch control. This standardization allowed diverse synthesizers to operate together.

Robert Moog again led developments in synthesizers throughout the 1970s, when he invented a version without the modular design but with a conventional musical keyboard. This instrument was portable and easier to use. Termed a prepatched synthesizer, this Minimoog was not only popular it also influenced the development of every synthesizer that followed. The integration of a keyboard, modulation wheel and pitch wheel became the model for synthesizers. Recognizing that it could include a keyboard made it appear to be a conventional instrument. These early analogue synthesizers were monophonic. That means they could only play one note at a time. By 1979, the first polyphonic music synthesizers appeared through Yamaha's GX1, CS-50, CS-60 and CS-80. Yet because of the size of microprocessors at the time, the sales for many of these models – except the Kurzweil 250 (K250) that was released in 1983 – were low. The moment of innovation in keyboard cultures arrived with the MIDI. In 1983 the Musical Instrument Digital Interface appeared, offering a communication protocol through a serial interface. It allowed the movement of data between devices, platforms and instruments in real time, including the selection of preset sounds, volume and effects, synchronized with other forms of data. The software standard for the MIDI was developed in 1991, but OpenSound Control (OSC) is being proposed as its Web 2.0 replacement as this was designed for networking.

Since the late 1980s synthesizers have been digitized, although analogue synthesizers still have their place. Through the movement from 'keyboard to keyboard' and percussive piano to computer interface, some of the strangest and most challenging experiments in popular music have taken place. From Rick Wakeman's 'Journey to the Centre of the Earth' to Depeche Mode's 'People are People', keyboard cultures remain the engine for innovative sounds and systems of instrumentation. While the guitar is an instrument of stability and continuity in popular music, the keyboard is the agent of change. Keyboard cultures include a child learning scales on a piano through to software packages that have rendered many of the functions of a recording studio redundant. The ability to hit a key and make a sound or hit a key and transform a sound has ensured that popular music, particularly after the 1970s, would always be more than rock music.

Key Questions

1. What makes the piano an unusual instrument?
2. Why did the Fairlight matter to popular music history?
3. Why does the Moog matter to popular music history?
4. What is a synthesizer?

Further Reading

Gorges, P. (2005) *Programming Synthesizers*. Bremen: Wizoo.

Schmitz, R. (2005) *Analog Synthesis*. London: Music Sales Corporation.

Shapiro, P. (2000) *Modulations: A History of Electronic Music*. Boston, MA: D.A.P./ Caipirinha.

Theberge, P. (1997) *Any Sound You Can Imagine*. Hanover, NH: Wesleyan University Press.

Sonic sources

Al Stewart (1976) *Year of the Cat*. RCA.

Kraftwerk (1978) *Das Model*. EMI/Kling Klang.

Little Richard (2002) *Get Rhythm*. Sony.

Rick Wakeman (1974) *Journey to the Centre of the Earth*. A & M.

Visual sources

Kraftwerk and the Electronic Revolution (2008) Plastic Head.

Moog (2004) Flexi.

Rick Wakeman: The Six Wives of Henry VIII (2009) Eagle Vision.

Theremin: An Electronic Odyssey (1993) Orion.

Web sources

Keyboard Magazine, http://www.keyboardmag.com/

Moog, http://www.moog.com/

Street, Rita, *Fairlight – A 25-year long fairytale*, IMAS Publishing Group, 2000, http:// www.audiomedia.com/archive/features/uk-1000/uk-1000-fairlight/uk-1000- fairlight.htm

Synth Zone, http://www.synthzone.com/

Drumming and Percussion

In Chuck Berry's famous lyrics for 'Hail Hail Rock and Roll', the guitar was not mentioned in the lyric. Instead, 'the beat of the drum' was 'loud and bold'. While rock music has been associated with screeching and soaring guitars, the core rhythm created through the drum kit has provided the backbeat and energy for the genre. The foundation of music is rhythm and the diversity of percussion deployed in popular music is beyond the limitations of a conventional drum kit, regardless of the size. Because of the burgeoning world of music, songs, sounds and performers, a range of objects can be rattled, struck, shaken and squeezed as part of popular music.

Rhythmic instruments confirm that music is much more than melody and harmony. The goal of percussion is to use a sound to mark out a recognizable musical pattern. The musical language of the drum crosses musical and geographical boundaries. Rhythm is a translator between genres and negotiates the relationship between noise and sound. There are many forms of percussion, including rattles and shakers, bells, chimes and drums, which are covered on one or both ends with a taut skin pulled over a frame. In the sections of an orchestra, drums are part of the percussion family of instruments. Described as a membranophone, this label is a reminder that drums require a membrane – also called a drum skin – to be stretched over some form of object, termed a drum shell. This shell is frequently circular with a wide drumhead. Timbales are open at one end. Other drums have both drumheads covered with membrane. This taut membrane is then struck – most frequently by a hand, foot pedal or stick – to produce a sound. A range of international examples uses this simple principle. The *bodhran* is an Irish frame drum played by hand or with a beater or stick termed a *cipin*. A tambourine is also part of the drum family, with its origins in the Middle East. This hand percussion is integral to many musical styles and genres. The tambourine is used in gospel, flamenco, samba and rock musics. Rattles and shakers have also been crucial to a range of dance musics, including the maracas in salsa music and the clapperless cowbell to create Latin rhythms and patterns. Cowbells are struck with a stick, but various tones can be created by hitting different parts of the bell and also muffling – or dampening – the sound.

Drums are the oldest musical instrument. With the development of new materials and musical styles, the design has remained remarkably constant. They are generally untuned instruments, but timpani and an increasing range of drums are now being tuned to a particular pitch. Roger Taylor from Queen famously played tuned drums. This decision to change the tone enlarges the function of drums beyond the chromatic and into the diatonic. The pitch is changed when the tension rods attached to the rim holding the skin over the drumhead are altered. These tension rods also enact a tuning function. The tighter the rods, the higher the frequency of the sounds and the lower the amplitude. The sound of a drum is formed through the shape and size of the shell, the material used for the drumhead, the tension and tuning applied to it, the location of the drum and the way in which the drumhead is struck. The steel pan, from the twin island nation of Trinidad and Tobago, produces clear pitches.

Drums have a specific role and function in popular music. Andrew Goodwin realized that 'nowhere is the link between music and memory more evident that in the case of drumming' (1998: 123). The goal of drumming – at its most basic – is to set and maintain the time for other performers. Once this primary task has been achieved, the next goal is to add depth and fill the spaces in the song. Such a characteristic is best observed by the small but remarkable group of singer drummers who use vocals, snares and cymbals in a distinct and innovative fashion. Levon Helm from The Band, Phil Collins from Genesis, Don Henley from The Eagles and Ringo Starr from The Beatles created new relationships between the beat and a vocal. Even for drummers who do not sing, there is a much greater part to play than being a metronome. Bernard Sumner, guitarist from Joy Division and New Order, remembers the role of Stephen Morris,

> To me, a drummer in the band is the clock, but Steve wouldn't be the clock, because he's passive: he would follow the rhythm of the band, which gave us our own edge. Live, we were driven by watching Ian dance; we were playing to him visually (Sumner in Savage, 1996: 364).

Morris was also a leader in the use of drum machines and programming. Drum machines imitate, extend and transform the sound of drums and percussion instruments, but often construct and execute rhythm patterns and combinations that are not physically possible using a human drummer. They offer a percussive sound that defamiliarizes the 'natural' rhythm. The point of sampling drumming patterns is that they create a trigger to popular music memory. Drum machines are not intended to sound like drums. They offer alternative percussive opportunities. In rock, drummers construct rhythm patterns within time signatures. Programming defamiliarizes the beat structure as drum machines create new rhythms that are not possible, even for the most experienced drummers. The best example is New Order's 'Blue Monday', a song that revolutionized rhythm. The bridge constructed a new patterning of beat that a drummer would not consider. Drum machines also provide new compositional opportunities. When working in compositional and mixing software environments it is customary to lay down a rhythm track first, with the melody and instrumentation being built on this base. This is distinct from analogue songwriting that often commences with the construction of a melody, chord progression or lyric. 'Blue Monday' began when Stephen Morris bought a new drum machine and tested out new rhythms. There are powerful and important distinctions between drums and drum machines, as realized by Tricia Rose.

> The drum machine has never sounded like drums because it isn't percussion: it's electronic current, synthetic percussion, syncussion … Electro ignores this hope

of emulating drums, and instead programs rhythms from electricity, rhythmatic intensities which are unrecognizable as drums. There are no snares – just wave-forms being altered. There are no bass drums – just attack velocities (1994: 62).

Drum machines create a percussion effect, productively shaping and creating space. They not only replicate existing rhythm patterns, they also alter tone and pitch and sustain on drums and cymbals.

The first drum machine – termed a rhythm machine – was produced by the musical innovator Léon Theremin. In the early 1930s, he was commissioned by Henry Cowell to invent an instrument that could generate multiple rhythm patterns that were too intri-cate to play on already existing keyboards. The Rhythmicon could generate 16 rhythms in a particular pitch. Publicly released in 1932, Cowell did not use it to its potential, and it is an under-written and under-researched part of both the history of rhythm and drumming cultures. The next drum machines focused on preprogrammed rhythms for particular styles of music, such as the mambo. The commercially available beat patterns were part of organs in the late 1960s, with a company called Ace Tone (later Roland) producing transistorized rhythm machines. The FR1 Rhythm Ace emerged in 1967 and was used by the Hammond Organ Company. It was not possible to modify the pre-programmed rhythms. Throughout the 1970s, other preset drum machines were released. Sly and the Family Stone were innovators, using these early models on their 1971 album, *There's a Riot Goin' On*.

The gulf between these early rhythm machines and modern derivatives is created because of the distinction between analogue sound synthesis and digitized sampling. The first programmable drum machine was the PAiA Programmable Drum Set, released in 1975 and needing to be built by users from a kit. The release of Roland's CR-78 (in 1978) and the Boss DR-55 (in 1979) ensured drum machines' entry into popular cul-ture. While the DR-55 only had four sounds, its price brought drum machines into the domestic market. The Linn LM-1 Drum Computer, released in 1980, was the first to use digital samples, but was priced at US$5000. Performers who used this model included Prince on *Purple Rain* and the Human League on their *Dare* album.

In the narrative of drumming cultures 1980 was the pivotal year that Roland released the TR-808. Although not digitally sampling sounds it would dominate dance musics for over a decade, particularly house, techno and hip hop. It had the capacity to create drum patterns by pressing trigger pads or by using step-sequencing, layering a rhythm pattern by adding individual sounds within a 16 bar cycle. DJs used the Roland to edit rhythmic patterns, sample sounds and add loops to the mix. An audio collage was created that referenced the history of music but also created something new through this combination. These techniques allowed disco and house music to survive until the present, being continually resampled and remixed. Gabber grew from the seed of techno. Trance extended the euphoric hook of house. Drum samples enabled the extension and stretching of these genres.

The future of drumming and percussion cultures will continue to evolve through both physical drums and digitized drum loops. Gaming industries are increasingly using music as part of interactive entertainment. The clearest example of this tendency is the Guitar Hero franchise. In 2008, drums became part of the seventh generation of consoles for the Wii, the XBOX 360 and Sony PS3. The Guitar Hero World Tour (GHWT), Rock Revolutions and Rock Band all feature drum controllers, building on the controllers included with sixth generation consoles on Game Cube. The new generations have the capacity to be both electronic drum kits and game controllers. While these controllers may not be musical instruments, they enlarge the parameters of sonic media and drumming cultures. The drum controller on GHWT includes cymbal pads, responsive pads and sticks. While it appears to be a toy, a third party drum controller – Drum Rocker – has been released and has the capacity to allow the pads to replicate the sounds and functions of a more conventional electronic drum kit. Indeed, compared to the guitar controller, which has a scant relationship with the actual playing of the instrument beyond the shape, the drum controller does feature similar skills that are applicable outside of a gaming environment. Once more, drumming cultures are expanding and creating new relationships not only between rhythm and melody or technology and songwriting, but also between game playing and playing music.

Key Questions

1. What are the characteristics of a percussion instrument?
2. Why was the Roland 808 influential in the dance music and electronica cultures?
3. What is the purpose of a drum machine?
4. How are programmable drum patterns used as a compositional tool in musical software?

Further Reading

Bazil, E. (2009) *Art of Drum Layering*. Thetford: PC Publishing.

Budofsky, A., Dawson, M. and Parillo, M. (2008) *The Drummer: 100 Years of Rhythmic Power and Invention*. Winona, MN: Hal Leonard.

Goodwin, A. (1998) *Drumming and Memory: Scholarship, Technology, and Music-making*. In T. Swiss, J. Sloop and A. Herman (eds), *Mapping the Beat: Popular Music and Contemporary Theory*. Malden: Blackwell.

Maffit, R. (2005) *Rhythm & Beauty: The Art of Percussion*. New York: Billboard.

Sonic sources

New Order (1983) *Blue Monday*.

Sly & the Family Stone (1968) *Dance to the Music*.

The Band (1968) *The Weight*.

Ting Tings (2008) *That's Not My Name*.

Visual sources

Classic Rock Drum Solos (2007) Proper Music Distribution.

Eve. *Tambourine, YouTube,* http://www.youtube.com/watch?v=sWUV71G5W8g

Percussion jamming, *YouTube,* http://www.youtube.com/watch?v=OT3l6JjmJtY

The Mick Fleetwood Story: Two Sticks and a Drum (2000) DVD UK.

Web sources

Drumming Web, http://www.drummingweb.com

Latin Percussion, http://www.lpmusic.com/

Percussive Art Society, http://www.pas.org/

The Tambourine Players Hall of Fame, http://www.stardustlanes.com/tambourine. html

Voice

This chapter in *Popular Music: Topics, Trends and Trajectories* requires some audience participation. Open up your database of music. It can be owned by you, your friends, your parents, your children or your fellow students. It can be on vinyl, cassettes, compact disc or downloads. Find some songs featuring the following voices. If possible, listen to these in the (often incongruous) pairs I have assembled.

Bob Dylan and Josh Groban
Duffy and Etta James
Axl Rose and Frank Sinatra
Donna Summer and Billie Holiday
Bon Scott and Johnny Cash
Aretha Franklin and Heather Small
Sam Cooke and Bob Marley
Pink and Edith Piaf
Odetta and Madonna
Youssou N'Dour and Otis Redding

The clash of tones, approaches and singing ambitions of these performers reveals stark differences. Some singers – like Groban and Sinatra – show remarkable diction and an emphasis on the lyric. Others – like Scott and Dylan – surrender the importance of their voice to the dominance of rhythm or other instruments such as the guitar or piano. Such an exercise shows that the voice in popular music is malleable, flexible and changeable. It stretches notes, reinforces rhythms, but also embeds emotion into melody and beat. The voice makes music into a song, taking a refrain from reality and representing it (Filippa, 1996: 328). The voice has a tentative, intimate and familiar quality that is difficult to record or capture. Alan Licht considered that 'in a sense, recording was an even more radical invention than photography in that the human voice was thought to be uncapturable, whereas human likeness has been captured to greater and lesser degrees in drawing and painting' (2007: 38). What he is suggesting is that recording the human voice is the ghost in the machine. It disconnects the voice from the diaphragm, lungs, throat and lips. It separates the body from the sound it makes.

The voice is part of our daily life. It is the basis of daily communication and dialogue. Our family and friends will use their voices to construct narratives and the stories of their lives. Social life also is built on the communicative capacity of the voice (Dolar, 2006: 13–17). For the sound to be converted into meaning, the products of the voice must be recognized as words. Accent, tone and timbre all influence the efficacy of a voice to communicate. When the speaking voice becomes a singing voice, it defamiliarizes the meaning system. Common words are stretched, enhanced or whispered. The speaking voice operates in a narrow band of normality in terms of tone and volume. The range of normality enlarges through singing. Volume, tone, accent and intonation all transform.

A piece of music with a role for the singing voice is termed a song. A singing voice is an instrument that can both mesh with and offer a lyrical commentary on other instruments. There is a power to a voice, such as with Frank Sinatra, Billie Holiday, Sam Cooke or Aretha Franklin. The coloratura and grain will summon spaces, emotion and views to listeners. When we hear a voice, we enter the world of a song through feeling. There are four vocal registers: the chest register, the head register, falsetto and the whistle register. While much singing within popular music is located in the chest register, the movement between registers can create a greater diversity of pitches and effects. Examples of movements between registers include Kate Bush's 'Wuthering Heights' and A-ha's 'Take On Me'. Falsetto was also used in many of the Bee Gees' disco tracks. Yodelling is an example of moving rapidly between registers. Frank Ifield's 'She Taught Me to Yodel' is one example of this vocal style. The human voice extends up to the whistle register. Although rarely featured in popular music, it has been used to great effect by Christine Aguilera and Mariah Carey. Perhaps the most famous pop deployment of the register was Minnie Ripperton's 'Loving You', released in 1975. It added an otherworldly – and unexpected – extension to the chorus.

As shown by these vocal registers, the voice fulfills a role in popular music that goes far beyond the act of singing. Many performers – such as Richard Harris, Neil Tennant and Leonard Cohen – speak over a musical accompaniment rather than sing with the melody. The role of rap in hip hop extends this principle. The goal is to capture an attitude and express a view. Direct communication is the aim. Jay Z and Kanye West offer articulate, direct and clear toned lyrics that comment on the world as much as the music. Other singers demonstrate the value of a rich and powerful tone, such as Frank Sinatra or Elvis Presley, who manage to trap loneliness and despair in the throat and express it through recording. Barney Hoskyns claimed that, 'Sinatra's of all voices is one that leads dignity to loneliness, makes it not just bearable but positively romantic' (1991: 8). The singer's life story is often a way to give meaning and history to the voice, opening up worlds and cultures of difference, desire, belonging and despair. Voices are also historical and move with fashion. Hearing the voices of Mario Lanza and Josh Groban demonstrates the different expectations we hold of a tenor in the twentieth and twenty-first centuries. A range of 'narrative' singers, such as Tom Waits and Bob Dylan, has enlarged the limits of popular music. Neither of these two sings well, but their growl, snarl and rough tone configure distinct and potent connotations to the lyrics.

Meanings in and from the voice emerge through the intricate and multiple combinations of tone and lyric, form and content, signifier and signified. While most singing involves shaping sounds into words, the voice is also used as a rhythmic instrument in jazz, blues and hip hop through scat and beat boxing. Slurs, breaths, pauses and trills are part of vocal sounds. Rapping is a distinct configuration of the human voice. It is still speaking, but this is more monotonal and rhythmic than is possible via the conventional voice in conversation. Syncopation is the key, moving words around the beat rather than creating a melody.

Singing is – at its most basic – the making of musical sounds with the human voice. Masculinity and femininity are performed, challenged and questioned through the human voice. Johnny Cash's bass-baritone voice in 'I Walk the Line' hits the low C with ease, captured masculinity through the volume and melody but betrayal and infidelity through the grain. Voices continue a life even after the death of the singer. Unlike hearing a track from a dead drummer or guitarist, there is an intimacy to a voice that provides a connection to a performer, even after demise. Listening to John Lennon's 'Imagine' after his murder amplified the message. Similarly, playing Tupac Shakur increases the poignancy when remembering the circumstances of his death in a drive-by shooting. Odetta's deep, troubling, other worldly voice becomes more disturbing and haunting. The voice is able to soak up memory and emotion, providing the conduit for audiences to apply popular music to their own lives.

Key Questions

1. What function does a voice hold in popular music?
2. What are the four vocal registers?
3. How does rap transform the history of the singing voice?
4. How has technological change affected how we record and hear the human voice?

Further Reading

Hines, J. (1990) *Great Singers on Great Singing*. New York: Limelight.

Hoskyns, B. (1991) *From a Whisper to a Scream: The Great Voices of Popular Music*. London: Fontana.

Potter, J. (2009) *Tenor: History of a Voice*. New Haven: Yale University Press.

Warner, J. (2007) *American Singing Groups: A History 1940 to Today*. Milwaukee, WI: Hal Leonard.

Sonic sources

Cohen, L. (1988) *First We Take Manhattan*.

Gladys Knight and the Pips (1973) *Midnight Train to Georgia*.

James, E. (1969) *I'd Rather Go Blind*.

Pet Shop Boys (1985) *West End Girls*.

Visual sources

Bush, K. 'Wuthering Heights,' *YouTube*, http://www.youtube.com/watch?v=BW3g KKiTvjs

Cohen, L. (2007) *I'm Your Man*. Lion's Gate.

Odetta, 'Water Boy,' *YouTube*, http://www.youtube.com/watch?v=VSDeROnTq64

Presley, E. (2006) *68 Comeback Special*. Sony BMG.

Web sources

Bee Gees, http://www.beegees.com/index.php

Marianne Faithfull, http://www.mariannefaithfull.org.uk/

Pet Shop Boys, http://www.petshopboys.co.uk/

Robert Wyatt, http://www.strongcomet.com/wyatt/

Turntablism

Even though the long-playing record only emerged in 1948, the musical platform of the twentieth century was the turntable. It became the means by which most consumers heard music (Holmes, 2008: 420). Significantly, when Thomas Edison invented phonography, he saw it as a way to record spoken word material (Elborough, 2008). Throughout the vinyl century, the platform was used to capture and record much more than words. The Beat Generation in particular created relationships between jazz and the reading of poetry. From its early history, experimentation was part of turntable history. In Rome, Composer Ottorino Respighi used a recording of nightingales for his 1924 performance of *The Pines*. Prescient of later turntablism, Paul Hindemith and Ernst Toch used the turntable as an instrument in Berlin's 1930 Neue Musik Festival. Throughout the twentieth century, the turntable moved from being a domestic platform for playing music to becoming a way to create and perform music. It changed from a means of playing music to an instrument in itself. Only in 2010, the same year that Sony stopped the Walkman, did Panasonic announce that it would no longer produce its Technics line of analogue turntables. Yet from the period the Technics SL 1200 was released in 1972 through to its death in 2010, it had become the basis of DJ culture. When used in a pair, different tracks were synchronized on Technics decks through beat matching. Surviving much longer than expected, as 'an analogue device in a digital world' (Peck, 2010: 9), the 1200 sustained not only an obsolete platform but also a nostalgia for vinyl.

Turntablism describes the creation of music using record turntables and a mixer. It is the basis of electronica, house music and its derivatives and – most importantly – hip hop. There are many DJ skills required for turntablism. Four major techniques include the basic skills of beat matching and beat mixing and the more complex abilities of scratching, which reverses the spin of the record by running the needle backwards over the vinyl's groove, and beat juggling, where two identical records, discs or samples are used to repeat the same sound for the breakbeat. Through such techniques, the turntable becomes – in effect – a manual, analogue sampler. By disrupting the passage of the stylus, new relationships are created between rhythms, lyrics and melody.

Turntablism is a term particularly associated with hip hop, although beat mixing and matching is also found in disco and post-house musics. Scratching was the key intervention, discovered by Grand Wizard Theodore but popularized by Grandmaster Flash. A famous early recording of scratching can be found on Herbie Hancock's 'Rockit' where DJ Grand Mixer DXT (appearing as DST) used different speeds by scratching records via two turntables, altering the pitch of the sound. This technique overcame one of the great restrictions of scratching: a narrow pitch range. Another technique, used by

DJ Spinbad, DJ Cash Money and DJ Jazzy Jeff, was to turn the fader on and off while moving the stylus over a portion of a record, particularly a riff or short lyric.

Specifically, turntablism emerged because the role of the DJ in hip hop crews started to decline as studio techniques were used. By the mid 1990s, the word turntablism was being used to describe this alternative role for the DJ, using a turntable and mixer to manipulate the music. New forms of scratching were invented and described, including the crab (by DJ Qbert) and orbit (by DJ Disk). All the techniques built on Kool DJ Herc's innovation: the invention of the break-beat. The break is a section of music in which the vocal drops away and percussion dominates. Kool Herc extended the break by repetitively switching between two identical records. This technique became not only the foundation of electronica but also the most influential technique in turntablism.

The rise of the MC in hip hop moved the DJ's role from functional accompanist to rapper and the realm of individual fame. Mark Katz described it as a 'musical practice in which prerecorded phonograph discs are manipulated in live performance' (2004: 115). The term turntablism was introduced in 1995 by DJ Babu, a member of the Beat Junkies crew. The goal in promoting this new term was to mark the boundary between turntablism and the DJ, with the former being a musician using the turntable as an instrument, while a DJ was playing already existing records. This distinction may not be as clear as that proposed by turntablists, with DJs using a diversity of creative techniques on and through their decks. The innovation in the practice is the recognition of how playing music develops into the creation of music.

Turntablism is an analogue practice, with direct contact between the hand and vinyl. CD players have been used in turntablism, with digital simulations of scratching. Final Scratch is the extension of this principle that enables the use of digital files alongside vinyl and turntables. The goal had been to build a bridge between the analogue control of vinyl through the hands, with the flexibility created through digital music files, particularly MP3 and WAV. The albums played on a turntable are encoded to trigger a digital signal at a particular point of the track. This means that thousands of samples and songs can be pulled and embedded from a hard drive, using the vinyl as the enabling technology (Werde, 2001). Many new descriptions are used for turntablists who are moving into digital experiments and away from the focus on vinyl alone. One is controllerism (Golden, 2007). Such a word makes a distinction from turntablism, because attention is focused on the manipulation of sounds with a computer as a platform rather than vinyl. However, with production ended on the Technics alternative platforms and practices will become more important.

While Final Scratch created new alignments between analogue and digital environments, turntablists and their instruments remained stalwarts for analogue techniques and skills in a digital age. While the iPod has erased the intermediary platform for playing music by downloading sonic files into a portable hard drive, the turntablist creates a direct connection between the hand and vinyl. For turntablists, the platform – the media – still matters. Importantly, vinyl was once a new media. Now it is old media, but its supercedence adds to the attraction. This practice of discovery and renewal means that music's history is continually freshened, by returning older tracks to a new mix.

One reason to search out rare vinyl records is to challenge other turntablists. International competitions now take place, revealing an extraordinary dexterity, skill and musical knowledge. Lyrics are often extracted and sampled from a track that conveys a statement of intent and also often a comment about the other turntablists. The goal is to be witty, aggressive, innovative and technically excellent. Not surprisingly, there are few female turntablists. This mode of sampling and creativity operates against a single songwriter, singer or musician. It cuts away context and builds new connections. Turntablism has an honesty to it, carrying history through the mix. It moves through spaces and structures. Such analogue sampling is a mode of referentiality, reflexivity and citation. Through turntablism, sampling and the DJ culture, remixes have transformed our understandings of originality and authenticity in popular music studies. Yet the use of found sounds – like found footage in documentary film making – offers an innovative and important way to reframe and reconsider the past.

Recently visual turntablism has entered the hip hop lexicon, which incorporates video and still pictures into live performances using a video mixer. There have also been important digital interventions in this analogue practice, with Pioneer, Gemini and Numark CD players digitally simulating scratching. Digitization permits a much wider range of manipulations of sound. With Final Scratch, DJs and turntablists are able to mix with MP3 and WAV files. While the analogue skills may be replaced, the dexterity, innovation and heightened sonic literacies displayed by turntablists mean that they have embodied the directive of the Web 2.0 age before digitization: listeners to music had become makers of music.

Key Questions

1. What is turntablism?
2. What is the difference between a DJ and a turntablist?
3. Which techniques are used by turntablists?
4. Why was Final Scratch important?

Further Reading

Haslam, D. (2001) *Adventures on the Wheels of Steel: The Rise of the Superstar DJs.* London: Fourth Estate.

Katz, M. (2004) *Capturing Sound: How Technology has Changed Music.* Berkeley: University of California Press.

Poschardt, U. (1998) *DJ Culture*. London: Quartet.

Webber, S. (2007) *DJ Skills: The Essential Guide to Mixing and Scratching*. Burlington: Focal.

Sonic sources

Afrika Bambaataa (1982) *Planet Rock*.

Grandmaster Flash (1981) *The Adventures of Grandmaster Flash on the Wheels of Steel*.

Jazzy Jeff (2007) *Return of the Magnificent*.

Showbiz and A.G. (2000) *D.I.T.C.*

Visual sources

Beat Junkies DJ Icy Ice & Numark Virtual Vinyl (2007) *YouTube*, http://www.youtube.com/watch?v=DP3Kn5Ch7bY

DJ 8–Ball vs DJ Noize – Supermen DJ battle for Supremacy (2007) *YouTube*, http://www.youtube.com/watch?v=KkoQOupR0CE

DJ Qbert. *Crab Scratch*, *YouTube*, http://www.youtube.com/watch?v=w5OeaC3rI-A

Star Wars DJ (2005) *YouTube*, http://www.youtube.com/watch?v=Uw0v6kkasMk

Web sources

DJ Battles, http://www.djbattles.com/

Old School, www.oldschoolhiphop.com

Scratching, DJ 101, http://www.discjockey101.com/scratching.html

Stanton, http://www.stantondj.com

iPod

After exploring the world of guitars, drums, keyboards and turntablism, it may seem odd for the iPod to conclude a section on instrumentation. As a platform for music, a player and recorder, uploader and downloader, it has transformed how music is heard, viewed, copied, remixed, sold and recorded. It is an instrument of and for change. The first iPod released with the touch wheel also featured a microphone slot for recording. While university lectures and amateur podcasts dominated these early recording opportunities, subsequent iPod accessories included a PA system, mixer and DJ desk, which had slots for two iPods. The player of music becomes the platform for recording music. It has been used for spoken word applications and audio books, with museums and galleries using the iPod with preloaded commentaries. These early iPods created 'reasonable' quality recordings. After the success of the iPod, a range of new recorders and sonic editing software has emerged. After 2005, the iPod's external microphones improved. Concurrently though, the price of alternative recording platforms has reduced. As sonic media devices and editing software have improved and evaluative mechanisms (particularly from the corporate branding of podcasts) and consumer expectations have become more demanding, a higher quality of sound is now required. For its time, the iPod was able to create recordings that were quick and easy to disseminate. It is now possible – at a reasonable cost – to develop and record higher quality materials. The Apple Powerbook G4, and subsequently the MacBook Pro, captured audio, using Apple's QuickTime Broadcaster. The iPhone also records voice memos. Similarly a range of affordable yet quality portable microphones also emerged, including the Zoom range with its H2, H4 and H4n, which is able to record in WAV 96kHz/48kHz/44.1kHz at 16-bit or 24-bit and MP3 to 320kbps and Variable Bit Rate (VBR) data formats. This is in advance of the early iPod's recording frequencies made possible through a Belkin or Griffin plug-in microphone.

Significantly, the iPod's screen, which was underutilized in the first five generations, became the basis for a revival of music videos, which are also downloadable from the iTunes store. The iTouch, iPhone and iPad allow a tight convergence between sound and vision, administered through touch, an underplayed sense in the history of popular music. The unexpected success of 'apps,' free and purchased applications for the iPhone, has further integrated what started as a listening device into the wider functions of daily life. Buying an iPod is not simply buying a musical device but a lifestyle accessory. Dan Frakes realized that, 'When you purchase an iPod, you're not just buying a killer portable music player. You're also gaining access to the most diverse and plentiful array of aftermarket accessories for any project I can remember' (2006: vii).

The iPod is an important instrument in the study of popular music history. While much attention has been paid to illegal downloading and the impact of the platform on compact disc sales, there has also been an underplayed discussion of the parallels between MP3-enabled platforms and cassette technology (Manuel, 1993). Connell and Gibson stated that the cassette 'was both an agent of homogeneity and standardization, but at the same time it was a catalyst for decentralization, democratisation and the emergence of regional and local musical styles' (2003: 168). This statement could have been written about the iPod. It became an international icon, logo and brand, but also created a range of local, customized and diverse ways of using the platform. The iPod has created new relationships between production and consumption. While, before the Web 2.0 environment, there was a separation between musicians and audience, the new software and hardware environment has not only meant that consumers produce, but also that producers are starting to behave like consumers. Indeed, Theberge expressed his concerns that 'popular musicians have become "consumers of technology"' (1997: 7). Significantly, Theberge made his statement before the iPod was even a possibility for Apple's designers.

Theberge's fear was embodied in Apple's marketing slogan of 'Think Different', which has been used to popularize many innovations in the history of computing, including colour screens, the mouse, CD Roms, variable fonts, intuitive navigation through icons and drop down menus. While recognizing this history of computing, the i-Pod made Apple a mainstream – rather than an alternative – brand. The white headphones marked a new form of music fandom, based on downloading, and transformed activities such as bus, train and airplane travel. Music charts morphed. The proliferation of the iPod transformed the music chart from simply being a physical count of the releases of singles from compact discs or seven-inch vinyl. It meant that any song from any point in popular musical history could be revived and become commercially successful. The significance of this transformation in music hardware, and the integration of the music industry and the computing industry, is difficult to underestimate. By 2009, 220,000,000 iPods had been sold internationally (Cheng, 2009). While the natural leveling of iPod sales emerged as the iPhone and iTouch infiltrated the market, the transformation of the music industry will not be as transitory. From February 2005, *Billboard's* Hot 100 chart included downloads. In the United Kingdom, from January 1, 2007, the singles chart did not require a physical release of music on CD single or vinyl to gain recognition. Digital downloaders became the determiners of popularity. Such a transformation further reduced the power of record companies, with downloaders being able to choose any track at any time to download, reducing the significance of the pre-packaged album. The iPod not only became an instrument for branding new and old music, it was also pivotal for new relationships between production and consumption, the original and the remix.

The iPod fragmented music, making it mobile and unstable. It permeated our daily lives. As Michael Bull stated, it was 'the first cultural icon of the twenty-first century, representing a sublime marriage between mobility, aesthetics and functionality, of sound and touch – enabling users to possess their auditory world in the palm of their hand' (2007: 1). The question now is how the player of music that enabled a wider array of consumerism than previously possible has also become an instrument – a platform – for music. Its small size and portability ensure that the iPod is firmly ensconced in our urban environment. As well as iTunes providing a range of music to buy, the iPod also shelters, selects and filters our sonic environment. It is an instrument of movement. It is an instrument of mobility. It is an instrument that aligns movement, music and identity. It not only plays music, it also restructures and reconstitutes our urban environment and identity. For a sonically-drenched community, the iPod privatizes sound and creates a track list to suit particular activities such as commuting, exercising, working or relaxing.

The music business has often moved through periods of crisis. The emergence of the gramophone record after the First World War saw the rise of record companies and a decline in sheet-music publishing. Much of the music business since that time has been based around making records popular soon after their release, for a particular period, and then – after a few weeks – replacing them with newer songs. Turntablism and compression files allow a much wider range of music to remain current, accessible and useable. The iPod has extended this history. The ubiquity of this platform has meant that music has transformed in its function to become what Kusek and Leonhard described as 'a kind of "utility"' (2005: x).

It is important – particularly in popular musical history – to avoid technological determinism. Yet the influence of the iPod must be noted. Described as 'Apple's twenty-first century Walkman' (Schlender, 2001), it is actually much more than a digital Walkman. It is an instrument for change. Clearly, the iPod did transform the production and consumption of music as well as our listening to it. There were precedents. The capacity to construct a personal play list was predated by analogue mix tapes. Like an analogue LimeWire, music was exchanged when Sony launched the cassette in 1966. At that time, the record industry complained that this format would destroy the business of music. It was the arrival of the compact disc in the early 1980s that changed the role and function of music. The moment that digitized music was available on CD, copies could be made of that release. The CD was an unprotected digital format, without Digital Rights Management. The CD-R, the recordable CD, allowed direct copying without a loss of quality. It was a warning for what would occur with the MP3. In the early 1990s, computing firms such as Dell, Compaq, Hewlett Packard and Apple saw an area of growth in their industry in the manipulation of audio files. The CD Rom started to be included in domestically-priced computers and computer speakers also improved. When a final element was added to the standard CD Rom and DVD Rom drives in computers – an internet connection – consumers could not only 'rip' music from legitimately bought compact discs, they could also move these MP3 files using the web. The development of the CD is not what altered the relationship between consumers and the music industry. This change in music was to emerge from the computing industry, not the music industry. Music became a utility to enable the sale of computer hardware. The way in which money was made from music – and the industries that profited from it – had changed.

Law is important to the digitized music scene and the iPod. Apple not only created the most significant design object of the twenty-first century – an instrument for playing music – they also made the most significant intervention in bringing music listeners back from 'illegally' downloaded music to accepting a purchase model for music. The iTunes music store was this intervention, and the five major record companies were convinced to license their songs to Apple. The majority of legally purchased music around the world is sourced from the iTunes store, with it also being a hub for free podcasts and iTunes U material.

The iPod and iTunes have altered our listening and the distribution patterns for music. The record industry has suffered, although the cause of this decline is contestable. Their business model was based on platform redundancy. The industry received an enormous bounce in the transfer from vinyl to eight track cassette, then cassette tape, and then on to compact disc. This replacement and redundancy pattern was exhausted by 2000, and the capacity of MP3 files and downloading returned music to a singles-fuelled market, rather than the CD-album built business. Because the record companies did not produce effective e-commerce portals to shape the new ways of listening and buying music, 'illegal' downloading platforms filled the void. The 'revolution' that created this change was not a revolution in music, but a revolution in computer hardware that facilitated the ripping and burning of CDs on personal computers.

This singles-driven musical culture means diverse sounds, genres and performers are finding new audiences. The notion of 'niche' and 'mainstream' is in transition. While the physical retailing of music has changed a new model of music, as a service rather than a product, is being formed (Kusek and Leonhard, 2005), along with a more direct relationship between musicians and consumers. The 'middle men' within record companies and music stores are becoming redundant. The movement to wireless connectivity ensures that musical consumption habits will enmesh with mobile living and listening.

The iPod's success in popular culture is due to at least three factors. Firstly, the design is sleek and modern. Secondly, it is functional, able to compress and carry a person's lifetime soundtrack in an object small enough to fit in a pocket or purse. Finally – and crucially – the iPod is mobile. In an age that blurs the boundaries between work and leisure, the iPod is carried through the diverse functions and stages of life. While miniaturization and transistorization were part of twentieth-century technological transformations that enabled portable radios, the electric guitar, minimoog, drum machine and cross fader, the iPod built on these innovations to embody the principle and practice of digital convergence.

The iPod has mediated our experience. It is also an instrument of change in how popular music has been produced, consumed and distributed. Fewer compact discs are purchased. That is not only because music can be obtained free of charge, but also because money is being spent on music on different platforms including video games and mobile phone applications. The audience is widening and diversifying.

> The youth market has repeatedly propelled the music business to new heights, from Elvis to The Beatles, from The Monkees to the boy bands, and from Eminem to Britney Spears. 'Kids' make up the single largest group of prospective music consumers and as a result, music fans aged over thirty-five had been relegated to the sidelines – a situation that has now changed drastically, with the arrival of file-sharing and digital music services (Kusek and Leonhard, 2005: 98).

While 'the long tail' is a cliché of e-commerce, it is also the lived reality of popular music. Music charts and record company marketing now have less influence than at any point in the post-war period. There are many pathways to finding 'new' music, even if it is only new for that particular consumer and was actually released forty years ago.

While the iPod as a platform will inevitably reduce in influence, with its market being infiltrated by its newer sisters the iTouch, iPhone and iPad, the scale of its transformation is clear. Music has become popular again and it can access and reclaim its history in new ways. The iPod shook up copyright law, the ownership of music, the rights of consumers and the relationship between sound, vision and touch. Each history and chapter in this book has been sharpened, changed or reorganized because of the presence of that first white object with a small screen and a fly wheel. Scrolling has created a new way of listening.

Key Questions

1. How has the iPod changed popular music?
2. What are the strengths and weaknesses of the iPod as a recorder?
3. Why was the iPod in particular an instrument for change?
4. Will the iPod and its derivatives continue to hold a central symbolic role in digitized popular music? What could trigger a post-iPod age?

Further Reading

Kahney, L. (2005) *The Cult of iPod*. San Francisco, CA: No Starch.

Katz, M. (2004) *Capturing Sound: How Technology Has Changed Music*. Berkeley: University of California Press.

Kusek, D. and Leonhard, G. (2005) *The Future of Music*. Boston, MA: Berklee.

Levy, S. (2006) *The Perfect Thing*. New York: Simon & Schuster.

Sonic sources

Apple (2006) 'iPod Tutorials,' podcast, iTunes.

S Net Networks (2006–2007) 'Apple Clips,' podcast, iTunes.

Sabella, T. and Root, T. (2007) The Business Side of Music, podcast, iTunes.

Spellman, P. (2007–) Music Career Juice, podcast, iTunes.

Visual sources

ARTS: Advice for a Future in the Music Industry, (2007) *YouTube*, http://www. youtube.com/watch?v=1TUZf0oBVZE&feature=PlayList&p=C67BD36D5E7 D29A7&playnext=1&playnext_from=PL&index=14

Brown, R. (2008) 'Want to know the future of the music industry? Look to the past', *YouTube*, http://www.youtube.com/watch?v=v6DmxUHH0zs&feature= related

Keynote with Jeffrey Veen – HighEdWeb 2008 Conference, (2008) *YouTube*, http:// www.youtube.com/watch?v=AcZQSGxnP-Y

Russ Solomon on Tower Records' Rise and Fall, (2007) *YouTube*, http://www. youtube.com/watch?v=iDpk74TX6fU

Web sources

Eaton, K. (2009) 'Are Slipping iPod Sales Bad News for the Recording Industry?' *Fast Company*, http://www.fastcompany.com/blog/kit-eaton/technomix/are-slipping-ipod-sales-bad-news-recording-industry-nope

iObserver, http://www.macobserver.com/tmo/features/iobserver/

iPod Lounge, http://www.ipod-lounge.com/ipodmovies/

Music Industry Today, iPod News, http://music.einnews.com/news/ipod

Section IV

Genre and Community

Country

Little Richard described country music as 'the white man's blues' (2008). Tex Sample termed it 'the soul music of rural and urban white working people' (1996: 13). As a form, it has a wide range of derivations sweeping through the southern United States. One cradle of the genre is the Appalachian Mountains. While country music is the current description, it has also been termed mountain music, bluegrass, cowboy music and hillbilly music. Bluegrass is a mode of American music with its origins in Kentucky. Founded by Bill Monroe and his Bluegrass Boys, it gained renewed popularity from the movie soundtrack of *O Brother, Where Art Thou?* Holding a range of genres within it, bluegrass is also a description for less well-known country music (Rosenberg, 1985). As with much 'marginal' music, the availability of downloadable MP3s has suited the genre. Neil Rosenberg confirms that, 'the advent of the Internet has suited bluegrass music well' (1985: xii). New audiences emerged for the genre that would never find the Stanley Brothers in a local record shop.

Another terminology used to describe this mode of music is 'country and western', referring to the distinctive musical styles from the southwestern United States. Such terms can block the realization that there were and are diverse sources for country, including Willie Nelson's base in Austin, Texas, and the Bakersfield Sound from Bakersfield in California, nearly 200 kilometers north of Los Angeles. Mobilizing honky tonk and swing, the hard-edge amplification of this style made it a tougher and sharper music. Merle Haggard and Buck Owens were also proponents of this style.

While much of country music is produced in and sourced from the United States, there are other nations with distinctive country music histories. Australia, for example, has a thriving country music industry, activating complex dialogues not only with folk, but also with indigenous music styles (Mitchell: 1996). Indigenous communities and Torres Strait Islander peoples have been both part of the audience and performers throughout Australia's national music history. This hybrid mode of music has also been termed 'bush music' or the 'bush ballad' (Stratton, 2003). 'Waltzing Matilda', a song about a drover stealing lifestock, is the unofficial Australian national anthem and is strongly locked in to the country and bush tradition. The performer Slim Dusty released hundreds of songs and albums to great acclaim in Australia. His best known song was released in 1957, entitled 'A Pub With No Beer'. There is a deep relationship in Australia between country and folk, fused together via their guitar-based foundations (Smith and Brett, 1998: 3). Irish musical traditions survive in Australian country music, often on a greater scale than has been witnessed in American country and western music.

Instrumentation is important and distinct in country music. The contributions of immigrants from the Appalachian Mountains introduced the fiddle, banjo and guitar to early country music. After being discovered by Ralph Peer and recorded in 1927, Jimmie Rodgers and the Carter Family were groundbreaking, building the sonic structures and literacies that we currently associate with country music. From 1938 electrified instruments, and particularly the steel guitar, started to transform the genre, exemplified by the Texas Wanderers' 'It Makes No Difference Now'. Unlike folk music, there has been no great controversy or debate about the use of amplified instruments. The lyrical content of country music is also distinctive. At its spangly, sparkly best, country music assembles a mock gothic grandeur that transforms marriage, divorce, love and loss into a narrative of catastrophic tragedy. Women's role in country music has always been more than standing by a man. A feminism that does speak its name, women in country music are continually disappointed by men. Not surprisingly, country music also has humour within it. The titles of songs, rousing sharp choruses, occupy the ambivalent space between irony and reality. Examples include Thom Sharpe's 'I Don't Know Whether to Kill Myself or Go Bowling', Waylon Jennings' '(Get Your Tongue out of my Mouth) I'm Kissing You Goodbye', Deana Carter's 'Did I Shave my Legs for This?' and Kacey Jones 'Every Man I Love is either Married, Gay or Dead'. The religious element in country music is also subject to humour, including Paul Charles Craft's 'Drop kick me, Jesus (Through the Goal Posts of Life)' and Mojo Nixon's 'Are You Drinking With Me Jesus?'

The audience for country music has been the target for both humour and misunderstanding. The complex relationship between country music and the white working class is (too) often simplified in the word 'redneck'. To offer two jokes as examples:

> How many country singers does it take to change a light bulb?
> Two, one to do it and one to sing a song reminiscing about all the good times he had with the old bulb.
> What happens if you play country music backwards?
> Your wife returns to you, your dog comes back to life, and you get out of prison (Country Music Jokes).

Country music, through much of its parallel history with rock music, has been demeaned as simple. Such a judgement is not demeaning of the music, but of the people who listen to it. Mary Bufwack and Robert Oermann instigated a study of women in country music and described the genre as the 'songs and styles of the working class' (1993: 7). While this audience has broadened, internationalized and diversified, the importance of the key instrumentation and musical structures, along with the lyrics of dislocation, loss, confusion and a desperate hope for a positive resolution, can be read socially and culturally. There is a strong critique of country music by credible rock critics, marginalizing, abusing and discounting the genre. It captures a trace of Tillie Olsen's realization about the culture of working people.

For our silenced people, century after century their beings consumed in the hard, everyday essential work of maintaining human life. Their art, which still they made – as their other contributions – anonymous; refused respect, recognition; lost (2003: vii).

Olsen is arguing that when disempowered communities create culture, it is rarely respected. Country is a commercialized music, but it also captures a productive (and occasionally destructive) nostalgia for a simpler life that should be understood critically and historically rather than dismissed as the longings of an undereducated audience.

The musical boundaries between country and 'mainstream' popular music are more intricate and complex than is the case with other musical genres discussed in this book. Country music entered not only popular culture but also popular music through Hollywood films (Chapman, 2000). The Nashville Sound in the 1950s and 1960s commercialized country music, with a smooth vocal and strings. Charlie Rich, Tammy Wynette, Patsy Cline and Jim Reeves were proponents of this style. In the 1990s, the size of this market became clear with Garth Brooks being both the top country artist and producing the top pop album in 1990, 1991 and 1992, enabled through music video as much as concert performances. Such success offers an important historical reminder of the smooth movements between rock, pop, blues and country. Chuck Berry's 'Maybelline' was released in 1955. It was one of only three releases in 1955 to enter the top ten of all three *Billboard* charts: country, pop and rhythm and blues (Ennis, 1992: 227). Significantly, Berry's original was number one on the R & B chart and reached number five on the pop chart. It was covered by Marty Robbins and then entered the country chart.

Such hybridity and movement is embodied by one phrase. Country Rock was a crossover musical formation, exemplified by The Byrds while Gram Parsons was a member and continued through his subsequent band, The Flying Burrito Brothers. Both Bob Dylan and Elvis Presley enabled the movement between these genres and The Eagles also worked in this unstable but productive genre. Although these bands and performers opened up a much more complex series of movements between popular music and country, there were and are controversies. The country music and rock communities were unsettled by unfamiliar importations of sounds and instrumentation. Peter Doggett described, 'that suspicion, bordering on hatred, that has shadowed every encounter between country and rock since the 1950s. From Elvis Presley through Bob Dylan and Willie Nelson to Garth Brooks, the result has been not just a merging of musical styles, but a clash of cultures – all the more intense because the protagonists know they are close cousins. The troubled relationship between country and rock has its roots in an American divide which was created by the Civil War of the 1860s, and which has never quite healed' (2000: vii). By the early 1970s, with an increasing number of performers moving between styles and instrumentations, the musical literacies of rock fans started to increase. The Band's *Music from Big Pink* in 1968 was the crucial album that – with subtlety and care – enlarged the parameters of both lyrical subjects and harmonies within popular music by exploring American roots music and sounds rather than following the excesses of psychedelia. Neil Young's *After the Goldrush* album in 1971 was another pivotal moment. While Dylan's *Nashville Skyline* was misunderstood, attacked and ignored in 1969, his later career in the 2000s showed how country music had remained part of his musical history, bringing forward skiffle and shuffle into the contemporary pop charts.

The relationship between country music and popular music remains important. It had moments of obvious crossover through Dolly Parton, John Denver, Johnny Cash and Garth Brooks. By the mid 1990s, however, a harder and edgier country music started to emerge that was less easily absorbed into the mainstream music charts. Alternative country (Alt country) worked against the 'Nashville sound'. Alt country was able to draw young and urban audiences back to the genre. Yet when listening to Carl Perkins, Elvis Presley, Jerry Lee Lewis and Johnny Cash, known as Sun's Million Dollar Quartet, the tissue of connectivity between country and rock, alternative and mainstream, is obvious. John Lennon famously stated, 'If there hadn't been an Elvis, there wouldn't have been a Beatles' (Lennon, 2010). Similarly, if there had not been a Johnny Cash, then Bob Dylan would not have happened, or he certainly would not have gained sustained success. Significantly, Dylan's thirty-second studio album, *Modern Times*, which was released in 2006, combined skiffle, bluegrass and country music. When it topped the charts, he became – at 65 – the oldest man to release a number one album in the United States. He also showed that country music remains part of popular music. If a song tells a story, then part of its narrative history comes from country.

Key Questions

1. From where is country music derived?
2. What is bluegrass?
3. Why does country music lack credibility?
4. What are the key musical instruments in country?

Further Reading

Fox, A. (2005) *Real Country: Music and Language in Working-class Culture*. Durham: Duke University Press.

La Chapelle, P. (2007) *Proud to Be an Okie: Cultural Politics, Country Music, and Migration to Southern California*. Berkerley: University of California Press.

Malone, B. (2002). *Don't Get Above Your Raisin': Country Music and the Southern Working Class*. Champaign: University of Illinois Press.

Peterson, R.A. (2000) *Creating Country Music: Fabricating Authenticity*. Chicago: Chicago University Press.

Sonic sources

Autry, G. (1939) *Back in the Saddle Again.*

Carter Family (1928) *Can the Circle be Unbroken.*

Cash, J. (1955) *Folsom Prison Blues.*

Parton, D. (1974) *Jolene.*

Visual sources

Grand Ole Opry at Carnegie Hall (2006) RCA.

Highwaymen Live (2006) Sony BMG.

Neil Young, Heart of Gold (2006) Paramount Classics.

Patsy Kline, Sweet Dreams Still (2006) Fastforward.

Web sources

Alternative Country, http://www.alt-country.org/

Bakersfield Sound Underground, http://blog.bakersfieldsoundunderground.com/

Country Music Hall of Fame, http://www.countrymusichalloffame.com/site/

e-fiddler, http://efiddler.com/loops_country.htm

Folk

There were two musical revolutions in the 1950s: the rock revolution and the folk revolution. Folk had a long and distinguished history before Bill Haley sang 'Rock Around the Clock'. Its influence on pop was enabled through singer songwriters like Joan Baez, Joni Mitchell and Tracy Chapman. These performers were continuing the legacy of Woody Guthrie, who added social commentaries and protest to popular music. He was followed by Pete Seeger, Bob Dylan and Donovan. In today's digitized, Web 2.0 environment, folk music continues to evolve. Musical technologies have enabled a wider dissemination of older, local, roots music. Folk music is more popular and easier to hear, play and research than at any point in its history (Bealle, 2005). Preservation and dissemination are enacted not only through the Smithsonian or the Library of Congress, but also via a range of online portals, such as Roger McGuinn's Folk Den project. He releases a folk song once a month from his website, without cost to the listener, with a wraparound from iTunes. Ironically, while debates have raged about electric folk (Sweers, 2005), it is digitized folk that will ensure the genre's survival and influence.

Such an accessible project from Roger McGuinn masks the often adversarial politics that have punctuated the history of modern folk. This divisiveness is best captured by the title of Florence Reece's song written in 1931: 'Which Side Are You On?'. The lyric asked listeners to make a choice. Such a song is a metaphor for folk: were the origins black or white? Is the future acoustic or electric? Is folk politically on the left or available for use by those on the right? Is it a genre of preservation or progressiveness? Throughout its history, folk has moved between these poles of debate. Songs have not only been collected by American folklorists but also recorded and released by corporate record companies. Material was archived by the Library of Congress from 1928 but used as an inspiration and database for popular cultural success by many singer songwriters, including Emmylou Harris, Suzanne Vega and Tracy Chapman.

The management of this dichotomy between authenticity and change, preservation and transformation, frames any discussion of folk music. Not surprisingly, diverse definitions limit and frame the genre. Ronald Cohen located five characteristics.

(1) its origins can perhaps be located in a particular culture or region; (2) authorship has historically been unknown, although authors did emerge over the past two centuries; (3) it has traditionally been performed by non-professionals, perhaps playing acoustic instruments; (4) its composition has been fairly simple, with perhaps little complexity so that it can be performed and shared communally; and (5) the songs have historically been passed down through oral transmission (2006: 2).

Such diverse definitions are important because they incorporate a range of (albeit acoustic) instruments, such as the guitar, mandolin, banjo, fiddle and harmonica and reveal the relationships with other genres, particularly blues, country and gospel. They capture the influence of folk, not only musically, but also lyrically and socially.

The arrival of electric folk, after the controversy of Bob Dylan 'plugging in' at the Newport Folk Festival, started to settle as the 1960s progressed. The Byrds created folk-rock, accompanied by Roger McGuinn's twelve string guitar, that fused the sound of The Beatles with the folk history of Leadbelly. Fairport Convention's 1967 album *Liege & Lief* featured the gentle voice of Sandy Denny with the biting electric guitar of Richard Thompson. Folk-rock (with or without the hyphen) enabled an easier transition between acoustic and electric instruments. When reviewing the controversies in folk music, it is necessary to grasp why electric instrumentation was a threat to the ideologies of the genre. Steve Waksman stated that, 'I am less interested in what Dylan's performance at Newport suggests about the folk music constituency, or about Dylan himself, than I am in what it suggests about the position of the electric guitar in the popular music of the 1960s' (1999: 1–2). Dylan's movement to an electric instrument both initiated and reinforced the value and meaning of the guitar for the rock decade. It also agitated the easy authenticity and politics that had been tethered to folk music. The loudness of the electric guitar shifted the relationship between sound and noise, lyric and rhythm, and what was acceptable to a listening audience.

The beacon and basis of much international folk music through the second half of the twentieth century was Pete Seeger. Second only to Woody Guthrie, Seeger embodied not only the mantle of the singer songwriter, he also infused folk music with the imperative for social justice. The scale of his role can be grasped when tracking his support for union organizations in the 1930s and 1940s, his membership of the Communist Party, being confronted by McCarthy's America and then reclaimed as the father of 1960s progressivist and civil rights movements. A version of US history can be gleaned from his autobiography (Winkler, 2009). He led a life of activism through song, protest and commitment. His songs and sounds were influential, both politically and musically. He enabled the early career of Bob Dylan, provided the foundational inspiration for Roger McGuinn and, as late as 2006, Bruce Springsteen released *The Seeger Sessions* on compact disc.

Through this folk connection from Guthrie to Seeger, Dylan to Springsteen, it is also clear that folk in North America is tethered to blues and country. The Carter Family in particular worked the relationship between folk and country (Zwonitzer and Hirshberg, 2002). Folk in Britain – although holding an independent history – was transformed by the arrival of American folk. Indeed, there was a parallel importation. While The Beatles and The Rolling Stones reintroduced American rock and blues back into the United States, Pete Seeger, Bob Dylan and The Byrds brought English folk back into British popular music. While Steeleye Span, Fairport Convention and Pentangle were producing influential British music, it was the repackaged 'foreign' folk that built relationships between folk and popular music (Sweers, 2005). Michael Brocken remembers that 'like many British youngsters in the 1960s, I was first drawn towards folk music by Americans ... if

I were brutally honest, it was the magnificent Byrds who had introduced me to the verities of (what one could do with) "traditional" material' (2003: ix). The Byrds were a band that translated between Britain and America, folk and rock. The cognate configuration of folk-rock questioned the limits of folk and the trajectories drawn from it.

The ideology of folk had a profound impact on rock's interpretation of itself. It allowed rock to gain some semblance of authenticity and separation from pop music (Middleton, 1990, 120). Folk also granted rock a political integrity and edge. Not surprisingly, academics and journalists have been drawn to its authenticity and meaning. Paul Hegarty noted, 'scholars' deep and often emotional and sensory attraction to folk song, narration and craft' (2002). The relationship between folk and popular music survives through every presentation of political protest through song. When there is a moment of pop protest, a flash of challenge to the powerful, a part of folk history returns to us.

Key Questions

1. Why is 'real folk' acoustic?
2. Why were there controversies when Bob Dylan played an electric guitar?
3. What is folk-rock (with or without the hyphen)?
4. How has folk music changed through digitization?

Further Reading

Alarik, S. (2003) *Deep Community: Adventures in the Modern Folk Underground.* Cambridge: Black Wolf.

Becker, J. (1998) *Appalachia and the Construction of an American Folk, 1930–1940.* Chapel Hill: University of North Carolina Press.

Brocken, M. (2003) *The British Folk Revival 1944–2002.* Aldershot: Ashgate.

Filene, B. (2000) *Romancing the Folk: Public Memory and American Roots Music.* Chapel Hill: University of North Carolina Press.

Sonic sources

Baez, J. (1968) *Love is Just a Four Letter Word.*

Dylan, B. (1963) *Blowing in the Wind.*

Fairport Convention (1968) *Meet on the Ledge.*

Guthrie, W. (1944) *This Land is your Land.*

Visual sources

Bob Dylan, *The Other Side Of The Mirror: Bob Dylan Live At The Newport Folk Festival* 1963–1965 (2007) Sony.

In Search of the English Folk Song (2008) Kultur.

Richard Thompson, 1000 Years of Popular Music (2006) Cooking Vinyl.

The Byrds, Under Review (2007) Chrome Dreams.

Web sources

Delta Blues Museum, www.deltabluesmuseum.org

Folk Den, www.folkden.com

Folk Music Archives, http://folkmusicarchives.org/

The Digital Folk Life, http://www.thedigitalfolklife.org/DigitalFolkLife1.htm

The Blues

'The Blues' is more than a genre. It is an attitude expressed through lyrics as well as a musicological structure. Twelve bar musical cycles are created by repeating two melodic and rhythm patterns, with a resolving third line. When continued through the length of a song, this structure is the basis of boogie woogie, swing, rhythm and blues, rock and soul. The dominant seventh chords provide the accented rhythm, creating the metre for the lead guitar using the blues scale. The blues has provided the basis and foundation of many – perhaps most – popular music genres. Like much of popular music, is a non-notated music, existing through performance and recording. It is a sonic catalogue and rewriting of slavery, oppression, discrimination and injustice. While slavery stripped a people of culture and language, through music there was an opportunity to reclaim, maintain and revise identity and history.

One way to understand how blackness and the blues align is by reviewing the career of Robert Johnson. As Peter Guralnick stated, his music 'remains the touchstone against which the achievement of the blues is measured' (1990: 5). His 'Sweet Home Chicago' and 'Cross Road Blues' connected the twelve bar blues and a wailing vocal. Johnson's songs and sound, unlike many of the early bluesmen, have continued to be influential. There are reasons for this fame. Firstly, through The Rolling Stones and Eric Clapton cover versions of Johnson's 'Love in Vain' and 'Crossroads', he remained modern and relevant. Secondly, his music has been reissued and repackaged, most noticeably in a box set in the 1990s, and has a strong presence on iTunes. His music is available to be both heard and purchased.

Building on this heritage of Johnson, the history of the blues is also bound up with the history of the guitar. Huddie Ledbetter – better known as Leadbelly – is pivotal to this developing blues (and guitar) tradition. While folk music has negotiated complex relationships between acoustic and electrified instruments, the blues shared with country the capacity to move between amplified and unamplified sounds without angst. The Mississippi Delta was the source of the Delta Blues and associated not only with rural and agricultural areas, but also with the workers in this region. This musical style was made possible through the availability of cheap guitars in the United States in the late nineteenth century. An early innovator, Charley Patton (1887–1934), recorded 'Pony Blues' in 1929 and worked with ragtime rhythms and country and spiritual genres. He was best known for open tuning and use of the slide. Throughout the 1920s, blues expanded from individual players to duos, small groups and bands. It also moved from rural to urban spaces. As an example of this, Buddy Guy grew up in Louisiana, but then moved to Chicago. He is best known for infusing the blues with irregular phrasing, biting riffs and melodic variety.

Many innovations from the blues have moved on to pop. Guitar picking styles have been particularly influential. While finger style players align both the base and melody, the great influence of the blues on the history of guitar was the use of the thumb to play the bass and mark the beat, while the fingers independently play the melody. This technique is still used by guitarists such as Mark Knoffler. 'Sultans of Swing' and 'Brothers in Arms' are clear examples. Blues also shows a distinct harmonic structure. The chords use dominant sevenths while the lead melody line works in the blues scale. The harmonic dissonance and disorder created through this combination means that the genre created new combinations of sound and sonic possibilities. This openness of the blues is different to folk. It is worthwhile remembering that when Bob Dylan played at the Newport Folk Festival in 1965 and 'went electric', his backing group was the Paul Butterfield Blues Band. A blues band that opened up new spaces in folk. The resultant audience attacks and controversies captured the ideology that links authenticity with acoustic and commercialism with electrified music. The blues is more open than folk genres and less troubled by debates about commercialization because so many popular music genres have borrowed from it. Indeed, when Albert Goldman asked Jimi Hendrix, 'what is the difference between the old blues and the new?' Hendrix answered, 'Electricity' (Goldman in Waksman, 2006: 65). This movement and openness also extended to the role of women. Unlike many genres, women have been a constant presence and influential through the history of the blues. Indeed, the first blues recording was by Mamie Smith, entitled 'Crazy Blues', on Okeh Records in 1920.

There are three pivotal moments in the history of the blues. The first, from the 1920s, is associated with the Mississippi Delta. Performers such as Blind Lemon Jefferson and Charley Patton are most associated with the form. The blues at this time created a series of myths that subsequent performers would use. Robert Johnson created the myth of 'the crossroads' where a performer sells his soul to the devil for his talents. This crucial and remarkable period in musical history also brought forward and modernized a history of slavery and southern work songs. These work songs – also known as 'call and response' – became the bedrock of the blues. A lyric was sung and a guitar would answer the call. Throughout the 1930s, these songs mirrored the loss and confusion between rural and urban lives, and the racism that continued to punctuate the lives of black men and women.

The second period in blues history was from the 1940s and 1950s and was centred on both Chicago and Memphis. Francis Davis realized that the blues had become a way to manage movement: 'a music that has always been about wanting to be someplace else but making the best of where you are' (1995: 255). It was an electrified music, released on the Sun and Chess labels, and featured performers like Howlin' Wolf and Muddy Waters. Jump blues moved the genre into rhythm and blues, which then built a scaffold into popular music because of the greater focus on singers and lyrics rather than instrumentalists. The electric blues of BB King, John Lee Hooker and T-Bone Walker added new techniques and sounds to the genre. King's string bending on his guitar Lucille and Muddy Waters' aggressive, masculine singing style offered a dominance and mastery of technique that would move the blues on to the next stage of the genre's evolution.

The third period formed a tight relationship between the blues and popular culture, and emerged through the 1960s and 1970s. Earlier tracks were re-released and re-performed. Bands such as The Rolling Stones, the early Fleetwood Mac and Eric Clapton's ensembles including Cream and Derek and the Dominoes brought forward this history. This complex period, which displayed the attraction of African American music to white Englishmen, folded the Mississippi Delta blues guitarists into the commercial packaging of white, English popular culture. They used solid body guitars and enormous amplifiers, building into the stack by the end of the 1960s. This influence was best symbolized by The Rolling Stones being named after a Muddy Waters song.

Throughout the 1970s blues as a pure genre declined, but its cross-popular cultural influence increased through Stevie Ray Vaughan, Gary Moore and Robert Cray. Still, it is important to remember that the blues was influential, but not popular, in the United States. It was The Rolling Stones and the subsequent 'British invasion' that ensured an integration of the blues with popular culture. The (dis)connection between the white experience in 1960s' England and the pain, discrimination and hardship from the treatment of slaves and the enduring institutional racism throughout the twentieth century created odd – and often productive – political dissonances. There is no doubt that when white performers covered black music, it increased the audience and awareness of these singers, guitarists and songs.

The blues expressed the changes to American society musically, racially, socially and technologically. Werner was clearer in his interpretation of the music than most: 'if you were white and honest, the blues revealed things the upbeat America of the early sixties assured you didn't exist' (2006: 65). Besides changing the consciousness of injustice, it is also possible to track the shifts in audio recording and urbanization using the practices of the blues. Blues increased its importance in popular music when it was reissued on compact disc. While, for the record companies, it was a way to remarket the back catalogue, it also allowed new listeners to dip into a history that could only be heard through covers. It created a reflection on the experience of African culture, the experience of slavery and how it lived and operated in the present. The most famous of these re-releases was the boxed set of Robert Johnson's *The Complete Recordings* released by Columbia in 1990. Once digitized in this fashion, these songs later became available for downloading from online portals.

Rhythm and blues not only captured the blues genre, it also created new connections with jazz and gospel. While there has been a (too simple) alignment of rhythm and blues with African American performers and consumers, Lawrence Cohn, Mary Aldin and Bruce Bastin argued in their book *Nothing But the Blues* that 'R & B' was invented by the musical industry for convenience sake to describe 'black music'. The only genres located outside of this race-based description were classical and religious musics, with gospel even a caveat to this blanket description (Cohn et al., 1993). Ray Charles's song 'I Got a Woman' was an example of gospel experimentation in a rhythm and blues context. 'Blues' was a description of a genre of music, whereas rhythm and blues was a label imposed on black musicians to marginalize their cultural production and form a more palatable replacement for the phrase 'race music'.

Throughout the latter half of the 1950s, material from the R & B charts started to move into the more general pop charts. As shown in the *Popular Music: Topics, Trends and Trajectories* chapter on Country Music, Chuck Berry's 'Maybelline' was crucial to this cross-over, as was Bo Diddley's self-titled song. From 1957 and the arrival of Elvis Presley, a non-African American artist had started to gain popularity in a musical category that had been developed to enclose and be limited to black performers. Further, with the arrival of Berry Gordy's Motown Records, the relationship between the pop and R & B charts became increasingly complex. During the 1970s, R & B included funk and some disco influences.

While rock music became a nostalgic music for baby boomers and conservative in structure, the blues continued to transform and merge with the genres of the day, with riffs circulating in hip hop and electronica. The blues has never been the primary genre of popular music, but it remains the foundation for rhythm, technique and style. Without the blues, rock and roll would not exist. However, as has happened throughout its history, the blues continues to change, transcend and influence.

Key Questions

1. From where was the blues derived?
2. When did the blues become part of popular music?
3. Which innovations in guitar technique were derived from the blues?
4. What is the difference between the blues and rhythm and blues?

Further Reading

Davis, F. (2003) *The History of the Blues: The Roots, the Music, the People*. Cambridge: Da Capo.

Gray, M. (2008) *Hand Me My Travelin' Shoes: In Search of Blind Willie McTell*. London: Bloomsbury.

Rolf, J. (ed.) (2007) *Blues: The Complete Story*. London: Flame Tree.

Wald, E. (2005) *Escaping the Delta: Robert Johnson and the Invention of the Blues*. New York: Harper Collins.

Sonic sources

Hooker, J.L. (1948) *Boogie Chillen*.

Johnson, R. (1937) *Cross Road Blues*.

Leadbelly (1938) *The Bourgeois Blues*.

Waters, M. (1956) *Got My Mojo Working*.

Visual sources

Legends of American Folk Blues Festival (2009) Tropical.

Martin Scorsese Presents The Blues: A Musical Journey (2004) Snapper.

The American Folk Blues Festivals 1963–1966 – The British Tours – Various Artists (2007) Universal.

The Story of the Blues: From Blind Lemon to B.B. King (2003) Quantum Leap.

Web sources

Blues news, http://www.blues.org/

Delta Blues, Museum, www.deltabluesmuseum.org

Desk Top Blues, http://www.desktopblues.lichtlabor.ch/

Shades of Blue, http://www.rhythmandtheblues.org.uk/public/

Rock and Roll

To understand rock music is to grasp the Anglo American dominance over international popular music after the Second World War. It is difficult to speak or write about popular music without engaging in a history of rock. Popular music has had a long history, both before and after Bill Haley counted in the first bar to 'Rock Around the Clock' in 1954. At its most basic, rock and roll is a genre of music that has its origins in the late 1940s and early 1950s. It used a boogie woogie blues rhythm with an emphasis on the back beat. Boogie woogie was grounded in a piano-based rhythm. Rock and roll was to signal the preeminence of the electric guitar in popular music. It was Little Richard who scaffolded this transition, using his piano-based rock and roll to create a strong back beat and enhance his gospel vocal style and extraordinary range. Rock and roll also sped up blues rhythms, emphasizing a second beat. Think about the opening of 'Rock Around the Clock': 'one TWO three O'CLOCK four O'CLOCK rock'. The stress on the second beat opened up new opportunities not only for rhythm and melody, but also for dancing.

Much of popular music dialogues with elements of United States history. While Canada and South American and European nations, along with the Asian and Pacific regions, added genres, instruments and ideologies to create local sounds and structures, American musical history overshadows and overwrites other national popular musics. British music is influential, but it is like a rhythm guitar riff drowned out by a scorching American lead guitar break. It can be heard, but it is often ignored and understated. American rock was not a form of imperialism, colonialism, globalization or domination. That is too simple a labeling of a complex musical history. Instead, it was a form of aural occupation.

This aural occupation was shaken by not only the influence of grunge and acid house, but also by the development of alternative academic languages and methods to think about music. Andrew Blake has been an outstanding theorist who has reminded students and scholars that popular music is much more than rock music. In 2007, he stated that,

> Anglo-American rock music was very old-fashioned. Performers played to paying audiences whose participation was limited to singing along, almost all of their music – songs, mainly – followed the harmonic and melodic rules of existing Western and African-American music; and they wrote and recorded within strict formal limits such as the time available on the vinyl single. Rock music journalists, acting in the same way as classical music or theatre critics employed by the more upmarket newspapers, arranged their work in a hierarchy of value which echoed those lists of old European composers. The lists changed every so often – for example, in the themed-1970s punk replaced progressive rock in importance for some listeners, and most critics – but it was a hierarchy of value none the less (2007: ix).

While rock music can be framed as conservative or radical, it is vital to recognize that popular music is much larger and more expansive than this label can contain. Rock and roll, which was abbreviated to 'Rock' through the 1960s, was a special form of music that captured this contradiction of being young and American. It transformed the negative, the restrictive and the oppressive limitations of 'youth' into a celebration of difference and pleasure. Rock and roll gave a generation language, rhythm and ideology. The 1950s saw the emergence of the teenager in wider popular culture through the iconic filmic status of Marlon Brando and James Dean. Rock and roll, along with leather jackets and an antagonistic attitude, provided a mode of socialization, turning individuals into gendered consumers dedicated to fun, passion and escape. Little Richard's 'Tutti Frutti' had a joyousness and power that came with the sense of sharing a secret that may have been offensive to parental sensibilities. The beat offered a way to manage identity, to create a sense of separateness from parental culture and build a space to understand the changes, displacements and ruptures in socio-economic structures. This was the first generation of young people to have readily available money, which meant they could become regular record buyers (Horricks and Slaven, 1980: 53).

In most histories, Alan Freed, a Cleveland-based DJ, is accredited with coining the phrase 'rock and roll' in 1951 to describe a new form of music. His innovation was to play rhythm and blues for a mixed-race audience. However, there are at least three songs from the late 1940s that featured 'rock and roll' as a phrase in their title: from Paul Bascomb in 1947, Wild Bill Moore in 1948 and Doles Dickens in 1949. The phrase 'rocking and rolling' was used as a pseudonym for both dancing and sex in black culture, exemplified by Trixie Smith's 1922 song 'My Man Rocks Me With One Steady Roll'. This double connotation of dancing and sex has permeated lyrics and ideologies of rock through to the present day. Rock and roll became a form of popular music that catalogued the development of a 'generation gap' between parents and youth.

Many songs have been acclaimed as the first rock and roll record, of which Ike Turner's 'Rocket 88', recorded by Sam Phillips in Memphis in 1951, has been the most accepted. However, Haley's 'Rock Around the Clock' is important to this history, as it was the first rock and roll song to top the *Billboard* charts in 1954. By February 1956, the changes to the music industry were confirmed when the charts were topped by Elvis Presley's 'Heartbreak Hotel' followed by Carl Perkins' 'Blue Suede Shoes' at number two.

Rock and roll – while gaining popular cultural traction in the mid-1950s with performers like Bill Haley, Chuck Berry, Elvis Presley and Jerry Lee Lewis – brought forward decades of history from blues, gospel, soul, country and folk. As an electrified form of music, it gathered its influences from Memphis, Chicago and New Orleans. It was the supreme genre for decades, yet attacked in the mid to late 1970s by punks for its bloated excesses. It had also reduced into an instrumental formula: two electric guitars, one lead and the other rhythm, a bass guitar and a drum kit. Some bands featured a piano and saxophone, increasing the melodic and rhythmic range. However, brass and keyboards remained minor instruments deployed by specific bands and songs. Rock remains a genre driven by guitar and drums. While progressive rock would return alternative instrumentations as seen in the work of Rick Wakeman, Mike Oldfield and Emerson, Lake and Palmer, it would remain a guitar-driven genre.

Rock and roll, as a hybrid musical style, carried new combinations of sound into popular music, including the amplification of guitars, an electric bass and an increase in the role of the drummer. A distinction and difference was forged from the era of strings. Simon Frith confirmed rock as 'a mass-produced, mass-consumed, commodity' (1981: 159). It poached and borrowed from rural and urban blues, jazz and big band vocal techniques, yet was signed to the large record labels and deployed corporate distribution practices.

While the early history of rock and roll played to and for a youthful audience, part of this narrative was to include tragic deaths. Buddy Holly, Ritchie Valens and the Big Bopper died in an airplane accident while traveling to the next gig. Eddie Cochran was killed in a car crash in the UK, which also injured Gene Vincent. Jerry Lee Lewis married his 13 year-old cousin and faced persecution on moral grounds and Chuck Berry was charged with transporting a minor over state borders. These stories of death, violence and transgression made Bill Haley's early success even more unusual. Aged thirty, married, and a father of five, he was very different from Elvis Presley's pulsating hips and style of presentation.

Lawrence Grossberg described the development of the rock as 'an entire range of postwar, "youth"-oriented, technologically and economically mediated, musical practices and styles. By describing it as a formation, I want to emphasise the fact that the identity and effect of rock depends on more than its sonorial dimension' (1994: 41). Grossberg was suggesting that it was not simply a musical style or genre. It moved into fashion, film and television, influencing language and building barriers between generations. But this was a temporary convergence between popular music and rock music. What the 2000s confirmed was that popular music was much more than rock music. Rock is not descriptive of the bulk of music that is now released, downloaded or listened to, it is instead an historical category with an established legacy.

The youthful freshness of rock and roll was brought to Britain. The images and sounds of rock music offered both a critique and mediation to an ageing, declining Britain that had suffered political scandals like the Profumo affair from 1961–3 and the balance of payment crisis in 1964. The Beatles offered a fresh and fashionable image and were able to align a version of American rock and roll that could operate in a transforming Britain. The response from fans was extended from the enthusiasm that greeted Elvis Presley's persona and voice. The success of The Beatles world wide was termed the 'British invasion' and the extent of their impact is difficult to overestimate. Their early recording career captured this cross-genre heritage. Rhythm and blues was confirmed through songs like 'She's a Woman' and 'Money'. Country and Western, Skiffle and rockabilly fed into 'I've Just Seen a Face'. Folk roots framed 'Hide Your Love Away' and 'I'll Follow the Sun'. Traditional ballads included 'If I Fell', 'And I Love Her' and 'Till There Was You'. Conversely, The Beatle's post-*Rubber Soul* releases explored the limits of sound, noise and music. 'A Day in the Life' accessed and activated a much wider cultural history beyond rock.

At the end of the 1960s, Arnold Shaw described the 'Rock Revolution' he had seen happen in the previous decade.

> The phrase rock revolution may sound like a metaphor or hyperbole. It is neither a figure of speech nor a rhetorical exaggeration. It quite literally characterized what has happened to American music in the 1960s – a complete upending of the pop music scene (1969: 1).

As rock and roll became rock, the genre continued to transform. Rock in the 1950s was attacked as a threat to family life, youth and morality. During the 1960s it became the soundtrack for change, hope and social transformation. It also signaled a standardization of verse, chorus and bridge structures. Similarly, it became more common throughout the 1960s that musicians started to both write and perform their own material. By the early 1970s, the fragmentation and hybridization of rock with folk, jazz, soul and blues had created psychedia, progressive rock and the androgynous complexities of Bowie, Roxy Music and Marc Bolan.

The Anglo–American dominance of popular music confirms the priority of particular languages, sonic literacies and ways of ordering melodic and rhythmic structures. It also reveals a critical tradition of writing and commentary that empowers and reinforces these formations. Since those remarkable screaming and pounding innovations of rock and roll in the 1950s and 1960s, rock has become part of the canon of popular music (Jones, 2008). The staged conflict between rock and capitalism, musicians and fans versus the recording company, has hampered the development of more intricate academic debates beyond credibility, authenticity and resistance. Indeed, many of the threats about illegal downloaders have been inserted into these tired debates about the authenticity of music and the fight against greedy record companies. However, rock has never been singular or authentic. Its permeability and changeability are verified by the number of adjectives that can be added to it: prog, punk, kraut, art, acid, folk, garage, soft and hard.

The impact of rock music – for the baby boomer generation – was extraordinary. Mark Crispin Miller remembered that,

> In the first flush of rock's excitement, we were amazed and delighted, eager to soar into rock and roll heaven, from whose heights we would look down at Dad, and laugh. There was something happening there, something unworldly and indefinable, as our superlatives suggested: out of sight, far out, too much. Now there is nothing left but after-images, which the critic tries to sort and measure. Having drifted back to earth, rock has been entombed in texts (1988: 176).

The contradiction of rock connoting rebellion while being funded by big business was to pepper popular music journalism and writing for the subsequent half century. Such generationalism and ageism always appears naïve in retrospect. A community who condemned supermaterialism has gone on to be the target market for hyperconsumerism. David Bowie – tottering in his stacked boots and smeared with Ziggy Stardust eyeliner, warned that 'rock and rollers' would 'get older' (1971). The 1960s' rock revolution itself became a marketable formation. As rock became a commodity, its greatest sons, Jagger, Richards, McCartney and Lennon, entered knighthood, sainthood or rehab. Rock performers became the museum artefacts of popular music. Rock is a can(n)on, firing at differences, with punk, grunge, indie and emo disavowing the rock status quo and inevitably ending up performing it. As Marcus Breen described Nirvana's 1991 album *Nevermind*:

> It marked a new engagement with physicality which opened up the constraints of rock's prevailing orthodoxy to an optimistic re-reading. This was rock that mattered (1996: 1).

The challenges from dance culture – disco and house – also affected rock. By 1994, Lawrence Grossberg suggested that 'rock's operating logic might no longer be either effective or possible' (1994: 56). While indie repeated and reinforced this operating logic, the impact of hip hop and rap – let alone the reality television ballad-based singing competitions – showed that the future will be post-rock. Yet Katha Pollitt's warning is important: 'as long as we're talking about white men competing with each other, we tacitly acknowledge that we live in a realistic world … add women and blacks into the picture, though, and suddenly the scene shifts' (1995: 83). This transformative capacity affected the status and role of rock in the wider terrain of popular music as can be seen in the careers of Beyonce Knowles and Lady Gaga, Dizzee Rascal and Kanye West.

In the period between 1956 and 1976, rock music dominated popular music and assembled a series of binary oppositions.

rock music	pop music
masculine	feminine
guitars	keyboards
listening	dancing
credibility	triviality

Rarely do such stark binary oppositions operate in popular culture. For nearly two decades, rock music was able to carry an intensity and credibility through young white men playing guitars that displaced and dismissed a range of other music as 'pop'. The impact of both punk and disco – leading through to acid house and drum 'n' bass – shook and shattered these categories. Nirvana offered a much more complex range of ideas about youth, masculinity, drugs and music than was available from Dire Straits or Bruce Springsteen at the time. Rock and roll has repeatedly developed a resistance from within. Punk and grunge spat with shrill rage at the complicity and conformity of rock. Inevitably though, this critique freshened up the genre, allowing it to reconfigure, change and survive. Rock is an historical formation, but it continues to make history.

Key Questions

1. What made rock and roll musically distinctive?
2. What is the relationship between rock and roll and youth?
3. What is emo? How does this style transform the genre of rock?
4. Is rock music still the music of youth?

Further Reading

Clover, J. (2009) *1989: Bob Dylan Didn't Have This to Sing About.* Berkeley: University of California Press.

Marcus, G. (2006) *Lipstick Traces: A Secret History of the Twentieth Century.* London: Faber and Faber.

Segalstad, E. and Hunter, J. (2009) *The 27s: The Greatest Myth of Rock and Roll.* Berkeley, CA: North Atlantic Books.

Wald, E. (2009) *How The Beatles Destroyed Rock n Roll: An Alternative History of American Popular Music.* Oxford: OUP.

Sonic sources

Big Brother and the Holding Company (1968) *Piece of My Heart.*

Presley, E. (1954) *That's Alright Mama.*

The Beatles (1963) *I Saw Her Standing There.*

The Rolling Stones (1965) *(I Can't Get No) Satisfaction.*

Visual sources

Blackboard Jungle (1955) Warner.

Electric Purgatory: The Fate of the Black Rocker (2005) Payback Productions.

The Last Waltz (1978) MGM.

Woodstock (2009) Warner Home Video.

Web sources

Rock and Roll Hall of Fame + Museum, http://www.rockhall.com/

Rock Band, http://www.rockband.com/

Rock Music Blogs, http://www.blogcatalog.com/directory/music/rock/

Rock Sound, http://www.rocksound.tv/

Soul

Soul is southern music, but this 'south' refers to much more than geography. It captures an ideology of disconnection that activates a history of displacement, marginalization and oppression. Soul is more community oriented and organized than most genres of music, and has close ties to gospel and blues. It also created a database of samples for rap that are used not only to recognize its specific history but also to construct affirmative and alternative narratives of blackness through rhythm and voice. Soul is a way of creating, singing and dancing to narratives of Black America. Southern soul was 'harder, grittier than the sweet sounds coming out of Detroit and Chicago' (Werner, 2006: 56). The rationale for this difference can be sourced from the engrained segregation in the south. Hearing Sam Cooke sing 'A Change is Gonna Come', the struggles of life and death are captured through the catch in his voice. The title suggests that optimism and equality are possible. At its best, it is 'the history of integration' (Shapiro, 2006: 366), but unfortunately there are also caveats to such a statement through such descriptions as 'blue-eyed soul'. If there is a political or social characteristic of soul, then it is the yearning for change. Even through the greatest injustices, soul is revelatory, affirmative and aspirational, and the bedrock of hip hop and electronica. Euphoria from despair lives in dance culture, but was born in soul. The foundation of soul was rhythm and blues, jump blues, gospel and jazz. The rhythmic and vocal tether between Ray Charles' 'I Got a Woman' (1954) and Otis Redding's 'Respect' (1967) is easy to hear.

Compared to the other genres discussed in this section, soul is the most diverse and transformative genre. While gospel has been integral to the vocal style, the tight instrumental arrangements, including punching countermelodies through a horn section, created a swooning, sweeping music of scale and grandeur, loss and hope. For James Brown, Smokey Robinson, Sam Cooke, Marvin Gaye and Curtis Mayfield, adult relationships and concerns entered the lyrical subject matter. Politics also had a critical presence. It is impossible to understand soul music without grasping the impact and consequences of the civil rights movement. At the time that Dylan released 'Blowing in the Wind' in 1963, Sam Cooke was translating the folk genre into soul, creating 'A Change is Gonna Come'. Channeling Dylan's ambiguity, Cooke created an anthem of hope and change for the future. This optimism would be tempered through struggle, captured in 1969 and 1970 by Nina Simone's 'To be Young, Gifted and Black' and Marvin Gaye's 'What's Going On?'.

Like blues, rhythm and blues and rap, soul was a genre incubated in and protected by independent record companies (Guralnick, 1996: 5). While Motown released much soul, R & B, blues and pop, the record company most associated with the genre was based in Memphis. Stax Records has been synonymous with soul and built a strong relationship with Fame Studios in Alabama where many artists including Percy Sledge, Aretha Franklin and Arthur Alexander recorded. Established in 1960, Stax was based in a disused theatre with a marquee featuring the slogan 'Soulsville USA'. This was a response to Motown's slogan, 'Hitsville USA'. Stax had a more specific focus than hits, with the company built on the success of both Otis Redding and the famed duo Sam and Dave (Samuel Moore and Dave Prater). Their dynamic and passionate live performances captured the ecstasy of soul, while also creating a package of danceable rhythms and riveting vocals built on the musicianship of Booker T and the MGs.

While Stax continued on with later success from Isaac Hayes and his Academy Award winning 'Theme from Shaft', soul as a genre fragmented after the 1960s and (arguably) never overcame the death of Redding. Sly and the Family Stone created new sounds and connections. The Staple Singers and Bobby Womack showed a complexity in both harmony and musical arrangement and released remarkable recordings. An infusion with disco rhythms and funk meant that Earth, Wind & Fire and The O'Jays gained chart success, continuing the history of both Stax and Otis Redding. Disco and hip hop instigated a metaphorical platform migration of soul, with the famous voices, rhythms and riffs surviving in the mix.

As with blues, soul was more popular in Britain than in its home country and continues to be influential. Booker T and the MGs' 'Green Onions' has been cited as influencing a range of dance music artists, including Shaun Ryder (Brabazon, 2005). Black Grape in particular created a hybrid, postmodern bricolage with soul. In the growth of 'urban music' in the United Kingdom, the confluence between contemporary R & B and soul became particularly obvious, with Joss Stone, Duffy and Amy Winehouse continuing the trajectory of strong female soul singers. They remain the soul daughters of Aretha Franklin.

Soul was part of the 1960s, but its reverberations travel beyond this decade. Soul had a short popular cultural history, conservatively dated from Booker T and the MGs' 'Green Onions' in 1962 through to Isaac Hayes' 'Shaft' in 1971. Between these songs, Otis Redding transformed how men should sing, dance and perform. Aretha Franklin shaped and sharpened the coloratura of the female voice, also lifting the value of women in a male-dominated industry. Most importantly, soul broadened out the emotional palette of popular music. From the four rhythmic trumpets that open the Four Tops' 'Walk away Renee' through to Stevie Wonder's 'Uptight', the anthem to love overcoming all injustice, soul added hope, texture and density to music.

Part of the fame of this southern soul music was – surprisingly – northern. A key movement in sustaining this genre was Northern Soul. Derived from the British mod scene, soul music gained great popularity in the north of England at the end of the 1960s. The journalist Dave Godin supposedly invented the phrase 'Northern Soul' in 1970, within the pages of *Blues and Soul* magazine. The music favoured in Northern Soul had two characteristics. Firstly, it maintained a fast tempo. Secondly, the dancers and collectors prized the rare songs on more obscure labels such as Okeh from New York, Golden World from Detroit and Mirwood from Los Angeles. It was a movement of reclamation, recycling and revival, taking older songs and bringing them into the present. When Motown was played, it was rare Motown. As Stephen Bardsley stated,

> Whereas 'Northern' and Motown are related and small amounts of Motown tracks are northern, the two genres are certainly different and due to much chart success, it might be said the majority of Motown is popular rather than Soul music (2010).

Such distinctions, while seemingly pedantic in retrospect, mattered and still matter to Northern Soul connoisseurs. Northern Soul was a movement of dancing and night-clubs, with the best known being the Twisted Wheel in Manchester, the Wigan Casino and the Highland Rooms at the Blackpool Mecca. The dancing, particularly from the men, was athletic and included flips, spins and backdrops.

The Twisted Wheel was originally a café termed the Left Wing. In 1963 the venue was bought by Ivor and Phil Abadi who used the shell of the building to run all-night parties. The important DJ at the Wheel was Roger Eagle. He collected imported soul and began to play innovative mixes of American music. Later on, as the demands for faster soul emerged, his mix of soul and jazz was not as popular. By the end of the 1960s, the 'all-nighters' had become famous throughout the United Kingdom. Under legal and social pressure because of drug use, the Wheel closed in 1971. New clubs were able to fill the space, spreading to Sheffield, Wigan, Bolton and Wolverhampton. At its peak in the mid 1970s, Northern Soul was a key part of British popular culture. In 1976, the Wigan Casino had 100,000 members (Winstanley and Nowell, 1996). In 1978, *Billboard* voted it as the best discotheque in the world (Brewster and Broughton, 2000: 99). Significantly, because of the size of the dance floor, it was necessary to construct a distinctive mix to suit the environment. Chris Hunt observed that,

> confronted by the biggest of Northern dancefloors, the DJs of Wigan needed to find the biggest of tunes to fill it. As a building the Casino was well past its heyday, but the best-kept dance floor that the circuit had seen – and with superb acoustics to match – it could have been tailor-made for Northern Soul. Its huge ballroom easily held 1200, the dance floor flanked on three sides by ornate balconies where the acrobatic dancers, illuminated by just two fluorescent lights suspended form the domed ceiling, could be watched from on high ... Wigan's dancers were demanding and the music has to be just right or they would walk ... With those kind of pressures dictating the playlist, Wigan's unique circumstances were shaping the music that was played, enabling the club to develop a style of its own, often out of keeping with what was happening elsewhere on the 'Northern' scene (2002).

Hunt had realized that there was an unusual and productive relationship created between a large dance floor, experienced and demanding dancers and responsive DJs. Their focus on rare records meant that it gathered a knowledgeable crowd. Like all the best clubs Wigan Casino also closed, in 1981.

Significantly, a trace of Wigan Casino's history remains online, but the lasting influence of Northern Soul continues with reissues and compilation albums. In the late 2000s, Terry Christian noted that Northern Soul was reviving (2008). The irony of Northern Soul is that songs that were overlooked in the United States eventually became the backbone of its success in England. Bill Brewster and Frank Broughton described it as 'a genre built from failures ... made by hundreds of singers and bands who were copying the Detroit sound of Motown pop' (2000: 86). This technique was best exemplified by The Tams' 1964 song 'Hey Girl Don't Bother Me', that became a UK number one song in July 1971. Just as The Beatles and The Rolling Stones took black American music and made it popular again, so did Northern Soul.

While soul music gained its energy from the civil rights movement in the United States of America, it has continued to survive and thrive offline and online. Soul survives because it is ideally suited to the digitized and fragmented nature of contemporary popular music. It is the foundation for samples in hip hop and house, yet it also serves as a reminder that music to dance to can also offer a soundtrack to think about after leaving the dance floor. Northern Soul was an incubator and translator for new generations of British performers to make soul modern and progressive. Lily Allen and Amy Winehouse write and sing a fusion of north and south, Britain and America, dancing and thinking.

Key Questions

1. Which genres fuse into soul?
2. Soul is often described as political pop, or the soundtrack for the civil rights movement. Why?
3. What was Northern Soul?
4. Why are contemporary female singers attracted to soul music?

Further Reading

Hewitt, P. (2000) *The Soul Stylists: Forty Years of Modernism*. Edinburgh: Mainstream.

Stickings, R. (2008) *Searching for Soul*. London: SAF.

Werner, C. (2006) *A Change is Gonna Come: Music, Race & The Soul of America*. Ann Arbor: University of Michigan Press.

Wilson, A. (2007) *Northern Soul: Music, Drugs and Subcultural Identity*. Uffculme: Willan.

Sonic sources

Booker, T. and the MGs (1962) *Green Onions*.

Hayes, I. (1972) *Shaft*.

Redding, O. (1965) *Mr Pitiful*.

Sam & Dave (1967) *Soul Man*.

Visual sources

Five Conversations about Soul (2003) Image Entertainment.

High Tech Soul – The Creation of Techno Music (2005) Pias.

Sam & Dave – The Original Soul Men (2008) Universal.

Strange World of Northern Soul (2003) Wienerworld.

Web sources

Motown, http://www.motown.com/

Soul or Nothing, http://ww.soul-source.co.uk

The Stax Site, http://staxrecords.free.fr/

Wigan Casino, http://www.wigan-casino.co.uk/

Reggae and Ska

Time Magazine voted Bob Marley and the Wailers' *Exodus* the album of the twentieth century ('The best of the century', 1999). This recognition, which is debatable, embodies the influence and debt owed to Jamaica from international popular music. When considering the impact of Cuban salsa and Jamaican reggae, these two small islands have had a social and musical impact beyond their seemingly small geographical size. Both have had to manage colonialism by America and Europe in different forms, and are creating new social, political and economic hybridities between Africa, the Caribbean, the Americas and Europe. Specifically, colonial Jamaica was a place that was dominated by a power struggle where an oppressed black majority was 'managed' by a white plantocracy. The musical history from this period is similarly hybrid with waves of discrimination. In the early twentieth century music drew together a range of social influences through mento, which blended African vocal and rhythmic patterns with mazurka, quadrille and lancer. This musical amalgam in turn created ska and rocksteady.

Ska is under-researched in popular music history. Ska's characteristics include a walking bassline and a piano or guitar-accented rhythm on the offbeat (Panter, 2007: 61). The first ska records were released in Jamaica in 1960 and were particularly important for the mod subculture in the United Kingdom. Like reggae, the look was just as important as the sound. Pork pie hats, white socks, two tone shoes and mohair suits created a cacophony of sonic and visual styles. The 2 Tone label was also important to this history, with The Specials, The Selector and The Beat (in North America, known as The English Beat) being released by this label. While often associated with the West Midlands in the United Kingdom, the Caribbean origins enabled a melodic bass that darted through sparse drumming. Ska was a hybrid music that brought together American rhythm and blues with Caribbean folk and gospel. Complex, intricate and politically aware, too often ska is marginalized as a novelty track.

When ska was slowed in tempo, the influence of the bass increased as did the emphasis on the offbeat. This new formation was renamed rocksteady. When slowed further, rocksteady provided the foundation for reggae. The two counter rhythms framed the melody and lyric. An accelerated double time organ was counterpoised against a half time bass and drum. Reggae is not simply part of a linear development in the rhythm of rocksteady and ska. Michael Veal described this as the match of 'density and sparseness' (2007: 34). The lyrical content also shifted to explore Africa as a homeland, with attention paid to black identity, colonization, racism, violence and class. Ska, rocksteady and what would be known as roots reggae were all in some way exploring history, race and nation. The effect of technology has been incredibly important as raggae was enabled through the internet and web, creating a 'digital Jamaica' (Veal, 2007: 190). This digital Jamaica created dub remixes of roots reggae. Digitization freshened and reconfigured the relationship between Jamaica and the African diaspora. Dub reggae worked with fragments of sound, opening up the pathway for electronica.

The bass guitar has been trivialized in the history of popular music. Too much attention is given to a wailing lead guitar or expansive vocal. Jamaican music shifted this narrative. Rocksteady, ska and reggae prioritized the bass, which – for ska and reggae – was syncopated. Rocksteady was slowed into reggae, but the complex and distinct rhythmic matrix was continued: a double time organ danced over the half time bass and drums. The lyrical content of reggae also changed from rock steady and ska, with a focus on colonialism and poverty. Developing through to the 1970s in the pioneering work of Clancy Eccles, Larry Marshall and Bob Marley and the Wailers, reggae transformed international music. Reggae is played in 4/4 time. It requires a symmetrical rhythm pattern for effective syncopation. Conventional drum kits are used for reggae and the snare drum is tuned to create the effect of a timbale. The drumming emphasis is on the third beat of the bar, usually with a snare or rim shot. Besides transforming the role of the bass guitar reggae is incredibly rare and special in the history of drumming patterns, as the first beat in the bar is empty. This rhythmic style has been credited to both Carlton Barrett of The Wailers and Winston Grennan. It also prioritizes the bass, with the upper frequencies of rhythm removed.

The impetus for reggae has been musical and social freedom. It was and is more than a style or genre of music. It is a movement, politics and mode of expression. The musician Prince Buster confirmed that,

> My music is protest music, music protesting against slavery, class prejudice, racism, inequality, economic discrimination, denial of opportunity and the injustice we were suffering under colonialism in Jamaica … We were taken from Africa where our fore-parents were kings and queens and brought to Jamaica on ships as slaves, where we were stripped of our names, our language, our culture, our God and our religion (Prince Buster in Bradley, 2000).

As Prince Buster confirms, reggae also captures a history of diaspora (Manuel, 2006). During the 1950s many Jamaicans left the island to travel to the United Kingdom and United States. One of the migrants who moved to London as Jamaica gained its independence in 1962 was Chris Blackwell. His Island label provided a hub for recording, distribution and the marketing of reggae. The influence of Island Records, formed in Jamaica in 1959 and relocating to the United Kingdom upon Blackwell's migration, increased the movement of reggae into diverse markets. Bob Marley and The Wailers' 'Catch a Fire' was released on Island Records in 1972. It became the key album for translating reggae into popular music.

Through the innovations and commitment of Island, the impact of reggae on contemporary music was immediate and positive and it moved around the world and created relationships and affiliations with other genres. Andrew Blake confirmed that,

Reggae ... was re-created in Britain partly because there were substantial numbers of British people of West Indian origin prepared to buy concert tickets and albums. However, reggae did not remain a specifically West Indian form; it was used in other music (1996: 182).

Blake's understanding of the 'use' of reggae is significant. For example, when Bob Marley toured Australia in 1979, indigenous musicians were inspired to create bands such as No Fixed Address. Indigenous musicians used the genre to reconfigure their own history through sound. The lyrical content of reggae was as innovative as the rhythmic construction. The lyrical complexity inspired through and by the Rastafari movement led to many subjects, such as poverty, injustice and faith, being tackled in Australian indigenous politics.

Jamaica created, housed and exported a music that influenced the rhythmic pattern of popular music, guitar technique, lyrical content and stage presentation. Lee 'Scratch' Perry and Bunny Lee developed dub while U-Roy and Big Youth – by talking over dub – created new sonic spaces for rap. Rock performers such as Eric Clapton covered material such as Bob Marley's 'I Shot the Sheriff'. Punk bands, particularly The Clash and The Slits, incorporated reggae into their sound. The important history of reggae in the United Kingdom dialogues with the immigration history of the former colonial power (de Koningh and Griffiths, 2003). The MV Empire Windrush arrived at Tilbury Dock on June 23, 1948, delivering 492 young Jamaican men and a few women to the UK. The migrants had left for a better life, as the Jamaican economy was vulnerable because of its reliance on the sugar market. This small group and those who followed were confronted with racism, suspicion and fear, and brought new complexities to British music. Through this migration Jamaican music continued to flow into the United States, enabled by Blackwell and Island Records. The impact was of such a scale that by 1985 the Grammy Awards had introduced the category of 'Best Reggae Album'.

This recognition was a little late. Bob Marley had died in 1981. From 1976, threats had been made on his life. After the most visible performer and activist for reggae had gone, the music industry moved away much of its money and interest. The major audiences for reggae in the United Kingdom had already transferred to hybridized genres that had originally led to reggae's development, particularly a return to ska. Lloyd Bradley commented that 'from 1979 onwards, the Two Tone craze supplied sufficient exoticism into the UK pop mainstream to hasten roots reggae's redundancy' (2000: 488). Arguably, Two Tone had been incredibly important as an incubator of reggae. It also provided a great service to (post)colonial Britain, attempting to create a multicultural future. Mark Bedford, bass player in Madness, remembers 'how "unequal" the end of the Seventies was' (Bedford in Eddington, 2004: 13). While reggae was able to capture and narrate colonial injustice and racial oppression in both postcolonial Jamaica and proto-multicultural Britain, ska was able to provide a soundtrack for an alternative Britain during Margaret Thatcher's TINA (There Is No Alternative) policies. While Madness was a doggedly London-based group The Specials were from Coventry and it was this city, two hundred miles from the capital, that was to become synonymous with ska's revival. Two Tone was utopic, a movement for social justice, racial equity and hope for the future. But it was also about more than music.

It was about sharp suits, asymmetrical haircuts and energized jagged dancing. The black and white checks were more than fashion. Paul Williams realized that this design 'was a statement of intent, and the black and white chequers symbolized the black of ska and white of punk in the mix of the music and the multiracial make up of the band' (2009: 31). This iconography fed into the social agenda. Richard Eddington recognized the priorities of this project: 'music, dancing, social comment, politics' (2004: 20). It was a way for a generation to think about important issues through music, like racism, sexism, urban degeneration and unemployment. It also provided a platform to consider a multicultural Britain of integration and transformation. It used the (mistaken) simplicity of reggae's rhythm and the lyrical rage from the early rock steady to create a progressive politics. Jerry Dammers of The Specials was clear about their goal: 'We've got two cultures in this country now, so the obvious thing is to go back to the roots of reggae and the roots of rock, and to try and form a new dance music' (Dammers in Eddington, 2004: 21). There was optimism with TwoTone. It offered racial fusion, a dancing philosophy that gave a politics to dance.

While The Specials and Madness are the most famous exponents of ska, there were actually three waves of the genre. The first pre-dated reggae, emerging in the late 1960s in Jamaica. This wave was exemplified by Prince Buster and Desmond Dekker. The second wave, from the late 1970s and early 1980s, had moved to the United Kingdom and was dominated by The Specials and Madness. The third wave emerged in America, where this Coventry-based music gained an international audience during the 1990s. No Doubt and the Mighty Mighty Bosstones created an alternative trajectory to post-grunge rock. The rhythm was bright, the vocals clear and the lyrics made up of clashing optimism and despair. Such a trajectory continues through to Lily Allen's music, where journalistic observations from the street weave with a bright and propulsive rhythm.

The greatest moment in the history of Ska, which continued reggae's history of protest, was 'Ghost Town'. It connected the race riots in Brixton and Toxteth with the destruction of British manufacturing industries by Margaret Thatcher's government. It conveyed the frustration of youth, the bleakness of desolate city centres and even the death of live music. From this one song, a history of racism, economic injustice and a unity through music can be mapped. The best of what popular music can be and achieve is sourced from ska and reggae. It is disturbing music. Within reggae's history, the under-represented parts of popular music – bass, dub, race and diaspora – have migrated to the present.

Key Questions

1. Which musical and social influence created reggae?
2. Which transformations to the bass guitar and drumming were instigated through reggae and ska?
3. What is ska? Why was it revived during Thatcher's Britain?
4. Why was *Catch the Fire* an important album for both reggae and popular music?

Further Reading

De Koningh, M. and Griffiths, M. (2003) *Tighten Up: The History of Reggae in the UK*. London: Sanctuary.

Eddington, R. (2004) *Sent from Coventry: The Chequered Past of Two Tone*. London: Independent Music.

Jahn, B. and Weber T. (1998) *Reggae Island: Jamaican Music in the Digital Age*. Cambridge: Da Capo Press.

Veal, M. (2007) *Dub: Soundscapes and Shattered Songs in Jamaican Reggae*. Middletown, NH: Wesleyan University Press.

Sonic sources

Madness (1980) *Baggy Trousers*.

Mighty Mighty Bosstones (1998) *The Impression That I Get*.

The Specials (1981) *Ghost Town*.

The Wailers (1973) *Slave Driver*.

Visual sources

Beats Of The Heart – Roots, Rock and Reggae (2007) Digital Classics.

Bob Marley – Catch A Fire (2006) Edgehill.

Ghost Town, YouTube, http://www.youtube.com/watch?v=RZ2oXzrnti4

No Doubt – Rock Steady (2003) Universal Island.

Web sources

Bob Marley, http://web.bobmarley.com/index.jsp

Reggae News, http://www.reggaenews.co.uk/

Scratch Radio, http://www.azevedo.ca/scratch/default.aspx

The Specials, http://www.thespecials.com/

Salsa

Derived from the Spanish language, salsa describes a spice or sauce. In other words, even at the level of metaphor, salsa is not a genre but a flavour or style given to other modes of music. It is a dynamic category to describe a mode of music but, like reggae, it performs diaspora and displacement. Salsa includes an expansive range of sounds, encompassing music of Cuban origin, but also incorporates rhythms that have moved around the world. Like Jamaica, Cuba is a small island nation whose sounds, rhythms and instrumentations have permeated the rest of popular music's genres, song writing, rhythm structures and performances. By the time slavery was abolished in Cuba in 1873, nearly one million Africans, mainly from Mozambique and the Congo, had been brought by Spanish settlers to the island and sold as slaves. This political and immigration history of exploitation and displacement created a melting pot for the fusion of new rhythms, building a unified identity from diverse cultural and musical practices. Salsa continued to develop through the migration of people from the Spanish-speaking Caribbean to Cuba and the United States.

The impact of Cuba's music history on pop's rhythmic structures is difficult to overestimate. But the term also captures a great diversity of musical styles, often encasing Cuban-derived genres such as the chachacha and mambo along with amalgamations of Puerto Rican folk forms. Currently, salsa describes a genre of popular music that has links with folk, jazz, rap and hip hop, house and disco. Its unifying principle is that salsa brings together a range of root musics and cultures, aligning African, European and Caribbean sounds.

Often forgotten is the diverse instrumentation that came to popular music through Cuba. Cuban songs, at the start of the twentieth century, created a new relationship between guitars and percussion and negotiated a new sonic space in eastern Cuba after the liberation from Spain. Even though there are diverse and innovative rhythmic patterns, the guitar is the core instrument for salsa. Its flexibility, providing both rhythm and melody, creates a rich and propulsive foundation for novel and original arrangements of percussion. What makes the role of the guitar unusual in salsa is that it creates the foundation and space for the distinctive beat and unusual instrumentation of the bongo and clave. Yet the Cuban revolution and resultant embargo by the United States meant that salsa had to operate independently, separated from direct economic and social assistance. The impact of this displacement and disconnection meant that, as Cesar Miguel Rondon has confirmed,

> Salsa was born in the Latino barrios of New York where the youth began to use it as the only music capable of expressing their everyday lives. They lived the ups

and downs of international pop culture, listening to rock music and absorbing the values disseminated by U.S. advertising, while desperately straddling authenticity and assimilation (Rondon, 2008: 18).

There are critiques of this narrative of authenticity through commercialization. Salsa was a misnaming – or remarketing – of Cuban music for a North American audience during an economic embargo. The US economic ban on Cuba after Castro's revolution in 1959 meant that 'salsa' became a way to counter the restrictions in a way that 'Cuban music' could not. It also reified, simplified and marketed a 'Latin' market for a 'non Latin' audience.

The reason why salsa has gained currency as a label is that it is a form of dance music, meaning that the Spanish-language lyrics are de-emphasized for an English-speaking audience. As music to accompany dancing, salsa lyrics are often underplayed in comparison to rhythm. A 4/4 time signature is common. The salsa instruments include cencerro (cowbells), congas, bongos, tamboras, maracas, guiro, quijango, batas, electric or double basses and piano. What makes the Latin instruments unusual is that they are – often concurrently – rhythmic, melodic and harmonic. The dense percussion creates the distinctive clave, the 1–2/1–2–3/1–2/1–2–3 rhythmic pattern. While all scholars must be wary of simplifying a complex musical history, some key characteristics of salsa have emerged. A tambora often shadows a melody in a way that harmonizes with vocals. Rhythm is supplied by bongos, congas and timbales.

Several salsa-based or influenced artists have moved these rhythms into popular music. These include Gloria Estefan, Jennifer Lopez, Marc Anthony and Rey Ruiz. These artists have increased the hybridity and movement by diversifying the instrumentation, particularly the percussion, while also invigorating older forms of dance music. Importantly, and propelled by the branding of salsa, singing in Spanish has also increased in popular music, created through an awareness of the international Latino audience, and the widening popular cultural visibility and acceptability of diverse voices and rhythms through world music. The distinctive salsa rhythms have been a sonic translator to enable new languages to emerge in the English-dominated popular music industry.

There are diverse interpretations of salsa rhythm through dance. Cuban and Colombian dancers start on the first beat. New York Latin and Puerto Rican dancers commence movement on the second beat. A range of salsa dances and rhythms – including the rumba, mambo and cha-cha-cha – has transferred from the clubs and the streets and into the formal ballroom dancing programme. While much of rock and most post-disco dancing involved unstructured and individualistic modes of movement, Salsa, propelled by heavy percussion, enables not only passionate movement, but also coordinated movement between partners (Lindop, 2008: 14). The mambo, with its forward and backward movements, is the simplest of steps, becoming increasingly complicated in the guapea, where the partners step back and forward with their palms pressing together.

The complex dialogue between 'Latin' and 'Salsa' – music and dancing – is productive, but also requires critical commentary. The key distinction is that salsa refers to a rhythm, but Latin describes an identity. The variants and debates about the currency and relevance of these simple categories must not be underestimated. The blended rhythm that forms salsa, called 'la clave', manifests itself differently in changing environments. Patria Roman-Velazquez explained that, 'salsa has been and is given different meanings through different time-space movements. Salsa's acceptance around the world is in part related to media exposure and distribution, and as this has taken place, salsa has been incorporated into international music networks, whilst creating (as in the case of London) a local salsa scene' (1999: 68). Unlike many of the genres and communities in this book, there is a tight grasp between the music form and the dancing style in salsa. While folk can be listened to and enjoyed, salsa remains a bodily expression through rhythm. How it is played and danced, contributes to the foundation of diverse music styles, genres and forms. The political questions raised by hybridity, migration and diasporic dialogues of salsa require further attention.

Key Questions

1. From where is salsa derived?
2. How did salsa travel around the world?
3. What are the characteristics of salsa? Is it a genre?
4. Which simplifications and problems emerge with our use of the term 'salsa'?

Further Reading

Leymarie, I. (2003) *Cuban Fire: The Story of Salsa and Latin Jazz*. London: Continuum.

Morales, E. (2003) *The Latin Beat*. Cambridge: Da Capo.

Roman-Velazquex, P. (1999) *The Making of Latin London: Salsa Music, Place and Identity*. Aldershot: Ashgate.

Waxer, L. (2002) *The City of Musical Memory: Salsa, Record Grooves, and Popular Culture in Cali*. Middletown, NH: Wesleyan University Press.

Sonic sources

Barretto, R. and Cruz, C. (1990) *Ritmo en el Corazon*.

Estefan, G. (2001) *Y-Tu-Conga*.

Manuelle, V. (2004) *La vida es un carnaval*.

Puente, T. (1963) *Oye como va*.

Visual sources

Beats of the Heart (2006) Digital Classics.

From Mambo to Hip Hop (2006) Wienerworld.

Lambada (1990) MGM.

Salsa: The Motion Picture (1988) MGM.

Web sources

Just Salsa Magazine, http://www.justsalsa.com/

Mucho Swing, http://www.muchoswing.com/

Salsa Community, http://www.salsacommunity.com/

Salsa Music, http://www.carnaval.com/music/salsa.htm

Metal

The 1980s featured two 'immoral' – or dangerous – musics: heavy metal and rap. Both were marketed to young men. The Parents' Music Resource Centre responded to the 'obscenity' of the language, extreme fashion, big hair and supposed sexism of these genres. In the case of metal it had it origins in the late 1960s and early 1970s, emerging from the fragmentation of blues-infused rock music. While some performers moved to country or psychedelic rock, reducing the volume and tempo, other bands lifted the amplification and distortion, reconfigured the relationship between guitars and drums and increased the speed and length of guitar solos. The criticisms directed at metal often ignore these roots in the blues. To create a folk (or more accurately metal) devil or moral panic, it is necessary to forget history and ignore context. The dialogue between blues-based rock and psychedelic rock created the foundation for much heavy metal. The popularity of the distorted guitar, exemplified through both The Kinks 'You Really Got Me', and Steppenwolf's 'Born to be Wild' created opportunities for new forms of amplified music. Comparisons can be drawn between the first two Cream albums *Fresh Cream* (1966) and *Disraeli Gears* (1967) and heavy metal, particularly because of the innovative fusions created by Eric Clapton's guitar, Jack Bruce's bass and the double bass drums of Ginger Baker. Similarly, Jimi Hendrix offered a model for the virtuoso guitar technique that was to follow.

The band configuration of metal continues the conventional rock formation, with a drummer, bass guitarist, rhythm guitarist, lead guitarist and singer. The overwhelming characteristic of metal is the extreme amplification of electric guitars. Distortion pedals create the 'heavy' sound. Faster, harder and louder than most rock music, other instruments occupy a secondary place to the guitar. Some bands, most notably Judas Priest and Iron Maiden, increased the number of guitarists to lift the sound and scale of the riff. The lead guitarist is the key to the genre, with intricate and complex solos a characteristic of most songs. Innovative sounds emerged, particularly from Black Sabbath guitarist Tony Iommi. A left-handed guitarist, an industrial accident injured the fingers of his right hand. To compensate, he deployed power chords and simplified his fingering of the fretboard. The consequence of his innovations was a new sound. This 'guitar hero' role downplayed the place of the singer who, in conventional rock music, was 'the frontman'. Similarly, the bass player in metal is integral to the heaviness of the sound. Nu metal and death metal bassists often use the five or six string models to add depth. The kits deployed in metal drumming are also much larger, with double bass drums and an increased number of cymbals and tom toms lifting the volume of sound. The lyrical subjects of metal are diverse, but do address the topics of sex, violence, love, lust and – ever so occasionally – Satanism. In the history of metal, Birmingham – often acclaimed as England's second city – has played a crucial role. It is a working class area dominated by (a cyclically declining) car industry. Black Sabbath was particularly important in establishing a role for music in the city. This trajectory was continued beyond the 1970s. In Birmingham, there was an indifference to punk, with the advent of Napalm Death, Extreme Noise and Heresy.

After the punk intervention in popular music in the mid to late 1970s, blues started to be less relevant to metal structures, with guitar thrash, speed and fretboard movements from the lead guitarist increasing in their complexity. This power, energy and endurance of heavy metal can be heard on AC/DC's albums. Formed in Australia in 1973, Angus Young – in his school uniform – became the archetypal guitar hero. Songs such as 'High Voltage', 'TNT' and 'Back in Black' show how metal can enter popular culture and maintain a large audience. While rarely acknowledged because metal is an unpopular music amongst journalists and academics as much as amongst morally conservative parental organizations, AC/DC has the second highest selling back catalogue of all time, second only to The Beatles' (Brown, 2009). 'Back in Black' has sold over 45 million copies ('News Archive', 2007).

Heavy metal found its archetypes in Led Zeppelin, Deep Purple and Black Sabbath. Remarkably, Black Sabbath would also develop and inspire the other subgenres of death metal and black metal. However, Led Zeppelin was the key sonic translator, moving heavy metal into popular culture through the album *Led Zeppelin II* and the single 'Whole Lotta Love'. After punk attacked extravagant and overproduced rock – of which metal was an obvious example – a 'New Wave' of heavy metal emerged, that included Iron Maiden, Motorhead and Def Leppard. The emphasis was on speed rather than the blues. Eddie Van Halen's guitar work on 'Eruption' from his self-titled album captured this combination of volume, speed and virtuosity. Through the exposure of metal bands on MTV and as videos from Def Leppard and Quiet Riot gained wider circulation, heavy metal had become a major component of American popular music by the mid to late 1980s. Guns 'n' Roses and Bon Jovi were able to align hard rock and glam metal to increase the proportion of women in the audience.

Metal continues to change, move and dialogue with this earlier history, to develop new audiences. From the breakthrough of heavy metal during the 1980s, particularly assisted by the rise of music video, the genre broke into subgenres, influenced by the popular success of Slayer and Metallica. Between 1988 and 1993, new forms of music and performance were developed with the splintering of thrash, heavy metal, speed metal, industrial and punk. Death metal, black metal, doom metal and grindcore in particular gained an independent following.

The history of metal is highly international, more than many of the genres described in this section, and covers the United Kingdom, the United States, Brazil, Poland, Sweden and Japan. European thrash in particular – from Kreator, Destruction and Celtic Frost – was built on the power chords from Black Sabbath to create a basic, deep and clean sound. Hybrids developed throughout the 1990s, with nu metal gathering its influences from hip hop. Bands such as Napalm Death, Death, Morbid Angel, Deicide, Cannibal Corpse, Carcass and Entombed provided the foundations for emotional punk or emo, which combined goth, metal and punk. Metallica became associated with this new genre, often being termed thrash metal. Nine Inch Nails and Marilyn Manson extended the industrial sounds of Throbbing Gristle by using the spoken and singing voice in new ways. Ironically – or perhaps not – both metal and rap expanded and created new relationships and links through bands like Korn and Limp Bizkit.

Heavy metal, as the founding sound for a range of genres, was and is excessive. It is the loudest, the most heteronormatively masculine but – conversely – the most performative. Alice Cooper, Marilyn Manson and Ozzy Osbourne cut across categories of acceptable masculine behaviour. Glam metal, performed by groups like the Motley Crew, captured the complex combination of new masculinity, makeup and shaggy and occasionally permed hair. Bodies – men's bodies – matter to metal communities. Sean Kelly argued that Iron Maiden 'was especially successful at reproducing the structure of the body as multiple sites of resistance, as a community in resistance' (2006: 160). Fan behaviour includes head-banging, slam dancing and air guitar, creating deviance, difference, defiance and a separation from conventional male behaviour.

This commitment of the body in and through music adds to the intensity of metal fandom. Fans are sometimes referred to as headbangers, which captures the violent movement of the head in time with the core metal guitar riff. While there is little step-based dancing to metal, physical gestures are common, including the headbang, raised arms with finger gestures including the devil horns, and air guitar. The behaviours in response to metal are rarely defined as 'dancing' because of its feminine connotations. Different genres encourage and frame distinct behaviours and physical commitments to rhythm, melody and lyric.

Significantly, the more that critics attacked metal bands, the more loyal and enthusiastic was the fan response. As an example, the *New York Times* popular music critic John Rockwell termed heavy metal as a 'brutally aggressive music played mostly for minds clouded by drugs' (1979). Such a statement misunderstands how music fandom offers new spaces for expression and the development of alternatives to conventional masculinity. The excessiveness of metal, welcoming an extreme, almost camp masculinity, has also provided the fodder for humour. *This is Spinal Tap* and *Anvil* both feature the journey of a heavy metal band, one fictional and the other less so.

Ironically, in common with electronica, metal as a genre is splintered and fragmented. The extreme metal scene emerged from a rejection of heavy metal. Bands like Venom tempered the melody from metal and spat loud, fast and staccato vocals. The separation of Thrash and Death Metal was an international movement from Norway to Brazil, with a focus on aggression, speed and screaming. Nu metal, best associated with Limp Bizkit and a range of sub bizkits, also merged goth and industrial music into metal. Linkin Park brought Eminem's vocal innovations into Metal. Formed in Southern California in 1998, they created relationships between rap and rock. Their reflexivity in terms of approach and process resulted in the 2000 album *Hybrid Theory*. While there are critiques of the singing ability of metal performers, the remarkable voice of Chester Bennington, front man and vocalist of Linkin Park, has created new modes of melodies and harmonies from metal.

Through all the success of the multiple forms of metal amongst its loyal audiences, the sound and its songs have been politicized beyond the genre and popular music. Violent imagery in lyrics has created moral panic about youth and crime. Yet such moral panics simplify the relationship between song and audience, music and its effects. The only way to demonize musics like metal is not only to decontextualize particular lyrics from the song that houses it, but also to avoid understanding the changes to masculinity, youth, work and family that create an audience for loud, aggressive and angry music. Bruce Johnson and Martin Cloonan stated that, 'musical violence is about the attempted exercise of power over someone else and the soundscape' (2008: 146). They may be right, but the humour and cartoon anger of the genre must not be ignored. Metal remains an important genre that can freshen and transform older styles of music. Faith No More produced covers of the Commodores' 'Easy' and the Bee Gees' 'I Started a Joke'. The mock seriousness and humour of metal, from comic Satanism to the pseudo heroism from surviving lost love, confirm the continuation of a genre that remains popular with fans and unpopular with critics.

Key Questions

1. What is heavy metal? How is it different from nu metal?
2. How do fans express their allegiance to metal?
3. What are the differences between metal and rock music?
4. Why has metal been attacked by moral conservatives? Are such attacks justified?

Further Reading

Arnett, J. (1996) *Metalheads: Heavy Metal Music and Adolescent Alienation*. Boulder, CO: Westview Press.

Christe, I. (2003) *Sound of the Beast: The Complete Headbanging History of Heavy Metal*. New York: HarperCollins.

Mudrian, A. (2004) *Choosing Death: The Improbable History of Death Metal And Grindcore*. Los Angeles, CA: Feral House.

Walser, R. (1993) *Running with the Devil: Power, Gender, and Madness in Heavy Metal Music*. Middletown, CT: Wesleyan University Press.

Sonic sources

AC/DC (1980) *Back in Black*.

Black Sabbath (1976) *We Sold Our Soul For Rock'n' Roll*.

Linkin Park (2003) *Numb*.

Metallica (1991) *Enter Sandman*.

Visual sources

Anvil (2008) Metal On Metal.

Get Thrashed – The Story of Thrash Metal (2008) Wienerworld.

Metal: A Headbanger's Journey (2006) Warner.

This is Spinal Tap (1984) Spinal Tap Productions.

Web sources

Anvil, http://www.anvilthemovie.com/

Classic Thrash, http://www.classicthrash.com/

Grindcore, http://www.grindcore.org/

Metal Hammer, http://www.metalhammer.co.uk/

Punk and Indie

Both punk and indie were and are guitar-fuelled sounds. Both are flushed with ideologies of authenticity and creativity, building a tight relationship between fans and performers. Both respond to 'commercial' dance music, with punk agitating against disco and indie problematizing post-house derivatives. The key attribute amongst musicians claiming this label was not their technical or musical skill, but a do-it-yourself attitude. As with early rock, punk and indie encouraged young people to play music rather than simply listen to it. The difficulty with this was that both gained so much success with audiences that they became part of the mainstream music that they were resisting. The radicalism and resistance were tamed and profitably marketed. Both genres have remained well represented in rock journalism and popular music scholarship. They perform the edgy, masculine resistance favoured in studies of youth and subculture. Often these genres are discussed in isolation, devoid of musical context. For example, the Sex Pistols emerged in the same year that the Eagles' 'Hotel California' was released to wide popular acclaim. It is important to ensure that critical credibility does not block an understanding of other popular musics that were successful at the time. It is easy to over-write and over-emphasize the resistance of punk and indie. According to Vivienne Westwood, 'punk is as comfortable as an old armchair these days' (Dickinson, 1997: 1). To describe punk as 'comfortable' is accurate but this masks the shock and outrage created in the first stage of its challenge. The use of language, hair and clothing created a shock of newness and challenged the crisp boundaries between music and noise.

Punk – in its clearest form – lasted for only eighteen months. It bounced between New York and London. It was a short sharp jolt within the music industry and transformed many of the relationships between genres and audiences in subsequent decades. Almost immediately derivatives such as Oi! and hardcore emerged. Arching from this moment, the word punk is still deployed as a descriptor of music. In the twenty-first century, bands such as Green Day summon the term as a statement of an attitude, musical style and a way of engaging an audience.

Many characteristics of punk do not involve music. A DIY ethic, along with anti-establishment values, provided a regeneration of a new youth culture as the baby boomers aged. The songs were fast, short and hard. Few instruments were used, often with simple arrangements. Lyrics were pivotal to punk. The words expressed rage at 'the system', with often nihilistic intent. In the late 1970s, punk was modern and modernizing, shredding, attacking and questioning earlier styles and modes of music. By 1976 in the United Kingdom, punk was being described as 'Year Zero' (Reynolds, 2005: 4). In December of that year, the British fanzine *Sideburns* showed three chord charts with the famous slogan: 'This is a chord, this is another, this is a third. Now form a band' (Savage, 1991: 280). Reducing popular music to basic chords confirmed that musicianship was not an aim for punk. The band – most often composed of an electric guitar, bass, drums and vocals – was about expression not musical excellence. Steve Jones stated that the Sex Pistols were bigger than music. Their goal was 'chaos' (Savage, 1991: 151).

The influence of the Sex Pistols is difficult to measure. Perhaps the best evidence for this statement is found on June 4, 1976, when they played at Manchester's Lesser Free Trade Hall. There were 40 people in the audience, many of whom would go on to form bands such as the Buzzcocks, Joy Division, The Fall and The Smiths. These bands were to be termed 'new wave' or 'indie'. The combination of floppy hair, youthful angst and evocative guitar riffs exemplified a body of work for bands such as The Smiths and Echo and the Bunnymen. Because of the DIY ethos, there was little separation between performers and fans. The key tactic was to trigger audience participation. This was encouraged through confronting and provoking the audience, as in the case of the Sex Pistols and the Dammed. Riotous stage invasions, spitting and shouting were part of the punk spectacle. While punk in the late 1970s remained an underground formation in the United States and Australia, for a brief moment it became the core of popular music and popular culture in the United Kingdom. The movement into 'new wave' in the early 1980s, a term used by bands as varied as The Police, The Stranglers, Human League, Talking Heads, Devo and Blondie, widened the audience. At the same time new wave also encompassed two tone and ska, along with the burgeoning new romantic movement. Considering the style of music and the fans, new wave is not an accurate or useful description to align such diverse individuals and groups as Elvis Costello, Duran Duran, The Jam and Depeche Mode. Yet with MTV and the success of music video, 'new wave' became a statement of innovation and changed the relationship between media, sound and vision.

There are as many origins as there are endpoints for punk. One root for both punk and indie can be found in the US-based garage band scene of the mid 1960s. Although bands like The Kingsmen, The Standells and The Swingin' Medallions lacked musical ability, the enthusiasm and energy within such songs as 'Louie Louie' created new relationships between performers and the audiences. The Stooges, with lead singer Iggy Pop, released a self-titled album in 1969 that was produced by John Cale, a former member of The Velvet Underground. The gruff and hostile vocal and minimal instrumentation offered a prescient introduction to the future of punk. Similarly, the New York Dolls released wild sounds and confrontational stage performances in the early 1970s. By 1974, the club CBGB had become a hub for confronting and challenging music, featuring Television, The Ramones and Blondie. The New York punk scene of the mid 1970s, building on the seminal influence of The Velvet Underground, Patti Smith, Talking Heads and Richard Hell and the Voidoids, generated a raw sound created through both the voice and guitar technique. Progressive rock was linked with musicianship and the 'rock god' guitar heroes, playing large venues with large amplification systems. New York – and later London and Manchester – punk rejected this mode and manner of playing music.

The Sex Pistols presented a loud and shocking music that demanded attention and sprang from a crumbling urban environment. The shock iconography provided the first deep critique of 'the Sixties' as an ideology and era. In the UK, punk erupted during the year that the first baby boomers turned thirty. The shocking objects included swastikas, syringes and suspenders. Women occupied a pivotal role in punk, attacking the hyper-masculinity of much rock. Siouxsie Sioux, The Slits and Poly Styrene from X-Ray Spex annexed the excessive masculinity of rock and reappropriated it for a confrontational femininity that was sexually demanding and judgemental of men's behaviour. The Slits particularly challenged the positioning of women on a stage, opposing the demure and silent archetypes through such songs as 'Typical Girls'.

Punk was different. It challenged mainstream culture. Jon Savage, the great music historian and journalist of punk, described the impact of its trajectory.

> Punk was beaten, but it had also won. If it had been the project of the Sex Pistols to destroy the music industry, then they had failed; but as they gave it new life, they allowed a myriad of new forms to become possible … History is made by those who say 'No' and Punk's utopian heresies remain its gift to the world (1991: 541).

Put another way, rock was a realist formation. Punk was modernist, opening up a new popular cultural economy based on subsistence rather than profit and an intent to shock rather than a desire to conform. While the audience for punk could be described as marginal or marginalized, the intensity of the public response marked it as different and perhaps dangerous. This was also determined by playing smaller venues, particularly pubs. A host of independent labels was spawned through punk including Rough Trade, Stiff and Factory. A series of genres were also formed including Oi!, new wave, post-punk, alternative rock and emo. By the early 1990s grunge had appeared as a revival of punk, with profitable and popular records released by Nirvana, Pearl Jam and Bad Religion. While not long lasting, Blink-182, Simple Plan and Good Charlotte – along with the success of Green Day's 'American Idiot' – continued punk's history in popular music.

The postpunk pop world was antagonistic towards rock music, with the dance floor rather than the safety pin being the symbol of alternative identities. The site of resistance became the subversive potential of sexuality. A denial of technological change became another method. A space for guitar-based music remained, through the keyboard and sample-fuelled dance floor domination. Matthew Bannister realized that 'indie's concentration on good old-fashioned electric guitars can be read as a kind of rock classicism, a return to tradition' (2006: 120). Continuing the intimacy of pub-based music, the DIY attitude of punk and the lyrical complexity of new wave, Indie music emerged. Indie was linked with 'alternative' music and slotted into the gap created by punk's short-lived intervention in popular music. As a plug in and play guitar-based music, it also rejected certain forms of technology, such as elaborate light shows and staging, and an (over) reliance on effects pedals. The ironically (considering the history of folk) 'natural' sound of an electric guitar meant that onstage equipment was minimal. It was lo-fi music during a period of digitization and technological change. Indie gained from this technological transformation, particularly with the availability of high quality home recording equipment. Home recording became part of the DIY aesthetic.

Indie – like punk – was a guitar-based sound, requiring only a minimal stage set-up and a more direct relationship between performers and consumers. Indie was not a genre of musical skill. It was a home for alternative music and tapped into the long-term ideologies for alternative music. Home recording equipment and mixing software allowed 'indie' music to gain an audience. Through YouTube and MySpace, lo-fi sounds have reached audiences using high tech wireless platforms. Like punk though, indie was quickly incorporated into the core of mainstream popular music.

The inability to cleanly define indie is because it is not, as such, a style of music or genre. It expresses a desire to operate outside of authority and high production values, reducing overdubbing in particular. It was a desire – after nearly two decades of the dominance of dance culture and the club – to return to the predominance of the live gig and the guitar. While punk suffered from challenges in distributing its music through conventional record companies and in gaining air time, indie was bolstered by the arrival of downloadable files and broadband. High tech distribution enabled low tech music.

With the success of indie bands in the last fifteen years, the artificial barrier between 'the mainstream' and 'the independent' evaporated. Bands like the Arctic Monkeys, Snow Patrol and Keane have entered popular culture, as have the vanguards of 'difficult' music – Radiohead. It is important to remember that resistance, difference and defiance have been part of popular music since Elvis Presley swung his hips and the cameramen on Ed Sullivan were prevented from panning down to show them. The key with both punk and indie was the ease and speed of transferability into commercialized and mainstream genres. The pretensions of difference, authenticity and radicalism were – and remain – short-lived and naive. The easiest example of this argument follows the story of the Arctic Monkeys on MySpace. Their song 'I Bet You Look Good on the Dance Floor' was ripe for a cover version. Predictably, high handbag house producer Belle Lawrence used the lyrical mentions of '1984', 'Electropop' and dancing like a robot as the hook into a remix. Even from the analogue bunker of indie there had come digitally remixed humour, pleasure and dancing.

Key Questions

1. What is the difference between 'mainstream' and 'indie' music? Are the edges between these categories patrolled? If so, by whom?
2. How do we – as scholars of popular music – know when 'alternative music' becomes 'mainstream'?
3. Why was punk so important to music writers, journalists and academics of popular music?
4. How 'low tech' is indie?

Further Reading

Bannister, M. (2006) *White Boys, White Noise: Masculinities and 1980s Indie Guitar Rock*. Aldershot: Ashgate.

Fonarow, W. (2006) *Empire of Dirt: The Aesthetics and Rituals of British Indie Music*. Middletown, CT: Wesleyan University Press.

Myers, B. (2005) *"Green Day": American Idiots and the New Punk Explosion*. London: Independent Music.

Thompson, D. (2009) *London's Burning: True Adventures on the Front Lines of Punk, 1976–1977*. Chicago, IL: Chicago Review.

Sonic sources

Arctic Monkeys (2005) *I Bet You Look Good on the Dance Floor*.

Radiohead (2008) *Nude*.

Sex Pistols (1977) *God Save the Queen*.

The Clash (1979) *London Calling*.

Visual sources

New York Doll (2005) First Independent Pictures.

The Great Rock and Roll Swindle (1980) Boyd's Company.

Punk Attitude (2005) Freemantle Media.

411 On The Independent Music Movement (2007) Music 4 Da Soul Records.

Web sources

Association of Independent Music, http://www.musicindie.com/

Indie Music, http://www.indie-music.com/

Indie Music for Life, http://www.indiemusicforlife.org/

Punk 77, http://www.punk77.co.uk/

Hip Hop

Hip hop is more than a musical genre. It enfolds a range of behaviours, attitudes and ideologies, including rapping, DJing, break dancing and graffiti. It is more than a style. As Nelson George observed, it 'is a product of post-civil rights era America' (1998: viii). It is a way to hear and see a different history of disempowerment and resistance. Russell Potter offered an important corrective for all writers, listeners and thinkers about this genre/style/social formation. He asked, 'can hip-hop be defined? Or is definition a kind of death, a refusal of the change that any evolving artform must embrace?' (1995: 25). The negation – the definitive 'no' – of hip hop, actualized through fashion, language and sound, is powerful and a foundational sound and stylistic shape for popular music more generally. Hip hop is as Russell Potter described it: a spectacular vernacular (1995). There are many hip hops and many raps in many countries. The transrap website reports on hip hop communities in 167 nations (Transrap, 2010). Most hip hop sold in France is in the French language (Beau, 2010).

Hip hop emerged in the 1970s. A speaking voice is overlaid on music created, by mixing records on two turntables. It draws influences from the toasting and sound systems in the Caribbean, United Kingdom and the United States in the 1960s and 1970s. Such a simple origin neither explains nor understands how hip hop resonates and engages with so many different audiences. Technology is important to this history. In the 1970s, a mixer was released that allowed the DJ to move sound from one turntable to another. While disco was propelled by this innovation it also had a profound impact on hip hop. Forged in the matrix between African American, Caribbean American and Latin American history, these narratives of difference and defiance came together in New York. While there are many influential cities, origins and performers, the most commonly cited narratives of hip hop mention Clive Campbell, a Jamaican-born DJ known as Kool Herc, who brought reggae and dancehall culture to New York. He also isolated the breaks – the rhythmic section – and developed break-beat deejaying. Grandmaster Flash and Afrika Bambaataa honed this technique. All three created rhythm by touching and moving records on turntables. Other techniques included beatboxing using the human voice as a percussion instrument. Rapping is a mode of expression that combines song, poetry and speech. The verbal dexterity and cleverness of rap, through a putdown or ridicule, blurs the relationship between art, pop, entertainment and business. It builds new relationships between technology and performance. Electronic music started to frame and influence hip hop culture when Africa Bambaataa and the Soulsonic Force released *Planet Rock* in 1983. Bambaataa used a drum machine and synthesizer to create a new hybrid music and sound system.

Hip hop is a diverse and changing genre. It deserves both an understanding of its history and a recognition of its dynamism and volatility. It captures, at its most trivial, a way of dressing and, at its most serious, a model of thinking about the past and present. It includes quotations, versions, samples and remixes that circulate and recirculate past sounds through recycling, repackaging and remixing. Hip hop acknowledges its history and past through old skool raps and samples. It offers provocative reclamations, revisions and reconsiderations of both Americanism and blackness. Greg Tate realized that 'perhaps the supreme irony of black American existence is how broadly black people debate the question of cultural identity among themselves while getting branded as a cultural monolith by those who would deny us the complexity and complexion of a community, let alone a nation' (1992: 153). Even Eminem reflected on his own whiteness and the reasons for his success in the lyrics of 'White America'. The development of 'conscious rap' – which often operates against 'gangster rap' – is an important moment in this history. Common, Mos Def, Talib Kweli and Lupe Fiasco probed the violence and misogyny of rap *through rap*. Another area of critique and commentary has been both the portrayal of women in rap and their place in the industry. Powerful female performers, such as Missy Elliott, Lil Kim, Queen Latifah and Salt-N-Pepa, continue to create and promote an affirmative, alternative femininity.

Besides gender and violence, race matters when thinking about hip hop. Basu confirmed that 'visual and aural representations of hip hop play a prominent role in shaping the public's imagination and perceptions of black youth. The much celebrated hype of rap moguls and artists livin' large in baronial splendor is deeply engrained in the fabric of hip hop's ghetto fabulous mythology' (2006: 27). The style, as much as the substance, has triggered a moral panic. While much attention and fear has been placed on homophobic or misogynistic lyrics, this judgement is not only a generalization but also an ignorance of how hip hop generally – and rap in particular – has transformed in the last decade. The diversity of topics, subjects and ideas can be represented through Kanye West's range of interests, which includes religion ('Jesus Walks'), the diamond trade in Sierra Leone ('Blood Diamonds') and resurrection ('Through the Wire'). While particular debates surround Tupac Shakur (2Pac), Eminem and the N.W.A., there is a mis-reading of the diversity of their subjects of interest. While Tupac recorded songs of violence such as 'Hit 'Em Up', he also spoke of his 'Dear Mama'. While there is misogyny carried through the lyric of 'How Do U Want It', there is also an affirmation of feminist empowerment in 'Keep Your Head Up'.

Earlier histories, languages and samples are brought forward in contemporary music, building into a 'diasporic dialogue' (Lipsitz, 1994: 41). While it is difficult to ascertain how and why rap has been singled out for criticism and commentary, part of the answer can be found in the question of race. While hip hop is connoted – often inaccurately – as the 'voice' and 'resistance' of black people, the majority of the audience who buy and download the tracks are white, young men. The complex negotiation between 'black texts' and 'white audiences' is a font for some of the controversy. Knife crime, gun crime, racism, sexism and homophobia existed before hip hop. They will also exist after hip hop. It is easier to blame music for social problems than to understand the complexity of the environments that created those problems.

While hip hop is part of mainstream music it also offers adversarial and biting attacks on conformity and normality. Rapping emphasizes flow and rupture, with words moving in and out of the rhythm. It is too easy – and inaccurate – to insert hip hop into the geographical confines of the United States of America. Jeffrey Decker realized that 'members of the hip hop nation form an "imagined community" that is based less on its realization through state formation than on a collective challenge to the consensus logic of U.S. nationalism' (1994: 100). This challenge is international in its construction. It survived through beat boxing on the streets of Perth in Western Australia whenever Downsyde played. It was summoned through Che-Fu's influential career in Aotearoa/ New Zealand, commencing as the frontman of Supergroove and continuing with the albums *2Bpacific* and *Navigator* that bounced around Dominion Road in Auckland.

If rock music is a colonial formation, then hip hop provides a decolonizing imperative. Although rap is over thirty years old and embedded into a range of popular musics, it maintains a complex function in academic writing. Tricia Rose recognized the disconnection between intellectual value, social value and rap.

> The department head rose from his seat and announced casually, 'Well, you must be writing on rap's social impact and political lyrics, because there's nothing to the music'. My surprised expression and verbal hesitation gave him time to explain his position. He explained to me that although the music was quite simple and repetitive, the stories told in the lyrics had social value. He pointed out rap's role as a social steam valve, a means for the expression of social anger. 'But,' he concluded, referring to the music, 'they ride down the street at 2:00am. with it blasting from car speakers, and (they) wake up my wife and kids. What's the point in that?' (1994: 62).

The point is clear when thinking about the politics of sound and space. Hip hop culture breaks through the boundaries between music and fashion, dancing and beat creation, speaking and singing. While based on African American experience, it has spread through Europe, Asia, the Pacific and the Middle East. The success of white rappers, from the Beastie Boys to Vanilla Ice and Eminem, created a culture of crossovers, but questions remain about cultural property and appropriation. From this heavily politicized debate about authenticity and credibility, hip hop and rap often had difficulty finding a space beyond the binarized thinking of black and white, gay and straight, bitches and bootie. Being both global and local, it has been critiqued because of its attention to consumption and affluence. It has even been blamed for the renewed popularity of fur in fashion (Day, 2009). Rap reconfigures a national history, with a focus on racial oppression. There is also a focus on independence, difference and defiance.

'Blackness' offers hybrid possibilities through language, sound and visuality. The historical experiences of colonization, penal settlements, slavery, settlement and assimilationist immigration policies created multiple and plural experiences of living and the understanding of history and politics. Blackness is not a product of nationalism. It is diasporic. Significantly, the hierarchies of race and culture are masked or questioned through affirmations of cultural hybridity. In that hybridity, hip hop is a fountain of renewal and challenge for all other musical genres. It remains a dynamic force in popular music.

Key Questions

1. What are the components of hip hop?
2. Is rap black?
3. Is rap American?
4. How would you argue against the misogyny and sexism of hip hop?

Further Reading

Basu, D. (2006) *The Vinyl Ain't Final: Hip Hop and the Globalisation of Black Popular Culture*. London: Pluto.

Chang, J. (2007) *Can't Stop Won't Stop: A History of the Hip-hop Generation*. London: Ebury.

George, N. (1998) *Hip Hop America*. Harmondsworth: Penguin.

Potter, R. (1995) *Spectacular Vernaculars: Hip-Hop and the Politics of Postmodernism*. New York: State University of New York Press.

Sonic sources

Eminem (2002) *Lose Yourself.*

Grandmaster Flash & The Furious Five (1981) *The Adventures of Grandmaster Flash on the Wheels of Steel.*

Missy Elliot (2001) *Get Ur Freak On.*

The Sugar Hill Gang (1979) *Rapper's Delight.*

Visual sources

Biggie And Tupac (2002) Optimum.

Hip Hop Story – Tha Movie (2002) Urban Entertainment.

Joel Turner, *YouTube*, http://www.youtube.com/watch?v=Ta-ATEOOo8M.

Wild Style – 25th Anniversary Special Edition (2007) Metrodome.

Web sources

Hip hop.com, http://www.hiphop.com/

Human Beatbox.com, http://www.humanbeatbox.com/

Muslim Hip Hop, http://www.muslimhiphop.com/

UGHH, http://www.undergroundhiphop.com/

Disco

Disco is a musical and sociological description of both a genre and venue. It also conveys a way of moving a body to rhythm. It is a maligned musical formation, with its origins in African American, Latino and gay dance cultures. Disco has moved and changed through a diversity of dance-oriented styles, including Hi NRG, house, techno, rave and jungle. It is no coincidence that Lady Gaga references the disco ball in her shows, videos and costumes. The sounds of disco live in present music through sampling. What makes disco so important to the dance and electronic music styles that followed is that it was developed on and for a dance floor (Butler, 2006: 37). Recording studios could only attempt to replicate the form, feeling and energy of the rhythms, vocals and production that had been designed for the nightclub environment.

Many genres discussed in *Popular Music: Topics, Trends and Trajectories* claim an American origin and pathway to popularity. Disco, with its roots in Philadelphia and New York soul, offers a distinctive trajectory through American musical history. Hearing songs such as Diana Ross and the Supremes' 'Love Child', Sly and the Family Stone's 'Dance to the Music' and Jerry Butler's 'Only the Strong Survive', the tether to disco can be heard, carrying forward sounds from the 1960s into the sexually experimental and permissive dance cultures of the 1970s. Using soul, salsa and funk, disco deployed and developed new technologies to provide the soundtrack for dancing. As Ulf Poschardt confirmed, 'disco is a forum for liberated bodies' (1998: 114). Significantly, the end of disco and the backlash against the genre also emerged in the United States, when rock musicians and fans started to attack the camp laughter, playful sexualities and synthesized sounds. July 12, 1979, has been described as the day disco died, when a Disco Demolition Night was staged at a White Sox game with 90,000 in attendance. Besides burning and exploding records, the stadium's grounds and seats were also destroyed. Still, in the years between 1974 and 1979, disco had transformed how music was made, recorded, remixed and played. It also offered new rhythms for dancing.

At its most basic, disco is based in a 4/4 time signature where a syncopated bass line operates with a hi hat opening on the offbeat. The vocals hover over the beat, often conveying lyrics of struggle but survival, as witnessed most famously in Donna Summer's 'Last Dance' and Gloria Gaynor's 'I Will Survive'. Giorgio Moroder is often credited with creating the first disco track with a completely synthesized composition. 'I Feel Love' allowed the warmth of Summer's vocals to bounce off cold keyboards.

Disco gained visibility and popularity throughout 1974 and 1975, with the Hues Corporation's 'Rock the Boat', LaBelle's 'Lady Marmalade', The Four Seasons' 'December 1963 (Oh What a Night)', and Barry White's 'Love Theme'. This period also saw the release of Gloria Gaynor's vinyl album of disco mixes, including 'Never Can Say Goodbye' and 'Reach Out (I'll be there)'. With Van McCoy's 'The Hustle' in 1975, the genre had its first choreography. The passage from a beat to a social movement can be traced to the release of the *Saturday Night Fever* film and soundtrack in December 1977. From this point, much of the playful gay sexuality was bled from the genre and the strings, bass lines and 4/4 rhythm that pervaded wider genres in both rock and popular music. Even The Rolling Stones recorded their version of disco with 'Miss You' in 1978. Barry Manilow released 'Copacabana' in the same year. Barbra Streisand recorded a duet with Donna Summer, 'No More Tears (Enough is Enough)'. Disco became heterosexual and mainstream.

Disco added three innovations to popular music. Firstly, it changed the content of music by transforming the love and romance of rock lyrics into overt sexuality and proliferating double entrendres. Secondly, disco altered the relationship between performers and producers/DJs, making way for the 'Celebrity DJ' movement of the late 1980s. Disco was the moment where DJs and producers increasingly gained as equal a profile as performers. Mel Cheren from Westend Records, Neil Bogart at Casablanca and Marvin Schlachter at Prelude created the space for Giorgio Moroder. An Italian producer, his best-known work has been in the genre of disco, particularly his collaborations with Donna Summer. Disco dialogued between experimentation and popularity, with the 17 minutes of 'Love to Love You Baby' providing an important entree into the sounds and sexuality of the genre. Thirdly, disco signaled the birth of the remix, at first using reel-to-reel tape machines. Songs were lengthened, stretched and remade to increase the intensity and duration of the dancing experience.

While much attention in the history of disco is still paid to performers such as Donna Summer and the proto-celebrity DJs, the genre was built on innovations in music engineering, technological innovation and technical dexterity. When trying to capture and enhance the dance floor experience in a studio, new strategies and techniques were needed. Much of this innovation in composition and technology was dependent on the work of mixing engineers. Unlike a great deal of rock music, disco deployed many more tracks in the recording studio to manage the diversity of instruments and vocal layering. What constitutes 'the disco sound' is actually the disco mix constructed by engineers. This provided the basis for genres that welcomed the remix: hip hop, house and techno. The goal of DJs and remixers was to reconstruct songs, adding percussion breaks, new melodies and sounds, to lengthen and intensify the experience of dancing. The DJs and remixers who changed the shape of music included Tom Moulton, David Mancuso, Larry Levan, Shep Pettibone and Frankie Knuckles who would go on to create house music. Disco was a club-based music. DJs would play a continuous mix of music, often accompanied by an elaborate light show that pulsated in rhythm with the music. Drugs, particularly cocaine, quaaludes and amyl nitrate, also saturated this sensory experience. With inhibitions lowered through seductive music, mirrors, flashing lights and drugs, promiscuity and public sex became part of disco's ideology.

Disco generated a specific sensibility, an intensely aural, corporeal and mobile world pulsating to a 4/4 beat. It played with the sex as much as the rhythm. From Divine to the falsetto-pitched Bee Gees, from Tom Robinson to Jimmy Somerville, disco created a space for an overt gay presence in popular music. Because of the specificity of disco, derived from the black and gay culture of New York, the gay voice was blatant, positive and ironic. Kodwo Eshun confirms that,

> Disco remains the moment when Black Music falls from the grace of gospel tradition into the metronomic assembly line. Ignoring that disco is therefore audibly where the 21st c begins, 9 out of 10 cultural critics prefer their black pop culture humanists and emphatically 19th C (1998: 6).

Eshun's critique is important here. Disco was naughty and transgressive. It created new roles for black and white, straight and gay. It mocked authenticity and credibility in favour of irony and playfulness.

Disco has not been the dominant music for three decades. Yet its instrumentation, sexualized lyrical excesses and flamboyant performances remain in the mix of contemporary music. Lady Gaga, the Pet Shop Boys, Kylie Minogue, Sophie Ellis-Bextor and Madonna continue to carry forward its traditions. When Madonna sampled Abba's 'Gimme! Gimme! Gimme! (A Man after Midnight)' in 'Hung Up', her first single from the album *Confessions on a Dance Floor*, she not only rebooted her career she also re-remembered a rhythmic history through a disco sample. Whenever a metaphoric and sonic wink is offered to a listener, whenever a stomping 4/4 rhythm pounds from a speaker, a splinter of disco cuts into the skin of the present.

Key Questions

1. What are the key innovations of disco as a musical genre?
2. What is a remix?
3. What contribution did disco make to contemporary music?
4. Why was sexual ambiguity important to disco?

Further Reading

Eshun, K. (1998) *More Brilliant than the Sun: Adventures in Sonic Fiction*. London: Quartet.

Fikentscher, K. (2000) *You Better Work! Underground Dance Music in New York City*. Connecticut: Wesleyan University Press.

Lawrence, T. (2004) *Love Saves the Day: A History of American Dance Music Culture, 1970–1979*. North Carolina: Duke University Press.

Shapiro, P. (2005) *Turn the Beat Around – The Secret History of Disco*. London: Faber and Faber.

Sonic sources

Gaynor, G. (1978) *I Will Survive*.

Summer, D. (1977) *I Feel Love*.

Sylvester (1978) *You Make Me Feel (Mighty Real)*.

Weather Girls (1982) *It's Raining Men*.

Visual sources

Disco – Spinning The Story (2005) Passport International.

Donna Summer – Live & More Encore (1997) Sony.

Saturday Night Fever (1977) Paramount.

Studio 54 (2005) Walt Disney Home Entertainment.

Web sources

DiscoMusic, http://www.discomusic.com/

Disco Music was Gay Music, http://brumm.com/gaylib/disco/

Disco Style, http://www.discostyle.com/

History of Disco Dance, Buzzle.com, http://www.buzzle.com/articles/history-of-disco-dance.html

House and Post-House Musics

For academics, writing about and researching dance music and cultures offers particular challenges. Because so much of popular cultural studies and media studies has emerged when the tropes of rock have been at their height, the flighty sexuality and geography of dance culture have not slotted into conventional structures and approaches. Electronic music links together sound studies and media studies, creating ways of listening and thinking. As Philip Sherburne realized, 'records in this tradition were not designed for home listening, but rather as fodder for performance in the hands of the DJ' (2004: 32). This musical economy of excess, drugs, dancing and profound – if transitory – happiness through popular music has fuelled governmental anxieties about ecstasy, youth and crime, meaning that once more 'yoof' has become a dancing folk devil. Irvine Welsh, in *The Acid House,* continued his drug-induced provocations from *Trainspotting,* by proclaiming that 'I think I'll stick to drugs to get me through the long, dark night of late capitalism' (1995: 240). Grasping such a maxim, the dancers to house and post-house musics fought for their right to party and to occupy micromoments of deviance, alternatives and difference.

Another way of describing house music and its aligned genres is as electronic dance music. This phrase encloses a range of musics, including house, techno, jungle, drum 'n' bass, gabba, ambient and trance. The innovations of this musical style emerged not only through listeners. Dancing and dancers were used to understand and interpret the music. What made both disco and house important as an intervention in popular music was that dancers moved to recorded music rather than a live band.

Post-disco dance music semiotically stripped popular music. Undressed of lyrics and the biography of an artist, it was cosmopolitan, transcultural and diasporic. Dance music has never revealed a clear centre – geographically or historically. As Michael Freedberg confirmed, 'One of the greatest challenges for a U.S.A.-based writer is that we live in a kind of "no-dance music zone." We have to travel, usually overseas, to hear the best 'dance music'" (n.d). Considering that disco and most genres and histories of popular music in this book have American origins or inflections, dance music flits around a different geography, creating links between cities rather than nations. Particular clubs are important, but the historical soundscape is invariably washed clean as a new venue, DJ or rhythm assumes ascendancy. While it is easy to focus on the big clubs, DJs and tracks, there is no centre for dance music: peripheries proliferate. Theorists must be watchful of any claims for purity or essentialism, particularly with regard to origin, race and nation.

Such a statement from Freedberg is ironic considering one of house's origins comes from Chicago in 1985 and 1986. Exfoliating disco down to its 4/4 rhythm, house brought forward the technological celebrations of Kraftwerk. For Kraftwerk, the voice was not central. There was no clear verse or chorus structure and the key foundation was a repetitive and mechanical rhythm. Afrika Bambaataa and Grandmaster Flash linked disco with Kraftwerk to provide a pathway to house. Two clubs were able to overcome and mobilize the inequalities of race and sexuality: Chicago's Warehouse and New York's Paradise Garage. The influence of these was so great that they branded the two types of music: house and garage.

While the history of house is international it is a music of cities, developing in clubs in New York, Chicago, Manchester and Detroit. It was built on disco's 12 inch vinyls. House reveals many characteristics, including the stutter technique as heard in Blackbox's 'Ride on Time': 'Tha-tha-thank you baby'. Other common soundscapes are large orchestral movements and a pounding piano. There were few lyrics in the genre. Jim Silk's 'Jack Your Body', released in January 1987, only featured the three words in its title. But it was Eiffel 65's 'Move Your Body' that propelled house from minority sounds and into popular culture in the United Kingdom. From 1988, and building on the innovative possibilities of the Roland 303, house diversified. Balearic house was a style of dj-ing that aligned pop and industrial music. Garage had a smoother sound, particularly through the influence of Marshall Jefferson. Yet the European interpretation remained strong. Starlight's 'Numero Uno' and Black Box's 'Ride on Time' were house's greatest moments. While dance culture reveals influences from Detroit techno and Chicago house, these sounds melted into the house rhythms from Spain, New Beat from Belgium, and German industrial music from Kraftwerk together with the Slovenian group, Laibach. Popular music remade itself within a European frame. The Europeanness of pop had always been present: The Beatles toured Hamburg and the mods derived much of their fashion sense from French style and fashion. Through house – and to paraphrase Kraftwerk – dance became a trans-European Express through popular music.

Technological change and innovation supported electronic dance music. The relationship between technology and music shaped how bodies moved to the output of machines. The layers and cuts of the DJ were enabled by the spaces provided in post-house music for weaving other beats and meanings. With house often framed as cold, impersonal and lacking authorship and authenticity, it also signaled the movement away from lyrics and towards instrumentality, creating a more obviously global series of sonic communities. Kraftwerk, for example, did not mask their nationalism. They did not relinquish their base in Düsseldorf and (West) Germany to construct what Tim Barr termed 'an Anglo-American veneer' (1998: 8). There was intention and consciousness in their decisions to be defiant and different. Ralf Hutter described the context in which Kraftwerk's music emerged.

> After the war, German entertainment was destroyed. The German people were robbed of their culture, putting an American head on it. I think we are the first generation born after the war to shake this off and know when to feel American music and when to feel ourselves. We are the first German group to record in our own language, use our electronic background, and create a Central European Identity for ourselves (in Bangs, 1988: 158).

Just as all modern folk artists nod to Woody Guthrie, all of electronic dance music draws its electricity from Kraftwerk. House has had a long life, birthing new styles such as techno, hard-core/gabber, club/mellow, trance and tribal. It also transformed how dancers danced, with both individuals and groups dominating the floor space. By the mid-1990s, dance mixes included funk, soul, hip hop, drum 'n' bass, ambient and techno, all held together through the rhythmic language of house.

The reason why dance has used so many descriptive terms is because to understand a sound, melody or rhythm, writers, journalists and researchers have had to translate it into words and sentences. Researchers use language to limit and frame music. That is why rock has dominated the writing about popular music. Rock is easy to write about because it has lyrics and charismatic performers and can claim a clear geographical and historical origin. House and its derivatives are proto- (or post-) linguistic. The mixes move between cities and the genres have intense relationships with disempowered communities, including citizens of colour, gay communities and women. Therefore, any delineation of genres imposed upon rhythm will be too simple. House also has a tension within it – carrying forward the tension in disco. The combination of the energy and passion of a diva warbling at the top of her range is crushed by the coldness and relentlessness of a synth riff. Remixed and synthesized with heavily layered computerized tracks, it is repetitive and hypnotic. House records use insistent repetition. The relentless, cold discipline of rhythm also leads into a range of new musical formations that may be described as a genre but are actually more organically tethered to house.

Techno was founded in Detroit's club scene. It was a way to break with – and challenge – the history of Motown. But it was also tethered to a European musical aesthetic that included the work of Giorgio Moroder, Tangerine Dream and – again – Kraftwerk. It was colder and more futuristic than house. Derrick May propelled the European synth pop of Kraftwerk forward in the mix. Indeed, at is height, Russell Potter was concerned that 'techno-rave was a sort of postmodern echo chamber' (1998: 41). As a colder, futuristic formation, black musicians such as Derrick May offered new renderings of Kraftwerk. Odd amalgamations of electronic noise and paganism were fused by The Orb, Orbital and Aphex Twin. As a mixture of many music styles, techno marked its differences from house not only by beats per minute, but also by the venues in which it was performed. Moving from the inner city warehouses, techno was played in open air locations.

Techno, hip hop, garage, big beat, trance, drum 'n' bass, handbag and jungle all connect with house. Jungle stretched the breakbeat, making the rhythmic pattern fill out the entirety of the song. Simon Reynolds stated that,

> Jungle contains a non-verbal response to troubled times, a kind of warrior-stance. The resistance is in the rhythms ... As such, its rhythmic innovations will pervade popular music well into the twenty-first century, as insidiously and insinuatingly as rock 'n' roll, funk and disco have done in the past (1998: 239).

Jungle digitized data from older sounds and recordings through an Akai S950 sampler and linked these to sequencing packages like Cubase. At its most basic, jungle was accelerated reggae, using both sampling and toasting. It was also a hybrid of hip hop and house. After 1994, the more musically and technological complex form of jungle was termed drum 'n' bass which was comprised of variants of house, reggae and techno and operated in the 175–185 beats per minute range. Associated with the Metalheadz, Moving Shadow and Prototype record labels, it was louder, harder and faster than both house and techno. Hardstep was a minimal form of jungle with a bare melody and clean breakbeat.

   Through all these house and post-house genres, dance music became popular music during the 1990s. Indeed, in 1998, 61 per cent of all single titles released in Britain belonged to the category of dance (Toynbee, 2000: 155). While indie brought back guitars and a fetishization of low tech and live performance, house music ensures that dance music remains part of popular music. Dance music will always offer great challenges for researchers and writers about popular music. It is very easy to quote lyrics and read significance from them, to pretend that the words that accompany music are actually poems in disguise. Dance music – because there are few lyrics – demands more honesty and appropriateness from writers. Kodwo Eshun captured this 'project' of writing about post-house dance culture.

> Since the 80s, the mainstream British music press has turned to Black Music only as a rest and a refuge from the rigorous complexities of white guitar rock. Since in this laughable reversal a lyric always means more than a sound, while only guitars can embody the zeitgeist, the Rhythmachine is locked in a retarded innocence. You can theorise words or style, but analyzing the groove is believed to kill its bodily pleasure, to drain its essence … dance-press writing also turns its total inability to describe any kinds of rhythm into a virtue, invoking a white Brit routine of pubs and clubs, of business as usual, the bovine sense of good blokes together (1998: 007).

Dance music is not pure. It is hybrid, plural, multicultural and cold. It creates a soundscape. It is also diverse, plural, hybrid and flexible in its distribution. It provides a lesson to all who write about music. The truth of music is not located through words. Our goal must be to create new ways, theories and methods that will give sound meaning rather than lyrics their significance.

Key Questions

1. What is the relationship between disco and house?
2. Why is house associated with particular cities?
3. Why is house and post-house music difficult to write about and research?
4. How did technological change enable dance music?

Further Reading

Butler, M. (2006) *Unlocking the Groove*. Bloomington: Indiana University Press.

Gilbert, J. and Pearson, E. (1999) *Discographies: Dance Music, Culture and the Politics of Sound*. London: Routledge.

James, M. (1997) *State of Bass: Jungle – The Story So Far*. London: Boxtree.

Rietveld, H. (1998) *This is Our House: House Music, Cultural Spaces and Technologies*. Aldershot: Ashgate.

Sonic sources

Blackbox (1989) *Ride on Time*.

Goldie (1995) *Inner City Life*.

Prodigy (1991) *Charly*.

Underworld (1995) *Born Slippy*.

Visual sources

24 Hour Party People (2002) Pathé.

High Tech Soul – The Creation of Techno Music (2005) Pias.

Human Traffic (2004) Prism.

Kraftwerk and the Electronic Revolution (2008) Plastic Head.

Web sources

Drum & Bass Arena, http://www.breakbeat.co.uk/

House Music, http://www.housemusic.com/

Kraftwerk, http://www.kraftwerk.com/

Ministry of Sound, http://www.ministryofsound.com/

World Music

Cultural imperialism follows popular music as melody follows rhythm. Local music can survive in an industry dominated by particular genres and nations, but there are often costs to pay for this sonic exposure. Protectionism by grants, funding or governmental policies can ensure that radio and television play a percentage of music from the home nation's performers. It is a conservative strategy to demand that 10, 20 or 30 per cent of music should be presented in a particular language or by a group of people maintaining a particular nationality. The goal of such media policy is understandable: to create a chance for local musicians to develop a career outside the interests of a few record companies based in the United States and the United Kingdom.

Another way to create a space for new music to be heard outside of protectionism is through rebranding. World music is a controversial categorization of sound. This odd phrase captures all 'non-Western' music. It spans from art to popular culture, folk to electronica. More precisely, it can refer to the music of indigenous musicians, but it also includes roots music, ethnic music and folk music. World music is a description of geography rather than a discussion of modernity. Japanese koto music, Tibetan chants and Indian ragas are incorporated into the definition, alongside indigenous performers' use of house and hip hop. Therefore, world music captures the music not sourced from the United Kingdom, the Americas and the colonizing populations of the world. It also captures local music in indigenous nations, creating an audience for these sounds through the transatlantic capitalism of record companies. World music is an example of how globalizing market forces structure and market local contexts and music (Cvetkovich and Kellner, 1997: 1–2) and it demonstrates the role of branding and e-commence in attracting a wider audience/market for marginal musics. There is even an 'app' to introduce iPhone and iPad users to world music.

World music is a marketing term with its origins in the 1980s, intending to brand 'foreign' sounds for a 'Western' consumer. World Music Day (*Fête de la Musique*) was first commemorated in France in 1982. Later, influenced by the release of Paul Simon's 1986 album *Graceland* which featured performers and sounds from southern Africa, WOMAD (World of Music, Arts and Dance) was formed in 1987 to initiate a marketing campaign to brand, label and promote performers, instruments and arrangements that were unfamiliar to the trans-Atlantic record buyer and radio listener. These projects provided an opportunity to 'discover' new music. Often, this was music disconnected from its context, with a song distanced from the culture and history that created it. The rapidity of disseminating technology created a post-local music industry with profound consequences for those sounds and songs not derived from Europe and the Americas. As there is a religious affiliation with many world musics, the song 'itself' can rarely be appreciated for its full importance. An example of this problem is the 'popular' Sufi music from such performers as Nusrat Fateh Ali Khan that became incorporated into world beat qawwali.

World music is a form of globalization capturing the benefits and problems of such a term. The contentiousness of globalization is part of a fear of unrestrained capitalism, or what Amartya Sen described as 'global Westernization' (2004: 16). The issue is not the efficiency of international trade or the digital divide. It is the imbalance in the global alignments of technology, markets and corporations. World music is part of globalization and therefore encounters inequalities and injustices when dialoguing with 'the other'. World music is also part of modernity and colonization: a discovery of difference and its packaging for the consumption of empowered consumers. Therefore, when scholars study world music, it is necessary to deploy diverse disciplinary frameworks compared to the study of other musical formations, including folklore studies, anthropology, post-colonial theory and ethnomusicology.

World music is part of a much wider concern of how cultural production on the periphery responds to the economic dominance of the centre. At the level of instruments and instrumentation, the movement of sounds is productive. For example, Ravi Shankar's influence on international popular music has been pervasive. Studs Terkel stated that 'Ravi Shankar is to the Indian sitar what Andres Segovia is to the guitar – the nonpareil' (2006: 81). When George Harrison featured the sitar on 'Norwegian Wood', he played the strings as if they were on a guitar. While the sound was innovative, Harrison's technique at this early stage was lacking. It was a colonization of an Indian instrument using a dominant technique, as if playing an electric guitar. Later collaborations and the relationship between Shankar and Harrison increased not only the awareness of Indian instruments, rhythms and sounds, they also instilled an understanding of how wider histories of music could play within pop. By the time *Sgt. Pepper's Lonely Heart's Club Band* and Harrison's 'Within You Without You' appeared, a more careful integration of sounds and technique was evident.

There is a long history of collecting music from 'the other'. A few examples of this process of collecting, preserving, transcribing and arranging foreshadowed many of the later challenges in world music. Johann Gottfried Herder Stimmen der Volker in Liedern and Volkslieder collected folk songs in the late 1770s. Achim von Arnim, Clemens Brentano and Des Knaben Wunderhorn in the early 1800s continued collecting folk, but gathered the lyrics without the music. This practice was continued by the influential John Philip Sousa, the band master of the US Marine Corp at the cusp of the twentieth century, who transcribed and (re)arranged global music. His linking of musical and military expansion has captured some of the later disquiet with the label of world music, with the claiming of sounds becoming synonymous with the claiming of territory. As recording mechanisms improved the collection and preservation of music increased by using wax cylinders. The World Fair in Chicago featured 103 recordings, including Turkish songs and music from the South Pacific. Early in the twentieth century, A.Z. Idelsohn created five volumes of the *Thesaurus of Hebrew-Oriental Melodies*, gathering and transcribing diasporic music.

There was a wider context for their practices. Throughout the twentieth century, ethnomusicologists gained a place and role in library collections. Frances Densmore recorded indigenous American communities, with her results being published by the Bureau of American Ethnology and the Library of Congress. This imperative to preserve 'disappearing' musics gained a greater audience and publicity through the Folkway recordings. Moses (Moe) Asch created the Folkway's label. He mobilized the new capacities of recording equipment to log the disappearances from folk culture. This collection is still maintained by the Smithsonian Institution and has been released on compact discs and as podcasts. Even UNESCO has a World Music Collection that releases musical anthologies.

Such a short narrative of the preservation of 'disappearing' music, often caused by colonization in the name of progress and modernism, confirms Philip Bohlman's critical belief that, 'the space between the West and its others has vexed ethnomusicology since its inception' (2002: 36). There is an array of binary oppositions to manage: between oral and literate cultures, popular and high culture, the international and local. As Tony Mitchell observed, 'most third world musics are already "contaminated" by their own appropriations of First World musical influences' (1996: 31). World music was a term that attempted to capture and create a space for non Anglo-American music. It did tend to overlay a nineteenth century trade route with a melody and rhythm route. As a label or genre, world music creates an exotic other. The question remains, what is *not* world music? The answer is that often the music from the United States and United Kingdom – or even more simplistically, the music produced by white people – is not world music. Russell Ferguson asked, 'when we say marginal, we must always ask, marginal to what?' (1990: 9). The possession of the exotic cultural objects of the other is deployed as an ethnographic specimen, work of art or commodity to freshen up the music market.

There are some musicological characteristics behind this branding of world music, including distinctions in scales and instrumentation. While mobility for some increased through air travel, the development of compression files and low cost sound recording devices meant that sounds could travel via the web even when people could not. Will Straw explored how these 'systems of articulation' operated in popular music, confirming that, 'The search for musical forms whose relationship to musical communities is that of a long-term and evolving expressivity will lead us to overlook ways in which the making and remaking of alliances between communities are the crucial political processes within popular music' (1991: 369). How 'the land' is understood and revered is incredibly important when conceptualizing difference. Our understanding of invasion or occupation through music can narrate the consequences of 'discovery' and 'settlement'. Therefore, how the past and history are written in and through music matters politically and socially. The positioning of indigenous music as 'roots' music is a form of meta-racism. Indigenous music is not a 'root'. It is fully formed, contemporary, dynamic and changeable. Indeed, the label of 'indigenous music' is reified and racist. Colonizers' music is not deployed as a label. Therefore, music from indigenous performers deserves to be complex, plural and defined by more than the singer's race or the marketing strategies of the empowered.

There is a more positive interpretation of world music, enabling migrant populations to gain visibility in their host cultures. Algerian, Cameroon and Moroccan musics have both a presence and audience in France, particularly in Paris. Their movement also offers a way to reconnect diasporic populations through music, assembling a sense of belonging and tradition and overcoming dislocation and displacement. New cultural relationships emerge in such an environment, often independent from the nation state. Migration and movement builds diverse sounds and identities and fractures clear categories of race and nation.

While recognizing these possibilities, the critiques of world music are clear. It can be seen not only as a generalized description of 'non-Western' music, but also as a form of sonic neocolonialism where English-speaking marketing executives label and exoticize the sounds of 'the other'. The role of David Byrne, Peter Gabriel and Paul Simon as facilitators for 'third world' music is complicated. In a post-authenticity, hybrid age, musical histories are becoming more ambivalent, incomplete and liminal. As an example, the use of the didgeridoo in popular music holds what Tony Mitchell described as a 'polemical function' (1996: 177). Yothu Yindi's song 'Treaty' was remixed into a house dance track, bringing forward in the mix samples of both didgeridoos and lap sticks. In 1992, it was remixed again by William Orbit. Most of the lyrics in the indigenous language were removed. While the overt politics were circumvented, Yothu Yindi made indigenous music part of popular culture in a way that Coloured Stone, No Fixed Address and the Warumpi Band did not manage. The danceable rhythm provided the basis for translation. The question here is whether world music makes the sounds, instrumentation and sonic structures of formerly colonized peoples 'acceptable' and fashionable to urban bohemian populations. More importantly, popular music scholars need to ask how much 'world' music is lost because the sound, lyric and politics are too uncomfortable for a white European or American audience. For every Youssou N'Dour singing '7 Seconds' with Neneh Cherry, there is an Archie Roach singing 'Took the Children Away'. One is smooth and comforting to popular cultural audiences. The other offers a more seething commentary.

Key Questions

1. What is world music? What is *not* world music?
2. What role has the digitization and downloading of cultures played in world music?
3. Is world music postcolonial or neocolonial?
4. Why did world music gain some popularity in the late 1980s?

Further Reading

Bohlman, P. (2002) *World Music: A Very Short Introduction*. Oxford: Oxford University Press.

Hutnyk, J. (2000) *Critique of Exotica: Music, Politics and the Culture Industry*. London: Pluto.

Manuel, P. (1988) *Popular Music of the Non-Western World*. New York: Oxford University Press.

Taylor, T. (1997) *Global Pop: World Music, World Markets*. London: Routledge.

Sonic sources

Paul Simon (1986) *Diamonds on the Soles of My Shoes*.

The Folkways Collection (2009) Smithsonian Institution, iTunes.

Yothu Yindi (1991) *Treaty*.

Youssou N'Dour with Neneh Cherry (1994) *7 Seconds*.

Visual sources

Essential World Music (2007) Sheer Sound.

Ladysmith Black Mambazo – Live (2009) Heads Up.

Sufi Soul – The Mystic Music Of Islam (2008) Riverboat.

Youssou N'Dour – Live At Montreux (2006) Eagle Rock.

Web sources

New World Music, http://www.newworldmusic.com/

Roots World, http://www.rootsworld.com/rw/

World Music Central, http://worldmusiccentral.org

World Music Network, http://www.worldmusic.net/wmn/news/

Section V

Debates

Intellectual Property

Popular music studies scholars deploy concepts like genre, audience, context and identity. Since 1997, after the arrival of the first Tony Blair government, new phrases like the creative economy, creative industries, copyright and intellectual property rights were summoned as the engine for economic stimulation and development. Popular music has gone from being a dynamic leisure practice of youth to a way to develop markets on diverse platforms to harvest intellectual property and copyright. Innovative soundscapes are interrupted, punctuated, controlled and restricted by law.

Intellectual property is a term derived from the law that refers to creative works including literary, artistic and musical formations. IP includes copyright, design, trademarks and patents and attempts to capture, monitor and market the bundling of ideas in a particular form. Ideas themselves do not designate rights. Instead, *the form* of the ideas designates specific rights to the authors, which they may or may not exercise. The entity that is owned is not a physical property but an abstract idea that has physical manifestations through designs, music and images. In IP law, the holder has rights that are dependent on the jurisdiction in which the property is located. In a digital environment, such jurisdictions became increasingly complex. For example, Kazaa's domain name was registered in Australia, with the servers in Denmark, software programmers resident in Estonia and the company registered in Vanuatu.

Using Kazaa as a metynomy for new styles of ownership and distribution, David Bowie's prescient realization is now reaching fruition.

> The absolute transformation of everything that we ever thought about music will take place within ten years, and nothing is going to be able to stop it ... I'm fully confident that copyright, for instance, will no longer exist in ten years, and authorship and intellectual property is in for such a bashing. Music itself is going to become like running water or electricity (Kusek and Leonhard, 2005: x).

Bowie's statement about revolution, technology and change raises questions about how music is written, owned and commodified. Of the three main types of intellectual property laws, copyright is the most relevant to popular music studies as it grants the holder exclusive rights to control how work is reproduced and adapted over a jurisdiction-specific period of time. Copyright maintains a rearguard action against technological change. Indeed, Lawrence Lessig stated that,

> copyright has always been at war with technology. Before the printing press, there was not much need to protect an author's interest in his creative work. Copying

was so expensive that nature itself protected that interest. But as the cost of copying decreased, and the spread of technologies for copying increased, the threat to the author's control increased. As each generation has delivered a technology better than the last, the ability of the copyright holder to protect her intellectual property has been weakened (2006: 172).

The shift from analogue to digital mattered in this context. There were two important changes. Firstly, digital copies were identical to the original. Secondly, the copies could be reproduced an infinite number of times and moved through the online environment. Because of the small files' size that comprises an MP3 popular music track, the mobility of songs without copyright permission was high. Therefore, content industries started to respond to the 'threat'. Importantly though, the stretch of copyright law has not only increased through digitization. As music has moved beyond composition and into live performance through to sound recordings – into what is termed 'neighbouring rights' – new forms of protection and infringement are being invented. Such protections are now limiting social activities and creative expressions based on earlier works. What has been called the public's right to 'fair dealing' and 'fair use', is now subject to new mechanisms from copyright owners restricting such phrases. Even more disturbingly, in an environment where copyright is increasingly regulated, the application of trademark protection has become more important. Trademark and copyright protection are different, but through trademark protection, content providers can restrict and commodify such ambiguous ideas such as performance, style and timbre (Demers, 2006: 25). The irony of such restrictions on popular music is that of all areas of popular culture and the creative industries, music is the most derivative, appropriated and allusory of earlier genres, riffs, rhythms, melodies, lyrical subjects and vocal styles. One of the ironic consequences of the ideology of authenticity and originality that travels through such genres as folk, punk and indie is that it has perpetuated the notion of an individual writing a song without references, context or history. It forgets the role of what Joanna Demers described as 'transformative appropriation' (2006: 4). She realized that, 'the fundamental change wrought by sound reproduction technologies of the twentieth century has been to enlarge the gray zone between plagiarism and allusion by introducing another category of imitation: mechanical reproduction' (2006: 29). Digitization has only increased the speed and capacity of borrowing, appropriation and remixing. But also, copyright over-emphasizes the appropriation and use of melody and lyric. This means that there is greater protection for a line of lyric or a phrase of notes rather than the deployment of a rhythm or bassline. Considering the impact of ska, reggae and 'Latin' rhythms, the legal balance towards words and melodies, rather than rhythms and instrumental mixes, is implicitly eurocentric. World music is particularly poorly protected. The line between recognizing non-European musics and exploiting these sounds is particularly vexed. Ethnomusicological field recordings are especially vulnerable (Demers, 2006: 103).

Over the last two decades copyright wars have flooded popular music studies, questioning the public use of songwriters' works. Each nation offers distinct laws and regulations. For example, the fair dealing provision of the England and Wales Copyright Act 1968 allowed the use of copyright materials without the copyright owner's permission. At issue here is the application and jurisdiction of the phrase 'fair dealing'. Importantly, there is a range of unexpected consequences of copyright law. Dick Weissman discusses the consequences of unfortunate copyrighting of folk recordings. John Lomax was a great preserver and promoter of American folk music and copyrighted a series of songs. The 'old' copyright law not only enabled these songs to be restricted for twenty-eight years – plus the twenty year renewal period – after Lomax's death in 1948, it also controlled music that should have been in the public domain. The Lomax family gathered not only publishing rights, but also songwriting fees for songs they did not write (Weissman, 2006: 21).

There are historical reasons why copyright has been such an issue in popular music, particularly as digitization has increased its influence. The economic, social and political protection of private property has been extended from physical property to privately owned lyrics, melodies and recorded performances (McLeod, 2003: 242). Copyright is based on assumptions and determinations of originality and authorship that were built on the framework triggered by the consequences of the printing press and print capitalism. Kembrew McLeod believed that 'copyright law only recognizes particular types of authorship as legitimate' (2003: 246). This type of law is tested in many ways, but particularly through the use of samples, which creates new originality from older originality. When a sample is used, two types of copyright fees are due: publishing fees and the mechanical fees that comes from the use of the 'master' recording. To avoid paying the mechanical fee, since the 1990s, hip hop musicians have utilized studio musicians to play a sample similar to the original, so that only the publishing fee is due to be paid (McLeod, 2003: 247).

Originally, copyright began its application to music by prohibiting any unauthorized copying of sheet music, but the deployment of the law has now increased in range. Joanna Demers confirmed,

> With respect to musical compositions, the law now enables copyright holders to enjoin public performances, broadcasting, the making of sound recordings in any medium, and, in many jurisdictions, the sharing of music with the aid of digital technology. Each of these exclusive rights can be separately assigned or multiply licensed for distinct purposes, potentially creating tangled webs of prohibition that fraught the use of music with dangers of litigation (2006: vii).

With the length of time increasing for the 'protection' of music, fewer works are entering the public domain, ensuring that the range of infringements and liabilities increases. While there is an array of laws ensuring the right for fair use of musical works, there are a number of litigants testing the limits of that use.

Popular music as an industry is based on intellectual property rights. By the 1980s, popular music had become a conventional (post) industrial economic product. Pretences of art and politics were a way to mask the commercial aspects. Raymond Horricks and Neil Slaven confirmed that by 1980, 'pop music as we know it is now an industry like any other – dispassionate, calculating and profit-conscious. It isn't always fun any more; but after all, it's only rock 'n' roll and we all like it' (1980: 70). Popular music is a business enterprise operated by corporations. It has always been reliant on consumerism and capitalism. While there have been moments within punk and reggae, indie and gospel, where there has been a denial of sales and commodification, this 'authenticity' has very quickly become a marketing device to sell a more 'radical,' 'resistive' and 'anti-corporate' product. Anti-branding and anti-marketing are ways to freshen up sales. However this resistance and difference served the interests of the market. Currently, and enabled through the odd relationship between consumer capitalism and digitization, there is what Christine Harold termed 'rhetorical sabotage in the new brand economy' (2007: 46).

The record industry did not predict the decline of interest in their product, particularly the album. Indeed, Simon Frith reported that 'in March 1988 the marketing director of HMV Records … told startled delegates at the annual meeting of the British Radio Academy that the single record would be obsolete within three years' (1988: 3). He was both right and wrong. All records would be obsolete. Albums would be obsolete. Singles would survive, but without a platform, being loaded directly onto a computer hard drive and portable devices. The goal for the recording industry was not simply the sale of music. Keith Negus wrote what was probably the last book before the impact of digital downloading became apparent to the record companies. Published in 1992, *Producing Pop: Culture and Conflict in the Popular Music Industry* explored 'the active work of recording personnel' (p. vi) in discovering and developing artists. He explored the era before the proliferation of cheap and intuitive home recording equipment and software, before the self promotion on MySpace and YouTube and distribution portals such as iTunes. In this pre-Napster and Kazaa environment, Negus reported that,

> Entertainment corporations are increasingly attempting to gain the maximum revenue possible from exploiting the ownership of copyright; using the mass communications media available to place recordings across multiple sites, and lobbying for the licensing of ever more public spaces where music is being used (such as shops, clubs, restaurants, pubs and hairdressing salons and supporting the deployment of copyright inspectors to enforce these policies and prosecute outlets engaging in the unlicensed use of music (1992: 13).

The goal for recording companies before the pervasiveness of digital compression was to own, control, monitor and diversify revenue sites by copyright regulation. When alternative collaborative and community media channels and social networking sites started to increase in scale and scope and the Creative Commons licensing procedure emerged, applications for ownership and copyright started to decline. Distribution through digital platforms meant that the business model of the recording industry transformed. One model for profit-making by recording companies was displaced. Compression files allowed music to move through the web and not be limited by a physical release. There are now millions of opportunities to hear, rip and download music without cost, or at least without paying a record company.

Music has been shared illegally for decades. Throughout the 1970s, the slogan 'home-out taping is killing music' attempted to educate consumers that shared music was stolen music. MP3s and Napster did not invent music sharing. It was digitization that increased the speed and scale of that sharing. The sale of compact discs has markedly declined and illegal sharing has increased, but there are other explanations for the decline of music sales. The increasing popularity of DVDs and computer games has meant that there is greater competition for the entertainment dollar. In this context, John Oswald believed that 'the real headache for the writers of copyright has been the new electronic contrivances, including digital samples of sound and their accountant cousins, computers' (2004: 132). This difficulty for regulators is not a musical problem. It is an issue of how technology is managed.

At each point of platform migration and change, there has been a fear expressed by those institutions that had gained financially from the prior medium and the laws that enabled a profit to be made. There was profound confusion between the different arms of the same corporations. Sony music and Sony hardware embody this contradiction, with the same company that sold MP3 players also attacking the purchasers of their hardware who then download MP3s. Keith Negus noted that, 'The struggles through which new technologies are produced and introduced can have a considerable impact on how contracts are drawn up and how the "product" of popular music is conceptualized' (1999: 33). The release of sheet music did not see the destruction of copyright laws. But the major fears, scares and revisions from the application of these Copyright Acts in analogue environments started to emerge with the arrival of digital music in the early 1980s. With the advent of the compact disc, it became possible to copy music without any loss in quality. Digitization ensured that the copy would be identical to the original. The CD was an unprotected digital format, without either Digital Rights Management or copy protection. By the early 1990s, the computing firms like Apple, Dell, Compaq and Hewlett Packard that manufactured hardware, saw future potential markets in sound technology. Computers started to include CD Roms, slowly replacing floppy disc drives. Concurrently, computer speakers improved. As the hardware improved through a combination of DVD and CD Rom drives and an internet connection, consumers could suddenly not only copy music from compact discs, they could also then move that music through the web. The speed of shifting MP3 files online was slowed because there was no index that could locate a particular song, performer and file. Shawn Fanning wrote this programme for MP3 file organization through Napster and that allowed the first peer-to-peer system. It was at this point that Universal, Warner, Sony BMG and EMI pursued legal action. With Napster curtailed, other improved file sharing applications emerged through Kazaa, Morpheus, iMesh, Grokster, Limewire and Bit Torrent. The profound paradox of copyright in peer-to-peer environments is that when a file is downloaded it is copied and not taken. As Mark Katz explained,

> File sharing does not necessarily deprive copyright holders of income. If every person who would have downloaded copyrighted music decided instead to buy

the CD, copyright holders would indeed stand to make huge sums of money. But that is not the same as saying that downloading is depriving copyright holders of that money (2004: 180).

Katz's point is an important one. The desire for music audiences to download free music is distinct from the desire to purchase music. It cannot be assumed that these audiences are of the same size or sociological profile. Put simply, the compact disc no longer became the convenient, viable and economical mode through which to purchase music. Digitized – but illegal – music was free. The selling of sonic content – via marketing models such as iTunes – may not be appropriate in the long term. Others models, based on membership or subscriptions, may become a new way to package music. James Boyle is clear on this. He states that, 'the goal of copyright is to encourage the production of, and public access to, cultural works. It has done its job in encouraging production. Now it operates as a fence to discourage access' (2008: 224). His worry is that all the attention of record companies and musicians is paid to controlling the availability and commercialization of old music, rather than to developing new performers, new sounds and new music. While the focus is on control and not access, the past rather than the present, popular music is a frontline topic in legal controls over cultural formations.

Intellectual property is a complex issue in popular music studies, as there are a finite number of notes, chords and time signatures. Repetition of melodies and rhythms is inevitable. Strange legal challenges have been waged about originality, such as the supposed relationship between The Chiffons' 'He's So Fine' and George Harrison's 'My Sweet Lord'. The judge ruled in 1976 that Harrison had 'subconsciously plagiarized'. While there was no link or relationship with the lyrics, the chord progressions were similar (Bright Tunes Music *vs.* George Harrison). Harrison paid Bright Tunes Music US$587,000 for the copyright violation and acquired the rights to 'He's So Fine' to avoid any such claims in the future (Song Fact, 2010). The Chiffons later recorded a version of 'My Sweet Lord' Popular music is embedded in the contradictions of popular culture with the demarcation between art and industry, and production versus consumption. Predictably, the ownership of music rather than the consumption of music will be a huge field for future debate, legislative threat and innovative rights management.

Key Questions

1. What are intellectual property rights?
2. Is sampling the 'theft' of a sound?
3. Why has IP become an even more important issue after the arrival of MP3s?
4. What is the difference between copying music and stealing music? Is there a difference?

Further Reading

Cloonan, M. (2007) *Popular Music and the State in the UK.* Aldershot: Ashgate.

Demers, J. (2006) *Steal This Music: How Intellectual Property Law Affects Musical Creativity.* Athens: University of Georgia Press.

Perelman, M. (2002) *Steal This Idea: Intellectual Property Rights and the Corporate Confiscation of Creativity.* New York: Palgrave.

Weintraub, A. and Yung, B. (2009) *Music and Cultural Rights.* Champaign: University of Illinois Press.

Sonic sources

Harrison, G. (1970) *My Sweet Lord.*

The Chiffons (1962) *He's So Fine.*

The Chiffons (1975) *My Sweet Lord.*

The Clash (1978) *I Fought The Law.*

Visual sources

Girl Talk: Everyone Borrows Intellectual Property, Even Kings of Leon, *YouTube*, http://www.youtube.com/watch?v=tQfHTHb2_Wg

Intellectual Property Rights Debate, *YouTube*, http://www.youtube.com/watch?v=H2jSabFiYQY

Lang, M. Understanding Intellectual Property and Copyright, *YouTube*, http://www.youtube.com/watch?v=Ngps0BnLlUg

Netanel, N. Understanding Music Copyrights with Neil Netanel, *YouTube*, http://www.youtube.com/watch?v=7r7zmSJW-n8

Web sources

Collins, K. (2008) 'Grand Theft Audio?: Video Games and Licensed IP'. Music and the Moving Image, 1.1: http://mmi.press.uiuc.edu/1.1/collins.html and http://www.gamessound.com/texts/collinsGTA.pdf

Copyright Infringement Project, UCLA Law, http://cip.law.ucla.edu/

Creative Commons, www.creativecommons.org

Musicians' Intellectual Law and Resource List, http://www.aracnet.com/~schornj/index.shtml

Censorship and Regulation

Most studies of popular culture play with categories of difference, deviance, subculture and resistance. A great area of neglect is the relationship between music and law, music and the market, and music and the state. Although Holly Kruse has suggested that this absence is particularly noteworthy in American popular music studies (1998: 187), it is widespread throughout the field.

Law regulates and disciplines popular culture. It creates criteria and boundaries by which popular culture are judged. There is what Steve Redhead describes as 'the fertile deconstructed terrain where legal theory, deviance and cultural studies collide' (1995: 100). Because much popular music has been targeted at a youthful audience, the sexual and violent content in lyrics has been the focus of conservative campaigns to ban, censor or repress. As Hebdige argued, 'youth is present only when its presence is a problem' (1988: 17). The challenge of MP3s and illegal downloading through peer-to-peer networks has transformed a practice or behaviour – rather than a group of people – into a trigger for intervention by international governments. Illegal downloading has created what Martin Cloonan has described as 'increasing interaction between the industry and government' (2007: 3). In the post-war period, national music policy was frequently handled by non-government organizations or Arts Councils, which ensured a certain level of disconnection between legislature and culture. The Second World War was a moment of reconsideration for many governments in building a relationship between art, culture and nationalism. In 1940, the British war-time government, in the midst of the Blitz, funded the Council for the Encouragement of Music and the Arts (CEMA). John Maynard Keynes became the chair in 1942 with the goal of maintaining high cultural standards, particularly in music, drama and painting. This organization became the Arts Council of Great Britain in 1945, with the goal of increasing the audience for high culture. There was a tension between access and excellence, with a systematic exclusion of popular culture. The imperative was for citizens to enjoy high art, but it resulted in the exclusion of pop, entertainment and commercial media from governmental funding. Popular music was particularly affected by this neglect. It was distanced from 'art' and because of its trans-national derivation and origins, could not be claimed as belonging to one country and developing national culture. It was only when creative industries modeling emerged through the first Tony Blair government in 1997 that economic development rather than social aspiration became a priority for 'arts' policy. Chris Smith was the Secretary of State for Culture at this time. One of his first acts in office was to abolish the Department of National Heritage and replaced it with the Department of Culture, Media and Sport.

Of all the industries, popular music is difficult to regulate or restrain by national borders. The determination of 'Canadian music,' 'New Zealand music' or 'German music' is difficult to define. Is it categorized by the nationality of the performers, the producers, the songwriters, the location of the studio, the primary audience or the national registration of the portal that enables the download of the song? While the music industry has focused on production and distribution, the new peer-to-peer networks blur the relationships between mixing and remixing, listening and producing. The increasing separation between the music industry and the recording industry ensures that regulation is more difficult to monitor and enforce. Because the attention was on production and nationalism rather than consumption and trans-local movements, it meant that audiences were operating beyond – and ignorant of – regulatory networks. The Department of Culture Media and Sport released a report in 2000, entitled *Consumers Call the Tune* (DCMS). This title belies the argument. The British Government took advice from record companies seeking to control illegal downloading to develop a market for legitimate purchases. This was a top-down initiative, rather than an attempt to understand the behaviour and rationale of online consumers.

Regulation can occur legally, financially, technologically or socially. One of the most rigid of regulatory models is censorship, which is based on legislation that restricts the circulation of sounds, images and ideas. It can also emerge through self-regulation by media industries. Censorship is a conscious process that requires a series of decisions to restrict the movement of particular platforms, media and ideas. Laws are socially constituted but institutionally enabled, rendering particular assumptions and ideas as legal or illegal. Censorship is not simply an instrument of the state. A series of media organizations will moderate, mediate and ban particular programmes and programming. For example, after September 11, thousands of Clear Channel Radio stations in the United States of America were directed not to play 160 songs, including The Bangles' 'Walk like an Egyptian', Phil Collins' 'In the Air Tonight' and – perhaps more predictably – The Clash's 'Rock the Casbah'. Other restricted titles included Carole King's 'I Feel the Earth Move' and John Lennon's 'Imagine' (Cloonan and Garofalo, 2003: 1).

Censorship determines particular materials to be harmful or objectionable and suppresses, restricts or removes them from circulation. Sounds and popular music are particularly vulnerable to regulation. While visual media are patrolled and controlled for the presentation of violence and sexuality, music is open to multiple interpretations. Particular words, rhythms and noises are excluded from particular places. Because music can convey many meanings it can be implicated in a range of social problems, from youth suicide to drug use, from sexual expression and experimentation to the raising of political consciousness. The Parents Music and Resource Center in America and Media Watch UK, which changed its name from the National Viewers and Listeners Association in 2001, have tried to restrict and 'improve' popular culture, often with a religious imperative, in order to promote and strengthen a particular version of marriage, family and morality. In November 1985, the Recording Industry Association of America (RIAA) signed an agreement with the PMRC so that albums with 'explicit' lyrics would include an advisory warning to parents. Such an initiative was built on the principle that there was an agreed definition of 'explicit' content along with an agreed notion that parents should control the listening habits of young people.

There are three main mechanisms to censor and control popular music. One method is to restrict the circulation of songs to particular age groups. Another is to regulate the content, to remove 'offensive' elements through editing or by changing a lyric, title or video. Two examples of this tactic include The Beatles' 'Ballad of John and Yoko' with the first word of the chorus being removed for radio play and Pulp's iTunes-housed video for 'Disco 2000', with the last word from the chorus of 'dance and drink and screw' being silenced from the purchased version. Another strategy is to repress a song, album or performer, removing it or them from national distribution. This last strategy is the one most obviously blunted by a web-based distribution of content. When taken together, restriction, regulation and repression can create a series of arbitrary but occasionally effective national standards about morality, quality and offensiveness. Increasingly, corporations are also operating as quasi-national arbiters of taste. For example, Walmart will not sell stock that its management determines to be 'obscene' (PBC). With record shops closing, supermarkets and department stores have become important points of sale for compact discs. Independent decisions by corporations, extending beyond national regulatory frameworks, are a mode of corporate censorship. The point of popular music is that it is indeed popular, with a diverse and large audience. If products are blocked from reaching a market, then such decisions will prevent a musical track or performer from becoming part of the wider culture.

The current difficulty with such a model is that a lot of popular culture circulates beyond national borders and national regulatory regimes. Enabled through digital compression, popular culture permeates through boarders. Also, censorship – while clear in its definition – is nebulous in its application, even in the analogue age. The famous example of this intricate and inaccurate model of censorship is the Sex Pistols' 'God Save the Queen'. While it was banned from airplay by UK radio and television stations, neither the government nor the courts took any action (Cloonan, 2003: 14). The reason for this ambiguity and confusion is that there are (at least) six different forms of censorship: self, social, legal, extralegal, voluntary and subterranean (O'Higgins, 1972: 12–13). The goal of these strategies is to transform arbitrary values about culture into a systematic process of restriction. There are diverse models that frame such a goal. The United States authenticates free speech through the First Amendment. Conversely, the United Kingdom operates 12 acts that restrict free speech.

Through much of popular music's history, censorship and regulation has been summoned to avoid moral harm to youth. Now censorship and regulation are being used to protect corporate interests so that content can be sold to youth within a nation state. Intriguingly, peer-to-peer music and video downloading services had been controlled by national copyright legislation. Such decisions were based on the assumption which national borders which had worked in enabling censorship of analogue content would also facilitate the restriction of media. The zonal coding of DVDs is a clear example of this strategy. With the world cut up into regions, a product purchased in one area may not necessarily operate in another (DVD Regions, 2010). In an Orwellian turn, while this is a form of Digital Rights Management (DRM), it is now being re-named with phrases such as Regional Code Enhancement (RCE), which further restricts the playing capacity of purchased products. The paradox is that throughout much of popular music's history, legislation has been deployed to restrict particular texts as dangerous. Now, legislation is categorizing particular technologies as dangerous.

Censorship emerges through the activation of federal or state laws and regulations. Increasingly, commercial interests are shaping market forces away from particular media products and towards others. Since September 11, and with a glut of user-generated content music from which to choose, both corporate and governmental forces have aligned to restrict the circulation of particular performers, sounds and songs. Certainly, copyright, as we explored in the last chapter, is a great financial enabler of creative industries strategies and a mechanism to control the circulation of popular music. Copyright holders can prevent a melody, lyric or sample from being used by other musicians. Steve Greenfield and Guy Osborn observed that 'without copyright protection for artists' work, the industry could not have developed commercially in the way it has done' (2003: 66). There are distinct copyrights for music, lyrics, the recording or the song. Each of these rights can be managed, bought or sold. Sampling adds a layer of complexity to this discussion. Greenfield and Osborn determined that 'these new technologies have heralded a new type of music culture, a culture that records changing relationships between performers, audiences and the form of representation' (1998: 65). Media law and policy trail behind the potentials and possibilities of technology. They are responsive, not initiators of change.

Obviously, music has always been copied. With the innovation of MP3s, the shrinking of file size and the arrival of Napster, Gnutella, Freenet, Morpheus and Kazaa file sharing software and services, the capacity to regulate, censor and control was severely restricted. The problems created because of downloading were in the business model, not the technology. The 'big six' record companies became the 'big four' in the 2000s. Reebee Garofalo stated that 'in its push toward globalization, the music industry has become significantly more concentrated at a time when technological advances demand a model of decentralization' (2003: 14). In other words, a few fordist companies were trying to control a post-fordist, decentralized, peer-to-peer practice of music sharing. They failed. The use of words like 'piracy' did not grasp that ownership is an historical and change-able formation. Lawrence Lessig realized,

Today we are in the middle of another 'war' against 'piracy'. The Internet has provoked this war. The Internet makes possible the efficient spread of content. Peer-to-peer (p2p) file sharing is among the most efficient of the efficient technologies the Internet enables. Using distributed intelligence, p2p systems facilitate the easy spread of content in a way unimagined a generation ago (2004: 17).

Lessig reiterated that notions of both piracy and creativity required a context and a history. Similarly, Chris Anderson realized that 'free' music – whether illegal or legal – had been naturalized by consumers.

> Between digital reproduction and peer-to-peer distribution, the real cost of distributing music has truly hit bottom. This is a case where the product has become free because of sheer economic gravity, with or without a business model. That force is so powerful that laws, copy protection, guilt trips, and every other barrier to piracy the labels could think of failed (and continue to do so) (2009: 29).

Volatile notions of copyright, when matched with a dynamic software and hardware environment and unreflexive and unresponsive business models, do not enable changes in consumerist practices.

Censorship became a way to control content, because copyright was unable to manage the movement of digital musical files. Just as youth was a folk devil through the post-war period of rock and roll, downloaders are today's new folk devils. Uncontrolled by national laws, they exchange 'inappropriate' content and operate outside of dominant institutions. The questions are, can censorship control digital listening spaces any more effectively than digital rights management and does freedom of speech include the freedom to download?

Key Questions

1. What is censorship?
2. Which particular forms of content are censored?
3. What is more difficult to censor: visual or sonic media?
4. Which difficulties confront censors in a digital environment?

Further Reading

Cloonan, M. and Garofalo, R. (eds) (2003) *Policing Pop*. Philadelphia: Temple University Press.

Greenfield, S. and Osborn, G. (1998) *Contract and Control in the Entertainment Industry: Dancing on the Edge of Heaven*. Aldershot: Dartmouth.

Redhead, S. (1995) *Unpopular Cultures: The Birth of Law and Popular Culture*. Manchester: Manchester University Press.

Scherzinger, M. (2007) 'Music censorship after 9/11,' in J. Ritter and J. Martin Daughtry (eds), *Music in the Post-9/11 World*. London: Routledge.

Sonic sources

The Beatles (1969) *The Ballad of John and Yoko*.

The Clash (1982) *Rock the Casbah*.

The Jaywalks (2004) *I Like Fat Chicks*.

The Sex Pistols (1977) *God Save the Queen*.

Visual sources

Rise – The Story of Rave Outlaw Disco Donnie (2004) Quantum Leap.

Smothered: The Censorship Struggles of the Smothers Brothers Comedy Hour (2002) New Video Group.

Soundtrack to War (2006) Revelation Films.

The Corporation (2006) In 2 Film.

Web sources

'Archive for the Music Censorship Category,' http://www.somebodythinkofthe children.com/category/music/

FreeMuse, www.freemuse.org

'Music and Censorship,' Noise between stations, http://www.noisebetweenstations. com/personal/essays/music_censorship.html

Taboo Tunes, http://www.tabootunes.com/gallery.html

Race, Appropriation and Commodification

In 1998, Madonna 'wore' a bindi for a bharatanatyam dance track. Was this an appropriation of symbolism or a mode of respectful, transformational politics? Was she being generous to other musicians, faiths and communities, or mining a symbolic system to freshen her image? We may never know. Such a question provides an entry into the fascinating and complex literature probing the relationship between race and popular music. Much of this academic material explores the role, place and value given to (and financial payments made to) African American performers for their too often unacknowledged and underfinanced contribution to jazz, blues, rock and rap. Increasingly, there are debates about the role of Hindi musical styles and forms in dance genres.

The history of popular music is punctuated by cycles of resistance and appropriation. Popular music involves movement in bodies, sounds and ideas. Terry Bloomfield realized that, 'in the West there has been a pattern that music, which at first expresses opposition to the social order, is then inexorably commodified by the capitalist structures of production' (1991: 81). Ironically, rock music has been a statement of political resistance, yet its origins in rhythm and blues capture a more complex history of resistance than the simple and supposedly radical action of young white men playing guitars. The commodification of music – the blues, hip hop or house – ensured that new and innovative sounds were marketed in a way that created an audience for a product and cut away more complex histories of blackness, colonialism and race. Marketing plans often meant that a sound or song that started 'black' became 'white' in order to enlarge its audience. While resistance to such a process is not difficult to find, the challenge in such a protest is determining the focus of that resistance. Is it the fault of record companies, white performers or fans? The problem – in cultural terms – is not appropriation, but a commodification of the music, imagery and the ideas of groups that because of social position and inequalities cannot make a profit from the sale of their sounds to an audience. In the 1950s, a political rhetoric of integration ensured that rock and roll together with rhythm and blues could dialogue. By the 1970s, political and social views on integrationism had polarized. Hip hop captured the collapse in the simple ideologies of anti-separatism and multiculturalism.

The issue of race is – literally – not a black and white issue. A range of mixed race bands like The Specials, UB40, Culture Club, The Thompson Twins and Massive Attack, to name a few examples, created a network of translation and challenge to the separation of black and white music. In the United Kingdom, there was a complex dialogue between different races in music. Most of the black community in the UK in the 1950s and 1960s did not come from the United States but from the Caribbean. Stuart Hall offered the key corrective to any discussion of blackness or whiteness in this context.

> What is at issue here is the recognition of the extraordinary diversity of subjective positions, social experiences, and cultural identities which compose the category 'black'; that is, the recognition that 'black' is a politically and culturally constructed category (1996: 166).

Hall demonstrates that for every assumption of unanimism, purity, primordialism and essentialism, there are counterflowing movements of hybridity, diaspora, cosmopolitism and translocalism.

When discussions of race, appropriation and commodification emerge, these signal an often uncomfortable realization that much of popular music has been based on the discovery of 'black music' by white musicians who have taken the songs, guitar patterns and genres and repackaged them with a marketing strategy for white audiences. Blackness is a complex and heterogeneous ideology within popular culture. It is part of a wider project of representation, where there is a masking of an honest and coherent debate about the function of whiteness, white power and colonization in contemporary life and popular culture (Mohanram, 1999). The role of black women in popular music, like Aretha Franklin, Whitney Houston, Donna Summer and Missy Elliot, links the projects of race and gender and occupies a particularly difficult role in popular music studies.

Black studies reveal important relationships with popular music, creating an intellectual space where there can be scrutiny of the histories of exiles, slavery and exploitation. Part of the affirmative action movement in the 1970s, it carried the politics of black power into the academy, changing universities into multiversities. Black studies explored slavery, movement and diaspora, probing the complexity of Black Britishness and Black Americanness. Popular culture and popular music were particularly important to this renaissance in Black history. While Alex Haley's *Roots* captured this movement, so did Gil Scott-Heron's 'The Revolution will not be Televised'. Reggae was particularly important in the early history of Black studies. It was young, political, historical and fashionable. The studies of reggae in this environment provided the framework to theorize rap and hip hop throughout the 1980s and 1990s (Baker, 1995).

In 1973, there were 200 Black studies programmes in the United States (Baker, 1995). While this number has now retracted, Black studies continue to fulfill its brief to ensure that theories and histories of blackness are enfolded into history and literature programmes. Initially it provided a space to raise provocative questions, such as expressed by Clarence Walker: 'What are "black ways" for thinking about history?' (1991: xviii). While such an inquiry may seem reified or simplistic, it provides the start for the development of consciousness, difference and defiance. Walker's question provokes us to consider if there are 'black ways' for thinking about popular music. While the master and slave relations have ended, institutional racism survives. Popular music is part of a black reconstruction of America, but most label owners, producers and promoters are still white.

Popular music – like all popular culture – is not a mirror for life. It does not give audiences the sounds of real and authentic experiences. Instead, sounds are selected, augmented, edited, cropped, remixed and overdubbed. Nevertheless, music initiates the capacity to change and transgress the real and create opportunities for a better future. In the history of blackness, popular music has a pedagogical function. It teaches and creates opportunities for learning. While musicians may not have intended to educate an audience about history or write about a productive and better future, there is no doubt that listeners and dancers learn about bodies, race, politics and difference through pop. The author and social activist bell hooks, through her *Reel to Real*, showed how this process operates in the cinema (1996: 2). Within popular music, we hear difference before seeing it. An iPod's Genius algorithm is not racist in its selection of the next song. The moment of racial bias occurs in the choice of compact discs that the listeners select, or in the purchase and downloading of a particular track and not another. In a digitized environment, the opportunities to hear new music have increased. So has the possibility of hearing difference.

Rock was a colonizing formation. Hip hop is decolonizing, agitating assumed differences between the trivial and authentic, colonizer and colonized. Rock, hip hop and techno were all genres that reworked race. The language of success in popular music is English and the accent is American, however this Anglo-American matrix is unstable. Rock music was not simply an appropriation of rhythm and blues. It was a hybridized form. Ewan Allison realized, 'the simple truth is that the white audience is a good deal happier when tapping its feet to the sounds of a white artist than a black' (1994: 440). Elvis Presley, Bill Haley and Jerry Lee Lewis exemplified his argument. Lawrence Grossberg realized that rock 'did not challenge the taken-for-granted terms of the ideologically and institutionally constructed racism of the U.S. and it most certainly did not offer any critique of the dominant ideology' (1991: 360–1). However, the relationship between black and white is dialectic, not linear or causal.

The hub of the debate is if, how and why hybridity and diaspora are marketed and consumed. Is it a concern that sounds and images are reified, simplified, appropriated, recut and sold? John Hutnyk created one of the most powerful and considerate theorizations of this difficult terrain in his *Critique of Exotica: Music, Politics and the Culture Industry*.

> In the search for authenticity it has become fairly commonplace to acknowledge that authenticity is a sham. Indeed, the more sophisticated poses available in the theory and tourist marketplace, not to mention in the popular music scene, hold that the conscious recognition of the staged character of 'authentic' performance does not compromise, but can in effect enhance, authenticity (2000: 90).

More precisely, he asks, 'can the Subaltern Dance?' (2000: 106). The followers of trip hop seemed to answer 'yes' to John Hutnyk's question. Based in Bristol, a port on a former slave route, it is populated by a diversity of citizens (including musicians) of African descent. The rise of trip hop, exemplified by Massive Attack's 'Blue Lines' and Portishead's 'Dummy' followed the path of punk and two tone. A slowed dub hip hop, trip hop was able to marry reggae and soul together. As revealed by trip hop, blackness operated in an unpredictable fashion in 1990s England through drum 'n' bass, reconfiguring dub reggae, jazz and techno.

The question is how these dialogues effect our listening to popular music. Appropriation of musical forms carries with it not only a betrayal of origins but also the exploitation of those whose sounds, ideas, rhythms and melodies have been disconnected from one context and presented in another. Ewan Allison was very clear on the modes of exclusion.

> Any thoughtful white listener should recognize that hip hop lives and breathes as a Black thing in ways simply not open to white experience, white thought ... To interrogate ourselves in this way is no easy task, inheriting a tradition of listening to Black music that reeks of disrespect (1994: 438).

The difficulty with Allison's argument here is that appropriation results in a diversification of music. Hip hop generally, and rap specifically, are not authentically black formations as have moved into a range of other genres and nations. In reality, sounds bleed through genres, histories and experiences. They are no longer 'a black thing'.

Appropriation is linked with discussions of cultural imperialism. The phrase suggests a one-way power relationship, signifying economic and social dominance. As the intellectual language moved from cultural imperialism in the 1970s through to globalization in the 1990s, there was a recognition that the relationship between the local and global, authentic experiences and marketed mediation, was complex and changeable. As an example, bhangra musical genres and styles have appropriated and transformed Anglo-American musical technologies. A clear example is 'Husan' by the Bhangra Knights. It is one of the most innovative hybrid house tracks, opening new sounds and spaces linguistically, musically and rhythmically. But the direction of the appropriation is unclear. A melting pot musical formation creates new sounds through a sonic dialogue. The profound problem remains that much greater demands to be 'representative' are placed on non-White performers. Rupa Huq was aware that 'much expectation is vested in the executants of the new Asian pop, much more than in their white counterparts who are not subjected to the same continual pressure to supply self-justifications' (2006: 203). In other words, white performers play music. When musicians of colour are involved, they are playing politics (and music).

Music is torn and twisted by the varied institutions with an interest in sound, noise and its multiple audiences. In attempting to refine the arguments about politics and music, John Hutnyk was adamant that 'the thing about appropriation is not authenticity or not, but rather the capacity to profit from culture' (2000: 9). In other words, attention should not be paid to the ownership of sounds, but rather to who profits from the product. Dominic Strinati asked a relevant follow-up question to that of Hutnyk: 'how do authenticity and inauthenticity affect the pleasures music can afford its audience?' (1995: 43). This is another fascinating issue. Does the knowledge of how Little Richard's or Chuck Berry's songs and styles were used to make a career and profit for white artists affect how we hear the original? Does guilt fill our headphones?

Perhaps it is not only a question of guilt or pleasure. Slavery and colonization stripped people of their language, social structures, histories and beliefs. Music enabled some communities to preserve elements of this culture and history. The problem here is that this preservation makes a profit for others. This is the key issue about appropriation. Cultural appropriation refers to the movement of ideas, music, language and identities from one location to another. Yet it is reliant on a notion of purity and originality that is tarnished or lost as it shifts in form and function. The political concern and critique emerges when there is an annexation by empowered groups over less powerful communities. Minorities often have clothing, language, religious beliefs, icons and music taken from a contextually-sensitive location and deployed in often inappropriate and commercial ways. Symbols and sounds lose meaning. At its best, this can be synonymous with cultural diffusion and multiculturalism. At its worst, complex belief systems and structures will be colonized and sold.

Writing about race and music has changed. Simon Frith insisted that, 'what was once an argument about cultural class, race and gender conflict, has been translated into a kind of celebratory pluralism' (1996: 6). The relationship between race and nation is differently constituted from hip hop to soul, techno to drum 'n' bass, rock to jungle. The concept of globalizing or global music does not provide sufficient subtlety to configure a study not only of local and regional cultures, but also of how local cultures move. Discussions of race, appropriation and commodification are volatile. Like the first verse of a rap, a challenge is issued to listeners, creating discomfort, movement and anxiety. This challenge should be productive, creating a thinking space in which to hear differently.

Key Questions

1. What is cultural appropriation?
2. How are earlier exploitations of black musicians to be resolved in the present?
3. How does the race of a performer effect how the music is consumed?
4. Is the iPod a colourblind platform?

Further Reading

Baker, H. (1995) *Black Studies, Rap and the Academy*. Chicago: University of Chicago Press.

Hutnyk, J. (2000) *Critique of Exotica*. London: Pluto.

Rose, T. (1994) *Black Noise: Rap Music and Black Culture in Contemporary America*. Hanover, NH: Wesleyan University Press.

Phinney, K. (2005) *Souled American: How Black Music Transformed White Culture.* New York: University of Pennsylvania Press.

Sonic sources

Beach Boys (1976) *Rock and Roll Music.*

Berry, C. (1955) *Rock and Roll Music.*

Boone, P. (1955) *Tutti Frutti.*

Little Richard (1955) *Tutti Frutti.*

Visual sources

Black Entertainment – A Celebration of Black Music (2001) IMC.

Jackson, M. (2003) 'Black or White', Epic.

Josh White – Free and Equal Blues (2001) Music Sales.

Rhapsody in Black (2004) Arrow.

Web sources

Brooks, D. (2008) Amy Winehouse and the (Black) Art of Appropriation, *The Nation,* September 10, http://www.thenation.com/doc/20080929/brooks

Honky Tonks, Hymns and the Blues (2006) http://www.honkytonks.org/showpages/blackandwhite.htm.

Narine, D. (1989) 'Blue-eyed soul': Are whites taking over rhythm & blues?, *Ebony,* July, http://findarticles.com/p/articles/mi_m1077/is_n9_v44/ai_7698861/

Neal, M. (2002) 'White Chocolate', *Pop Matters,* 17 December 2002, http://www.popmatters.com/columns/criticalnoire/021217.shtml

Girl Groups and Feminism

Every era and genre of popular music has featured an extraordinary woman who transformed and challenged audiences. Rock had Janis Joplin. Soul featured Aretha Franklin. Hip hop summoned Queen Latifah. Celine Dion rejuvenated the power ballad. Beyonce Knowles and Lady Gaga extended the legacy of Donna Summer. Such extraordinary women block the supposition that popular music is primarily a male experience. The women who have been successful in rock history – like Suzi Quatro and Joan Jett – have tended to masquerade masculinity with whisky-stained voices, leather trousers and shock-cut hair. To understand the complex relationship between women and popular music requires great analytical subtlety. Contemporary critics are fortunate. In 1984, one of the finest texts on femininity in music was published. It was written by Sue Steward and Sheryl Garratt and was titled *Signed, Sealed and Delivered: True Life Stories of Women in Pop*. They argued that women have often been invisible in the history of popular music. While they have a role as singers, female instrumentalists are marginalized. Indeed, particular instruments are accepted as being available solely for masculine performance.

There have been visible, confrontational, strange and complex women who have changed the parameters of popular music and women's role in history. While women's history is often belittled, ignored or silenced, pop has provided a small but highly visible space for women to dress, dance, scream and sing. Dusty Springfield, Stevie Nicks, Gloria Gaynor, Siouxie Sioux, Courtney Love and Lady Gaga have stretched the acceptable behaviour of women through clothing, hair, makeup and voice. From Springfield's beehive to Beyonce Knowles dance routine in 'Single Ladies', women in popular music have twisted the voyeuristic masculine gaze into the pleasure and power of being watched. Such a strategy is often temporary, a frozen moment when an empowered woman and popular music align. A powerful – if ephemeral – reconfiguration of the gender order is implemented.

While it is difficult to establish a solid and long-lasting connection between empowered women and a career in popular music, it is similarly difficult for female journalists, researchers and academics to claim expertise in popular music. Indeed, most books that students read about popular music are written and/or edited by men. There is a reason for this. Norma Coates conceded that,

> for women to be heard, they must temporarily assume the expert position normally held by men in the formation. That is, they must talk like a man, or more accurately, as if they were men (1998: 83).

The relationship between rock and feminism is complex. Feminism's second wave emerged at the same time as the great 'rock' decade concluded. This meant that feminist popular music studies had to respond to and critique a fully formed and empowered discourse of both masculinity and music. Feminist musicians and commentators played catch up, responding to already formed genres and modes of singing.

Women's voices have offered a staunch critique of the male domination of the industry. A strong example is the song 'Respect'. Written and initially performed by Otis Redding, it was performed by Aretha Franklin six months before Redding's death. In its cover version, the track moved from a hypermasculine demand for a man's right to the domination of women in marriage into becoming a feminist anthem (Guralnick, 1986: 332). This transformation – through Franklin's voice and body – provides a key example of how the same words and melody can be reshaped in a new way, to create a new political environment.

In the 1980s, Peter Christenson and Jon Brian Peterson argued that, 'gender is central to the ways in which popular music is used and tastes are organized' (1988: 282). Their use of the word 'organized' is incisive and informative. Gender is an organizing force in music, the punctuation of pop. While almost every genre – except perhaps disco and country – is associated with men, women offer a counterflow of imagery and sounds that transforms 'business as usual'. Rock music was not the same after Janis Joplin's 'Another Piece of My Heart'. Affirmative black masculinity was shriveled by Salt 'n' Pepa's 'Push It'. Punk had a wider effect, changing how women were seen in popular music, but their role as backing singers and non-instrumentalists remained constant. This exclusion was intentional, pronounced and structural. Through much of the history of popular music, women had a role as fans, girlfriends, and occasionally singers. Sara Cohen claimed that 'there were very few "ways into" the music scene for a woman, and being a girlfriend was still the easiest' (1991: 210). Such a statement is disturbing because there remains a pivotal role for music in the socialization of young women. The pedagogic function of music teaches women about femininity, masculinity, love and relationships. Deanna Sellnow wrote that,

> Music as an authentic popular voice, as a means for argument, as a way to combine verbal and emotional elements are discussed … Music can function effectively as an authentic voice for women as a marginalized group (1999: 66).

Popular music validates the views of dominant groups and dominant ideas about romance and love although oppositional discursive messages are possible. The importance of polysemy and intertextuality provides spaces for women to construct alternative stories and views. This negotiation of supposedly 'safe' pop is found in the configuration of girl groups.

The history of girl groups is not only a narrative of performers. It is also a story of producers and songwriters who created melodic and romantic pop songs. The wide scale instrumentation and orchestration that backed girl bands rendered early rock and roll more complex (Unterberger, 2003: 843). While many girl groups can be claimed as the first, The Chantels should be in consideration, with their song 'Maybe' in 1958. With the Shirelles' 1960 song 'Will You Still Love Me Tomorrow?', the genre would be created: dense harmonies, an expansive orchestra and a pensive and evocative lead vocal. The song was written by Gerry Goffin and Carole King. This songwriting team would launch many of the best-known girl groups. The final element in the girl group story is Phil Spector. He created the Wall of Sound – a dense and layered studio formation – that became associated with The Ronettes and The Crystals. Significantly, many of these early girl groups were African-American, bringing forward and together the histories of both doo wop and rhythm and blues. Even with the British 'invasion', The Supremes and Martha & the Vandellas were able to survive.

A girl group is composed of a series of female singers. This description does not include a group including instrumentalists. It is a generic and often derogatory term, but it does signify a lead vocal with backing harmonies and often 'the girls' will dance as well as sing. Many of the recorded songs involve romance, love and loss. Tracking back to The Andrews Sisters, key examples of girl groups include The Ronettes, The Supremes, The Pointer Sisters, Destiny's Child, The Spice Girls, Girls Aloud and The Pussycat Dolls. Motown contributed – besides The Supremes – The Marvelettes, Martha and the Vandellas and The Crystals. Girl groups have been black and white but most importantly, they have been transitory. Girl groups bounce into popular culture, look beautiful, sing well and dance smoothly. They gain an audience of tween and teen young women and often thirty-something gay men. Then the groups break up, caused by either a decline in sales or the individual success of one of the performers. Diana Ross from The Supremes and Beyonce Knowles in Destiny's Child are examples of the standout performer entering a solo career. When 'the girls' attempt to regroup as women, as was the case with The Spice Girls reunion in the late 2000s, it rarely works. The point is that girl groups are finite. They all must end. They rarely provide a foundation or basis for extended fame and fortune. For every Beyonce Knowles, there are hundreds of wannabes who have neither the talent nor the trajectory for a musical career. This affirmation of girliness, rather than womanhood, is contradictory to many contemporary goals of feminism. Girl groups are an attempt to stop the biological, ideological and chronological clocks. In affirming adolescence, without any desire for womanhood, this is a way to keep femininity in a subordinate role.

Feminism is a politically and theoretically useful paradigm in popular music studies because it focuses women's attention on their oppression, rather than subjugating their identity to the needs of others. Girl groups have been able to reveal playful physicality and a safe eroticism. Women's sexuality provokes discussions of repression and control, with hints of pleasure and agency. Once The Spice Girls started affirming the importance of 'Girl Power', they transformed from being another trivial, manufactured girl group and became a threat. This (re)clamation of feminism in pop plays with issues of credibility. While Courtney Love had 'cred', The Spice Girls were (and still are) lacking this critically-recognized judgement. Part of the fame of girl groups is based on extreme fashion. From The Ronettes' beehives to Geri Halliwell's Union Jack dress, clothes have built relationships between girls and women, femininity and feminism. These women, because of their glamour and transitory celebrity, were often attacked through tabloid environments for their sexuality and physicality. As one example of this sexism, when 'Sporty Spice' Melanie Chisholm gained some weight, she was mocked in the tabloids as 'Sumo Spice' (Dougherty, 2000).

Women are essential to the music industry and this role is often trivialized or ignored. Women's role as fans is paramount for the survival of the music market. Sheryl Garratt remembered that 'most of us scream ourselves silly at a concert at least once, although many refuse to admit it later, because like a lot of female experience, our teen infatuations have been trivialized, dismissed and so silenced' (1984: 140). The contribution of women to popular music – relative to the success of Elvis Presley, The Beatles, Michael Jackson and Justin Timberlake – has been under-valued. When performers become 'serious', it is a signifier that they have finally attracted male fans. Groupie is a word that undermines women's fandom. The real and credible audience is male. Many women – at some point in their life – will be prone to becoming fixated on a group of young men. The reasons for this attraction are many, but one cause is the role – and repressions – of young women in families and social life. As Simon Reynolds remarked, 'There's a "truth" of pop music to be found in the wet seats at Beatles or Stones concerts – as much as in the pantheon of Lennon's songwriting or the vicissitudes of the counter culture' (1990: 45).

There is another interpretation of these wet seats that connects with feminism. Although women purchase most pop records and the related merchandise, such as posters and postcards, women who are in popular music are restricted to the role of 'fan'. Pop fandom does grant women a voice, a politics and some space. There is a moment of clarity and awareness that occurs through the cynicism of a comment about wet seats at Beatles' concerts, Madonna wannabes, young fans of The Spice Girls singing that 'you gotta get with my friends' and Lady Gaga's monsters who follow her on Twitter. The experimentations with popular music are both physical and internalized, of the body and mind. While punk increased women's visibility, through reinscribing leather, rubber, suspenders and bondage gear, popular culture is a sphere where women can 'be and do' what is not expected or permitted within the non-pop social domain. They can dance. They can scream. They can look. They can laugh with their friends.

Girl groups have revealed a subversive sexual/political site. They occupy space and perform the contradictions between the private, popular and a public. They are loud, physically active and successful. There is an important political goal in forming a fashionable, truly popular feminism. Girl groups in popular music are part of this project. If women, as much as girls, can maintain the friendship, dancing, laughter and success, then girl groups can have a lasting trajectory which should improve the status of women in popular music. They do not provide a feminist future, but a pathway to different models of femininity.

Key Questions

1. What is feminism? What is the relationship between feminism and popular culture?
2. Why are most of the women in popular music singers in bands? Why are there so few female instrumentalists?
3. Were The Spice Girls feminists? Was 'Girl Power' a form of feminism?
4. Why is the popularity of girl groups short lived?

Further Reading

Leonard, M. (2007) *Gender in the Music Industry*. Aldershot: Ashgate.

Raha, M. (2004) *Cinderella's Big Score: Women of the Punk and Indie Underground.* Berkeley, CA: Seal.

Steward, S. and Garratt, S. (1984) *Signed, Sealed and Delivered: True Life Stories of Women in Pop*. London: Pluto.

Whiteley, S. (1997) *Sexing the Groove: Popular Music and Gender*. London: Routledge.

Sonic sources

The Crystals (1963) *He's a Rebel*.

The Ronettes (1964) *Be My Baby*.

The Shirelles (1960) *Will You Still Love Me Tomorrow?*

The Spice Girls (1996) *Wannabe*.

Visual sources

Dreamgirls (2006) Paramount Home Entertainment.

Girl Groups: The Story of a Sound (1983) MGM.

Spice World: The Movie (1993) Universal.

The Crystals, *Da doo run run*, *YouTube*, http://www.youtube.com/watch?v= dqgtsai2aKY.

Web sources

Feminism/Popular Culture, http://afeministresponsetopopculture.blogspot.com/

Girl Groups, http://www.girl-groups.com/

Motown Webring, http://welcome.to/the-motown-webring

Spectropop, http://www.surf.to/girlgroups

Boy Bands and Men's Studies

Much of popular music has stretched and probed the limits and boundaries of conventional masculinity. Elvis Presley's pelvic movements, The Beatles' haircuts, David Bowie's dip into the Ziggy Stardust's paintbox, Duran Duran's shiny suits and gelled hair, 'N Sync's tattoos and piercings and Kanye West's sunglasses are all memorable. In the late 1950s and early 1960s, earnest young men like Pat Boone, Ricky Nelson, Paul Anka, Bobby Darin, Frankie Avalon and Fabian created and commodified romance, confidence, fashion and intimacy. They created a safe masculinity of love and adoration rather than sexual threat. These models of masculinity are important. Popular music has not only shaped how generations of men think about their bodies, fashion, love and sex, but also how generations of women configure their expectations of men.

'Boy band' was a phrase used in the 1990s to describe a singing group. The term became a cliché, but its usage commenced with Maurice Starr's creation of New Edition and New Kids on the Block. It signified artificiality, a group of young men brought together by a record company or an ambitious manager. The audience for boy bands was and is clearly defined. It is young and female. The Back Street Boys, Take That, 'N Sync, New Kids on the Block and Boyzone are all groups that fulfil this definition. Male singing groups – to whom 'boy bands' as a phrase was not applied – include The Platters, The Temptations and The Bee Gees. This is a significant distinction. Being 'boys' in a band is not enough to summon the description. The Jackson 5 danced better than Take That. The Platters had tighter harmonies than Boyzone. Significantly, a 'boy band' implies artificiality and constructedness. Artifice is part of the project. They play with fame, celebrity, music and masculinity. Boy bands also create a different way of performing, with highly choreographed dancing that goes beyond The Platters' synchronized movements. This dancing can mask a lack of musicianship. However, the other key characteristic is that boy bands feature young men singing in tight harmony.

Different members of boy bands occupy archetypes of the good boy, the bad boy, the athlete, the quirky one and the 'Ringo role,' the 'I am happy just to be here' member. They rarely write their own material. Cover songs dominate their list of hits. Take That are the exception here. Through their reconstitution as a male singing group without Robbie Williams, they shed the definition of 'boy band' to become a singing group in the tradition of The Temptations. In Take That 2.0, all members of the band write music and play instruments. To move away from a boy band and become men in pop required less dancing, more singing, more musicianship and an honest discussion of their constructed, commercialized and ironic past. Intriguingly, when Williams returned to Take That recently, the dialogue between past and present became more awkward.

Boy bands rarely have longevity. As their audience ages, tastes transform. Band members, such as Justin Timberlake, Brian McFadden, Robbie Williams and Ricky Martin, frequently leave for a solo career. When prominent members move on, the boy band may stagger on for a time, but will eventually fade and then fold. The completely predictable construction and narrative of the boy bands was critiqued with savage irony in Aotearoa/New Zealand. The Edge, a New Zealand radio station, developed a boy band – called Boyband – in 2006. They labelled members with their literal categories. Bad Boy was matched with Mummy's Boy, Gay Boy, Fat Boy and Hot Boy. They even attained a number one song in their home charts – for one week – with a cover of The Kinks' 'You Really Got Me'.

Boy bands have charted the transformations to masculinity, often initiated through the changing societal role of women. Popular music offers a way to monitor the reconstruction of masculinity. The relationship between men and music is invariably more revealing and meaningful in terms of power and social structure than understanding the secondary place of women in rock. Boy bands are part of what Jackie Cook termed 'a range of fully developed popular genres of new-masculinities representations, within both visual and textual modes' (2000: 171). New forms of masculinity were not a response to femininity or women, but to earlier models of masculinity.

This responsive and responding masculinity had a wider context in the 1990s. After the second wave of feminism, men had to find new ways of constructing an identity that was not based on the subjection and marginalization of women. This movement emerged at the same time as manufacturing jobs, historically dominated by men, declined and the service sector, dominated by women, started to predominate. The rise in the divorce rate, the reduction in the size of families and the increasing education level of the population, particularly of women, initiated new expectations of masculinity. Men's studies is an academic discipline that grew throughout the 1980s and 1990s to develop the serious study of men and masculinity that was not always attendant to feminism research. Despite the input of feminist theory and politics that informed and inflected men's studies, the major project was to create more independent modes and ideologies of masculinity. This reflection on the nature of masculinity created many popular cultural manifestations and responses. John Gray's *Men are from Mars, Women are from Venus* was one example, as was Robert Bly's *Iron John*. While some men withdrew to earlier models of masculinity – returning to ideologies of the breadwinner and the strong and impassive head of the household – popular culture created a diversity of voices and views. Boy bands were one such response, providing a packaged, controllable and safe masculinity for the consumption by young women. This packaging has always existed. The Beatles, The Monkees and The Rolling Stones all attracted a large female audience. But during the 1990s, the domination of boy bands in the charts showed that there was a huge audience for a safe and non-threatening form of masculinity, 'boys' who sang and danced, smiled and waved. The 1990s were the era of broken masculinity, unemployment, underemployment, *Fight Club*, divorce and self help. Boy bands emerged from this culture, creating non-threatening, charming, dancing young men for a female audience.

Popular culture has a powerful role in changing masculinity. Kevin Goddard argued that, 'Men's identities are not monolithically determined and … they are inextricably linked to their understanding of what it is that women expect of them' (2000: 34). The boy bands presented men as loyal, in love and who will sacrifice anything to remain in the relationship and be with the woman forever. In many popular cultural environments, such as film and soap opera, the man in crisis has been a staple narrative (Sandell, 1996). However, boy bands feature good looking young men, singing well constructed pop songs. They are not in crisis but they are in the process of development, waiting for a good woman to enter their lives to complete them.

Throughout much of the history of popular music, the default audience has been female. What the boy band era confirmed was the truth of popular music history. The 'serious' critics require audiences to be male. In actuality, the audience is female. The real audience dances, screams, sings along and feels the pleasure of being part of popular culture. While patriarchal culture is organized around the presentation of a female body for the consumption by men, boy bands were different and disruptive, structured to enable, celebrate and encourage the female gaze on a male performer's body.

Take That are the survivors of the boy band era. They offer an original and remarkable story in the history of both boy bands and popular music. After Robbie Williams went on to solo fame, the band split. They eventually regrouped for a ten-year anniversary. They recalled their actual experiences of fame and loss in a documentary, inadvertently revealing both the arrogance and ruthlessness of Robbie Williams when describing his former bandmates. Through this exposure, which added depth to the superficiality of their boy band fame, the four members (without Williams) regrouped and moved beyond nostalgia to create their own tribute act. Williams' career has never recovered. Take That forged a new type of career, more in keeping with Motown's male singing groups rather than their former selves. The key moment in this rebranding was the music video for 'Patience' where the four remaining members renegotiated their former selves and history through the platform that created their fame. After becoming the first post-boy band, they may indeed be back for good. The role of Williams in this future remains unpredictable and unstable.

Key Questions

1. What is a boy band?
2. Why were boy bands particularly important to the 1990s music industry?
3. What do boy bands tell popular music researchers about the relationship between masculinity and the popular music industry?
4. Are we now post-boy bands?

Further Reading

Gray, T. (2008) *The Hit Charade: Lou Pearlman, Boy Bands, and the Biggest Ponzi Scheme in U.S. History*. New York: HarperBusiness.

Hawkins, S. (2009) *The British Pop Dandy: Male Identity, Music and Culture*. Aldershot: Ashgate.

hooks, b. (2003) *We Real Cool: Black Men and Masculinity*. London: Routledge.

Jarman-Ivens, F. (2007) *Oh Boy! Masculinities and Popular Music*. Abingdon: Routledge.

Sonic sources

Backstreet Boys (1997) *Everybody (Backstreet's Back)*.

New Kids on the Block (1990) *Step by Step*.

Take That (1992) *A Million Love Songs*.

Take That (2006) *Patience*.

Visual sources

Backstreet Boys: Black & Blue Around the World (2001) Jive.

New Kids On The Block – Hangin' Tough ~ Live (1989) Cherry Red.

'N Sync PopOdyssey (2001) BMG.

Take That For the Record (2006) BMG.

Web sources

All I know about marriage I learned from pop music, *YouTube*, http://www.youtube.com/watch?v=kq3acv-Rsp8

Boy Bands, Bubblegum.com, http://www.bubblegun.com/culturepop/boybands.html

Boy Bands, http://www.orizon.co.uk/index.html

Sing Star Boy Bands vs Girl Bands, Playstation, http://uk.playstation.com/games-media/games/detail/item120747/SingStar%C2%AE-Boybands-vs-Girlbands/

Gay, Lesbian, Bisexual and Transgenderist Musics

Keith Richards described rock as 'music for the neck downwards' (Richards in Evans, 2006: 19). Popular music, throughout its history, has featured a series of moments of sexual instability where the normative rules of love, romance, sex, marriage, family and children were questioned, probed or attacked. Even Johnny Cash, that bastion of heterosexual American masculinity, recorded a song titled 'A Boy Named Sue'. Its first performance at San Quentin Prison created a disturbing, amusing, volatile and complicated relationship between singer, song and audience that was captured on audio and video tape. A hard man was singing to other hard men about carrying a woman's name through life. This single moment showed that even the most popular and heterosexual of popular cultural performers could agitate and shatter normal behaviour and judgements.

Thinking about sexuality and popular music can invoke easy narratives about identity and complicated discussions about history. It is easy to list and label a series of performers, noting their sexuality and then 'explaining' how this identity has framed their music. K.D. Lang, Neil Tennant, Melissa Etheridge and Tom Robinson have managed and transgressed such simple categorizations throughout their professional careers. It is much more difficult to think about how a voice, lyrics, and a particular selection of instruments or rhythms can create a space for social and sexual instability.

For example, The Kinks are lauded in the pantheon of rock greats. Lacking the influence of The Beatles and The Rolling Stones, they were always more complicated and risk taking than their compatriots in the 1960s' British 'invasion'. If possible, listen to three songs from The Kinks before progressing with this chapter. The three tracks are

'You Really Got Me'
'Lola'
'Waterloo Sunset'

The first is a proto-metal rock classic: hard riffs, gruff vocal, and brutal and complex drumming patterns. A link can be drawn from this track through to later metal genres. Yet even in the midst of this heteronormative narrative, punctuated by aggressive power chording and rhythm guitar patterns, the supposedly dominant heterosexual man is not running this romantic/sexual encounter. He is not in control. The gap between the distorted guitars playing chords that would satisfy a Metallica fan and the lyric that presents a heterosexual woman dominating a man and a sex life offers a moment of instability and ambivalence.

This disjuncture between instrumentation and lyric is twisted into the queer sphere through 'Lola'. In the discourse of rock, this song is one of the strangest, cleverest, funniest and sexually disruptive to enter popular culture. Lola 'walks like a woman'. She 'talks like a man'. The transgenderist experience is explained through the extraordinary lyrical realization that 'girls will be boys and boys will be girls'. 'Lola' is a dangerous song – much more dangerous than parental warnings on rap may realize. It provides a narrative and context for a range of sexualities and identities. It is a song of predictions and surprises, both musically and lyrically.

Finally there is 'Waterloo Sunset', which is often claimed as The Kinks' masterpiece, which presents as a gentle, lilting song with a light, treble-enhanced strumming of the guitar and heavy cymbals, rather than snares, on the drum kit. Ray Davies' voice is effeminate, a voyeuristic watcher of the beautiful people in 1960s' London. Famously, the 'Terry' and 'Julie' in the narrative refer to Terence Stamp and Julie Christie. The watcher simply looks 'at the world from my window'. Uninvolved and disconnected from personal relationships, The Kinks' created an aura of aloof disconnection that would create a pattern for The Pet Shop Boys. They were to spend much of their musical career watching others behind their sunglasses and from under hats. There is more than a geographical relationship between 'Waterloo Sunset' and 'West End Girls'.

These three examples produced from a single – if extraordinary – band show that sexuality is important to popular music and very difficult to understand and analyze. The promise of love, intimacy and sex provides the lyrical juice for a range of genres, from teen idols through to rap. The consequences of loss, betrayal and break ups fuel country and emo. Country music – with its extravagant narratives of love, betrayal, demons and death – has offered some strange interventions in popular music. Songs such as 'Every Man I Love is Married, Gay or Dead' by Kacey Jones or Travis Tritt's 'Here's a Quarter, Call Someone who Cares' add humour and mock grandeur to interpersonal relationships. Popular music also provides narratives about normality and difference, as is the case with boy bands and girl groups, while constructing an emotional language to understand the nature of masculinity, femininity and the discourses of sexuality.

Sexuality is controllable when powerful institutions like religion, families, schools and universities encircle and control it. Doctors, psychologists and religious leaders construct normal sexual behaviours, categorizing and judging difference and deviance. Popular culture most frequently reinforces dominant ideologies, while leaving spaces for dissent, resistance and reinterpretation. The overwhelming majority of popular music celebrates heterosexual love, romance, sex and family, constructing narratives of 'normal' emotional development. Simon Frith examined the consequences of excluding – through intention or ignorance – sexual diversity.

The absence of gays from the subcultural pop myth reflects, then, the fantasy involved: what academic commentators long to do is place themselves in a utopia of innocence ... The cultural study of popular music has, after all, always rested on a valorization of youth – youth not as a sociological category but as a state of being (1992: 181).

Frith is making an important point here. A denial of sexuality is a denial of maturity, a refusal of ageing. To offer a deep, mature discussion of the ambivalence, liminality and confusions of sexuality in popular music is to enter an adult world of betrayal, disappointment and loss. By constructing a more complex understanding of musical audiences, the simple relationships between 'youth' and 'popular music' can be studied.

In 1992, the year where AIDs entered popular culture and sexual ambiguity became an issue that could not be ignored but dare not speak its name, John Godfrey proclaimed from the pages of *The Face*, '"say it loud, I'm neither gay or straight but I'm proud," may be the ultimate statement in post-modern sexuality, but it leaves a lot to be desired. Like who am I?' (1992: 109). The movement between male and female, fuelled by sexual experimentation and a fear of death, transformed bodies into a performative canvas. Madonna experimented, probed and pouted. The Pet Shop Boys watched. Duran Duran and Spandau Ballet invested in clothes rather than relationships. The commitment to fashion, hair and makeup adorned bodily surfaces with play and performance, but also masked and silenced the more concrete and difficult discussions of sexuality that may have emerged.

From Cliff Richard to The Beatles, Wham to Duran Duran, and from Everything but the Girl (EBTG) to Alicia Keys, popular music has activated an exploration of sexuality and identity and has also strongly connected with the idea of community. Occasionally in popular music this commitment to a sexual community is overtly political, as in the case of Jimmy Somerville and The Communards. Committed to the act of coming out, an unambiguous homosexuality was declared. They wished to provide a role model and spoke on behalf of the gay community at a time when it was vulnerable after the scare campaigns encircling HIV and AIDs. Perhaps holding a more lasting – if more politically ambivalent – role is Frankie Goes to Hollywood. Releasing – excluding the endless repackaging – a single album, their songs 'Relax', 'Two Tribes' and 'The Power of Love' combined war, sex, death and violence in a way that extended beyond even the most extreme operatic performance. Frankie Goes to Hollywood brought sex to the masses, unencumbered by love, marriage or family. Comprising both gay and straight men from Liverpool, they were witty, funny and well dressed. They sang and performed as if the last days of the Roman Empire were upon us. Like the Sex Pistols of sexuality, Frankie Goes to Hollywood were only in existence for a short period, but their influence has proved lasting. Even in the midst of AIDs, they showed that sexuality could still provoke humour and deep thought rather than death.

The portrayal of gayness – even when summoned by heterosexual performers – matters to popular music. It provides opportunities for rebooting and renewal. Like Frankie Goes to Hollywood, The Scissor Sisters in the mid-2000s were also able to provide a new way to think about identity, sexuality and music. Like queer Spice Girls, each member of the band took on a character and role. Their musical contribution, from the extraordinary reconfiguration of Pink Floyd's 'Comfortably Numb' through to the Drag Queen 101 of 'Filthy Gorgeous' and the brutal understatement of 'Return to Oz', invested the surfaces of popular music with a camp humour and political possibility. As with Frankie Goes to Hollywood, their intervention in popular music was not long lasting, but their enabling capacity in popular music was important, providing opportunities for more adult discussions of sexuality in its diversity and plurality.

Most of the performers in The Scissor Sisters were gay, with a straight male drummer and the heterosexual singer/performance artist, Ana Matronic. Similarly the two most visible members of Frankie Goes to Hollywood were gay. There is a reason for this outwardly visible gay presence. Popular music, in its post-disco formation, has always had a strong connection with gay clubs. So many dance tracks have smacked of gay irony: Sinitta's 'So Macho', Eartha Kitt's 'I Love Men' and anything by the Village People. Popular culture does grant a space for the culturally invisible and while it has been associated with youthful rebellion and protest, in addition it is commodified and heavily marketed. Lady Gaga has continued this history. Popular music provides listeners/viewers with public discourses about the nature of social relationships. In the space between song and audience, there is the potential for disruption and dissonance. Music is part of a politics of enunciation, marking sexual, racial, classed and generational differences. It also creates spaces of telling, listening, dancing and thinking.

Queer theory is appropriately applied to popular music. It is a theory invested in the surfaces of culture, revealing the assumptions that enable and promote binary oppositions like straight and gay, black and white, old and young. Queer theory disconnects signifier (form) from signified (content), raising the possibilities of many interpretations of images, ideas and sounds. Validating plurality and diversity, queerness is unstable, playful and unravels the clear relationship between sexual identity and sexual behaviour. Such an approach helps to understand the social and sexual relationship between performers and fans like Morrissey, Kylie Minogue, The Pet Shop Boys and Lady Gaga. The categories of straight and gay rarely sit comfortably when analyzing fan communities. The applications of the word 'queer' have been a site of controversy in gay and lesbian politics. While seemingly part of identity politics and an attempt to build coalitions, it can be configured as a denial of affirmative action and political resistance. These debates are part of popular cultural studies. The controversies about whether a musician is 'out' – having declared their sexual identity – are matched by the fear of ghettoizing music as 'gay'. Actually, sexual identity is much more than sexual practices. It involves a collection of fleeting and often arbitrary choices about clothing, hairstyle and music. Queer theory has shown that behaviour can be disconnected from identity, and the surfaces of popular culture provide great opportunities for social and sexual experimentation.

At its best, popular music provides a soundlab for stretching and testing the limits of our identity. It offers narratives of possibilities and alternatives. These moments of difference and defiance may be short lived. Indeed – except for Madonna and The Pet Shop Boys – these radical ruptures in the socio-sexual fabric have been transitory. These explorations, experiments and commitments may be fleeting, but in disconnecting the simple and assumed alignment between identity and sexuality, popular music can provide a soundtrack for a new way of living.

Key Questions

1. What is the function and role of the performer's sexuality in the 'reading' of popular music?
2. Why do most tracks in popular music express heteronormative narratives of love and sex?
3. How can queer theory assist our understandings of sexuality and popular music?
4. How can popular performers and songs disrupt the assumptions about love, marriage and heterosexuality?

Further Reading

Burns, L. and Lafrance, M. (2001) *Disruptive Divas*. London: Routledge.

Gill, J. (1995) *Queer Noises: Male and Female Homosexuality in 20th Century Music.* London: Continuum.

Smith, R. (1995) *Seduced and Abandoned: Essays on Gay Men and Popular Music.* London: Continuum.

Whiteley, S. (1997) *Sexing the Groove: Popular Music and Gender.* London: Routledge.

Sonic sources

Lady Gaga (2008) *Just Dance.*

The Kinks (1970) *Lola.*

The Pet Shop Boys (1987)*It's a Sin.*

The Smiths (1985) *How Soon Is Now?*

Visual sources

Eurythmics – Ultimate Collection (2006) Sony.

Frankie Goes To Hollywood – Hard On – Live Portraits (2006) Zyx.

Red Hot And Blue – A Benefit For AIDS Research And Relief (1994) BMG.

We Are the Scissor Sisters And So Are You (2004) Polydor.

Web sources

National Sexuality Resource Centre, http://nsrc.sfsu.edu/

New Now Next, http://www.newnownext.com/

Queer Music, YouTube Channel, http://www.youtube.com/group/queermusic

Queer Music Heritage, http://www.queermusicheritage.us/

Digitization, User Generated Content and Social Networking

In 2008, Lush T-Shirts increased their 'Geek' range. A new and very popular shirt was released with the emblazoned slogan 'Legal downloads are killing piracy' (Lush, 2008). Such inversion creates not only humour but also an awareness of the fast history that has been written in the last ten years. For much of the 2000s record companies have been at war with their own consumers, targeting people who they have identified as sharing music online. Often termed digital musical piracy, such a description is a denial of much of the history of popular music.

Being a fan of popular music is about sharing knowledge, ideas and passion. To be a fan is to make a stand about some form of music and to display through words, clothes, posters or Facebook profiles that particular songs or groups are of personal relevance and importance. For thirty years, cultural and media studies theorists have granted audiences a large and wide role in constructing meaning, difference and identity. In the analogue age journalists and academics framed an audience as 'active', because it was argued they interpreted the text in a way that decoded its message to suit their environment. The Web 2.0 environment created a suite of opportunities for fans to write, sing, remix and share their passion in new and creative ways. One of the most remarkable examples of how older music can return to popularity through social networking sites is Eleanor McEvoy's song 'Sophie'. The lyric details a young woman fighting anorexia nervosa. The soundtrack has been used by fans and activists to create YouTube videos exploring eating disorders. The comments left in response to these videos increased awareness of a particular song and meant it gained new audiences and listeners.

Web 2.0 describes the creation and distribution of content by an online and computer literate population. While the focus is on content creation, very often it is content selection and movement. The uploading of content – songs, footage and videos – that is created by others but used and reused by consumers initiates a widespread copyright infringement. Such a 'crime' is justified through corporate revenge. Michael Faber argued that,

> Record companies paid colossal advances they could never recoup; they over-charged shamelessly for albums, phased out singles, recorded music to digital information stored in generic discs, then reeled in shock when consumers figured

out that it was much cheaper to copy the digits on their PCs than to pay a wad of cash for those same zeroes and ones in a plastic case. The corporations' response? Sue their customers. Hide virus-breeding rootkits inside 'copy protected' discs. Pray for another *Thriller* to rescue them. Sign desperate deals with supermarket chains such as Wal-Mart, whose discounts then drove thousands of record shops out of business. Legal downloads, introduced 10 years too late, proved lucrative for Apple and Amazon, but their emphasis on individual songs further eroded the status – and the revenue – once commanded by albums (2009: 38).

In other words, record companies made many mistakes. Consumer behaviour through software and hardware 'solved' these problems for personal – rather than corporate – benefit. Digital Rights Management (DRM), a form of technological protection measures (TPMs), was one way for producers to control 'illegal' behaviour. A concurrent consumer development was not only the use of Bit Torrent and Pirate Bay, but also the creative uses of digital recordings (Fisher, 2004: viii).

Re-editing, remixing and mash-ups reconfigure original content. Lessig termed this environment a *Remix Culture* (2008). However, it is necessary to remember that this digital creativity is based on copyright infringement. There is a clash between the legal controls over publishing and copyright and the appropriation and remixing of copyrighted components. Put another way, this is a conflict between Digital Rights Management versus the Creative Commons licensing procedure. The key question remains how consumers can be encouraged, facilitated or forced to pay for digitized content that they have not created, re-edited or enhanced. A range of innovative schemes is emerging, where musicians have disconnected from record companies and are finding ways to make a living from their songs, performances and songwriting (Dolan, 2005). Concurrently, many bands and musicians have exhibited a high degree of acceptance of pirated music. The Grateful Dead are a clear example of performers who allow piracy, knowing that it enables alternative income streams. By not pursuing bootleggers, they are aware that such practices have facilitated the purchase of other products (Pfahl, 2001).

While illegal downloaders have been demonized and legally pursued by record companies, there needs to be a much more careful understanding of the information this community provides about the new media environment. Yes they wanted free music, but this desire was also a response to decades of overpriced and overpackaged music that was unsustainable, either economically or environmentally. It also captured a desire for social networking and post-geographical alignments between music consumers. By 2001, Napster was the largest music fan community in the history of music. Sean Ebare was aware that 'an understanding of the "user-driven" dynamics of music audience subcultures is an invaluable tool in not only forecasting the future of online music consumption patterns but in understanding other online social dynamics as well' (2005). In other words, even while demonizing the downloaders, it was important for record companies to understand the message that was being sent to them about new relationships between music and its audience. Through much of the history of popular music, there has been an assumption that its audience was young. In particular there has been an assumption that 'rock music' had an audience from 'youth culture'. However both phrases were shaken and shattered in a Web 2.0 environment. The mobility of music has increased the plurality of consumers. Even as late as 2006, Dan Laughey stated that 'music is delivered and sold to youth audiences' (2006: 1). However social networking sites, along with the ease of downloading individual singles, have dislocated and distorted linear and chronological popular music history. Pop time has always been cyclical rather than linear. Now that the software and hardware has caught up with the desire of fans to jump between genres and performers and times, it is no longer possible to either label or track a specific sociological group with a particular mode or form of music. Indeed, the speed has increased between the production and the consumption of music, facilitated by turntablism and innovative domestic software that encourages remixing (Ebare: 2005).

In 1994, Roy Shuker reflected that 'rock critics continue to function as significant gatekeepers and arbiters of taste' (1994: 72). In the subsequent two decades, the development of web-based fan sites, blogs, social networking sites and the portfolio of participation that is described as Web 2.0 has created a range of new voices and views. This participatory culture has displaced and decentred this gatekeeper function. Keith Negus acknowledged that 'the struggles through which new technologies are produced and introduced can have a considerable impact on how contracts are drawn up and how the "product" of popular music is conceptualized' (1999: 33). Developments in the decade since Negus wrote these words have intensified his argument. Music can be written, recorded, mixed and distributed from home. It can be downloaded, free of charge from YouTube and Facebook. Apple iTunes can be used as a quasi-record company to recompense artists (and/or the corporation) for each download.

The statistics about downloading behaviour – legal or illegal – are volatile. Even as early as 2005, the PEW Internet and American Life study reported that 27 per cent of American internet users (36 million people) admitted to downloading either music or video files. Half of those surveyed worked outside of peer-to-peer networks or paid online services to swap songs. Seven million adults – or 19 per cent of the online population – admitted that they had downloaded files from someone else's iPod or MP3 player (Madden and Rainie, 2005). The restrictions on peer sharing through commercial sites such as iTunes via Digital Rights Management have been effective in a limited sense, but there are so many options for gaining free music files. Every barrier intended to control software and hardware creates new opportunities for the development of hardware and software that enables consumers to gain products without payment. The business model for many online services is a free one. As Chris Anderson has realized, with sonic files available at no cost, consumers will pay for extras and special editions to the material they can freely attain. He classified this as 'Freemium', which can operate within the gift economy and piracy (2006: 26–29).

Music is one element in a wider culture of social networking in the online environment. Participants/consumers share video, links, stories and sounds. With all files digitally created, uploaded and downloaded, new cultures are created based on sharing interests, literacies, software and hardware. Fans will comment, rank and judge, talking between themselves rather than valuing a key review from an esteemed journalist in a music magazine. They will also take a file, remix it, re-edit it and upload it for further development and commentary. The question is one of money. For every case like the Arctic Monkeys who gave their music away on MySpace only to gain international success and fame (and a recording contract), there are millions of performers and bands who provide free content – music – for the pleasure of consumers but never receive payment. This gift economy – this culture of free – does affect the possibilities of a revenue stream for the artists and performers who create the music in the first place. While the users may *generate* the content, they will rarely pay for it.

Key Questions

1. What is user generated content?
2. Why do music consumers 'steal' free music?
3. Is a model of illegal downloading sustainable?
4. How have music journalists been affected by the 'comment culture' of blogs?

Further Reading

Anderson, C. (2009) *The Future of a Radical Price*. New York: Random House.

Fisher, W. (2004) *Promises to Keep: Technology, Law, and the Future of Entertainment*. Stanford: Stanford University Press.

Harold, C. (2007) *Ourspace: Resisting the Corporate Control of Culture*. Minneapolis: University of Minnesota Press.

Lessig, L. (2008) *Remix Culture: Making Art and Commerce Thrive in the Hybrid Economy*. New York: Penguin.

Sonic sources

Appleton, J.J. (2006) *Downloader's Blues*.

Days, D. (2009) *My YouTube Song*.

Remix Culture (2009) Center for Social Media, American University, iTunes U.

The Afters (2008) *MySpace Girl*.

Visual Sources

Charlie Rose – Jake Tapper/Lawrence Lessig (2008) Charlie Rose Inc.

Chris Anderson with Will Hearst: The Long Time Tail (2007) Whole Earth Films.

Michael Jackson: Fan's Camera Footage (2009) Music Video Distribution.

Rip: A Remix Manifesto (2009) EyeSteelFilm.

Web Sources

Dixon, P. (2007) 'Future of Music Industry,' YouTube, http://www.youtube.com/watch?v=hmP64KjRims&feature=related

Free! Why $0.00 is the Future of Business (2008), YouTube, http://www.youtube.com/watch?v=RZkeCIW75CU

How To Download Free Music (2007), YouTube, http://www.youtube.com/watch?v=SB22fUUVkVs&feature=related

Remix: Lawrence Lessig on IP in the Digital Economy (2008), YouTube, http://www.youtube.com/watch?v=nS6IC5AWh5c

Music: Politics, Resistance and Protest

In 2003 and from a London stage, Natalie Maines of the American country trio The Dixie Chicks abused the then President Bush. After doing so, she received death threats, bomb threats and the band's songs were removed from the play list of hundreds of radio stations, many owned by Clear Channel Corporation. While The Dixie Chicks' music had rarely been considered 'political' in the fashion of either Bob Marley or The Clash, the challenge they posed to a serving administration and Republican supporters was stark.

There was a reason for these attacks. There has been an assumption, particularly since the 1960s, that music has a message. In the merging of music, culture and politics, trivial and ephemeral pop was loaded with significance, gravity and resistive potential. The phrase 'progressive rock' connoted through the adjective 'progressive' that this style of music was improving, changing and moving. Simon Frith, in a prescient statement, confirmed that,

> the cultural study of popular music has been, in effect, an anxiety-driven search by radical intellectual and rootless academics for a model of consumption – of the perfect consumer, the subcultural idol, the mod, the punk, the cool commodity fetishist, the organic intellectual of the high street who can *stand in for them* (1992: 180).

Many performers provide 'the message' required by left-leaning and progressivist academics and journalists. As the people who define, label and review 'important' music, these writers will select particular bands and performers that they consider to be contributing to the worthiness and importance of music. Often the chosen performers will express the views of the writer, with popular music fans becoming a ventriloquist puppet, mouthing the political views of a specific journalist or researcher. John Lennon's 'Power to the People', Bob Dylan's 'Masters of War', Marvin Gaye's 'What's Going On', Crosby, Stills, Nash and Young's 'Ohio', Elvis Costello's 'Shipbuilding', The Pet Shop Boys' 'I'm With Stupid' and Aretha Franklin's 'Respect' are a few examples where a track resonates not only with its context, but also with the political imperatives of academics and journalists.

Such links between music and politics are too simplistic. For too long, the default assumption has been that 'rock' is a mode of radicalism and resistance. Actually, the overwhelming majority of popular music is signed to and distributed by corporations with the singular goal of selling products to audiences. While the lyrical content of popular music may suggest radicalism and defiance, the means of production for this music are based on conservative exchanges of money for a product. Music is part of a capitalist exchange, buying and selling a range of products, including downloads, DVDs, concert tickets and compact discs. While Bob Dylan's music is used as the soundtrack for a range of social movements for social justice, he remains – with only a slight detour to Asylum – signed to Columbia Records. But he has also sold the rights to his songs and his personal image to a range of companies, including the use of 'Love Sick' for a Victoria's Secret commercial and the granting of permission to use 'Sunday Baby' to advertise Apple's iPod and iTunes.

Throughout the history of post-rock popular music, there has been a concurrent growth in the branding of popular culture. In the history of cinema, for example, product placements have been a crucial income stream for the industry. James Bond is synonymous with Aston Martin, Smirnoff, Omega and Rolex. Popular music is part of this branded, commodified entertainment. Performers advertise a range of goods aligned with the youth market, including soft drinks, fast food, portable music players and a range of gaming products. In the last two decades there has been an increased integration of brand and song. Occasionally this has been initially unsponsored and unsolicited, in the case of Janis Joplin's song 'Mercedes Benz'. Although it was not released with this intention, by the 1990s it was being used in a campaign to market the vehicle. Brands are mentioned in song lyrics without sponsorship to capture everyday experience rather than confirm marketing deals. Sheryl Crow's mention of a 'Bud buzz' in 'All I Wanna Do' is an example. There has been a complex alignment of musicians as 'celebrities' with a particular product. Michael Jackson's and Britney Spears' advertisements for Pepsi are two obvious examples. In this case, brand placement aligned with corporate culture and the development of celebrity. Fergie from the Black Eyed Peas is reputed to have signed a US$4 million contract to endorse Candies fashion through a 'product placement' in lyrics (*Song Lyrics*, 2007).

Product placement can be visual or audible. Visual brand management is more successful and longer lasting, particularly in an era of audience fragmentation and dispersal. In an environment that uses both digital video recorders and TiVo, viewers can ignore the advertisements and advance the footage to the required content. Apple has used conventional television advertisements and urban billboards, featuring artists such as Bob Dylan, to manage the iPod brand. Jean-Marc Lehu confirmed that 'the Apple communications budget is tiny compared with that of HP, Dell, NEC or Microsoft. This is why, in line with its positioning, Apple has always tried to communicate differently' (2009: 62). Such sponsorship deals are becoming increasingly important as conventional advertising in breaks between programming is being ignored, critiqued, avoided and questioned through social networking sites. Such avoidance strategies increase the need to integrate and naturalize placements on a range of platforms, including those developed for music. This tight alignment of music, performer and corporate culture has raised critical objections both inside and outside the music industry, but such a stance is increasingly difficult to maintain as brands pervade the landscape. A demarcation between 'music' and 'commerce' has rarely – indeed very rarely – existed. Therefore resistance to distributors and corporate 'interests' is difficult to mobilize. It is ironic that much of the rock music being used as a soundtrack for overthrowing the state has been paid for by corporations. Resistance and radicalism became a marketing device to sell music.

The 1960s mattered to the construction of a relationship between rock and politics. Terry Bloomfield confirmed,

> Classic rock … reflects the dominance of white adult male definitions of popular music; in part, too, many commentators are of an age that they remember sixties music as a sentimental accompaniment to excursions into adulthood, while many more were swept up at that time by the enthusiasm for cultural revolution (1991: 60).

Rock expressed the narratives and alienations of youth. Bob Dylan's songs throughout the 1960s were and are still scrutinized in detail by rock journalists, seemingly intensified through Dylan's opaqueness to journalistic commentary. Significantly, it was the legendary broadcaster and writer Studs Terkel who enabled Dylan to explain the song that is often cited as his most political: 'A Hard Rain's A-gonna Fall'.

> I'll tell you how I come to write that. Every line in that really is another song. Could be used as a whole song, every single line. I wrote that when I didn't know how many other songs I could write. That was during October of last year [1962] and I remember sitting up all night with a bunch of people someplace. I wanted to get the most down that I knew about into one song, so I wrote that. It was during the Cuba trouble, that blockage, I guess is the word. I was a little worried, maybe that's the word (Dylan in Terkel, 2006: 204).

There can seem to be a literal link between lyrics and the historical context. Such easy relationships also serve to undervalue a more complex alignment of place, politics and music. Other forms of music – like dance and country – are neglected. Richard Dyer realized that 'the prestige of folk and rock, and now punk and (rather patronizingly, I think) reggae, still holds sway. It's not just that people whose politics I share don't like disco; they manage to imply that it is politically beyond the pale to like it' (1990: 169). Dance music – including disco, house and its derivatives – has been attacked for its apolitical or anti-political status. For example, Angela McRobbie described 'rave' (rather than techno) as 'a culture of avoidance' and containing 'nothing like the aggressive political culture found in punk music' (1993: 423). Such statements are based on colonial and rock-infused definitions of both social change and politics. Outside of disco, electronica and dance musics, rock erupted with anger rather than passivity. In 1976, Rock against Racism was formed by rock photographer Red Saunders after the rise of the National Front, enhanced via supportive comments by Eric Clapton towards Enoch Powell. Three years later Margaret Thatcher was in office and promoted a British nationalism based on colonial heritage rather than multiculturalism. In such an environment 'protest music' can empower and unify a group, motivating them to share struggles and subvert rules through formal and informal resistances and participatory politics. Frequently, there is creative thought and a desire for change, but with no prepared plan or strategy to activate concrete structural interventions on the basis of this transformation in consciousness.

Most of popular music is not protesting against anything. There are celebrations of love, or mourning the loss of a romance, or building soundtracks for dancing and enjoyment. Indeed, Deena Weinstein believed that 'while so many celebrate and enumerate various rock protest songs, I want to account for the myth of their ubiquity and their relative rarity, specifically in the United States' (2006: 3). Most musicians, at a critical point in their career, will disconnect from a desire for social change because the goal of personal success becomes attainable and important. Some communities, such as indigenous groups, are much more committed to expressing rage and injustice. The Australian indigenous performers Archie Roach in his 'Took the Children Away' and Ruby Hunter with 'Proud, Proud Woman' more directly connect music, identity and protest. Commercial success was less relevant than the making of a political statement. The cost of such affirmations often leads to a loss of an audience. In Australia, where an overwhelming majority of the population are not indigenous, a reminder of indigenous history through music creates discomfort rather than pleasure. This statement does not suggest that such sonic interventions should not be made, but that there are costs and consequences.

Blackness is a complex formation and slices through popular music. While rap may express an authentic and clear black voice, the politics of Soul II Soul or Massive Attack was and is more difficult to pinpoint. This realization is not only applicable to scholars in media and cultural studies, but also to the wider range of academics and journalists who take popular music as their topic. While there is much attention given to the relationship between men, rock, blackness and politics, Sarah Thornton has asked that researchers in popular music broaden their definitions.

> Rather than de-politicising popular cultures, a shift away from the search for 'resistance' actually gives fuller representation to the complex and rarely straightforward politics of contemporary cultures (1995: 1).

In other words, looking for 'resistance' actually deflects popular music researchers from understanding more complex concepts and ideas of consciousness and community. In the early history of rock music, the beat was as important as the lyrics. The protest through rhythm was generational. Lyrics detailed subjects like cars, girls and parents. Eddie Cochrane's 'Summertime Blues' tapped most of these topics. Jerry Lee Lewis and Little Richard conveyed a generational protest through their look, via a drape jacket, winkle-picker shoes, drain-pipe trousers and slim ties. While too much focus has been placed on 'reading' lyrics and resistance through rhythm, what has been under-discussed is the attention paid to the role of volume, clothes and hair styles.

Such stories of resistance are difficult to research and understand. It is easier to assume that music is a soundtrack for political protest. Folk music has maintained a culture of dissent through lyric and instrumentation. Bob Dylan's 'Chimes of Freedom' and Phil Ochs' 'I Ain't Marching Anymore' are examples of this genre. Judy Collins, Joan Baez and Peter, Paul and Mary popularized 'protest music' even further, aligning civil rights and popular culture. Rock music in the 1960s offered a way to align antiwar resistance and the counterculture. While much of the anti-establishment lyrics dissipated with the advent of psychedelic music, there have remained songs for the working class, indigenous peoples, citizens of colour, women, prisoners and gay and lesbian communities from performers such as Johnny Cash, Bruce Springsteen, Tracy Chapman and Tom Robinson. While protest and resistive music is often associated with left wing and progressivist musical forces, there has also been protest music from the right. Charlie Drake's 'Welfare Cadillac' attacked those claiming governmental support and Merle Haggard's 'The Fightin Side of Me' was an anti-pacifist song. Invariably, this 'easy' conceptualization of politics was conveyed through lyrics with music, particularly national anthems, being used by the establishment to create bonds between listeners. They can also be a force for anti-establishment communities, attacking war, racism, sexism and homophobia. 'We Shall Overcome' – most famously performed by Pete Seeger and Joan Baez – became the soundtrack for the civil rights movement.

Protests, marches, riots and revolutions will often have a soundtrack. Political change can create musical change. In Cuba, after Castro's 1959 revolution, there was a movement away from American jazz and towards Mozambique, pilón and pacá rhythms. Similarly, the Velvet Revolution in Czechoslovakia in 1989 used Frank Zappa's Mothers of Invention and The Velvet Underground, both banned by the government in the 1960s, as the music of dissent. After Václav Havel became president of the Czech Republic in 1993, he met Lou Reed and stated 'Did you know that I am president because of you?' (Havel in Welch, 2003).

Events like Live Aid, Live 8 and Live Earth have raised 'awareness' and 'consciousness' about world poverty and environmental damage. Their long-term impact is difficult to measure. Most of the literature within popular music studies exploring 'politics' invariably focuses on the lyric rather than the music. Rock and roll music featured lyrics. There were famous instrumentals from The Shadows and The Telstars, but the lyric was on the ascent through the 1960s, only being undermined by acid house, techno and drum 'n' bass from the 1980s that was rhythm heavy and word light. Essentially, a particular history of protest was promoted and confirmed through lyrics. Another type of dissent – through drugs, bodies and dancing – emerged when literal interpretations of lyrics were not possible.

The politics of music must also include rhythm, censorship, cultural wars over appropriation, intellectual property and ownership. However, there are profound problems when connecting a minority of musics with political change. Most of popular music can unintentionally change our understandings of bodies, masculinity, femininity, sexuality, race and nation. Suzanne Moore offered a profound critique of this authentic, male model of politics.

I blame the Left for this ... for continuing to believe that culture is the spoonful of sugar that helps the medicine go down. The medicine is, of course, politics in the old-fashioned sense of the word. That a pop song moves people more than the average party politics broadcast is something that we still absolutely refuse to see. I am not saying that a popular song is therefore equivalent, but I am saying that culture rather than politics is now the space in which we have our most moving experiences both collectively and personally (1991: 11).

Music has been integral to the project of nationalism through anthems, and songs of war through military band music. It provides narratives and histories of men, women, love, loss, retribution and renewal. Listening to an extraordinary song can provide a moment of insight, an inspiration for how we could live our lives. Moore captures a truth of popular music that all researchers should remember.

> With the mantra of class/race/gender in one hand and a checklist of proper ideo-logical contents in the other, we end up with an analysis that fails to grasp all that makes popular culture popular (1991: viii).

While we earnestly mobilize checklists about class, race and gender in particular genres, researchers must ensure that we do not lose what makes popular music part of popular culture. Scholars need more honesty in understanding the 'protest' and 'resistance' in popular music. There is a story that the protest singer Julius Lester was reminded in 1967 that Woody Guthrie's guitar featured the slogan 'This Machine Kills Fascists', replied, 'Maybe his did. Mine didn't. The fascists just applauded me' (Lester in Rodnitsky, 2006: 25).

We commenced this chapter with The Dixie Chicks. They sang one melody of America and American history. There are many Americas in popular culture. Some are conservative. Some are radical. Nearing the end of the twentieth century, Simon Frith asked,

> The question becomes whether America can continue to be the mythical locale of popular culture as it has been through most of this century. As I've suggested, there are reasons now to suppose that 'America' itself, as a pop cultural myth, no longer bears much resemblance to the USA as a real place even in the myth (1991: 268).

As the twenty-first century progresses, there have been changes and movements in the posi-tion of 'America' in the world. Many of these changes have emerged through foreign policy rather than popular music. However, one feature of the iPodification of popular music is not only that more music is available throughout the world, but also that more music that is American is available. The Long Tail, as popularized by Chris Anderson (2006), may be clichéd and overdrawn, but it does capture the shape of contemporary music commerce. A greater diversity of music is sold. The key variable is whether this diversity is determined by time (history) or space (geography), or more accurately, a combination of both. Different Americas are being circulated in local environments, but a key to rewriting our present pol-itics with past music may be to reclaim and hear music beyond the borders of rock history.

There is a symbolic connection between the internet environment and popular music. URLs – Uniform Resource Locators – do not mark American identity. While all other nations – like the United Kingdom (.co.uk), Australia (.com.au) and Singapore (.com.sg) – declare a national identity through URLs, for almost all American websites they are 'the norm,' the standard and the unmarked sign. Amazon.com, Apple.com and Yahoo.com confirm this tendency. Such a confirmation of power and location through absence in American URLs was based on the British system of postage stamps, where British national identity did not need to be declared. Every other state had a national allegiance written on the stamp. Popular music is similar. The default setting of musical origin is American, with British music a secondary source. Other national musics need to negotiate with this default sonic setting. Digitization may broaden out both the source and sound of music. Such innovative listening spaces may create a potential protest that is not 'Blowing in the Wind' but heard through earphones.

Key Questions

1. Why are lyrics the focus for journalist and researchers in determining the protest in music?
2. Is protesting through music effective? How do you evaluate this effectiveness?
3. Which genres are particularly valued when assessing the protest in music?
4. Is it possible to protest through rhythm?

Further Reading

Peddie, I. (2006) *The Resisting Muse: Popular Music and Social Protest*. Aldershot: Ashgate.

Rose, T. (1992) *Black Noise: Rap Music and Black Culture in Contemporary Culture*. Hanover: Wesleyan University Press.

Sakolsky, R. and Ho, F. (eds) (1995) *Sounding Off! Music as Subversion/Resistance/Revolution*. Brooklyn: Autonomedia.

Wiseman-Trowse, N. (2008) *Performing Class in British Popular Music*. London: Palgrave.

Sonic sources

Sam Cooke (1965) *A Change is Gonna Come*.

Crosby, Stills, Nash and Young (1970) *Ohio*.

Bob Marley (1973) *Get Up, Stand Up.*

Pete Seeger (1963) *We Shall Overcome.*

Visual sources

Pete Seeger: The Power of Song (2008) Genius.

Pet Shop Boys – A Life In Pop (2006) EMI.

Rhythms of Resistance (2007) Digital Classics.

Woodstock (2009) Warner.

Web sources

Centre for political song, http://polsong.gcal.ac.uk

Freemuse: Freedom of musical expression, http://www.fremuse.org

Music of Social Change, http://www.metascholar.org/MOSC/

Pop Justice, http://www.popjustice.com/

Conclusion

Walking Off the Dance Floor

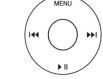

Marcus Breen, a great music writer, believed that 'pop is like a stick of chewing gum, you take it and chew on it when you need it. The cost is low, yet the benefits are substantial' (1996: 5). While assumptions are made about visual media proliferating through the multiple screens in our lives and the increasing importance of appearance in our celebrity-fuelled culture, the early iPods revealed the lie of such statements. The voice, rhythm and melody have never been so immersed in our daily lives. Blind media generally, and sonic media particularly, require distinct modes of engagement. When we listen, we think about and understand content differently than when vision is involved. While seeing is believing – and visual media are verifiable media – sonic media hold a different social and semiotic function. Sound is a communication platform of potential, possibilities, imagination and suggestions.

Sonic media are also a cultural space of change. The ipodification of culture is volatile and dynamic. By the second half of 2009, it was clear that the sale of iPods was declining, including the Nano and the Classic. The purchases of the iTouch and iPhone were meanwhile increasing (Arthur, 2009: 1). The iPad burst on the market in 2010 with a splash of publicity, seemingly prioritizing the screen over sound. Such a change triggered crisis and fear once more, as has punctuated the history of digitization of music. The decline of the stand-alone digital music player (DMP) was caused by the cannibalization of its own market. The competition is increasing for interactive, connected handheld devices that play a range of media and include telephony, texting and camera capacities. Digital music continues to be important, not only as a self-standing industry, but also as an enabler of a range of new, interactive, dynamic and connected functions for users.

Studying popular music in colleges and universities is challenging and difficult. It manages two key problems. Firstly, it is part of popular culture and suffers all the biases, prejudices and cultural assumptions that value high culture and elite behaviours and practices. The other challenge is one of categorization, as popular music is also a part of sonic media. It is composed of sounds and not written words. That is why the least effective analyses of pop attempt to anchor the ephemeral intangibility of sound to a discussion of lyrics as if they were a form of debased poetry. Actually, if scholars can shake off the predominance of the word and improve their auditory literacies, then a range of innovative disciplines can extract innovation, passion, dynamism and energy from popular music. Cultural and media studies, journalism studies, musicology, ethnomusicology, politics, history, sociology, postcolonialism and anthropology, alongside national studies like Canadian studies, New Zealand studies and Australian studies, all offer an innovative approach to music. With all these paradigms and theories it is necessary to understand what makes popular music popular, to interpret the emotional connection of a listener to the sound and the dancer to a rhythm.

Popular music is messy. It is cross cultural and open to the vagaries of technology. If pop music scholars present our histories using a chronological narrative – Elvis, Dylan, The Beatles, Sex Pistols, Nirvana, Green Day, The Ting Tings, Lady Gaga – then we deny the complexity in both sounds and meaning. The record industry as an institution has deployed a business model that has been critiqued and unsettled by both legal and illegal downloading practices. For the last twenty years dance music has depended on the relationship between supply and demand, musicians and consumers. The ideology of rock has not only been sustained but also challenged by indie. World music has remained a category that sells exoticism. Music promotes political ideas but also maintains a clear economic function as a product to be sold.

A book on or 'about' popular music can never be inclusive or definitive. There is simply too much music – even in a post-rock, post-house setting – to hold it in our analytical palm. Popular music research and writing requires specific skills. It is the most ephemeral of.media, moving and changing at an intense speed, requiring the scholar to continue to discover the new, the innovative and the novel. Significantly, it will continue to carry its history forward into new mixes and movements. The survival and increasing popularity of Bob Dylan was the surprise of the twenty-first century. The documentary *No Direction Home* rebooted his career for a new audience. He could sing about *Modern Times* while remembering the past. Similarly, The Beatles Rock Band brought the fab four to life and allowed the ghosts of Lennon and Harrison to continue to play their Rickenbackers. Lady Gaga compressed the history of David Bowie, Queen and Madonna into a tight package that both embodied celebrity culture and attacked it.

It has been an exciting time to write a book about popular music. Ulf Poschardt stated that 'Pop culture is a bastard. It can't decide whether it is a counterculture or the dominant culture. Generally, pop is both, and mostly it is the instrument with which counterculture is turned into dominant culture' (1998: 401). New and old genres combine in innovative ways. The marketing and branding of music has become more unstable and dynamic. In the current climate, there is a great opportunity to discuss a range of songs and sounds, knowing that readers are only a click away from hearing any track. *Popular Music: Topics, Trends and Trajectories* has mapped the changes and continuities in the history of sound, showing that the 'iPod moment' has had an effect on most entries. It is important with all the attention on technology to remember the emotional investment placed in the platform for music. Nelson George captured this emotional and social connection with musical technology.

For those too young to remember, there were once vinyl records. New. Unscratched. Smooth. You tore open the plastic wrapping, pulled it out of the white paper inner sleeve and the sturdy cardboard jacket cover and in your hand was a black vinyl circle with a hole in the middle. Around the hole was paper with a design and words printed upon it. You placed it on your turntable and through stereo speakers the music played just like a CD. Forgive my nostalgia – I still love vinyl (1998: 5).

The pleasures of popular music are ephemeral, but in those moments of intense commitment and connection, the songs are desperately real and incredibly important. Beyond nostalgia, the history of music in the twentieth century exhibited much continuity: performers played live, a physical musical platform was developed that enabled the listening to music and music was played on the radio. The twenty-first century has seen the revision and loss of these earlier realities. Compressed files are downloaded, having been bought or obtained free from alternative and illegal file sharing networks. Some genres continued to value live performances, but the impact of house music, sampling and remixing and its derivatives means that the notion of the original, the authentic and the live performance is lost or discredited. Finally, listening to radio in real time, along with commercial interruptions, is decentred in favour of individually selected track listings constructed either manually or through 'genius' programming for mobile music platforms and podcasts.

There have also been transformations to the music itself. The post-Fordist fragmentation of genres, audiences and markets means that 'rock music' is neither the core of popular music nor the most important part of the industry. There remains a residue of guitar-based 1960s music through performers like U2. Similarly, Anglo-American music is augmented and transformed by new musical and social movements and relationships. The soundtracks and rhythms from Hindi musicals have dialogued with house music and electronica. What creates the pleasure from music is the capacity to repeat familiar and comfortable elements like genre, chord structures, a catchy chorus or a familiar melody or sample. Having the capacity to instigate a moment or element of change is what continually invigorates a genre.

While the protestations from the record industry in the last few years have shrieked crisis, threat and trauma, popular music is actually one of the most suitable and sustainable visions for a new economy. The ideal commercial model for new music in the new economy has yet to be formulated. Jim Shorthose and Gerard Strange made the observation that

At its most general level, this new economy can be identified as being increasingly global; increasingly about intangibles such as knowledge, information, images and fantasies; and increasingly decentralized, and characterized by networks and flexibility (2004: 43).

This 'managed creativity' (Shorthose and Strange, 2004: 47) is a way to moderate and manage a deskilled, Fordist workforce with the flexibility required for a changing economy and a globalizing of finance capital. Specific local histories, musics and rhythms are being lost unless they can be commodified through international global networks. New relationships are formed between independence and commercialization. At their best, creative industries' initiatives develop policy interventions to provide an incentive for innovative cultural production (Jones, 2005: 5–12).

Music has always formalized social activities. Anthems are created for nations, political organizations and schools. Music creates a consciousness of space and identity. It differs from almost every other popular cultural formation. Reading newspapers and magazines, watching television, surfing the internet and playing computer games encourage a sedentary lifestyle. Music encourages physical movement: dancing, singing along, mouthing lyrics, air guitar or – in the combination of gaming and music through Rock Band – a physical connection between activity and noise. Popular music is special, different and defiant. Our role as researchers and writers about popular music is to understand the pleasure from pop as much as the protests and politics created from it.

At the conclusion of this journey through popular music at this moment of change, transformation and transition, it seems appropriate to note Dick Hebdige's advice at the opening of his innovative, powerful and intellectually stretching *Cut 'n' Mix: Culture, Identity and Caribbean Music*. He stated that, 'this book doesn't try to tell the whole story because the whole story can't be told … every day new connections are being made that create potentialities that are unimagined here' (1987: 10). His advice is appropriate for all researchers who write about what we hear. The study of popular culture can and should be part of understanding the multimodality of communication, including the linguistic, the sonic and the visual. Songs are the sonic landmark of our emotional lives. Instead of building monuments to the great moments of rock, our role as scholars is to understand how music is being used socially, culturally and economically. It may also be worthwhile remembering Bob Dylan's comment on popular music: 'I remember when that Napster guy came up across, it was like, "Everybody's getting music for free." I was like, "Well, why not? It's ain't worth nothing anyway"' (Dylan in Lethem, 2006). Worth, like meaning, is determined by the ear of the listener as much as by the history of the hardware. But with software, revelations through sound are a single click away.

Key Questions

1. What is the relationship between hearing and believing (particularly when compared to seeing and believing)?
2. How will the post-iPod music industry transform? How is the mobile phone changing the consumption of music?
3. How is studying popular music different from other forms of popular culture?
4. How will you decide what is important popular music? What are your criteria?

Further Reading

Franklin, M. (2005) *Resounding International Relations: On Music, Culture and Politics.* London: Palgrave.

Katz, M. (2004) *Capturing Sound: How Technology Has Changed Music.* Berkeley: University of California Press.

Klein, B. (2009) *As Heard on TV: Popular Music in Advertising.* Aldershot: Ashgate.

Tschmuck, P. (2006) *Creativity and Innovation in the Music Industry.* Berlin: Springer.

Sonic sources

Fluyd (2005) *Post Music Phantoms.*

REM (1987) *It's the End of the World as We Know It.*

Talking Heads (1985) *Road to Nowhere.*

The Doors (1967) *The End.*

Visual sources

Desperate Man Blues: Discovering the Roots of American Music (2006) Dust to Digital.

Good Charlotte: the Fast Future Generation (2006) Sony.

The Future Is Unwritten (2008) Sony Legacy.

The Strat Pack − The 50th Anniversary of the Fender Stratocaster (2004) Eagle Rock.

Web sources

Arts House Music, http://www.artistshousemusic.org/Home

Future Producers, http://www.futureproducers.com

Mashable: the social media guide, http://mashable.com/2009/04/18/social-sharing-music/

Tweet the future, http://tweetthefuture.com/q.php?q=music

References

'2008 Gaming Industry Data,' (2009) *Seeking Alpha*. (January 6), http://seekingalpha.com/
article/115107–2008-gaming-industry-data-growth-not-stopping-just-slowing.

Acoustica Mixcraft, http://www.acoustica.com/mixcraft/.

Adorno, T. Adorno about popular music, *YouTube*, http://www.youtube.com/
watch?v=Wn_lF3o8QXQ&feature=PlayList&p=96735ED98C0DA542&index
=14&playnext=2&playnext_from=PL.

Against pop, http://nomuzak.co.uk.

Alarik, S. (2003) *Deep Community: Adventures in the Modern Folk Underground.*
Cambridge: Black Wolf Press.

Alderman, J. (2001) *Sonic Boom*. Cambridge: Perseus.

All I know about marriage I learned from pop music, *YouTube*, http://www.youtube.
com/watch?v=kq3acv-Rsp8.

Allison, E. (1994) 'It's a Black Thing: Hearing How Whites Can't,' *Cultural Studies*,
8(2): 438–6.

Alsop, W. (2005) *SuperCity*. Manchester: Urbis.

Alternative Country, http://www.alt-country.org/.

Anderson, C. (2009) *Free: The Future of a Radical Price*. New York: Random House
Business Books.

Anderson, C. (2006) *The Long Tail*. New York: Hyperion.

Anvil, http://www.anvilthemovie.com/.

Apple Corporation, http://www.apple.com.

'Archive for the Music Censorship Category,' http://www.somebodythinkofthechildren.
com/category/music/.

Arnett, J. (1996) *Metalheads: Heavy Metal Music and Adolescent Alienation*. Boulder, CO:
Westview Press.

Arthur, C. (2009) 'Twilight of the iPods,' *Technology Guardian*. September 10: 1.

Arts House Music, http://www.artistshousemusic.org/Home.

Association of Independent Music, http://www.musicindie.com/.

Audacity, http://audacity.sourceforge.net/.

Audition, http://www.adobe.com/products/audition/.

Austerlitz, S. (2007) *Money for Nothing: A History of the Music Video from The Beatles to
The White Stripes*. London: Continuum.

Baker, H. (1995) *Black Studies, Rap and the Academy*. Chicago: University of Chicago
Press.

Bakersfield Sound Underground, http://blog.bakersfieldsoundunderground.com/.

Bangs, L. (2000) in J. DeRogatis, *Let it Blurt: The Life and Times of Lester Bangs*. London: Bloomsbury.

Bangs, L. (1988) 'Kraftwerk feature,' in G. Marcus (ed.), *Lester Bangs: Psychotic Reactions and Carburettor Dung*. London: Minerva.

Banks, J. (1996) *Monopoly Television: MTV's quest to control the music*. Boulder, CO: Westview Press.

Bannister, M. (2006) *White Boys, White Noise: Masculinities and 1980s Indie Guitar Rock*. Aldershot: Ashgate.

Bardsley, S. (2010) 'What is Northern Soul?' http://home.iprimus.com.au/stephenbardsley/Northern%20Soul%20page.htm.

Barfe, L. (2004) *Where Have All the Good Times Gone? The Rise and Fall of the Record Industry*. London: Atlantic.

Barr, T. (1998) *Kraftwerk*. London: Ebury Press.

Basu, D. (2006) *The Vinyl Ain't Final: Hip Hop and the Globalisation of Black Popular Culture*. London: Pluto Press.

Bauman, Z. (2000) *Liquid Modernity*. London: Polity.

Bazil, E. (2009) *Art of Drum Layering*. PC Publishing.

Bealle, J. (2005) *Old-Time Music and Dance: Community and Folk Revival*. Bloomington: Indiana University Press.

Beau, M. (2010) *Hip Hop and Rap in Europe*, http://www.icce.rug.nl/~soundscapes/DATABASES/MIE/Part2_chapter08.shtml.

Becker, J. (1998) *Appalachia and the Construction of an American Folk, 1930–1940*. Chapel Hill: University of North Carolina Press.

Bee Gees, http://www.beegees.com/index.php.

Bell, D. and Hollows, J. (eds) (2005) *Ordinary Lifestyles: Popular Media, Consumption and Taste*. Milton Keynes: OUP.

Bennett, A. and Dawe, K. (2001) *Guitar Cultures*. Oxford: Berg.

Bennett, A. and Peterson, R. (2004) *Music Scenes: Local, Translocal and Virtual*. Nashville: Vanderbilt University Press.

Berk, M. (2000) 'Technology: analog fetishes and digital futures,' in P. Shapiro (ed.), *Modulations: A History of Electronic Music*. New York: Caipirinha, pp. 188–204.

Berland, J. (2003) 'Radio space and industrial time: the case of music formats,' in J. Lewis and T. Miller (eds), *Critical Cultural Policy Studies: A Reader*. Malden: Blackwell, pp. 230–239.

Beyonce (2009) 'Single Ladies', *YouTube*, http://www.youtube.com/watch?v=x1nixz YHDus.

Blake, A. (2007) *Popular Music: The Age of Multimedia*. London: Middlesex University Press.

Blake, A. (1996) 'The echoing corridor,' in T. Butler and M. Rustin (eds), *Rising in the East*. London: Lawrence and Wishart, pp. 197–214.

Bloom, A. (1987) *The Closing of the American Mind*. London: Penguin Books.

Bloomfield, T. (1991) 'It's sooner than you think, or where are we in the history of Rock Music,'? *New Left Review*, No. 190, http://www.newleftreview.org/?view=1657.

Blues news, http://www.blues.org/.

Bob Marley, http://web.bobmarley.com/index.jsp.

Bohlman, P. (2002) *World Music: A Very Short Introduction.* Oxford: Oxford University Press.

Bowie, D. (1971) 'Changes,' *Honky Dory.* RCA.

Boy Bands, http://www.orizon.co.uk/index.html.

Boy Bands, Bubblegum.com, http://www.bubblegum.com/culturepop/boybands.html.

Boyle, J. (2008) *The Public Domain.* New Haven: Yale University Press.

Brabazon, T. (2005) 'Off World after the cabaret,' in T. Brabazon, *Liverpool of the South Seas.* Perth: UWA Press.

Bradley, L. (2000) *This is Reggae Music: The Story of Jamaica's Music.* New York: Grove.

Breen, M. (1996) 'Woof, Woof: The real bite of Reservoir Dogs,' *The UTS Review.* 2.2: 1–9.

Brewster, B. and Broughton, F. (2000) *Last Night A DJ Saved My Life: The History of the Disc Jockey.* New York: Grove Press.

'Bright Tunes Music vs George Harrison,' UCLA Law and Columbia Law Copyright Infringement Project: http://cip.law.ucla.edu/cases/case_brightharrisongs.html.

Brocken, M. (2003) *The British Folk Revival 1944–2002.* Aldershot: Ashgate.

Brooks, D. (2008) 'Amy Winehouse and the (Black) Art of Appropriation', *The Nation*, September 10, http://www.thenation.com/doc/20080929/brooks.

Brooks, R. in S. Reich (2008), 'An introduction, or my (ambiguous) life with technology,' in P. Miller (ed.), *Sound Unbound: Sampling Digital Music and Culture.* Cambridge: MIT Press.

Brown, P. (2009) 'Fab Four still waiting for net gains,' *The Guardian,* April 19, http://www.guardian.co.uk/technology/2009/apr/16/beatles-filesharing.

Brown, V.V. (2009) 'The DIY Soul Queen,' *The Observer*, October 11, p. 11.

Brunt, R. (1992) 'Engaging with the popular: audiences for mass culture and what to say about them,' in L. Grossberg, C. Nelson and P. Treichler (eds), *Cultural Studies.* New York: Routledge, pp. 69–80.

Buckland, T. (2006) *Dancing from Past to Present: Nation, Culture, Identities.* Madison: University of Wisconsin Press.

Budofsky, A. Dawson, M., Parillo, M. (2008) *The Drummer: 100 years of Rhythmic Power and Invention.* Hal Leonard.

Bufwack, M. and Oermann, R. (1993) *Finding Her Voice: The Saga of Women in Country Music.* New York: Crown.

Bull, M. (2007) *Sound Moves: iPod Culture and Urban Experience.* London: Routledge.

Bull, M. (2002) 'The seduction of sound in consumer culture,' *Journal of Consumer Culture*, 2(1): 81–101.

Bull, M. and Back, L. (2004) 'Introduction: into sound,' in M. Bull and L. Back (eds), *The Auditory Culture Reader*. Oxford: Berg, pp. 1–17.

Burns, L. and Lafrance, M. (2001) *Disruptive Divas*. London: Routledge.

Butler, M. (2006) *Unlocking the Groove*. Bloomington: Indiana University Press.

Camp Jitterbug, http://www.campjitterbug.com/.

Carr, R. (1996) *Beatles at the Movies*. London: Collins.

CBGB's Online, http://www.cbgb.com/.

Centre for Political Song, http://polsong.gcal.ac.uk.

Chaffee, S. (1985) 'Popular music and communication research: an editorial epilogue,' *Communication Research*, 12(3): 413–424.

Chambers, I. (1986) *Popular Culture – The Metropolitan Experience*. London: Methuen.

Chang, J. (2007) *Can't Stop Won't Stop: A History of the Hip-Hop Generation*. London: Ebury.

Chapman, R. (2000) *Guitar: Music, History, Players*. London: Dorling Kindessley.

Cheng, J. (2009) '"Rock and Roll" Apple iPod Event,' *Arts Technica*, September 9: http://arstechnica.com/apple/news/2009/09/liveblog-rock-and-roll-apple-ipod-event.ars.

Christe, I. (2003) *Sound of the Beast: The Complete Headbanging History of Heavy Metal*. New York: HarperCollins.

Christenson, P. and Peterson, J. (1988) 'Genre and Gender in the Structure of Music Preferences,' *Communication Research*, 15.3: 282–301.

Christian, T. (2008) 'The Return of Northern Soul,' *The Times*, August 27: http://entertainment.timesonline.co.uk/tol/arts_and_entertainment/music/article 4613377.ece.

Chtcheglov, I. (1981) 'Formulatory for a new urbanism,' in K. Knabb (ed.), *Situationist International Anthology*. Berkeley: Bureau of Public Secrets, pp. 1–4.

Classic Thrash, http://www.classicthrash.com/.

Clayton, M., Herbert, T. and Middleton, R. (2003) *The Cultural Study of Music*. New York: Routledge.

Cloonan, M. (2007) *Popular Music and the State in the UK*. Aldershot: Ashgate.

Cloonan, M. and Garofalo, R. (2003) 'Introduction,' in M. Cloonan and R. Garofalo (eds), *Policing Pop*. Philadelphia: Temple University Press, pp. 1–11.

Cloonan, M. (2003) 'Call That Censorship? Problems of Definition,' in M. Cloonan and R. Garofalo (eds), *Policing Pop*. Philadelphia: Temple University Press, pp. 13–29.

Clover, J. (2009) *1989: Bob Dylan Didn't Have This to Sing About*. Berkeley: University of California Press.

Club Equinox, http://clubequinox.com/index.html.

Coates, N. (1998) 'Can't we just talk about music? Rock and gender on the internet,' in T. Swiss, J. Sloop and A. Herman (eds), *Mapping the Beat: Popular Music and Contemporary Theory*. Oxford: Blackwell Publishers, pp. 77–99.

Cohn, L., Aldin, M. and Bastin, B. (1993) *Nothing But the Blues: The Music and the Musicians*. New York: Abbeville Press.

Cohn, N. (1969) *Awopbopaloobop Alopbamboom*. London: Weidenfeld and Nicolson.

Cohen, R. (2006) *Folk Music: The Basics*. New York: Routledge.

Cohen, S. (1991) *Rock Culture in Liverpool: Popular Music in the Making*. Oxford: Claredon Press.

Coleman, N. (2009) 'There is something unquestionably sad about the news,' The *Independent*. (January 2): http://www.independent.co.uk/arts-entertainment/music/features/legendary-olympic-recording-studio-to-burn-out-1220725.html.

Collins, K. (2008) 'Grand Theft Audio?: Video Games and Licensed IP'. Music and the Moving Image, 1.1: http://mmi.press.uiuc.edu/1.1/collins.html and http://www.gamessound.com/texts/collinsGTA.pdf.

Collins, P. (2004) *No Jacket Required tracks and credits*: http://www.philcollins.co.uk/jacket1a.htm.

Connell, J. and Gibson, C. (2003) *Soundtracks: Popular Music, Identity and Place*. London: Routledge.

Cook, J. (2000) 'Men's Magazines at the Millennium: new spaces, new selves,' *Continuum*, 14.2: 171–186.

Cook, R. (1999) 'Playing safe,' *New Statesman*, (December 6): 46.

Copyright Infringement Project. UCLA Law, http://cip.law.ucla.edu/.

Coryat, K. (2008) *Guerrilla Home Recording*. New York: Hal Leonard.

Country Music Hall of Fame, http://www.countrymusichalloffame.com/site/.

'Country Music Jokes.' Yuks 'R' Us: http://www.yuksrus.com/music_country.html.

Cox, and Warner, D. (2004) *Audio Culture: Readings in Modern Music*. New York: Continuum.

Crawford, R. (2001) *America's Musical Life in New York*. London: W.W. Norton and Company.

Creative Class, http://creativeclass.com/.

Creative Commons, www.creativecommons.org.

Crenshaw, M. (1994) *Hollywood Rock: A Guide to Rock 'n' Roll in the Movies*. London: Plexus.

Crisell, A. (2006) 'General introduction,' in A. Crisell (ed.), *More Than a Music Box: Radio Cultures and Communities in a Multi-media World*. New York: Berghahn Books, pp. vii–xiv.

Cvetkovich, A. and Kellner, D. (1997) 'Introduction: thinking global and local,' in A. Cvetkovich and D. Kellner (eds) *Articulating the Global and the Local: Globalisation and Cultural Studies*. Boulder: Westview Press, pp. 1–30.

Daly, A. (2002) *Critical Gestures: Writings on Dance and Culture*. Hanover: Wesleyan University Press.

'Dancing about architecture.' (2002) *ilix.com*, http://www.ilxor.com/ILX/ThreadS electedControllerServlet?boardid=41&threadid=4185.

Davis, F. (1995) *The History of the Blues*. Cambridge: Da Capo Press.

Dawe, K. and Bennett, A. (2001) 'Introduction: guitars, cultures, people and places,' in A. Bennett and K. Dawe (eds), *Guitar Cultures*. Oxford: Berg, pp. 1–8.

Day, E. (2009) 'Would you rather go naked? Not any longer'. *The Observer*. November 22: http://www.guardian.co.uk/lifeandstyle/2009/nov/22/fur-rather-go-naked

Decker, J. (1994) 'The state of rap', in A. Ross and T. Rose (eds), *Microphone Fiends: Youth Music and Youth Culture*. New York: Routledge, pp. 99–121.

de Koningh, M. and Griffiths, M. (2003) *Tighten Up: The History of Reggae in the UK*. London: Sanctuary.

Delta Blues Museum, www.deltabluesmuseum.org

Demers, J. (2006) *Steal this Music: How Intellectual Property Law Affects Musical Creativity*. Athens: University of Georgia Press.

Denisoff, R.S. and Romanowski, W. (1994) *Risky Business: Rock in Film*. New Brunswick: Transaction Publishers.

Department of Culture, Media and Sport (2000) *Consumers Call the Tune*: http://www.culture.gov.uk/images/publications/consumerscalltune.pdf.

Desk Top Blues, http://www.desktopblues.lichtlabor.ch/.

Desmond, J. (2006) *Meaning in Motion: New Cultural Studies of Dance*. Durham: Duke University Press.

Dickinson, B. (1997) 'There is a light that never goes out: Joy Division,' in C. Hutton and R. Kurt (eds), *Don't Look Back in Anger: Growing Up with Oasis*. London: Simon and Schuster, pp. 1–14.

DiscoMusic, http://www.discomusic.com/.

Disco Music was Gay Music, http://brumm.com/gaylib/disco/

Disco Style, http://www.discostyle.com/.

Dixon, P. (2007) 'Future of Music Industry,' *YouTube*, http://www.youtube.com/watch?v=hmP64KjRims&feature=related

DJ Battles, http://www.djbattles.com/.

DJ Download, www.djdownload.com.

Doggett, P. (2000) *Are you Ready for the Country: Elvis, Dylan, Parsons and the Roots of County Rock*. London: Penguin.

Dolan, D. (2005) 'The big bumpy shift: digital music via mobile internet,' *First Monday*. 1 (July 4), http://firstmonday.org/htbin/cgiwrap/bin/ojs/index.php/fm/article/view/1452/1367

Dolar, M. (2006) *A Voice and Nothing More*. Cambridge: MIT Press.

Doty, A. (1988) 'Music sells movies: (Re)new(ed) conservativism in film marketing,' *Wide Angle*. 10(2): 70–79.

Dougherty, S. (2000) 'Bitter Season,' *People*, November 27, 54.22, http://www.people.com/people/archive/article/0,20133083,00.html.

Drum & Bass Arena, http://www.breakbeat.co.uk/.

Drumming Web, http://www.drummingweb.com.

Du Noyer, P. (2002) *Liverpool: Wondrous Place Music from Cavern to Cream*. London: Virgin.

DVD Regions (2010) *Home Theater Info*, http://www.hometheaterinfo.com/dvd3.htm.

Dyer, R. (1990) *Only Entertainment*. London: Routledge.

Dylan, B. (2006) in J. Lethem (2006) 'The genius of Bob Dylan,' *Rolling Stone*. August 21:   http://www.rollingstone.com/news/story/11216877/the_modern_times_of_bob_dylan_a_legend_comes_to_grips_with_his_iconic_status/printe-fiddler, http://efiddler.com/loops_country.htm.

Eaton, K. (2009) 'Are Slipping iPod Sales Bad News for the Recording Industry?' *Fast Company*, http://www.fastcompany.com/blog/kit-eaton/technomix/are-slipping-ipod-sales-bad-news-recording-industry-nope.

Ebare, S. (2005) 'Digital music and subculture: sharing files, sharing styles,' *First Monday*. Special Issue 1 (July), http://firstmonday.org/htbin/cgiwrap/bin/ojs/index.php/fm/article/view/1459/1374.

Eddington, R. (2004) *Sent from Coventry: The Chequered Past of Two Tone*. London: Independent Music Press.

Elborough, T. (2008) *The Long-player Goodbye*. London: Hodder & Stoughton.

Ennis, P. (1992) *The Seventh Stream: The Emergence of Rocknroll in American Popular Music*. Hanover: Wesleyan University Press.

Eno, B. (2004) 'Ambient music,' in C. Cox and D. Warner (eds), *Audio Culture*. New York: Continuum, pp. 94–97.

Eno, B. and Chilvers, P. (2009a) 'Bloom,' iPhone Application, October.

Eno, B. and Chilvers, P. (2009b) 'Trope,' iPhone Application, December.

Erlmann, V. (ed.) (2005) *Hearing Cultures*. Oxford: Berg.

Eshun, K. (1998) *More Brilliant than the Sun: Adventures in Sonic Fiction*. London: Quartet Books.

Evans, M. (2006) *Rock & Roll*. London: AAPPL.

Evolution of Dance, *YouTube*, http://www.youtube.com/watch?v=dMH0bHeiRNg.

Faber, M. (2009) 'Record losses,' *The Guardian Weekly*, August 21: 38.

Fairlight Instruments. (1982) *Fairlight Users Manual*. Sydney: Fairlight.

Fake Bands, http://www.fakebands.co.uk/.

Faithfull, M., http://www.mariannefaithfull.org.uk/.

Fantasia, http://www.fantazia.org.uk/.

Fasoldt, A. (1998) *A sound idea: MPEG Layer 3 keeps improving,* January 25, http://aroundcny.com/technofile/texts/tec012598.html.

Feminism/Popular Culture, http://afeministresponsetopopculture.blogspot.com/.

Fender, http://www.fender.com/.

Ferguson, R. (1990) 'Introduction: Invisible Centre,' in R. Ferguson, M. Gever, T. Minh-ha, C. West (eds), *Out There: Marginalisation and Contemporary Cultures*. Cambridge: MIT Press, pp. 8–14.

Fiestad, S. (2007) *Blue Book of Electric Guitars*. Minneapolis: Blue Book Publications.

Fikentscher, Kai (2000) *You Better Work! Underground Dance Music in New York City*. Hanover: Wesleyan University Press.

Filene, B. (2000) *Romancing the Folk: Public Memory and American Roots Music*. Chapel Hill: University of North Carolina Press.

Filippa, M. (1996) 'Popular songs and musical cultures,' in D. Forgacs and R. Lumley (eds), *Italian Cultural Studies: An Introduction*. Oxford: Oxford University Press, pp. 327–343.

Finnegan, R. (2007) *The Hidden Musicians: Music-making in an English Town*. Middleton: Wesleyan University Press.

Fisher, W. (2004) *Promises to Keep: Technology, Law and the Future of Entertainment*. Stanford: Stanford University Press.

Fitzgerald, R. (2007) *Clublife*. New York: HarperCollins.

Florida, R. (2005) *Cities and the Creative Class*. New York: Routledge.

Florida, R. (2002) *The Rise of the Creative Class*. New York: Basic Books.

Folk Den, www.folkden.com.

Folk Music Archives, http://folkmusicarchives.org/.

Fonarow, W. (2006) *Empire of Dirt: The Aesthetics and Rituals of British Indie Music*. Middletown: Wesleyan University Press.

Fox, A. (2005) *Real Country: Music and Language in Working-class Culture*. Durham: Duke University Press.

Foxwell, K. Ewart, J., Forde, S. and Meadows, M. (2008) 'Sounds like a whisper: Australian community broadcasting hosts a quiet revolution,' *Westminster Papers in Communication and Culture*, 5(1): 5–24.

Frakes, D. (2006) *Your iPod Life*. Berkeley, CA: Peachpit.

Franklin, M. (2005) *Resounding International Relations: On Music, Culture and Politics*. London: Palgrave.

Free! Why $0.00 is the Future of Business (2008) *YouTube*, http://www.youtube.com/watch?v=RZkeCIW75CU.

Freedberg, M. (n.d.) 'Writing About Dancing: Disco Critics Survey,' Rock Critics Archive: http://rockcriticsarchives.com/features/discocritics/discocritics10.html.

Free Internet Radio, http://www.shoutcast.com/.

Freemuse, www.freemuse.org.

Frith, S. (1996) *Performing Rites: On the Value of Popular Music*. Cambridge: Harvard University Press.

Frith, S. (ed.) (1993) *Sound and Vision: Music Video Reader*. Abington: Routledge.

Frith, S. (1992) 'The cultural study of popular music,' in L. Grossberg, C. Nelson and P. Treichler (eds), *Cultural Studies*. New York: Routledge, pp. 174–186.

Frith, S. (1991a) 'He's the one,' *Village Voice*, (October 29): 18.

Frith, S. (1991b) 'Anglo-America and its discontents,' *Cultural Studies*. 5: 263–9.

Frith, S. and Goodwin, A. (1990) 'Groundworks,' in S. Frith and A. Goodwin (eds), *On Record: Rock, Pop and the Written Word*. London: Routledge: 1–4.

Frith, S. (1988) 'Introduction,' in S. Frith (ed.), *Facing the Music*. New York: Pantheon.

Frith, S. (1981a) 'The magic that can set you free,' in R. Middleton and D. Horn (eds), *Popular Music One: Folk or Popular? Distinctions, Influence, Continuities*. Cambridge: Cambridge University Press, pp. 159–68.

Frith, S. (1981b) 'The sociology of rock – notes from Britain,' in D. Horn and P. Tagg (eds), *Popular Music Perspectives: Papers from the First International Conference on Popular Music Research*. Amsterdam: de Gruyter.

Frith, S. (1978) *The Sociology of Rock*. London: Constable.

Frow, J. (1995) *Cultural Studies and Cultural Value*. Oxford: Oxford University Press.

Future Producers, http://www.futureproducers.com.

Gammond, P. (1980) 'Coming of age: recording in the LP Era,' in P. Gammond and R. Horricks (eds), *The Music Goes Round and Round: A Cool Look at the Record Industry*. London: Quartet Books.

Gammond, P. and Horricks, R. (1980a) 'Prologue,' in P. Gammond and R. Horricks (eds), *The Music Goes Round and Round: A Cool Look at the Record Industry*. London: Quartet Books.

Gammond, P. and Horricks, R. (1980b) 'The pop explosion,' in P. Gammond and R. Horricks (eds), *The Music Goes Round and Round*. London: Quartet Books.

Garofalo, R. (2003), 'I want my MP3: who owns internet music,' in M. Cloonan and R. Garofalo (eds), *Policing Pop*. Philadelphia: Temple University Press, pp. 87–103.

George, N. (1998) *Hip Hop America*. Harmondsworth: Penguin.

Gibson.com (2009) 'Inspirational past, exciting present, revolutionary future' (October 21): http://www.gibson.com/en-us/Lifestyle/Features/innovation-1020/.

Gibson Les Paul, http://www.lespaulguide.com/.

Gibson, C. and Connell, J. (2005) *Music and Tourism: On the Road Again*. Bristol: Channel View Publications.

Gibson, C. (2008) 'Recording studios: relational spaces of creativity in the city,' *Built Environment*, 31(3): 192–207.

Gilbert, J. and Pearson, E. (1999) *Discographies: Dance Music, Culture and the Politics of Sound*. London: Routledge.

Gill, J. (1995) *Queer Noises: Male and Female Homosexuality in 20th century Music*. London: Continuum.

Girl Groups, http://www.girl-groups.com/.

Goddard, K. (2000) 'Looks Maketh the Man': The Female Gaze and the Construction of Masculinity,' *Journal of Men's Studies*, 9.1, Fall: 23–39.

Godfrey, J. (1992) 'The new camp,' *The Face*, 51, December: 109.

Godin, D. (2001) 'Foreword,' in K. Rylatt and P. Scott (eds), *CENtral 1179: The Story of Manchester's Twisted Wheel Club*. London: Bee Cool Publishing.

Godin, D. (1970) 'The Up-North soul groove,' *Blues & Soul*, June 1970, from *Rock's Back Pages*, http://www.rocksbackpages.com/article.html?ArticleID=12041.

Golden, E. (2007) 'Musical Maneuvers,' *Remix*. (October 1): http://remixmag.com/performance/dj_tips_techniques/music_maneuvers_digital_dj/.

Goldman, A. (2006) in S. Walksman (2006) 'Black Sound, Black Body' in A. Bennett, B. Shank and J. Toynbee (eds), *The Popular Music Studies Reader*. London: Routledge, pp. 64–70.

Goodwin, A. (1998) 'Drumming and memory,' in T. Swiss, J. Sloop and A. Herman (eds), *Mapping the Beat: Popular Music and Contemporary Theory*. Oxford: Blackwell, pp. 31–46.

Gorbman, C. (2000) 'Film music,' in J. Hill and P. Church Gibson (eds), *Film Studies: Critical Approaches*. Oxford: Oxford University Press, pp. 43–50.

Gorges, P. (2005) *Programming Synthesizers*. Bremen: Wizoo.

Gotfrit, L. (1991) 'Women dancing back: disruption and the politics of pleasure,' in H. Giroux (ed.), *Postmodernism, Feminism and Cultural Politics*. Albany: State University of New York, pp. 174–195.

Gray, M. (2008) *Hand Me My Travelin' Shoes: In Search of Blind Willie McTell*. London: Bloomsbury.

Gray, T. (2008) *The Hit Charade: Lou Pearlman, Boy Bands, and the Biggest Ponzi Scheme in U.S. History*. New York: HarperBusiness.

Greenfield, S. and Osborn, G. (1998) *Contract and Control in the Entertainment Industry: Dancing on the Edge of Heaven*. Aldershot: Dartmouth.

Greenfield, S. and Osborn, G. (2003) 'Remote control: legal censorship of the creative process,' in M. Cloonan and R. Garofalo (eds), *Policing Pop*. Philadelphia: Temple University Press, pp. 65–78.

Grindcore, http://www.grindcore.org/.

Grossberg, L. (1994) 'Is anybody listening? Does anybody care?,' in A. Ross and T. Rose (eds), *Microphone Fiends: Youth Music and Youth Culture*. New York: Routledge, pp. 41–58.

Grossberg, L. (1991) 'Rock, territorialization and power,' *Cultural Studies*, 5: 358–367.

Guitar Hero, http://hub.guitarhero.com/.

Guralnick, P. (1990) *Searching for Robert Johnson*. London: Secker & Warburg.

Guralnick, P. (1996) *Sweet Soul Music: Rhythm and Blues and the Southern Dream of Freedom*. London: Penguin.

Hall, S. (1996) 'New Ethnicities,' in H. Baker, M. Diawara and R. Lindeborg (eds), *Black British Cultural Studies*. Chicago: University of Chicago Press, pp. 163–172.

Hall, S. (1978) 'Popular culture, politics, and history,' *Popular Culture Bulletin*, 3: 6–7.

Hall Hansen C. and Hansen, R. (1990) 'The influence of sex and violence on the appeal of rock music videos,' *Communication Research*, 17(2): 212–234.

Hanson, M. (2006) *Reinventing Music Video: Next-Generation Directors, Their Inspiration and Work*. Cheadle: Rotovision.

Hansson, H. and van de Bunt-Kokhuis, S. (2004) 'E-learning and language change – observations, tendencies and reflections' (August) *First Monday*, 9(8): http://firstmonday. org/htbin/cgiwrap/bin/ojs/index.php/fm/article/view/1168/1088.

Harold, C. (2007) *Our Space: Resisting the Corporate Control of Culture*. Minneapolis: University of Minnesota Press.

Harris, J. (2009) 'Don't look back,' *The Guardian* (June 29) http://www.guardian. co.uk/music/2009/jun/27/music-writing-bangs-marcus.

International Association for the Study of Popular Music, http://www.iaspm. net/.

Harris, J. (2009) 'I got a new head, and I'm fine,' *The Guardian*, June 19: 3.

Haslam, Dave. (2001) *Adventures on the Wheels of Steel: The Rise of the Superstar DJs*. London: Fourth Estate.

Haslam, D. (1999) *Manchester England: The Story of the Pop Cult City*. London: Fourth Estate.

Havel, V. (2003) in M. Welch (2003) 'Velvet President,' *The Free Library*. May: http://www.thefreelibrary.com/Velvet+president:+why+Vaclav+Havel+is+our+era's+George+Orwell+and+more-a099933033.

Hawkins, E. (2002) *Studio-in-a-Box*. Vallejo: EMBooks.

Hawkins, S. (2009) *The British Pop Dandy: Male Identity, Music and Culture*. Aldershot: Ashgate.

Hebdige, D. (1987a) *Cut 'n' Mix: Culture, Identity and Caribbean Music*. London: Comedia.

Hebdige, D. (1987b) 'Hiding in the light,' *Art and Text*, 26: 67–78.

Hebdige, D. (1988) *Hiding in the Light*. London: Routledge.

Hegarty, P. (2002) 'Noise threshold,' *Organised Sound*. 6.1:193–200.

Hegarty, P. (2008) *Noise/Music: A History*. New York: Continuum.

Herbert, T. (2001) *Music in Works: A Guide to Researching and Writing about Music*. London: Associated Board of the Royal Schools of Music.

Hewitt, P. (2000) *The Soul Stylists: Forty Years of Modernism*. Edinburgh: Mainstream Publishing.

Heylin, C. (1992) *The Penguin Book of Rock & Roll Writing*. London: Penguin.

Hickey, D. (1997) *Air Guitar*. Lost Angeles: Art Issues Press.

Hill, L. (1996) *Easy Rider*. London: British Film Institute.

Hines, J. (1990) *Great Singers on Great Singing*. New York: Limelight.

Hip hop.com, http://www.hiphop.com/.

History of Disco Dance, Buzzle.com, http://www.buzzle.com/articles/history-of-disco-dance.html.

Holmes, T. (2008) *Electronic and Experimental Music: Technology, Music, and Culture*. New York: Routledge.

Honky Tonks, Hymns and the Blues (2006) http://www.honkytonks.org/showpages/blackandwhite.htm.

hooks, b. (2003) *We Real Cool: Black Men and Masculinity*. London: Routledge.

hooks, b. (1996) *Reel to Real: Race, Sex and Class at the Movies*. London: Routledge.

Home Recording, http://homerecording.com/.

Hopper, D. (2004) 'Sequences,' *Sight and Sound*, 4(9): 46.

Horricks, R. and Slaven, N. (1980) 'The Pop Explosion,' in P. Gammond and R. Horricks (eds), *The Music goes Round and Round: A Cool Look at the Record Industry*. London: Quartet Books.

Hoskyns, B. (1997) *Beneath the Diamond Sky: Haight-Ashbury 1965–1970*. London: Bloomsbury.

Hoskyns, B. (1991) *From a Whisper to a Scream: The Great Voices of Popular Music.* London: Fontana.

House Music, http://www.housemusic.com/.

How To Download Free Music (2007) *YouTube*, http://www.youtube.com/watch? v=SB22fUUVkVs&feature=related.

Hubbard, P. (1996) 'Urban Design and City Regeneration: social representations of entrepreneurial landscapes,' *Urban Studies*, 33(8): 1441–1461.

Human Beatbox.com, http://www.humanbeatbox.com/.

Hunt, C. (2002) 'The story of Wigan Casino,' *Chrishunt.biz*, Spring: http://www. chrishunt.biz/features05.html.

Huq, R. (2006) 'Asian Kool? bhangra and beyond' in A. Bennett, B. Shank and J. Toynbee (eds), *The Popular Music Studies Reader*. London: Routledge, pp. 201–7.

Hutchinson, T. (2008) *Web Marketing for the Music Business*. Boston: Focal Press.

Hutnyk, J. (2000) *Critique of Exotica: Music, Politics and the Culture Industry*. London: Pluto.

Ihde, D. (2007) *Listening and Voice: Phenomenologies of Sound*. New York: State University of New York.

Indie Music, http://www.indie-music.com/.

Indie Music for Life, http://www.indiemusicforlife.org/.

Ingram, A. (2001) *A Concise History of the Electric Guitar*. Pacific: MelBay.

iObserver, http://www.macobserver.com/tmo/features/iobserver/.

iPod Lounge, http://www.ipod-lounge.com/ipodmovies/.

Jahn, B. and Weber, T. (1998) *Reggae Island: Jamaican Music in the Digital Age.* Cambridge: Da Capo Press.

James, M. (1997) *State of Bass: Jungle – The Story So Far*. London: Boxtree.

Jarman-Ivens, F. (2007) *Oh Boy! Masculinities and Popular Music.* Abingdon: Routledge.

Jensen, E. and LaBelle, B. (2007) *Radio Territories*. Los Angeles: Errant Bodies.

Johnson, B. and Cloonan, M. (2008) *Dark Side of the Tune: Popular Music and Violence.* Aldershot: Ashgate, pp. 149–162.

Johnson, J. (2002) *Who Needs Classical Music?* Oxford: Oxford University Press.

Jones, D. (1994) 'Dark Star,' *Arena*, May/June: 39.

Jones, D. (2005) *iPod, Therefore I Am*. London: Weidenfeld and Nicolson.

Jones, G. (2009) *Last Shop Standing: Whatever Happened to Record Shops?* London: Proper Music.

Jones, Wyn (2008) *The Rock Canon*. Aldershot: Ashgate.

Jones, P. (2005) 'Music education and the knowledge economy: developing creativity, strengthening communities,' *Arts Education Policy Review*, 106(4): 5–12.

Just Salsa Magazine, http://www.justsalsa.com.

Kahn, D. (2001) *Noise, Water, Meat: A History of Sound in the* Arts. Cambridge: The MIT Press.

Kahney, Leander (2005) *The Cult of iPod*. San Francisco: No Starch Press.

Katz, M. (2004) *Capturing Sound: How Technology Has Changed Music*, Berkeley: University of California Press.

Katz, B. (2007) *Mastering Audio: The Art and the Science.* Amsterdam: Focal Press.

Kelly, S. (2006) 'Communities of resistance: heavy metal as a reinvention of social technology,' in I. Peddie (ed.), *The Resisting Muse: Popular Music and Social Protest.* Aldershot: Ashgate.

Keyboard Magazine, http://www.keyboardmag.com/.

Klein, B. (2009) *As Heard on TV: Popular Music in Advertising.* Aldershot: Ashgate.

Knopper, S. (2009) *Appetite for Self-destruction: The Spectacular Crash of the Record Industry in the Digital Age.* New York: Simon & Schuster.

Kraftwerk, http://www.kraftwerk.com/.

Kruse, H. (1998) 'Fields of practice: musical production, public policy and the market,' in T. Swiss, J. Sloop and A. Herman (eds), *Mapping the Beat: Popular Music and Contemporary Theory.* Oxford: Blackwell, pp. 187–201.

Kusek, D. and G. Leonhard (2005) *The Future of Music: Manifesto for the Digital Music Revolution.* Boston: Berklee Press.

La Chapelle, P. (2007) *Proud to Be an Okie: Cultural Politics, Country Music, and Migration to Southern California.* Berkeley: University of California Press.

Laing, D. (1971) *Buddy Holly.* London: Studio Vista Limited.

Latin Percussion, http://www.lpmusic.com/.

Laughey, D. (2006) *Music and Youth Culture.* Edinburgh: Edinburgh University Press.

Lawrence, T. (2004) *Love Saves the Day: A History of American Dance Music Culture, 1970–1979.* Duke University Press.

Leadbeater, C. (1999) *Living on Thin Air.* London: Viking.

Leadbeater, C. and Oakley, K. (1999) *The Independents.* London: Demos.

Legal downloads are killing piracy (2008) London: Lush, http://www.lushtshirts.co.uk/legal-downloads-are-killing-piracy-tshirt-p-642.html?osCsid=d8ac41c52dda76367c6471c521782728.

Lehu, J. (2009) *Branded Entertainment: Product Placement & Brand Strategy in the Entertainment Business.* London: Kogan Page.

Lennon, J. (2010) Sun Star Studios, http://www.sunstarstudios.com/elvis1.html.

Leonard, M. (2007) *Gender in the Music Industry.* Aldershot: Ashgate.

Lessig, L. (2004) *Free Culture: The Nature and Future of Creativity.* New York: Penguin.

Lessig, L. (2006) *Code 2.0.* New York: Basic Books.

Lessig, L. (2008) *Remix: Making Art and Commerce Thrive in the Hybrid Economy.* New York: Penguin.

Lester, J. in Rodnitsky, J. (2006) 'The decline and rebirth of folk-protest music,' in I. Peddle (ed.), *The Resisting Muse.* Aldershot: Ashgate, pp. 17–29.

Levy, F. (2008) *15 Minutes of Fame: Becoming a Star in the YouTube Revolution.* New York: Alpha.

Levy, S. (2006) *The Perfect Thing.* New York: Simon & Schuster.

Lewis, J. and Miller T. (eds) (2003) *Critical Cultural Policy Studies: A Reader*. Malden: Blackwell.

Leymarie, I. (2003) *Cuban Fire: The Story of Salsa and Latin Jazz*. London: Continuum.

Licht, A. (2007) *Sound Art: Beyond Music, Beyond Categories*. New York: Rizzoli.

Lindberg, U., Gudmundsson, G., Michelsen, M. and Weisethaunet, H. (2005) *Rock Criticism From the Beginning: Amusers, Bruisers and Cool-headed Cruisers*. New York: Peter Lang.

Lindop, G. (2008) *Travels on the Dance Floor*. London: Carlton.

Lipsitz, G. (1994) *Dangerous Crossroad*. London: Verso.

Little Richard (2008) *The Last Great American*. Manchester: BBC 4: http://www.bbc.co.uk/programmes/b0074s4x.

Live 365, http://www.live365.com/index.live.

Luckman, S. (2003) 'Going Bush and finding one's 'tribe': raving, escape and the bush doof,' *Continuum*, 17(3): 315–330.

Luhrmann, B. (2001) in G. Fuller's 'Strictly red,' *Sight and Sound*, 11(6): 16.

Madden, M. and Rainie, L. (2005) *Music and video downloading moves beyond P2P*, PEW Internet and American Life Project, http://www.pewinternet.org.PPF/r/153/report_display.asp.

Maffit, Rocky (2005) *Rhythm & Beauty: The Art of Percussion*. New York: Billboard.

Malone, B. (2002) *Don't Get Above Your Raisin': Country Music and the Southern Working Class*. Champaign: University of Illinois Press.

Manuel, P. (1988) *Popular Music of the Non-Western World*. New York: Oxford University Press.

Manuel, P. (2006) *Caribbean Currents*. Philadelphia: Temple University Press.

Manuel, P. (1993) *Cassette Culture: Popular Music and Technology in North India*. Chicago: University of Chicago Press.

Marcus, G. (2006) *Lipstick Traces: A Secret History of the Twentieth Century*. London: Faber and Faber.

Marcus, G. (1999) *Dead Elvis*. Cambridge: Harvard University Press.

Marcus, G. (1998) *Stranded: Rock and Roll for a Desert Island*. Cambridge: Da Capo Press.

Marcus, G. (1993) *In the Fascist Bathroom*. London: Penguin.

Mashable: The Social Media Guide (2009) http://mashable.com/2009/04/18/social-sharing-music/

Massey, H. (2000) *Behind the Glass*. San Francisco: Backbeat.

McCarthy, C. (2008) *Fly by Night: The New Art of the Club Flyer*. London: Thames and Hudson.

McLeod, K. (2003) 'Musical production, copyright, and the private ownership of culture,' in J. Lewis and T. Miller (eds), *Critical Cultural Policy Studies: A Reader*. Malden: Blackwell, pp. 241–252.

McRobbie, A. (2006) 'Dance narratives and fantasies of achievement,' in J. Desmond (ed.), *Meaning in Motion: New Cultural Studies of Dance*. Durham: Duke University Press, pp. 207–31.

McRobbie, A. (1993) 'Shut up and dance: youth culture and changing modes of femininity,' *Cultural Studies*. 7(3): 406–426.

Merriden, T. (2001) *Irresistible Forces: The Business Legacy of Napster*. Oxford: Capstone.

Metal Hammer, http://www.metalhammer.co.uk/.

Mewton, C. (2001) *All You Need to Know about Music and the Internet Revolution*. London: Sanctuary.

Middleton, R. (1990) *Studying Popular Music*. Philadelphia: Open University Press.

Millard, E. (2004) 'Introduction,' in A. Millard (ed.), *The Electric Guitar: A History of an American Icon*. Baltimore: Johns Hopkins University Press, pp. 1–15.

Millard, A.J. (2004) *The Electric Guitar*. Baltimore: John Hopkins University Press.

Miller, M. (1988) *Boxed In – The Culture of TV*. Evaston: Northwestern University Press.

Miller, P. (ed.) (2008) *Sound Unbound: Sampling Digital Music and Culture*. Cambridge: MIT Press.

Milner, G. (2009) *Perfecting Sound Forever: The Story of Recorded Music*. London: Granta.

Ministry of Sound, http://www.ministryofsound.com/.

Missingham, A. (2007) *Why Games are Bigger than Rock 'n' Roll*. London: Youth Music.

Mitchell, T. (1996) *Popular Music and Local Identity*. London: Leicester University Press.

Mohanram, R. (1999) *Black Body: Women, Colonialism and Space*. St Leonards: Allen and Unwin.

Moog, http://www.moog.com/.

Moore, A. (1997) *The Beatles: Sgt. Pepper's Lonely Hearts Club Band*. Cambridge: Cambridge University Press.

Moore, S. (1991a) 'Art vs Arnie,' *Marxism Today*. October: 11.

Moore, S. (1991b) *Looking for Trouble: On Shopping, Gender and the Cinema*. London: Serpent's Tail.

Moore, T. (2004) *Mix Tape: The Art of Cassette Culture*. New York: Universe Publishing.

Morales, E. (2003) *The Latin Beat*. Cambridge: Da Capo Press.

Morley, P. (2003) *Words and Music*. London: Serpent's Tail.

Motown, http://www.motown.com/.

Motown Webring, http://welcome.to/the-motown-webring.

Mott, T. (2007) 'We're putting the band back together,' *Edge Magazine*. October 24: http://www.edge-online.com/magazine/feature-rock-band.

Morris, S. (2003) *On Writing Hit Songs*. Wellington: Four Winds.

Movie Music.com, http://www.moviemusic.com/.

Mucho Swing, http://www.muchoswing.com/.

Mudrian, A. (2004) *Choosing Death: The Improbable History of Death Metal and Grindcore*. Los Angeles: Feral House.

'Music and Censorship,' Noise between stations, http://www.noisebetweenstations.com/personal/essays/music_censorship.html.

'Music and The Beatles,' Visit Liverpool.com, http://www.visitliverpool.com/site/experiences/music-and-the-beatles.

Music Industry Today, iPod News, http://music.einnews.com/news/ipod.

Music of Social Change, http://www.metascholar.org/MOSC/.

Music Video Games, http://www.musicvideogames.net/.

Musicians' Intellectual Law and Resource List. http://www.aracnet.com/~schornj/index.shtml.

Muslim Hip Hop, http://www.muslimhiphop.com/.

Myers, B. (2005) *'Green Day': American Idiots and the New Punk Explosion*. London: Independent Music Press.

MySpace, www.myspace.com.

Nancy, J. (2007) *Listening*. New York: Fordham University Press.

Narine, D. (1989) 'Blue-eyed soul': Are whites taking over rhythm & blues?, *Ebony*, July, http://findarticles.com/p/articles/mi_m1077/is_n9_v44/ai_7698861/.

National Sexuality Resource Centre, http://nsrc.sfsu.edu/.

Neal, M. (2002) 'White Chocolate' *Pop Matters*, 17 December 2002, http://www.popmatters.com/columns/criticalnoire/021217.shtml.

Negus, K. (1999) *Music Genres and Corporate Cultures*. London: Routledge.

Negus, K. (1992) *Producing Pop: Culture and Conflict in the Popular Music Industry*. London: Edward Arnold.

New Now Next, http://www.newnownext.com/.

New World Music, http://www.newworldmusic.com/.

News Archive (2007) Blabbermouth.net. December 21: http://www.roadrunner records.com/blabbermouth.net/news.aspx?mode=Article&newsitemID=87144.

Nguyen, M. (2009) 'Writing about popular music,' Suite 101, April 11, http://maga"zinepublishing.suite101.com/article.cfm/writing_about_music.

Noise Abatement Society (2009) http://www.noiseabatementsociety.com.

Noise Act (1996) http://www.opsi.gov.uk/acts/acts1996/ukpga_19960037_en_1.

Noise Pollution (2009) Environmental Protection Agency, http://epa.gov/air/noise.html.

Oakley, K. (2004) *Developing the Evidence Base for Support of Cultural and Creative Activities in the South East*. SEEDA.

O'Higgins, P. (1972) *Censorship in Britain*. London: Thomas Nelson and Sons.

Old School, www.oldschoolhiphop.com.

Olsen, T. (2003) *Silences*. New York: Feminist Press.

Osborne, J. (2009) *Radio Head: Up and Down the Dial of British Radio*. New York: Simon and Schuster.

Oswald, J. (2004) 'Bettered by the borrower: the ethics of musical debt,' in C. Cox and D. Warner (eds), *Audio Culture*. New York: Continuum, pp. 131–137.

OverClocked ReMix: Game Arrangement Management Community, http://www.ocremix.org/.

Panter, H. (2007) *Ska'd for Life: A Personal Journey with The Specials*. London: Macmillan.

PBC. (n.d.) *Store Wars: When Walmart Comes to Town*, http://www.pbs.org/itvs/storewars/stores3_2.html.

Peck, T. (2010) 'Out of the groove: digital age silences DJ turntable of choice,' *Observer*, November 10: 9.

Peddie, I. (2006) *The Resisting Muse: Popular Music and Social Protest.* Aldershot: Ashgate.

Percussive Art Society, http://www.pas.org/.

Perelman, M.I. (2002) *Steal This Idea: Intellectual Property Rights and the Corporate Confiscation of Creativity.* New York: Palgrave.

Peterson, R.A. (2000) *Creating Country Music: Fabricating Authenticity.* Chicago: Chicago University Press.

Pet Shop Boys, http://www.petshopboys.co.uk/.

Pfahl, M. (2001) 'Giving away music to make money: independent musicians on the internet,' *First Monday*, 6(8), http://firstmonday.org/htbin/cgiwrap/bin/ojs/index.php/fm/article/view/880/789.

Phinney, K. (2005) *Souled American: How Black Music Transformed White Culture.* New York: Abe Books.

Pickering, M. and Green, T. (1987) *Everyday Culture: Popular Song and the Vernacular Milieu.* Milton Keynes: Open University Press.

Pierlejewski, S. (1997) 'The death of a disco dancer,' in C. Hutton and R. Kurt (eds), *Don't Look Back in Anger: Growing Up with Oasis.* London: Simon and Schuster.

Pini, M. (2001, 95) *Club Cultures and Female Subjectivity: The Move From Home to House.* Houndmills: Palgrave.

Podcast Alley, http://www.podcastalley.com/.

Podcast.com, http://podcast.com/.

Pollitt, K. (1995, 83) *Reasonable Creatures.* London: Vintage.

Pop Justice, http://www.popjustice.com/.

Poschardt, U. (1998) *DJ Culture.* London: Quartet Books.

Positive Soundscapes, http://www.positivesoundscapes.org/.

Potter, J. (2009) *Tenor: History of a Voice.* Yale: Yale University Press.

Potter, R. (1995) *Spectacular Vernaculars: Hip Hop and the Politics of Postmodernism.* Albany: State University of New York.

Potter, R. (1998) 'Not the same: race, repetition, and difference in hip-hop and dance music,' in T. Swiss, J. Sloop and A. Herman (eds), *Mapping the Beat: Popular Music and Contemporary Theory.* Oxford: Blackwell, pp. 31–46.

Pressing, J. (1992) *Synthesizer Performance and Real-time Techniques.* Oxford: Oxford University Press.

Pride of Manchester, http://www.prideofmanchester.com/music/.

Punk Rock Academy, http://www.punkrockacademy.com/

Punk 77, http://www.punk77.co.uk/.

Queer Music, *YouTube* Channel, http://www.youtube.com/group/queermusic.

Queer Music Heritage, http://www.queermusicheritage.us/.

Raha, M. (2004) *Cinderella's Big Score: Women of the Punk and Indie Underground.* Berkeley, CA: Seal.

Redhead, S. (1995) *Unpopular Cultures: The Birth of Law and Popular Culture*. Manchester: Manchester University Press.

Redhead, S. (1993) 'Disappearing youth?' *Theory, Culture & Society*, 10(3): 191–200.

Regal, B. (2005) *Radio: The Life Story of a Technology*. Westport: Greenwood.

Reggae News, http://www.reggaenews.co.uk/.

Remix: Lawrence Lessig on IP in the Digital Economy (2008) *YouTube*, http://www.youtube.com/watch?v=nS6IC5AWh5c.

Revogaming, www.revogaming.net.

Reynolds, S. (2005) *Rip It Up and Start Again: Postpunk 1978–1984*. London: Faber and Faber.

Reynolds, S. (1998) *Energy Flash*. London: Macmillan.

Reynolds, S. (1996) 'A philosophical dance stance,' *The Australian Higher Education Supplement*, (December 11): 35.

Reynolds, S. (1990) *Blissed Out: The Raptures of Rock*. London: Serpent's Tail.

Richards, K. (2006) in N. Holt (ed.) (2006) *The Wit and Wisdom of Music*. King's Sutton: House of Raven Book Services.

Rickenbacker, http://www.rickenbacker.com/.

Rietveld, H. (1998) *This is Our House: House Music, Cultural Spaces and Technologies*. Aldershot: Ashgate.

Rock and Roll Hall of Fame + Museum, http://www.rockhall.com/.

Rock's Backpages, http://www.rocksbackpages.com/.

Rock Band, http://www.rockband.com/.

Rockcritics.com, http://rockcritics.com/.

Rock Music Blogs, http://www.blogcatalog.com/directory/music/rock/.

Rock Sound, http://www.rocksound.tv/.

Rockwell, J. (1979) 'From 'Doo-wop' to 'Shlock Rock'; A Rock Glossary,' *New York Times*. February 4: http://select.nytimes.com/gst/abstract.html?res=F10F17F93 95511728DDDAD0894DA405B898BF1D3&scp=1&sq=J.%20Rockwell,%20 %E2%80%9CFrom%20'Doo-wop'%20to%20'Shlock%20Rock';%20A%20 Rock%20Glossary,%20&st=cse.

Rodriguez, C. (2001) *Fissures in the Mediascape: An International Study of Citizens' Media*. Cresskill: Hampton Press.

Rogers, R. (1997) *Cities for a Small Planet*. London: Faber.

Rolf, J. (ed.) (2007) *Blues: The Complete Story*. London: Flame Tree Book.

Roman-Velazquez, P. (1999) *The Making of Latin London: Salsa Music, Place and Identity*. Aldershot: Ashgate.

Romney, J. and Wootton, A. (1995) *Celluloid Jukebox: Popular Music and the Movies Since the 50s*. London: British Film Institute.

Rondon, C. (2008) *The Book of Salsa*. Chapel Hill: University of North Carolina Press.

Roots World, http://www.rootsworld.com/rw/.

Rose, T. (1994) *Black Noise: Rap Music and Black Culture in Contemporary America*. Hanover: Wesleyan University Press.

Rosenberg, N. (1985) *Bluegrass: A History*. Urbana: University of Illinois Press.

Ross, A. (1994) 'Introduction,' in A. Ross and T. Rose (eds), *Microphone Fiends: Youth Music and Youth Culture*. New York: Routledge, pp. 1–16.

Ross, A. (2008) *The Rest is Noise: Listening to the Twentieth* Century. London: Fourth Estate.

Ross, A. (2009) *The Rest is Noise*. http://www.therestisnoise.com/audio/.

Ryan, J. and Peterson, R. (2001) 'The guitar as artefact and icon: identity formation in the babyboom generation,' in A. Bennett and K. Dawe (eds), *Guitar Cultures*. Oxford: Berg, pp. 89–116.

Sakolsky, R. and Ho, F. (eds) (1995) *Sounding Off! Music as Subversion/Resistance/Revolution*. Brooklyn: Autonomedia.

Salsa Community, http://www.salsacommunity.com/.

Salsa Music, http://www.carnaval.com/music/salsa.htm.

Sample, T. (1996) *White Soul: Country Music, the Church and Working Americans*. Nashville: Abington Press.

Sandell, J. (1996) 'Reinventing Masculinity: The Spectacle of Male Intimacy in the Films of John Woo,' *Film Quarterly*, 49.4: 223–35.

Savage, J. (1996) *Time Travel*. London: Chatto and Windus.

Savage, J. (1992) *The Hacienda Must Be Built*. London: International Music Publications.

Savage, J. (1991) *England's Dreaming: The Sex Pistols and Punk Rock*. London: Faber and Faber.

Schafer, R.M. (2004) 'Open ears,' in M. Bull and L. Back (eds), *The Auditory Culture Reader*. Oxford: Berg, pp. 25–28.

Schafer, R.M. (2004) 'The music of the environment,' in C. Cox and D. Warner (eds), *Audio Culture*. New York: Continuum, pp. 29–39.

Scherzinger, M. (2007) 'Music censorship after 9/11,' in J. Ritter and J. Daughtry (eds), *Music in the Post-9/11 World*. London: Routledge.

Schlender, B. (2001) 'Apple's 21st-century Walkman' (November 12) *Fortune*: http://money.cnn.com/magazines/fortune/fortune_archive/2001/11/12/313342/index.htm.

Schmitz, R. (2005) *Analog Synthesis*. London. Music Sales Corporation.

Schwartz, L. (2007) *Making Music Videos: Everything you Need to Know from the Best in the Business*. New York: Billboard.

Scratch Radio, http://www.azevedo.ca/scratch/default.aspx.

Scratching, DJ 101, http://www.discjockey101.com/scratching.html.

Segalstad, E. and Hunter, J. (2009) *The 27s: The Greatest Myth of Rock and Roll*. Berkeley: North Atlantic Books.

Sellnow, D. (1999) 'Music as persuasion: refuting hegemonic masculinity in "He thinks he'll keep her",' *Women's Studies in Communication*, 22.1, Spring: 66–84.

Sen, A. (2004) 'How to judge globalism,' in F. Lechner and J. Boli (eds), *The Globalization Reader*. Oxford: Blackwell, pp. 16–21.

Shades of Blue, http://www.rhythmandtheblues.org.uk/public/.

Shank, B. (1994) *Dissonant Identities: The Rock 'n' Roll Scene in Austin, Texas.* Hanover: Wesleyan University Press.

Shapiro, P. (ed.) (2000) *Modulations: A History of Electronic Music.* New York: Caipirinha.

Shapiro, P. (2006) *The Rough Guide to Soul and R&B.* London: Rough Guides.

Shapiro, P. (2005) *Turn the Beat Around – The Secret History of Disco.* London: Faber and Faber.

Shaw, A. (1969) *The Rock Revolution.* New York: Crowell.

Sherburne, P. (2004) 'Digital Discipline: Minimalism in House and Techno,' in C. Cox and D. Warner (eds), *Audio Culture.* New York: Continuum, pp. 16–21.

Shneiderman, B. (1998) *Designing the User Interface.* MA: Addison–Wesley Publishing.

Shorthose, J. and Strange, G. (2004) 'The new cultural economy, the artist and the social configuration of autonomy,' *Capital and Class.* 84: 43–59.

Shuker, R. (1994) *Understanding Popular Music.* London: Routledge.

Sing Star Boy Bands vs Girl Bands, Playstation, http://uk.playstation.com/games-media/games/detail/item120747/SingStar%C2%AE-Boybands-vs-Girlbands/.

Skullcandy (2009) http://www.skullcandy.com/.

Smith, G. and Brett, J. (1998) 'Nation, Authenticity and Social Difference in Australian Popular Music: Folk, Country, Multicultural' in R. Niles and R. Evans (eds), *Everyday Wonders, A Special Issue of Journal of Australian Studies.* 58:3–17.

Smith, J. (1998) *The Sound of Commerce: Marketing Popular Film Music.* New York: Columbia University Press.

Smith, M., Snay, M. and Smith, B. (2004) 'Talking sound history,' in M. Smith (ed.), *Hearing History: a reader.* Athens: The University of Georgia Press, pp. 365–404.

Smith, R. (1995) *Seduced and Abandoned: Essays on Gay Men and Popular Music.* London: Continuum.

SoloH (N.D.) *Mpeg Encoder,* http://www.euronet.nl/~soloh/mpegEnc/#update.

Song Fact. 'He's so fine by The Chiffons': http://www.songfacts.com/detail.php?id=1215.

Songkick, www.songkick.com.

'Song Lyrics: an unlikely form of advertising,' (2007) *Right Celebrity,* http://celebrity.rightpundits.com/?p=1321.

Sonic Architecture, www.sonicarchitecture.com.

Sony, http://www.sony.com.

Soul or Nothing, http://ww.soul-source.co.uk.

Soundscapes, http://soundscapes.info/.

Soundtrack.net, www.soundtrack.net.

Soundtrack Collector, www.soundtrackcollector.com.

South by Southwest, http://sxsw.com/.

Space Weather, www.spaceweather.com.

Spectropop http://www.surf.to/girlgroups.

Stanton (2009) http://www.stantondj.com.

Steinem, G. (1995) *Outrageous Acts and Everyday Rebellions.* New York: Owl Books.

Steward, S. and Garratt, S. (1984) *Signed, Sealed and Delivered: True Life Stories of Women in Pop*. London: Pluto.

Stickings, R. (2008) *Searching for Soul*. London: SAF Publishing.

STLyrics, http://www.stlyrics.com/.

Stratton, J. (2003) 'Whiter rock: the 'Australian sound' and the beat boom,' *Continuum*, 17. 3: 331–346.

Straw, W. (1991) 'Systems of Articulation, Logics of Change,' *Cultural Studies*, 5.3:361–375.

Street, R. (2000) *Fairlight – a 25-year long fairytale*, IMAS Publishing Group, http://www.audiomedia.com/archive/features/uk-1000/uk-1000-fairlight/uk-1000-fairlight.htm.

Strinati, D. (1995) *An Introduction to Theories of Popular Culture*. London: Routledge.

Sweers, B. (2005) *Electric Folk: The Changing Face of English Traditional Music*. Oxford: Oxford University Press.

Swiss, T., Sloop, J. and Herman, A. (1998) *Mapping the Beat: Popular Music and Contemporary Theory*. Malden: Blackwell Publishing.

Synth Zone, http://www.synthzone.com/.

Szendy, P. (2008) *Listen: A History of Our Ears*. New York: Fordham University Press.

Taboo Tunes, http://www.tabootunes.com/gallery.html.

Tagg, P. (1982) 'Analysing popular music: theory, method and practice,' *Popular Music*, 2.

Talbot, D. (2007) *Regulating the Night: Race, Culture and Exclusion in the Making of the Night-time Economy*. Aldershot: Ashgate Publishing Limited.

Tate, G. (1992) *Flyboy in the Buttermilk*. New York: Fireside.

Taylor, T. (1997) *Global Pop: World Music, World Markets*. London: Routledge.

Terkel, S. (2006) *And They All Sang:* London: Granta.

Theberge, P. (1997) *Any Sound You Can Imagine: Music Making/Consuming Technology*. Hanover: Wesleyan University Press.

'The Best of the Century,' *Time Magazine*, December 31, 1999, http://www.time.com/time/magazine/article/0,9171,993039–2,00.html.

The Digital Folk Life, http://www.thedigitalfolklife.org/DigitalFolkLife1.htm.

The Quentin Tarantino Files, http://www.tarantino.info/.

The Specials, http://www.thespecials.com/.

The Stax Site, http://staxrecords.free.fr/.

The Tambourine Players Hall of Fame, http://www.stardustlanes.com/tambourine.html.

This business of dance and music, http://www.thisbusinessofdanceandmusic.com/.

Thomas, H. (2003) *The Body, Dance and Cultural Theory*. Houndmills: Palgrave.

Thompson, D. (2009) *London's Burning: True Adventures on the Front Lines of Punk, 1976–1977*. Chicago: Chicago Review Press.

Thornton, S. (1995) *Club Cultures: Music, Media and Subcultural Capital*. Cambridge: Polity.

Toop, D. (2004) *Haunted Weather*. London: Serpent's Tail.

Toop, D. (2000) 'Hip Hop: iron needles of death and a piece of wax,' in P. Shapiro (ed.), *Modulations: A History of Electronic Music*. New York: Caipirinha, pp. 90–101.

Toop, D. (1995) *Ocean of Sound*. London: Serpent's Tail.

Toynbee, J. (2000) *Making Popular Music*. London: Hodder Headline.

Transrap. (2010) http://www.transrap.com/.

Tschmuck, P. (2006) *Creativity and Innovation in the Music Industry*. Berlin: Springer.

Tweet the future, http://tweetthefuture.com/q.php?q=music.

Twyman, J. (2004) *(Inter)facing the Music: The History of the Fairlight Computer Musical Instrument*. Bachelor of Science (Honours) Thesis, University of Sydney, 2004.

UGHH, http://www.undergroundhiphop.com/.

Unterberger, R. (2003) 'Girl Group,' in V. Bogdanov, J. Bush, C. Woodstra and S. Erlewine (eds), *All Music Guide to Soul: The Definitive Guide to R&B and Soul*. San Francisco: Backbeat Books.

Urban sounds, http://www.urbansounds.com.

Veal, M. (2007) *Dub: Soundscapes and Shattered Songs in Jamaican Reggae*. Middletown: Wesleyan University Press.

Vernallis, Carol (2004) *Experiencing Music Video: Aesthetics and Cultural Contexts*. New York: Columbia University Press.

Video Cure.com, http://www.videocure.com/.

Waksman, S. (1999) *Instruments of Desire*. Cambridge: Harvard University Press.

Wald, E. (2005) *Escaping the Delta: Robert Johnson and the Invention of the Blues*. New York: Harper Collins.

Wald, E. (2009) *How The Beatles Destroyed Rock n Roll: An Alternative History of American Popular Music*. Oxford: OUP.

Wall, T. (2003) *Studying Popular Music Culture*. London: Hodder Arnold.

Walker, C. (1991) *Deromanticising Black History: Critical Essays and Reappraisals*. Knoxville: University of Tennessee Press.

Walser, R. (1993) *Running with the Devil: Power, Gender, and Madness in Heavy Metal Music*. Middletown: Wesleyan University Press.

Wareham, D. (2004) 'Introduction,' in T. Moore (ed.), *Mix Tape: The Art of Cassette Culture*. New York: Universe Publishing, pp. 1–18.

Warner, J. (2007) *American Singing Groups: A History 1940 to Today*. Milwaukee: Hal Leonard.

Waxer, L. (2002) *The City of Musical Memory: Salsa, Record Grooves, and Popular Culture in Cali*. Middletown: Wesleyan University Press.

Webber, S. (2007) *DJ Skills: The Essential Guide to Mixing and Scratching*. Burlington: Focal Press.

Weinstein, D. (2006) 'Rock protest songs: so many and so few,' in I. Peddie (ed.), *The Resisting Muse: Popular Music and Social Protest*. Aldershot: Ashgate, pp. 3–16.

Weintraub, A. and Yung, B. (2009) *Music and Cultural Rights*. Champaign: University of Illinois Press.

Weissman, D. (2006) *Which Side Are You On?* New York: Continuum.

Welsh, I. (1995) *The Acid House*. London: Vintage.

Welsh, I. (1996) *Ecstasy*. London: Vintage.

Werde, B. (2001) 'The D.J.'s New Mix: Digital Files and a Turntable'. *New York Times*. (October 25): http://query.nytimes.com/gst/fullpage.html?res=9B04E1DA1531 F936A15753C1A9679C8B63.

Werner, C. (2006) *A Change is Gonna Come: Music, Race & the Soul of America*. Ann Arbor: The University of Michigan Press.

Wheeler, T. (2007) *Celebrating 60 years of Fender Amps*. Milwaukee: Hal Leonard.

Whiteley, S. (1997) *Sexing the Groove: Popular Music and Gender*. London: Routledge.

Wigan Casino, http://www.wigan–casino.co.uk/.

Williams, P. (2009) *You're Wondering Now: The Specials from Conception to Reunion*. London: Cherry Red.

Wilson, A. (2007) *Northern Soul: Music, Drugs and Subcultural Identity*. Uffculme: Willan Publishing.

Winkler, A. (2009) *To Everything There is a Season: Pete Seeger and the Power of Song*. New York: Oxford University Press.

Winstanley, R. and Nowell, D. (1996) *Soul Survivors: The Wigan Casino Story*. London: Robson Books.

Wiseman–Trowse, N. (2008) *Performing Class in British Popular Music*. London: Palgrave.

Wittkower, D. E. (2008) *iPod and Philosophy: iCon of an ePoch*. Chicago: Open Court.

World Music Central, http://worldmusiccentral.org/.

World Music Network, http://www.worldmusic.net/wmn/news/.

Wyatt, R. http://www.strongcomet.com/wyatt/.

YouTube, www.youtube.com.

Zwonitzer, M. and Hirshberg, C. (2002) *Will You Miss Me When I'm Gone? The Carter Family and their Legacy in American Music*. New York: Simon & Schuster.

Sonic Sources

A Guy Called Gerald (1988) 'Voodoo Ray'.

AC/DC (1980) 'Back in Black'.

Afrika Bambaataa (1982) *Planet Rock*.

Apple (2006) 'iPod Tutorials,' podcast, iTunes.

Appleton, J.J. (2006) 'Downloader's blues'.

Arctic Monkeys (2005) 'I Bet You Look Good on the Dance Floor'.

Autry, G. (1939) 'Back in the Saddle Again'.

Backstreet Boys (1997) 'Everybody (Backstreet's Back)'.

Baez, J. (1968) 'Love is Just a Four Letter Word'.

Barretto, R. and Cruz, C. (1990) 'Ritmo en el Corazon'.

Beach Boys (1976) 'Rock and Roll Music'.

Berry, C. (1955) 'Rock and Roll Music'.

Berry, C. (1964) 'You Never Can Tell'.

Big Brother and the Holding Company (1968) 'Piece of My Heart'.

Black Sabbath. (1976) 'We Sold Our Soul for Rock'n' Roll'.

Blackbox (1989) 'Ride on Time'.

Bocelli, A. (1995) 'Time to Say Goodbye'.

Booker, T. and the MGs (1962) 'Green Onions'.

Boone, P. (1955) 'Tutti Frutti'.

Bowie, D. (1977) 'Sound and Vision'.

British Library Sound Archive (2009) http://www.bl.uk/nsa.

Buggles (1979) 'Video Killed the Radio Star'.

Carter Family (1928) 'Can the Circle be Unbroken'.

Cash, J. (1955) 'Folsom Prison Blues'.

Chic (1978) 'Le Freak'.

Chubby Checker (1961) 'Let's Twist Again'.

Clash (1979) 'London Calling'.

Cohen, L. (1988) 'First We Take Manhattan'.

Cooke, Sam (1965) 'A Change is Gonna Come'.

Corner House Studio, podcast, iTunes.

Costello, E. (2002) 'Dancing about Architecture'.

Crosby, Stills, Nash and Young (1970) 'Ohio'.

Days, D. (2009) 'My YouTube song'.

Dylan, B. (1963) 'Blowing in the Wind'.

Edison Media Research (2008) *Music Royalties*, iTunes.

Electronic Arts (2006–), podcast, iTunes.

Eminem (2002) 'Lose Yourself'.

Eno, B. (1983) *Apollo: Atmospheres and Soundtracks*.

Enya (1988) 'Orinoco Flow'.

Estefan, G. (2001) 'Y-Tu-Conga'.

Etchart, M. (2006) *Sound and Vision Radio*, podcast, iTunes.

Fairport Convention (1968) 'Meet on the Ledge'.

Fat Boy Slim (1998) 'You're Not From Brighton'.

Fluyd (2005) 'Post Music Platforms'.

Future Sound of London (1996) *Dead Cities*.

Gaynor, G. (1978) 'I Will Survive'.

Gladys Knight and the Pips (1973) 'Midnight Train to Georgia'.

Goldie (1995) 'Inner City Life'.

Grandmaster Flash (1981) *The Adventures of Grandmaster Flash on the Wheels of Steel*.

Guthrie, W. (1944) 'This Land is Your Land'.

Jazzy Jeff (2007) *Return of the Magnificent*.

Showbiz and A.G. (2000) *D.I.T.C.*

Haley, B. and the Comets (1954) 'Rock Around the Clock'.

Harrison, G. (1970) 'My Sweet Lord'.

Hayes, I. (1972) 'Shaft'.

Hear in this place (2009) Public Radio International, iTunes.

Henry Jenkins, Johanna Blakley, David Carr, Stephen Duncombe. (2009) 'Politics and popular culture,' MIT/ iTunes U.

Highland, J. (2008) *notPopular.com*, iTunes.

Hooker, J.L. (1948) 'Boogie Chillen'.

Jackson, M. (1983) 'Thriller'.

James, E. (1969) 'I'd Rather Go Blind'.

Jazzy Jeff (2007) *Return of the Magnificent*.

Johnson, R. (1937) 'Cross Road Blues'.

Joy Division (1979) 'Digital'.

Joy Division (1979) 'Transmission'.

Joy Division (1980) 'Love Will Tear Us Apart'.

Kraftwerk (1974) 'Autobahn'.

Kraftwerk (1978) 'The Model'.

Kusek, D. (2005) *The future of music*, iTunes.

Lady Gaga (2008) 'Just Dance'.

Leadbelly (1938) 'The Bourgeois Blues'.

Linkin Park (2003) 'Nobody's Listening'.

Linkin Park (2003) 'Numb'.

Little Richard (2002) 'Get Rhythm'.

Little Richard (1955) 'Tutti Frutti'.

Long, M. *Home Studio and Audio Review*, podcast, iTunes.

Madness (1980) 'Baggy Trousers'.

Manuelle, V. (2004) 'La vida es un carnaval'.

Marley, B. (1973) 'Get Up, Stand Up'.

Martha Reeves and the Vandellas (1964) 'Dancing in the Street'.

Maximo Park (2007) 'Books from Boxes'.

Metallica (1991) 'Enter Sandman'.

Mighty Mighty Bosstones (1998) 'The Impression That I Get'.

Miller, D. and Chick, D. *Inside home recording*, podcast, iTunes.

Ministry of Sound Podcast (2007) iTunes.

Minogue, K. (2004) *Body Language*.

Missy Elliot (2001) 'Get Ur Freak On'.

Moonah, J. (2007–8) *Online music marketing*, iTunes.

Morley, Paul (2007) 'Control: the podcast,' iTunes.

Mr Fingers (1986) 'Can You Feel It?' Trax Records.

New Kids on the Block (1990) 'Step by Step'.

New Order (1983) 'Blue Monday'.

New York Dolls (1973) 'Personality Crisis'.

No Place Like Home Studios, podcast, iTunes.

Parton, D. (1974) 'Jolene'.

Pet Shop Boys (1987) 'It's a Sin'.

Pet Shop Boys (1985) 'West End Girls'.

Pink Floyd (1973) *Dark Side of the Moon*.

PLAY, *Sound Salon*, iTunes podcast.

Presley, E. (1954) 'That's Alright Mama'.

Prodigy (1991) 'Charly'.

Puente, T. (1963) 'Oye como va'.

Quail, M. (2006) *The music law podcast*, iTunes.

Radiohead (2008) 'Nude'.

Redding, O. (1965) 'Mr Pitiful'.

Reed, L. (1989) *New York*.

REM (1987) 'It's the End of the World as We Know It'.

Remix Culture (2009) Center for Social Media, American University, iTunes U.

Roxy Music (1974) *Country Life*.

S Net Networks (2006–2007) 'Apple Clips,' iTunes.

Sabella, T. and Root, T. (2007–) The Business Side of Music, iTunes.

Sam & Dave. (1967) 'Soul Man'.

Seeger, P. (1963) 'We Shall Overcome'.

Sex Pistols (1977) 'God Save the Queen'.

Showbiz and A.G. (2000) *D.I.T.C.* Tommy Boy.

Simon, P. (1986) 'Diamonds on the Soles of Her Shoes'.

Simply Syndicated (2007–) 'Albums you should hear,' iTunes.
Sly & the Family Stone (1968) 'Dance to the Music'.
Snap (1998) 'Rhythm is a Dancer'.
Spellman, P. (2007 -) Music Career Juice, podcast, iTunes.
Spice Girls (1996) 'Wannabe'.
Steppenwolf (1968) 'Born to be Wild'.
Stewart, A. (1976) 'The Year of the Cat'.
Summer, D. (1977) 'I Feel Love'.
Sylvester (1978) 'You Make Me Feel (Mighty Real)'.
Take That (1992) 'A Million Love Songs'.
Take That (2006) 'Patience'.
Talking Heads (1985) 'Road to Nowhere'.
Tangerine Dream (1974) 'Phaedra'.
The Afters (2008) 'MySpace Girl'.
The Baud (1968) 'The Weight'.
The Beatles (1963) 'I Saw Her Standing There'.
The Beatles (1967) *Sgt. Pepper's Lonely Hearts Club Band*
The Beatles (1969) 'The Ballad of John and Yoko'.
The Beautiful South (2006) 'Manchester'.
The Chiffons (1962) 'He's So Fine'.
The Chiffons (1975) 'My Sweet Lord'.
The Clash (1978) 'I Fought The Law'.
The Clash (1979) 'London Calling'.
The Clash (1982) 'Rock the Casbah'.
The Crystals (1963) 'He's a Rebel'.
The Doors (1967) 'The End'.
The Folkways Collection (2009) Smithsonian Institute, iTunes.
The Jaywalks (2004) 'I Like Fat Chicks'.
The Kinks (1970) 'Lola'.
The Music of Grand Theft Auto IV (2008).
The Pete Tong Tongcast (2005) iTunes.
The Rolling Stones (1965) '(I Can't Get No) Satisfaction'.
The Rolling Stones (1971) *Sticky Fingers*. Atlantic.
The Ronettes (1964) 'Be My Baby'.
The Shirelles (1960) 'Will You Still Love Me Tomorrow'.
The Sims 2 (2005-) iTunes.
The Smiths (1985) 'How Soon is Now?'
The Specials (1981) 'Ghost Town'.
The Sports (1978) 'Who Listens to the Radio'.
The Sugar Hill Gang (1979) 'Rapper's Delight'.
The Velvet Underground (1968) 'The Velvet Underground'.
The Wailers (1973) 'Slave Driver'.

The Who (1965) 'My Generation'.

The Who (1971) 'Won't Get Fooled Again'.

The Q Podcast (2006-) iTunes.

Ting Tings (2008) 'That's Not My Name'.

Trance Tuesday Podcast (2009) iTunes.

Travis (1999) 'Writing to Reach You'.

Utravox (1981) 'Vienna'.

Undertones (1978) 'Teenage Kicks'.

Underworld (1995) 'Born Slippy'.

Wakeman, R. (1974) 'Journey to the Centre of the Earth'.

Waters, M. (1956) 'Got My Mojo Working'.

Weather Girls (1982) 'It's Raining Men'.

Yothu Yindi (1991) 'Treaty'.

Youssou N'Dour with Neneh Cherry (1994) '7 Seconds'.

Williams, R. (2009) *Reality Killed the Video Star.*

Visual Sources

24 Hour Party People (2002) Pathe.

411 On The Independent Music Movement (2007) Music 4 Da Soul Records.

AC/DC, 'Rock and Roll ain't noise pollution,' *YouTube*, http://www.youtube.com/watch?v=3HyxdRO2i9o.

'Adorno about popular music,' *YouTube*, http://www.youtube.com/watch?v=Wn_1F3o8QXQ&feature=PlayList&p=96735ED98C0DA542&index=14&playnext=2&playnext_from=PL.

Air Guitar Nation (2008) Contender Entertainment Group.

Anime Music Videos, http://www.animemusicvideos.org/home/home.php.

'An interview with Lawrence Grossberg,' (2007) http://www.youtube.com/watch?v=NZoDG6tfxHg.

Anvil (2008) Metal On Metal.

ARTS: Advice for a Future in the Music Industry (2007) *YouTube*, http://www.youtube.com/watch?v=1TUZf0oBVZE&feature=PlayList&p=C67BD36D5E7D29A7&playnext=1&playnext_from=PL&index=14.

Authors@Google: Greil Marcus (2007) *YouTube*, http://www.youtube.com/watch?v=J0O9ISIAbCE.

Backstreet Boys: Black & Blue Around the World (2001) Jive.

Beat Junkies DJ Icy Ice & Numark Virtual Vinyl (2007) *YouTube*, http://www.youtube.com/watch?v=DP3Kn5Ch7bY.

Beats Of The Heart – Roots, Rock And Reggae (2007) Digital Classics.

Beyonce, 'Single Ladies (put a ring on it),' music video, iTunes.

Biggie And Tupac (2002) Optimum.

Black Entertainment – A Celebration of Black Music (2001) IMC.

Blackboard Jungle (1955) Warner.

Blue (1993) Basilisk Communications Ltd.

Bob Dylan – The Other Side Of The Mirror: Bob Dylan Live At The Newport Folk Festival 1963–1965 (2007) Sony.

Bob Marley – Catch A Fire (2006) Edgehill.

Brown, R. (2008) 'Want to know the future of the music industry? Look to the past,' *YouTube*, http://www.youtube.com/watch?v=v6DmxUHH0zs&feature=related.

Bush, K. 'Wuthering Heights,' *YouTube*. http://www.youtube.com/watch?v=BW3gKKiTvjs.

CBGB Final Night. *YouTube*, http://www.youtube.com/watch?v=7bZkFkJRBQs&feature=related.

Charlie Rose – Jake Tapper/Lawrence Lessig (2008) Charlie Rose Inc.

Chris Anderson with Will Hearst: The Long Time Tail (2007) Whole Earth Films.

Classic Rock Drum Solos (2007) Proper Music Distribution.

Cohen, L. (2007) *I'm Your Man.* Lion's Gate.

Crystals, 'Da doo run run,' *YouTube*: http://www.youtube.com/watch?v=dqgtsai 2aKY.

Desperate Man Blues: Discovering the Roots of American Music (2006) Dust to Digital.

DJ 8-Ball vs DJ Noize – Supermen DJ battle for Supremacy (2007) *YouTube*, http:// www.youtube.com/watch?v=KkoQOupR0CE.

DJ Qbert, 'Crab Scratch.' *YouTube*, http://www.youtube.com/watch?v=w5OeaC3rI-A.

Dirty Dancing (1987) Vestron.

Disco – Spinning The Story (2005) Passport International.

Donna Summer – Live & More Encore (1997) Sony.

Dreamgirls (2006) Paramount Home Entertainment.

Duran Duran, 'Rio,' music video, iTunes.

Dylan, B. (2006) 'Someday Baby' iTunes Commercial. *YouTube*, http://www.youtube. com/watch?v=X450KgAlgIQ.

Electric Purgatory: the fate of the black rocker (2005) Payback Productions.

Essential World Music (2007) Sheer sound.

Eve, 'Tambourine'. *YouTube*, http://www.youtube.com/watch?v=sWUK1G5W8g.

Everything You Need to Know About Setting Up a Bedroom Studio (2006) Wise.

Eurythmics – Ultimate Collection (2006) Sony.

Extreme Guitar Metal Edge (2008) Quantum Leap.

Five Conversations about Soul (2003) Image Entertainment.

Florida, R. (2003) 'Richard Florida: The Rise of the Creative Class,' *YouTube*, http:// www.youtube.com/watch?v=iLstkIZ5t8g.

Frankie Goes To Hollywood – Hard On – Live Portraits (2006) Zyx.

From Mambo to Hip Hop (2006) Wienerworld.

Get Thrashed – The Story of Thrash Metal (2008) Wienerworld.

Ghost Town. *YouTube*, http://www.youtube.com/watch?v=RZ2oXzrnti4.

Girl Groups: The Story of a Sound (1983) MGM.

Girl Talk: Everyone Borrows Intellectual Property, Even Kings of Leon, *YouTube*, http://www.youtube.com/watch?v=tQfHTHb2_Wg.

Good Charlotte: the fast future generation (2006) Sony.

Good Morning Vietnam (1988) Walt Disney.

Grand Ole Opry at Carnegie Hall. (2006) RCA.

Green Day, 'Wake me up when September ends,' music video, iTunes.

Good Rockin' Tonight: The Legacy of Sun Records (2001) Image Entertainment.

Grease (1978) Paramount.

Great Rock and Roll Swindle (1980) Boyd's Company.

'Greil Marcus on the shape of things to come' (2007) *YouTube*, http://www.youtube. com/watch?v=n4CnseuDLtw&feature=PlayList&p=346E2C690F02E6D4&pla ynext=1&playnext_from=PL&index=4.

High Fidelity (2000) Bueno Vista Home Entertainment.

High School Musical (2006) Disney.

High Tech Soul – The Creation of Techno Music (2005) Pias.

Highwaymen Live (2006) Sony BMG.

Hip Hop Story – Tha Movie (2002) Urban Entertainment.

Home Recording Basics (2006) Hal Leonard.

Human Traffic (1999) Fruit Salad Films.

Icke, D. (2004) *The Freedom Road*. UFO TV.

Il Divo (2006) Encore, Sony.

I'm Not There (2007) Paramount.

In Search of the English Folk Song (2008) Kultur.

Intellectual Property Rights Debate, *YouTube*, http://www.youtube.com/watch?v= H2jSabFiYQY.

International Association for the Study of Popular Music (IASPM), http://www. iaspm.net.

Jackson, M. (2003) 'Black or White,' Epic.

Jailhouse Rock (1957) Metro Goldwyn Mayer.

Jasonmit, 'Music Today Sucks,' *YouTube*, http://www.youtube.com/watch?v= nGvkSFWr1qs.

Jobs, S. (2001) 'Apple Music Event 2001,' *YouTube*, http://www.youtube.com/ watch?v=kN0SVBCJqLs.

Joel Turner, *YouTube*, http://www.youtube.com/watch?v=Ta-ATEOOo8M.

Josh Groban in Concert (2002) WMV.

Josh White – Free and Equal Blues (2001) Music Sales.

Keynote with Jeffrey Veen – HighEd Web 2008 Conference (2008) *YouTube*, http:// www.youtube.com/watch?v=AcZQSGxnP-Y.

Kraftwerk and the Electronic Revolution (2008) Plastic Head.

Ladysmith Black Mambazo – Live (2009) Heads Up.

Lambada (1990) MGM.

Lang, M. Understanding Intellectual Property and Copyright, *YouTube*, http://www. youtube.com/watch?v=Ngps0BnLlUg.

Legends of American Folk Blues Festival (2009) Tropical.

Legends of Bottleneck Guitar (2003) Music Sales.

Martin Scorsese Presents The Blues: A Musical Journey (2004) Snapper.

Metal: A Headbanger's Journey (2006) Warner.

Michael Jackson: Fan's Camera Footage (2009) Music Video Distribution.

Moog (2004) Flexi.

Morrissey – who put the 'M' in Manchester? (2008) Sanctuary Visual Entertainment.

Moulin Rouge (2001) 20th Century Fox.

Neil Young, Heart of Gold (2006) Paramount Classics.

Netanel, N. Understanding Music Copyrights with Neil Netanel, *YouTube*, http:// www.youtube.com/watch?v=7r7zmSJW-n8.

New Kids On The Block – Hangin' Tough ~ Live (1989) Cherry Red.

New York Doll (2005) First Independent Pictures.

Nirvana: Spirit of Seattle (1995) S. Gold and Sons.

No Doubt – Rock Steady (2003) Universal Island.

Noise.io – The iPhone Synthesizer (2008) *YouTube*, http://www.youtube.com/watch?v= u8yhQHJUll8.

Nsync-Popodyssey (2001) BMG.

Odetta, 'Water Boy,' *YouTube*, http://www.youtube.com/watch?v=VSDeROn Tq64.

Patsy Kline, Sweet Dreams Still (2006) Fastforward.

'Percussion Jamming', *YouTube*, http://www.youtube.com/watch?v=OT816JjmJtY.

Pet Shop Boys – A Life In Pop (2006) EMI.

Pete Seeger: The Power of Song (2008) Genius.

'Podcasting in plain English,' *YouTube*, http://www.youtube.com/watch?v=y-MSL-42NV3c.

Presley, E. (2006) *'68 Comeback Special*. Sony BMG.

'Pulp Fiction Dancing,' *YouTube*, http://www.youtube.com/watch?v=zoUEMZ nibS8.

Punk Attitude (2005) Freemantle Media.

Radio Days (1986) MGM.

Red Hot And Blue – A Benefit For AIDS Research And Relief (1994) BMG.

Rhapsody in Black (2004) Arrow.

Rhythms of Resistance (2007) Digital Classics.

Richard Thompson's 1000 Years of Popular Music (2006) Cooking Vinyl.

Rick Wakeman: The Classical Connection (2004) Beckman Visual Publishing.

Rick Wakeman: The Six Wives of Henry VIII (2009) Eagle Vision.

Rip: A Remix Manifesto (2009) EyeSteelFilm.

Rise – The Story of Rave Outlaw Disco Donnie (2004) Quantum Leap.

Russ Solomon on Tower Records' Rise and Fall (2007) *YouTube*, http://www.you-tube.com/watch?v=iDpk74TX6fU.

Sam And Dave – The Original Soul Men (2008) Universal.

Salsa: The Motion Picture (1988) MGM.

Saturday Night Fever (1977) Paramount.

Shadowplayers: Factory Records 1978–81 (2006) LTM.

Shine a Light (2008) Paramount Vantage.

'Simon Reynolds discusses rip it up and start again,' (2008) *YouTube*, http://www.youtube.com/watch?v=W1Ov09YdchQ.

Smothered: The Censorship Struggles of the Smothers Brothers Comedy Hour (2002) New Video Group.

Soundtrack to War (2006) Revelation Films.

Something in the Water (2008) WBMC.

Spice World: the movie (1993) Universal.

Star Wars DJ (2005) *YouTube*, http://www.youtube.com/watch?v=Uw0v6kkasMk.

Steppenwolf, 'Born to be wild,' *YouTube*, http://www.youtube.com/watch?v= rMbATaj7Il8.

Strange World of Northern Soul (2003) Wienerworld.

Studio 54 (2005) Walt Disney Home Entertainment.

Studio 54, YouTube http://www.youtube.com/watch?v=_dl726_FKhc&feature= related.

Sufi Soul – The Mystic Music Of Islam (2008) Riverboat.

Take That for the Record (2006) BMG.

The Beatles (2009) 'The Beatles Rock Band Twist and Shout Trailer,' *YouTube*, http://www.youtube.com/watch?v=h3YlnQze028.

The Blackboard Jungle (1955) Metro Goldwyn Mayer.

The Boat that Rocked (2009) Universal.

The Byrds – Under Review (2007) Chrome Dreams.

The Corporation (2006) In 2 Film.

The Future Is Unwritten (2008) Sony Legacy.

The Last Waltz (1978) MGM.

The Mick Fleetwood Story: Two Sticks and a Drum. (2000) DVD UK.

Theremin: An Electronic Odyssey (1993) Orion.

The Strat Pack: Live in Concert – 50 Years of the Fender Stratocaster (2005) Eagle Rock.

The American Folk Blues Festivals 1963–1966 – The British Tours – Various Artists (2007) Universal.

The Story of the Blues: From Blind Lemon to B.B. King (2003) Quantum Leap.

This is Spinal Tap (1984) Embassy.

Tom Dowd & the Language of Music (2003) Palm Pictures.

Ultravox (1980) 'Vienna,' music video, iTunes.

We Are the Scissor Sisters And So Are You (2004) Polydor.

White Noise for iPhone and iPod Touch (2008), *YouTube*, http://www.youtube.com/ watch?v=s9h-sWQRC0k.

Wild Style – 25th Anniversary Special Edition (2007) Metrodome.

Woodstock (2009) Warner Home Video.

Youssou N'Dour – Live At Montreux (2006) Eagle Rock.

Index

A-ha 20, 79, 111
   Take On Me 20, 79, 111
Abba 78, 178
   Gimme! Gimme! Gimme! (A man after midnight) 178
Abbey Road, 64
AC/DC 52, 162, 165
   Back in Black 162
   High Voltage 162
   TNT 162
Anderson, Chris 204, 230–1, 238
   Long Tail, the 238
Andrew Sisters 214
Anka, Paul 218
Arctic Monkeys 169–70, 231
   I Bet You Look Good on the Dance Floor 169
Astaire, Fred 25, 71, 73
Avalon, Frankie 218

Back, L 13, 17
Bad Religion 168
Baez, Joan 3, 132, 134, 236, 237
   We Shall Overcome 237
Band, the 62, 106
   Music from Big Pink 129
   The Weight 109
Bauman, Zygmunt 6
   Liquid Modernity 6
Beastie Boys 173
Beatles, The 10, 19–21, 31, 35, 57, 67–8, 72, 77–8,
   94–5, 97, 106,121, 130, 133, 143, 150, 162, 181,
   202, 215, 218–19, 222, 224, 242
   Ballad of John and Yoko 202
   Paperback Writer 77
   Penny Lane 77
   Rain 77
   Rubber Soul 143
   Sgt. Pepper's Lonely Heart Club 19, 35, 186
   Strawberry Fields Forever 77
   Yellow Submarine 72
Bee Gees, the 111, 113, 164, 178, 218
Bennett, A 8, 56, 93, 98
Berry, Chuck 75, 105, 129, 139, 142–3, 209, 211
   Hail Hail Rock and Roll 105
   Maybelline 129

Big Bopper 143
Big Pink 62, 64, 129
   Music from Big Pink 129
Bill Monroe and his Bluegrass Boys 127
   O Brother, Where Art Thou? 127
Bit Torrent 88–9, 197, 229
Black Ark studio 62
Black Sabbath 161–2, 165
Blackwell, Chris 153–4
   see Island Records 153–4
Blink-182 21, 168
Blondie 68, 78, 167
Bloom, Allan 14, 18, 19, 247
bluegrass 68, 95, 127, 130
blues, the 8, 41, 68, 77, 95–7, 111, 127, 129, 131, 133,
   135, 136–44, 147–8, 152, 161–2, 206, 208, 211,
   214, 231, 236, 245
   Blues and Soul 148
Bo Diddley 139
Bohlman, P 187, 189
Booker T and the MGs 64, 148, 151
   Green Onions 148, 151
Bowie, David 71, 74, 80, 144, 193, 218, 242
   The Man who Fell to Earth 71
   Labyrinth 71
boy bands 121, 218–21, 223
Boyzone 218
Brando, Marlon 142
British Radio Academy 196
Brooks, Garth 129–30
Brown, James 147
Brown, V.V. 59
   Travelling Like the Light 59
Bull, M 13, 17, 48, 90, 119
Burchill, Julie 41
bush ballad 127
Bush, Kate 101, 111, 113
   Babooshka 101
   Wuthering Heights 111
Butler, Jerry 176
   Only the Strong Survive 176
Butler, M 25, 176, 184
Butterfield, Paul 137
Buzzcocks, the 55, 167

Byrds, The 96, 98, 129, 133–5
Byrne, David 188

Cabaret Voltaire 55
Carey, Mariah 111
Cash, Johnny 62, 74, 93, 100, 110, 112, 130–1,
    222, 237
    A Boy Named Sue 222
    Get Rhythm 100
    I Walk the Line 112
Cavern Club, The 67–8
censorship 9, 200–5, 237
Chantels, The 214
Chapman, Tracy 132, 237
Charles, Ray 74, 138, 147
    I Got a Woman 138, 147
Chiffons, The 198–9
    He's So Fine 198
Clapton, Eric 94, 136, 138, 154, 161, 235
    Crossroads 136
    I Shot the Sheriff 154
    Love in Vain 136
    While my Guitar Gently Weeps 94
Cloonan, M 164, 199–204
clubs 3, 7, 8, 18, 20, 26–7, 35–41, 51, 53, 55–6,
    66–71, 78, 149, 158, 167, 169, 176–7, 180–3,
    186, 196, 225
Coates, Norma 41, 212
Cohen, Leonard 111
Cohn, Nik 41
    Awopbopaloobop Alopbamboom 41
Collins, Judy 236
Collins, Phil 102, 106, 201
    No Jacket Required 102
colonialism 27, 62, 141, 152–3, 206
Coloured Stone 188
Communards, the 224
compact discs 15–16, 20, 36, 59, 62, 86–90, 110,
    115–16, 119–21, 133, 138, 197–8
Connell, J 52, 64, 119
Cook, Norman 74
    Moulin Rouge 74
Cook, Richard 83
Cooke, Sam 110–11, 147, 239
    A Change is Gonna Come 147
copyright 33, 54–5, 62, 87, 122, 193–9, 202–4,
    228–9
    see Lomax, John 195
Costello, Elvis 36, 167, 233
    Shipbuilding 233
country music 8, 68, 71, 95–7, 127–31, 133, 136, 139,
    142–3, 148, 161, 213, 223, 233, 235
country rock 129
Cray, Robert 138

Cream (band) 138, 161
    Disraeli Gears 161
    Fresh Cream 161
Cream (club in Liverpool) 55
creative class 10, 53
    see also Florida, Richard
creative commons 196, 199, 229
creative industries 7, 33, 51, 53–5, 57, 66, 193–4, 200,
    203, 244
Crosby, Stills, Nash and Young 233
    Ohio 233
Crystals, The 214, 216

dance culture 24–5, 40, 69, 74, 79, 145, 147, 169, 176,
    180–3
    Dancing with the Stars 24
    Strictly Come Dancing 24
dance films
    Fame 26, 74
    Flashdance 26, 74
    High School Musical 18, 26, 74
    Saturday Night Fever 26
dance music 8, 23–9, 37, 39, 42, 51, 67, 105–8, 148,
    150, 155, 158, 166, 178, 180–4, 233, 235
dancing 2, 3, 6, 7, 23–9, 31, 33, 36, 40, 42, 66–8, 76,
    141–2, 145, 147, 149–50, 155, 158–9, 163, 169,
    171, 173, 177–8, 180, 204, 215, 218–19, 225,
    236–7, 244
DAT (digital audio tapes) 60
Davies, Ray 223
    see Kinks, The 77, 161, 219, 222–3, 226
Davis, Sammy 62
Dean, James 142
De Burgh, Chris 14
Department of Culture, Media and Sport 200
Detroit 8, 53, 55–6, 66, 71, 147–8, 150, 181–2
Diana Ross and the Supremes 176
    Love Child 176
Digital Audio Broadcasting (DAB) 15
Digital Rights Management (DRM) 55, 89, 120, 197,
    203–4, 229–30
digitization 4, 5, 9, 15, 31, 54, 59, 61, 86–7, 96–8,
    116, 134, 153, 169, 188, 194–7, 228–9,
    231, 239, 241
disco 24, 26, 68, 107, 111, 114, 139, 145, 148, 157–8,
    166, 171, 176, 183, 213, 225, 235
Dixie Chicks, the 233, 238
DJ (disc jockey) 18–19, 61, 68, 82, 89, 114–18, 142,
    149, 171, 177, 180–1
    Donnie Darko 72, 74–5
Donovan 132
downloading, illegal 5, 7, 64, 89, 119, 121, 144, 200–1,
    229, 242
Downsyde 173

Drake, Charlie 237
   Welfare Cadillac 237
drum 'n' bass 23, 27, 55, 145, 180–84, 209–10, 237
drum machine 106–8, 121, 171
drumming 8, 105–09, 142, 152–3, 155, 161, 222
Duffy 110, 148
Duran Duran 78, 80, 167, 218, 224
Dusseldorf 8, 181
DVD 20, 72, 109, 120, 197, 202–3, 234
Dylan, Bob 3, 10, 14, 73, 77, 110–11, 129–137, 146–7,
   233–6, 242, 244
   A Hard Rain's a-gonna Fall 235
   Blowing in the Wind 134, 147
   Chimes of Freedom 236
   Dont Look Back 77
   Love Sick 234
   Masters of War 233
   Modern Times 130
   Nashville Skyline 130
   No Direction Home 242
   Subterranean Homesick Blues 77
   Sunday Baby 234

Eagles, the 106, 129, 166
   Hotel California 166
Easy Rider 72–3
Eddington, R 154–56, 252
electronica 59, 62, 68, 89, 108, 114–15, 139, 147,
   153, 163, 185
Ellis-Bextor, Sophie 178
Eminem 71, 121, 163, 172–3
   8 Mile 71
   White America 172
emo (emotional punk) 8, 26, 84, 145, 163, 223
Eno, Brian 21, 49, 52, 60
Eshun, K 25, 38–9, 42, 178, 183
Estefan, Gloria 158
Etheridge, Melissa 222

Fabian 218
Facebook 1, 7, 16, 41, 87, 228, 230
Factory Records 58, 63, 68–9
Fairlight 101–04, 252, 266–7
Fall, The 55, 167
fandom 3–4, 8, 41, 64, 119, 163, 215
Farlowe, Chris 15
fashion 3, 18, 25, 27, 38, 53–4, 79, 106, 111,
   143, 155, 161, 171, 173, 181, 209, 214, 218,
   224, 234
Fatboy Slim 21
feminism 28, 128, 212–17, 219
   see also Girl Groups
Fender 48, 94, 96–7, 99
Fender, Leo 96

Fleetwood Mac 109, 138
Florida, Richard 7, 10, 53–4
Flying Burrito Brothers 73
folk 2, 3, 127, 132–7, 142–4, 147, 152, 157, 168, 182,
   185–7, 194–5, 204, 235
Fonda, Peter 73
Frankie Goes To Hollywood 224–6
Franklin, Aretha 110–11, 148, 207, 212–13
   Respect 233
Freed, Alan 142
Frith, S 22, 31–3, 40, 143, 196, 210, 223–4,
   233, 238
funk 139, 148, 176, 182

Gabriel, Peter 20, 77, 101, 188
   Sledgehammer 20, 77
Gammond, P 19, 37
Garland, Judy 71
Garofalo, R 201, 203–4
Garratt, S 212, 215–16
gay and lesbian dance culture 26, 68, 173, 176,
   222, 227, 237
gay and lesbian film 26, 177
gay and lesbian music 128, 178, 182, 214, 219,
   222–7, 237
Gaye, Marvin 147, 233
   What's Going On 233
Gaynor, Gloria 176–7, 179, 212
   I Will Survive 176
   Never Can Say Goodbye 177
   Reach Out (I'll Be There) 177
genre 125–190
   blues 8, 41, 68, 77, 95–7, 111, 127, 129, 131, 133,
      135–44, 147–8, 152, 161–2, 206, 208, 211,
      214, 231, 236, 245
   country 127–131, 139, 248, 250, 253, 258–9,
      262, 264
   disco 24, 26, 68, 107, 111, 114, 139, 145, 148,
      157–8, 166, 171, 176, 183, 213, 225, 235
   electronica 59, 62, 68, 89, 108, 114–5, 139, 147,
      153, 163, 185
   folk 2, 3, 127, 132–37, 142–44, 147, 152, 157, 168,
      182, 185–7, 194–5, 204, 235, 246
   funk 139, 148, 176, 182
   hip hop 18, 38, 51, 61, 71, 89, 107, 111, 114–16,
      139, 145, 148, 150, 157, 160, 171–5, 177,
      182–3, 185, 195, 206–10, 212
   house music 51, 57, 68–9, 107, 114, 177, 180–84,
      243, 245,
   indie music 166, 168–70, 216
   metal 8, 26, 50, 83–4, 161–65, 222, 246
   punk 8, 26, 35, 39, 41–2, 50, 55, 61, 68, 87, 141–5,
      154–5, 162–3, 166–70, 194, 196, 208, 213,
      215–6, 233, 235

genre *cont.*
    rave 25, 27, 39, 51, 69, 176, 182, 205, 235
    reggae 30, 62, 83–4, 95, 152–7, 171, 183, 194,196,
        207, 209, 235
    rock and roll 8, 39, 41–2, 50, 52, 62, 71–73, 105,
        139, 141–6, 170, 206, 211, 237
    salsa 105, 152, 157–60, 176
    soul 8, 59, 68, 127, 136, 142, 144, 147–51, 170, 176,
        182, 184, 189, 209–12, 236
    world music 38, 105, 158, 185–9, 194, 242
Gibson, C 52, 63–4, 119
Gibson guitar 63, 94–7
Girl Groups 212–17, 223
    see also feminism
Girls Aloud 214
globalization 8, 27, 50, 54, 57, 83, 93, 141, 173–4, 181,
    185–6, 203, 209–10, 243–4
Godin, D 40, 148
Goffin, Gerry 214
    Will You Still Love Me Tomorrow 214
Good Charlotte 168
Goodwin, Andrew 3, 32, 106, 108
gramophone 18, 82, 120
Green, Al 72
    Ain't No Sunshine 72
Green Day 21, 81, 166, 168, 170, 242
    American Idiot 168
Greenfield, S 203–4
Groban, Josh 35, 110–11
Grossberg, L 31, 43, 143, 145, 208
guitar culture 3, 6, 8, 33–6, 40–1, 48, 50, 55, 73, 79,
    93–100, 103–12, 118, 121, 127–8, 133–9, 141–5,
    152–7, 161–2, 166–70, 183, 186, 206–7, 222–3,
    238, 243–4
Guitar Hero 34, 97–9, 161–2, 167
guitar magazines 98
guitars
    Fender Stratocaster 48, 63, 94, 96–7, 99, 245
    Gibson 63, 94–7
    Martin 94
    Rickenbacker 63, 94–7, 99, 242
Guralnick, P 136, 147, 213
Guthrie, Woody 132–3, 182, 238

Haçienda, The 8, 55–6, 68–70
Haggard, Merle 127, 237
    The Fightin Side of Me 237
Haley, Bill 71, 75, 94, 97, 132, 141–2, 208
    Bill Haley & the Comets 71, 75, 94
    Rock Around the Clock 71, 75, 94, 132, 141–2
    The Blackboard Jungle 71
Hall, S 2, 207
Halliwell, Geri 215
Hanson, M 22, 80

Happy Mondays, the 55–6, 68
Harold, C 196, 231
Harris, Emmylou 132
Harris, Richard 111
Harrison, George 95, 186, 198–9, 242
    My Sweet Lord 198
    Norwegian Wood 186
Haslam, J 55, 117
Hebdige, D 23, 28, 41, 200
    Cut 'n' Mix: Culture, Identity and Caribbean
        Music 244
Hegarty, P 50, 52, 134
Helm, Levon 106
Hendrix, Jim 50, 96–8, 137, 161
    The Star Spangled Banner 50
Herbert, T 34, 36, 249, 256
hip hop 18, 38, 55, 61, 71, 89, 107, 111, 114–16, 139,
    145, 148, 150, 157, 160, 171–5, 177, 182–3, 185,
    195, 206–10, 212
Holiday, Billie 110–11
Holly, Buddy 94, 97, 143
home recording 4, 60–3, 78, 169, 196
    see also recording
honky tonk 127, 211
Hooker, John Lee 137, 139
Hopper, Dennis 73
Horricks, R 37, 142, 195
Hoskyns, B 53, 111–12
house music 51, 57, 68–9, 107, 114, 177, 180–84,
    243, 245
Human League 55, 107, 167
    Dare 107
Hunter, Ruby 236
    Proud 236
Hutnyk, John 189, 208–10

Ifield, Frank 111
    She Taught Me to Yodel 111
indie music 166, 168–70, 216
indigenous music 127, 154, 185, 187–8, 236
    Hunter, R 236
    Roach, A 186, 236
Inspiral Carpets 55–6
intellectual property 9, 54, 55, 193–5, 197–9, 237
International Association for Study of Popular Music
    10, 32, 35
iPad 1 2, 6, 18–19, 79, 118, 122, 185, 241
iPod 1–9, 13–17, 19, 28, 36, 51, 60, 82–4, 89–90, 115,
    118–23, 210, 230, 234, 241–2
Island Records 153–4
    see Blackwell, Chris 153

Jackson, Michael 77, 211, 215, 232
    Thriller 20, 77, 229

Jackson 5, The 218
Jagger, Mick 15, 145
Jahn, B 156
Jarman, Derek 75
Johnny Thunder and the Heartbreakers 68
Johnson, Bruce 164, 257
Johnson, Julian 19, 257
Johnson, Robert 67, 136–40
   Crossroads, 136
   Cross Road Blues, 136
   Love in Vain, 136
   Sweet Home Chicago 136
Jolson, Al 71
   Mammy 71
   The Jazz Singer 71
Jones, Dylan 90
Jones, Graham 57
Jones, Kasey 128, 223
   Every Man I Love is Married, Gay or Dead 223
Joy Division 10, 17, 55, 72, 75, 106, 167
   Love will Tear Us Apart 72, 75
Just Salsa Magazine 160

Kahn, Douglas 49, 51
Kahney, Leander 122
Katz, Bob 63
Katz, Mark 115–16, 122, 197–8, 245
Kazaa, 87–8, 193, 196–7, 203
Kelly, Sean 163
keyboard 8, 30, 100–104, 107, 118, 142, 145, 168, 176
Keyboard Magazine 104
King, B.B. 137, 140
King, Carole 201, 214
   I Feel the Earth Move 201
King Stubby studio 62
Kinks, The 77, 161, 219, 222–3, 226
   Dead End Street 77
   Happy Jack 77
   Lola 222
   Waterloo Sunset 222
   You Really Got Me 161, 219, 222
Kitt, Eartha 225
   I Love Men 225
Knopfler, Mark 137
   Brothers in Arms 137
   Sultans of Swing 137
Knopper, S 9, 258
Knuckles, Frankie 68, 177
Kraftwerk 8, 16–17, 79, 104, 180–2, 184, 247
Kusek, D 83, 90, 120–2, 193

LaBelle, B 84, 176
Lady Gaga 18, 27, 145, 176, 178, 212, 215, 225–6
Lang, K.D 222

Lanza, Mario 111
latin 26, 94, 105, 109, 158–9, 171, 194
Laughey, Dan 8, 230
Leadbeater, Charles 7, 53
Leadbelly 5, 95, 133, 136, 139
   aka Ledbetter, Huddie
Led Zeppelin 162
   Led Zeppelin 11 162
   Whole Lotta Love 162
Lennon, John 130, 145, 242
   Imagine 112
   Power to the People 233
Leonard, Hal 65, 108, 216
lesbian and gay dance culture 26, 68, 173, 176, 222,
   227, 237
lesbian and gay music 128, 178, 182, 214, 219,
   222–7, 237
Lessig, Lawrence 4, 62, 193, 203–4, 229, 231–2
Lewis, Jerry Lee 62, 100, 130, 142–3, 208, 236
Licht, A 49, 52, 110
Little Richard 100, 104, 127, 141–2, 209, 211, 236
   Get Rhythm 100
   Tutti Frutti 142
Liverpool 32, 53, 55, 57, 68, 224
Liverpool Institute of Performing Arts 32
Lola 222–3, 226
Long Tail, the 122, 238, 246
Lopez, Jennifer 158
Luhrmann, Baz 73–4

McCartney, Paul 32, 145
   Liverpool Institute of Performing Arts 32
McGuinn, Roger 94–5, 132–3
   see Folk Den Project 132
   Mr Tambourine Man 94
McRobbie, A 23, 235
Madden, M 90, 230
Madonna 68, 74, 77–8, 110, 178, 206, 215, 224–5, 242
   Confessions on a Dance Floor 178
   Hung Up 178
   Material Girl 74
Manchester 8, 40, 53, 55–8, 63, 66, 69, 71, 149, 167,
   181, 204, 246
Manuel, P 119, 153, 189
Marcus, G 39, 41, 43, 146
   Dead Elvis 39
   Stranded: Rock and Roll for a Desert Island 39
   The Fascist Bathroom 39
Marley, Bob 110, 154–6, 233, 240
   Catch a Fire 153
   I Shot the Sheriff 154
   Bob Marley and the Wailers 152–153
   Exodus 152
Martin, George 60

Martin guitar 94
Martin, Ricky 219
Marvin, Hank 96
  see also Shadows, The 96
Massive Attack 206, 208, 236
Maximo Park 18
Mayfield, Curtis 147
MCL (Music Composition Language) 101
Merseybeat 68
metal 8, 26, 50, 83–4, 161–5, 222, 246
Middleton, R 32, 34, 134
MIDI (Musical Instrument Digital Interface) 61, 96,
  100–01, 103
Milner, G 15, 59, 65
  Perfecting Sound Forever: The Story of Recorded Music 59
Ministry of Sound 85, 184
Minogue, Kylie 27, 102, 178, 225
  Body Language 102
  Sweet Music 102
Mississippi Delta 136–8
  see Blind Lemon Jefferson 137
  see Patton, Charley 136–8
  Pony Blues 136
Mitchell, Joni 132
Mitchell, T 38, 127, 187–8
Monkees, The 20, 103, 121, 219
Moog 48, 101–04
  see minimoog 121
Moore, Gary 138
Moore, Samuel 148
  see Sam and Dave 148
  with Prater, Dave 148
Morley, P 17, 41, 43
Morris, S 30, 106
Morrissey 225
  see Smiths, The
Motown 29, 64, 139, 147–51, 182, 214, 217, 220
MP3 player 83–4, 86, 89, 197, 230
Mr Tambourine Man 94, 98
MTV 18–19, 72, 77, 79–80, 162, 167
music and censorship 204–05, 246, 260
music industry 4, 5, 8, 53–7, 60, 63–4, 78, 86,
  89, 102, 119–20, 123, 127, 142, 154, 158,
  166, 168, 185, 196, 201, 203, 215–16, 220,
  232, 234, 245
music video 19–22, 33, 73, 75, 77–81, 129, 162, 167,
  220, 232, 246
music writing
  academic 3–4, 13, 26, 31–42, 56, 64, 67, 134,
    141, 162, 173, 180, 206, 212, 228, 233
  journalism 3, 7, 26, 31, 36–42, 55–6, 63, 67, 134,
    141, 144, 148, 155, 162, 166, 168–9, 212, 231,
    233, 235–6, 242
MySpace 7, 16, 21–2, 78–9, 83, 87, 169, 196, 230–1

N'Dour, Youssou 110, 188–9
Napster 5, 87, 90, 196–7, 203, 229, 244
Nashville sound, the 129–30
National Sexuality Resource Centre 227
nationalism 173, 181, 200–1, 235, 238
Negus, K 35, 196–7, 230
Nelson, Ricky 218
Nelson, Willie 127, 129
New Kids on the Block 218, 221
New Order 55–6, 68, 78, 106, 109
  Blue Monday 106
Newport Folk Festival 133, 135, 137
Nicholson, Jack 73
night-time economy 53, 66
Nirvana 58, 145, 168, 242
  Nevermind 145
No Fixed Address 154, 188
Noise Abatement Society, the 17
Noise Act 17
noise pollution 17
Northern Soul 148–51

Oakley, Kate 7, 53
Odetta 110, 112–13
Olsen, T 128–9
Orbison, Roy 62

Parsons, Gram 129
  see Byrds, The
Parsons, Tony 41
Paul, Les 96–9
Pearl Jam 168
Pennebaker, D.A 73, 77
  Dont Look Back 73, 77
percussion 94, 100, 103, 105–9, 115, 157–8, 171, 177
Percussive Art Society, the 109
Perkins, Carl 142
  Blue Suede Shoes 142
Perry, Lee 62
  see Black Ark studio 62
Pet Shop Boys, the 27, 75, 100, 113, 178, 223–6, 233, 240
  I'm With Stupid 233
  West End Girls 223
Peter, Paul and Mary 236–7
Peter's Friends 72
Pink Floyd 19, 225
  Dark Side of the Moon 19
Platters, the 218
podcast 15, 22, 43, 52, 65, 80, 82–5, 90, 118, 121–2,
  187, 243
Pointer Sisters, The 214
politics 8–10, 25, 27–8, 33, 130, 132–3, 147, 153–5,
  173–4, 184, 188–9, 195, 206–9, 215, 219, 225,
  233, 235–8, 242, 244–5

popular culture 2, 3 ,4, 10, 20–25, 30, 32, 36, 38, 40,
57, 74, 82, 90, 97, 107, 121, 129, 138, 142, 145,
149, 159, 162, 167, 169, 174, 181, 185, 188, 194,
198, 200–04, 207–8, 214–20, 223–5, 234, 237–8,
241, 244,
Poschardt, U 116, 176, 242
Presley, Elvis 62, 71, 97, 111, 113, 129–30, 139, 142–3,
146, 169, 208, 215, 218
Heartbreak Hotel 142
Jailhouse Rock 71
Prince 107
Purple Rain 107
Prince Buster 153, 155
pubs 3, 7, 39, 53, 66–9, 78, 127, 168, 183, 196
see also clubs
punk 8, 26, 35, 39, 41–2, 50, 55, 61, 68, 87, 141–5, 154–5,
162–3, 166–70, 194, 196, 208, 213, 215–6, 233, 235
Punk Rock Academy 35
Pussycat Dolls, the 27, 214

Queen 78, 105, 242
Bohemian Rhapsody 78
queer theory 225–6

race 9, 28, 31, 38, 47, 62, 138, 142, 150, 152, 155,
172–3, 180–1, 188, 206–11, 237–8
radio 14–18, 22, 47, 50–1, 77, 79–80, 82–5, 121, 156,
185, 196, 201–2, 219, 233, 243
Ramones, the 68, 167
rave 25, 27, 39, 51, 69, 176, 182, 205, 235
recording 78, 86–8, 103, 110–11, 114, 118, 123,
136–8, 143–4, 148, 153, 176–7, 183, 186–7,
194–5, 201, 203, 229, 231
see also home recording
Redding, Otis 110, 147–8, 151, 213
Respect 147
Redhead, Steve 33, 200, 204
Reece, Florence 132
Which Side are You On? 132
reggae 30, 62, 83–4, 95, 152–7, 171, 183, 194, 196,
207, 209, 235
Reggae News 156
Reynolds, S 36–7, 39, 43, 166, 182, 215
Richard, Cliff 71, 224
Richards, K 15, 48, 94, 145, 222
Rickenbacker 63, 94–7, 99, 242
Roach, Archie 188, 236
Took the Children Away 188, 236
Robeson, Paul 20
Robinson, Smokey 147
Robinson, Tom 178, 222, 237
rock and roll 8, 39, 41–2, 50, 52, 62, 71–3,105, 139,
141–6, 170, 206, 211, 237
Rock and Roll Hall of Fame 146

Rogers, R 50, 55, 66
Towards an Urban Renaissance 50
Rolling Stones, The 19, 133, 136, 138, 146, 150, 177,
215, 219, 222
Crossroads 136
Love in Vain 136
Rolling Stone (magazine) 37, 39
Ronettes, The 214–16
Rooney, Mickey 71
Rose, T 106, 173, 210, 239
Ross, A 17, 23, 52
Ross, Diana 176, 214
see also Diana Ross and The Supremes 176
Love Child 176
Roxy Music 18–19, 144
Country Life 19

salsa 105, 152, 157–60, 176
Savage, Jon 41, 70, 106, 167–8
Schafer, M 13
Schlender, Brent 6, 120
Scissor Sisters, the 224–5, 227
Scorsese, Martin 73, 140
Scott, Bon 110
Seeger, Pete 132–3, 237
We Shall Overcome 237
Segovia, Andres 186
Sex Pistols 166–8, 170, 202, 205, 224, 242
God Save the Queen 202, 205
Shadows, the 96, 237
see Marvin, Hank 96
Shakur, Tupac 112, 172
Dear Mama 172
Hit 'Em Up 172
How Do U Want It 172
Keep Your Head Up 172
Shank, B 55–6, 58
*Dissonant Identities: The Rock 'n' Roll Scene in
Austin, Texas* 56
Shankar, Ravi 186
Shapiro, P 65, 104, 147, 178
Shirelles, The 214
Simon, Carly 15
You're So Vain 15
Simon, Paul 188
Graceland 185
Simone, Nina 147
To Be Young, Gifted and Black 147
Simple Plan 168
Sinatra, Frank 110–11
Sinitta 225
So Macho 225
ska 84, 152–5, 167, 194
Ghost Town 155

Skullcandy 9, 15
Slaven, N 142, 195
slavery 38, 136–8, 153, 157, 173, 207, 210
Sloop, J 58, 108
Sly & the Family Stone 107, 109, 148, 176
    Dance to the Music 176
    There's a Riot Goin' On 107
Smith, Chris, Secretary of State for Culture 200
Smith, Mamie 137
    Crazy Blues 137
Smith, Patti 68, 167
Smith, Trixie 142
    My Man Rocks Me With One Steady Roll 142
Smiths, the 55, 75, 94, 167, 226
    see Morrissey 225
    The Queen is Dead 75
Smithsonian Institution 132, 187, 189
Somerville, Jimmy 178, 224
Sonic Architecture 47, 48, 51–2
sonic media 1, 47, 49, 51, 71, 108, 118, 204, 241
Sound Art 48, 52
soundscapes 47–49, 51, 156, 164, 180–1, 183, 193
Sony 14, 48, 62, 88, 90, 114
Sony Walkman 6, 14–15, 18, 48, 51, 88, 114, 120
soul 8, 59, 68, 127, 136, 142, 144, 147–51, 170, 176,
    182, 184, 189, 209–12, 236
    see also Northern Soul 148–51
Soul II Soul 236
Spector, Phil 60, 214
Spice Girls, the 214–16, 224
Springfield, Dusty 212
Springsteen, Bruce 133, 145, 237
Starr, Ringo 106
Stax (Records) 64, 147–8, 151
Steppenwolf 72–5,
    Born to be Wild 72–5, 161
Stewart, Al 18
    The Year of the Cat 18
Stone, Joss 148
Stone Roses, The 55–6
Strawberry Studios 64
Studio 54 68, 70, 179
Summer, Donna 29, 102, 110, 176–7, 179, 207, 212
    I Feel Love 102
    Last Dance 176
    Love to Love You Baby 177
    No More Tears 177
Sun Records 62–3, 65, 137
Supremes, the 214
Swiss, T 58, 108
synthesizer 17, 61, 87, 100–04, 171

Take That 218, 220–1
Talking Heads 68, 167, 245

tambourine 105, 109
    Mr Tambourine Man 94, 98
techno 8, 23–4, 26, 42, 55–6, 69, 107, 151,
    176–7, 180–4, 208–10, 235, 237, 265
Telstars, The 237
Temptations, the 218
Tennant, Neil 111, 222
Terkel, Studs 42, 186, 235
The Band 62, 106, 129
    Music from Big Pink 129
    The Weight 109
The Quentin Tarantino Files 76
The Who 77
    Dead End Street 77
    Happy Jack 77
Theberge, P 65, 104, 119
Theremin, Leon 52, 101, 104, 107
Thompson, Richard 35, 133, 135
Thompson Twins, the 206
Thornton, S 67, 236
Timberlake, Justin 27, 215, 219
Toop, David 3, 51, 61
turntablism 67, 114–18, 120, 230
    Final Scratch 115–16
24 Hour Party People 70–1
Twisted Wheel, The 40, 149
Twitter 1, 7, 215

Valens, Richie 143
Vanilla Ice 173
Vaughan, Stevie Ray 138
Velvet Underground, The 19, 167, 237
    The Velvet Underground 19
Village People, the 225
vinyl 6–7, 16, 19, 35, 67, 86, 88–9, 110, 114–7, 119,
    121, 135, 141, 174, 177, 181, 242
voice 1, 2, 8, 14–15, 42, 62, 73, 82, 93, 102,
    110–13, 118, 133, 143, 147–8, 158, 163–4,
    167, 171–2, 178, 180, 212–3, 215, 219, 222–3,
    230, 236, 241
Voidoids, The 68, 167
    aka Richard Hell and the Voidoids

Walkman 6, 14–15, 18, 48, 51, 88, 114, 120
    see Sony
Walker, T-Bone 137
Wakeman, Rick 35, 100, 103–4, 143
Warehouse, The 68–9, 181
Warhol, Andy 21
Warumpi Band, the 188
Welsh, I 27, 180
    Ecstasy 27
    Trainspotting 27
Wigan Casino 149–51

Wild Bill Moore 142
Williams, Robbie 80, 218–20
   Take That 218, 220–1
Wilson, Brian 60
Wilson, Tony 69
Winehouse, Amy 148, 150, 211
world music 38, 105, 158, 185–9, 194, 242

Yothu Yindi 189
Young, Angus 162
Young, Neil 130–1, 233
   After the Goldrush 130
YouTube 1, 7, 21–2, 78–9, 83, 87, 169, 196, 228, 230

Zappa, Frank 36, 237